A Schema
for Unifying Human Science

A Schema
for Unifying Human Science

Interdisciplinary Perspectives on Culture

Rick Szostak

SUP

Selinsgrove: Susquehanna University Press
London: Associated University Presses

Associated University Presses
2010 Eastpark Boulevard
Cranbury, NJ 08512

Assoicated University Presses
16 Barter Street
London WC1A 2AH, England

Associated University Presses
P.O. Box 338, Port Credit
Mississauga, Ontario
Canada L5G 4L8

The paper used in this publication meets the requirements of the American National Standard for Permanence of Paper for Printed Library Materials Z39.48-1984.

Library of Congress Cataloging-in-Publication Data

Szostak, Rick, 1959–
    A schema for unifying human science : interdisciplinary perspectives on culture / Rick Szostak.
        p. cm.
    Includes bibliographical references and index.
    ISBN 1-57591-060-8 (alk. paper)
    1. Culture. 2. Culture—Study and teaching. 3. Anthropology. 4. Social Sciences. I. Title.

GN357 .S96 2003
306—dc21   2002021751

Contents

Preface

ONE OF THE JOYS OF BEING AN ACADEMIC IS THAT ONE CAN READ — AND then hope to build upon—the exciting ideas of so many others. It is a shame that the pressures to publish and to specialize, and the time constraints inherent in a life of teaching, research, and administration, cause many scholars to do very little reading outside of their area of specialization. I have always sought to read works that seemed only tangentially related to my research focus of the moment, and often found therein ideas that would have escaped me otherwise. Moreover, when early in my career I occasionally found myself wondering what to do next, I eschewed the temptation to plunge into the first research project that presented itself, and rather took the time to read across various disciplines; I always found inspiration in the process (though there were many days when I wondered if this would be the case).

How does one identify works in related disciplines—or of an interdisciplinary nature—that might shed a novel light on one's own research or teaching interests? It seemed to me that this was much harder to do than it needed to be. If one is driving from Chicago to New York, one can glance at a map and quickly identify several possible points of interest along or nearly along the way. But there is—or at least was—no map of human science that could provide a similar service to the interdisciplinary traveller.

At the time that the vague idea of constructing such a map was taking form in my mind, I became involved in some committee work at the University of Alberta which, among other things, forced me to think a great deal about the commonly observed problem that students have difficulty in integrating material across different courses. This problem may loom largest at institutions which rely heavily on "breadth requirements," so that students must take courses from several different disciplines or areas of study. But even at institutions which make the effort to provide core courses of an interdisciplinary nature, students are generally left to their own devices in figuring out how one course might be related to another. Not surprisingly, I came to appreciate that the solution to the students' problem could be the same as the solution to the researcher's

7

problem: if we could create a map of human science, students would find it much easier to see how different courses were related. (It would also help them integrate material *within* courses, which can be problematic too, especially when courses are team-taught). From there it was a small step to a recognition that such a map could greatly facilitate "lifelong learning" for us all.

The map would not, of course, look quite like a road map, but it would have a common base in the identification of "places" or, more precisely, the phenomena of interest to human scientists. At first glance, one might think that a list of such phenomena would have two problems: it would be inordinately long, and as a result would provide limited guidance to either student or scholar in drawing connections among those phenomena. But it soon became obvious that the list of phenomena could be organized hierarchically, with a handful of broad categories disaggregated (to use the terminology of economists) or unpacked (to use the terminology of realist philosophers) into a set of subsidiary phenomena, and these in turn further disaggregated (often to one or more additional levels of disaggregation). Note that the hierarchy refers only to the level of aggregation, and thus involves no implicit judgment of the relative importance of diverse phenomena. Such a hierarchical organization makes the list much more user-friendly, as we shall see, while also giving each phenomenon studied by human scientists a unique place within it.

When I later came to read the works of others—Parsons, Barber, and Brady in particular—who had also had the idea of developing some sort of map, I found that they too had recognized the hierarchical structure of phenomena. They had not, though, identified more than a handful of the most aggregated phenomena. Since, as we shall see, most causal links occur among phenomena at lower levels of aggregation, this inevitably meant that their systems were of limited utility. Developing a more extensive list was conceptually straightforward, but required me to read extensively across human science.

As I read, it was clear to me that I would need not only to develop a map or "schema," but that I would then have to show that it was both valid and valuable. This could only be done by using the schema as a device for organizing our understanding of a diversity of causal links (that is, understandings of how one or more of the phenomena in my schema influence one or more others). While the human science enterprise should strive for a coherent comprehension of the causal links which exist between virtually every pair of phenomena identified in my schema, it would have been an unmanageable task for me to have attempted a summary of such a comprehensive scope. I decided instead to focus on the links to and from one of my broad categories of phenomena: culture. I chose "culture" for a variety of reasons. The "personal" reason was that I had long had a strong interest in culture, and a strong feeling that those writing on culture often talked past each other due to conflicting definitions of the relevant terminology. The "scholarly" reasons are dealt with in more detail in chapter one but include the importance of culture, its prominence in discussions of curricular reform, and the advantages which the schema provides for a comprehension of culture. I will in the concluding chapter discuss six broad insights into the study of culture which emerge from this analysis. The first lesson is that we can only comprehend the role of culture in human societies by unpacking culture into its constituent phenomena. Unpacking, as we shall see in chapter 3, also allows us to sail between the twin dangers of cultural bigotry (where one argues that one's culture is superior to another) and cultural relativism (where one eschews criticism of any cultural element, even cannibalism or wifebeating, in any society). The second lesson is that a full understanding of culture requires the study of hundreds or thousands of causal links. It is folly to think that any one theory or method can guide us. I know of no other book that does or could bring this point home as forcefully. The third lesson follows from the second: while unifying theories or methods are attractive due to a false promise of simplicity, they inevitably guide us to ignore much that is crucial to our understanding. The fourth lesson is that cultural phenomena both influence and are influenced by other phenomena: the all too common practice of treating culture as only cause or effect is thus inherently misguided. The fifth is that our schema serves as a crucial antidote to the siren song of grand theory and oversimplification. And the sixth lesson is that the schema serves an important pedagogical role.

The book has two goals, then: to use the study of culture as both a test and an exposition of the accuracy and value of my schema, and in turn to use the schema to provide a structure which can enhance understanding, and thus both teaching and research, in the area of culture. With respect to the first, I should note that I cannot "prove" the exhaustiveness of the schema: I can but show that a huge range of scholarly analysis can comfortably be placed within it (and can argue further that the schema's flexibility ensures that any future discoveries will also find a place). Once we accept that proof is impossible in science (see chapter 2), this evidence should appear compelling. With respect to the second broad goal of the book, the utility of the schema will only be apparent to those who are ready to embrace complexity. Those who cling to the mistaken and misleading idea that some one theory or method can tell us all that we need to know will shrink from an approach that encourages us to view each of hundreds of causal links with a fresh mind. But the world is a complex place, and each causal link is unique, and thus it is better to face complexity than run from it. Without the use of the schema, it would be difficult to organize such diverse material, and thus far too easy for both scholar and student to simply ignore many important linkages.

This book has a slightly unusual format. Rather than building gradually toward a set of conclusions, I will discuss in the first chapter the basic goals and orientation of the book, review some relevant philosophical considerations in the second chapter, and then devote nine chapters to the unpacking of each of my categories and analysis of relevant links, before providing a set of conclusions in the final chapter. That is, there is a large block of material in the middle chapters in which the ideas developed at the outset are applied to different human science categories, and the concluding chapter draws equally on each of these.

There is, intentionally, no unifying theoretical or methodological perspective to what follows. I will discuss the advantages in general of theoretical and methodological flexibility in chapter 2. Scholars and students who would prefer a false simplicity may thus find the book daunting. The simple fact is that different links are best illuminated by different theories, and these in turn evaluated by a range of methods. To pretend otherwise is to follow the chimera of grand theory (or methodological orthodoxy), and must impose a huge arbitrary constraint on the pursuit and transferance of understanding.

My style of presentation inevitably differs by link. For links that have been the subject of considerable scholarly debate, I attempt a concise and evenhanded overview of differing positions. For links that have received less attention (or for which I have uncovered only a small part of the relevant literature), I reprise what seems to me the dominant point of view. For links that have been largely ignored, I draw on related research in order to suggest fruitful lines of inquiry. To attempt to deal with such distinct scenarios in similar fashion would be to seek an artificial and misleading unity. With style, as with theory and method, the schema itself provides an organizing and unifying device which spares us from the temptation to pretend to other kinds of unity. My approach thus mimics (but improves upon) the state of affairs in human science itself, where we lavish attention on some links (sometimes because we perceive them to be more important, sometimes because they are amenable to the preferred theory or method of one or more disciplines), devote sporadic attention to others (and thus risk reinventing the wheel as past research on little-studied topics is forgotten), and virtually ignore others.

I provide a philosophical justification for my approach, especially in terms of realist philosophy, in chapter 1. I also discuss postmodernism. I embrace the key insight of postmodernism, that the world is a complex place, and the key implication of this postmodern insight, that we should thus pursue diverse theories and methods as well as diverse empirical studies. I argue that the schema allows us to (better) pursue this postmodern agenda without agreeing with those postmodernists who would suggest that increased understanding is impossible, that all we can do is engage in subjective argumentation, and that we may as well emphasize style over substance in our writing. I view this book as a challenge to this unduly pessimistic strand of postmodern thought (which is more common in the study of culture than elsewhere in human science). I hope to show that, by using the schema as an organizing device, we can pursue a diversity of research agendas, and yet link our detailed understanding of diverse causal links into a greater whole. Moreover, I hope to show that our understanding of particular links can be expressed in everyday language, without unnecessary stylistic flourish. We can thus collectively embrace complexity (and also a diversity of perspectives) without having to also embrace despair.

Given the finite time and energy constraints facing any scholar, all scholarly enterprises (even those involving many scholars) must trade off depth versus breadth. The clear bias in modern academia is toward depth: the scholar who specializes in a narrow area can claim to master all that lies within that domain (though often being unaware of work in closely related areas). The danger, of course, is that overspecialized academics fail to put the pieces together. This book chooses breadth over depth. In its coverage of culture it offers breadth of two sorts: coverage of a wide range of causal linkages, and reference to scholarly works from all human science disciplines. The inevitable cost is that the author cannot claim, like the specialist, to know *everything* about a particular link (though, of course, the work of such specialists is cited throughout). I am confident that I am accurate in my representation of every scholarly argument covered, but suspect that I have missed some important point here or there. Space constraints would have necessitated this even had knowledge constraints not been binding. I believe that a student (and especially scholar) of culture should be exposed to the breadth of argument of this book, and hope that readers will be encouraged to pursue further research on links of particular interest (and generally provide references to aid this quest). I think it easier for a student or scholar to add depth once exposed to breadth than to accomplish the reverse process of fitting together little bits of analysis into a coherent whole. And I believe that the advance of scientific understanding requires an interaction between specialist research and attempts to tie this together into a broader "big picture." I would hope that, even if the reader disagrees with my treatment of particular links, they will still appreciate my illustration of the importance of that link.

There is no objective criteria by which to determine how much space to devote to any particular link. Some links undoubtedly "deserve" more space than others, though any two scholars might disagree on which to emphasize. The coverage here undoubtedly reflects my own interest and expertise. I hope to show that a comprehensive understanding of the influences both on and of culture require some attention to each of the links covered; I readily confess that more could be said about each of them.

The intellectual history of recent centuries is littered with failed attempts to unify human science theoretically, and a few tentative efforts to do so schematically. The value of interdisciplinarity to research, teaching, and public policy analysis is now widely recognized, but we lack a "map" of the terrain. I hope that this book, which shows how human science research can be tied together by an organizing schema (and only by an organizing schema), will be of interest to a wide range of scholars, students, and citizens.

A book with the extensive scope of this one would be impenetrable to even the most learned of scholars if it utilized the scientific jargon of each field it encountered. I have thus eschewed the use of jargon throughout. The book can be used as a text for interdisciplinary courses (or as a background text for a series of courses), especially but not exclusively those with a cultural focus. All instructors (and most authors, for that matter) inevitably emphasize certain aspects of any subject they teach: those with which they are most familiar and/or those which they think of greatest importance. The ever-present but rarely appreciated danger is that students will think that they have been exposed to the "big picture" rather than just parts of it. Students familiar with the schema would be unlikely to make such an error; indeed they would and should likely be encouraged to pursue other linkages in their assignments, papers, or presentations.

We speak a lot these days of "lifelong learning," but devote very little effort to a consideration of how best to facilitate independent learning. I would argue that the most valuable service we can provide is to give learners a structure into which they can readily place new bits of information. The human brain seeks patterns in all the information it acquires. Our schema thus facilitates the retention of lots of information (both within and beyond the material covered in this book), by giving the brain a handy means of categorizing diverse bits of information. We should thus also increase people's confidence in their ability to add to their understanding through life. Moreover, such a structure can and should guide them as to where to search for new information as they face novel problems in life. We can all too easily think that the links with which we are familiar are everything, unless confronted with a map which identifies the areas we have not explored. The schema on which this book is based can greatly facilitate lifelong learning across the entire subject matter of human science. If it seems difficult at first, it will yield a lifetime of benefits.

Acknowledgments

WHILE ACADEMIA IS FULL OF INCENTIVES TO PURSUE NARROW AND POPU-
lar research agendas, it does provide the freedom (at least for those of us
well along in our careers) to pursue projects of a broad scope that catch our
interest. Still, I would like to thank Mel McMillan and Ken Norrie, my
department chairs for most of the last several years, for their steadfast
support and encouragement for my pursuit of projects that took me far
beyond the boundaries of Economics. I would also like to thank Patricia
Clements, the longtime Dean of Arts, for putting me on all those
committees.

I have benefitted enormously from participation in interdisciplinary
conferences over the last few years, as I proceeded to formalize my ini-
tially vague ideas. I have presented this material at the 1996 and 1998
conferences of the Centre for Interdisciplinary Research in the Liberal
Arts, the 1997 and 1999 conferences of the Association for Integrative
Studies (AIS), the 1999 conferences of the Association for General and
Liberal Studies and Social Science History Association, and the 2000
conferences of the American Association for Behavioral and Social Sciences, National Social Science Association, and Canadian Historical Association. While I am indebted to a large number of participants at these
conferences for both advice and encouragement, I would single out a few
for special recognition: Ross Emmett, Bruce Janz, Steve Nickel, Ray Miller, Francine Navakas, Kathleen Maloney, Ronald King, and Rosemary
Ommer.

Michael Bowler invited me to make a presentation at St. Mary's University of Minnesota in 1999, and Peter Caws invited me to make presentations in both faculty and graduate seminars at George Washington University that year. I learned a lot both from these gentlemen and from the
presentations.

When I first contacted the Association for Integrative Studies, Bill Newell made extensive comments on the paper I sent. This exchange encouraged me to join the AIS, a group from whom I have learned a great deal.
After my first presentation at an AIS conference, Stan Bailis encouraged
me to submit a paper to *Issues in Integrative Studies*. Stan and Jay Went-

13

worth gave me a great deal of editorial advice on that paper, which is in turn reflected in this book. I would thank the AIS for permission to use material from "Toward a Unified Human Science," *Issues in Integrative Studies,* 2000, in this book.

I would like to thank Hans Feldmann and the editorial committee of Susquehanna University Press for both publishing this book and suggesting some valuable final revisions. I am also grateful for helpful comments from anonymous referees. Any errors that remain after all of the advice I have received are entirely my fault.

Finally, I thank my wife Anne-Marie and our children, Mireille, Julien, and Theodore, for their patience and support. I owe them more than words can express.

A Schema
for Unifying Human Science

1

The Big Picture

IMAGINE THE DIFFICULTY OF TEACHING A COURSE (OR WRITING A BOOK) in North American geography without recourse to maps. A lecture or two could be devoted to each of the major regions of the continent and the students told where each was located with reference to a couple of other regions (e.g., The Great Lakes lie to the northwest of the Appalachians and south of the Canadian Shield). On the final exam you ask the students to describe how to get from Chicago to the ocean and are disappointed when some of them wind up in Canada. If they had just had a map from the outset, they would have found it so much easier to see how each topic in the course related to the others.

Interdisciplinary scholars have done much in recent decades to break down barriers among the disciplines in the social and behavioral sciences and humanities (hereafter human science). It is now widely recognized that no one discipline has all the answers to pressing public policy problems. Yet in our efforts both to research cross-disciplinary interactions and to teach our students about interdisciplinary linkages, we lack a cognitive map which describes how the subject matter of human science fits together. Like the imaginary geography student of the opening paragraph, both researchers and students have no easy way of seeing how the topic they are focused on today fits into a broader whole.

Conceptually, however, constructing such a map is far from impossible. Research in human science almost without exception involves describing how phenomena influence one another (leaving to one side for a moment the philosophical concerns of some scholars with how the world should be or with how scholars do and should behave methodologically, and the efforts of others to describe or measure phenomena). This broad similarity in approach may not be obvious simply because different scholars focus on different sets of phenomena. Moreover, they differ in the sorts of influence which they perceive as important.[1] And as Elster (1989, 4) bemoans, much human science research fails to make clear the causal mechanisms involved.

An organizing schema for human science can be constructed, then, by providing a list of the key phenomena of interest to human scientists and describing the types of influence which one phenomenon could exert on another. In a broad sense the latter part of this task has already been performed by philosophers of science. The first part of the task has been suggested by several scholars over the past decades, but none have been so bold as to actually propose a list (see below). They have recognized, though, that such a list can and should be structured hierarchically with a small set of major categories subdivided into a larger set of phenomena, which in turn can be disaggregated, and so on.[2]

The next section of this chapter tackles definitional issues. How exactly do I define "organizing schema," "phenomena," or "influence"? Although I believe that these terms become clearer in usage, it is useful to provide precise definitions at the outset. One of the key problems facing inter-disciplinary scholars is the diverse meanings attached to words like "culture." I will argue that one advantage of our schema is that it provides precise definitions of phenomena.

In the third section of this chapter I will begin to develop a hierarchical structure of phenomena. I start with a set of ten broad categories which together exhaust the subject matter of human science. These will each be disaggregated in later chapters, yielding a list of over one hundred "second-level" and "third-level" phenomena (see Table 1). While it turns out that the vast bulk of human science research can be understood in terms of these phenomena, I will for many of them describe how further disaggregation could proceed.

The organizing schema (cognitive map) requires more than a list of phenomena. In the fourth section of this chapter, I briefly review the sorts of influence which phenomena can exert on each other. To stop there, however, would risk leaving the impression that human science is a much less complex undertaking than it actually is. While there are only a few broad categories of influence (or causation), the precise mechanisms by which one phenomenon affects another display a huge variety.

Not only are causal links (influences) generally unique but they are ubiquitous. Only rarely can we look at two phenomena and not see some way in which each affects the other.[3] Crime is a good example. While scholars in some disciplines emphasize the individual-level causes and scholars in other disciplines emphasize the society-level causes, the scholarly community as a whole has shown how various aspects of our common genetic base, personality, culture, the natural environment, the economy, politics, social structure, technology, health and population, and even art have an effect on crime. Exposure to this knowledge should render us less susceptible to arguments that there is one solution to the problem of crime (even allowing for the fact that some influences are more important than others). Familiarity with the schema as a whole should encourage healthy skepticism with respect to all major public policy issues.

While it is possible to sketch causal links between almost any two phenomena, it is obvious that scholarly attention has been lavished on some links while others have been virtually ignored. Nor can the relative scholarly attention devoted to particular links always be comprehended in terms of their importance (note also that even links that are of trivial importance at any point in time may still have a huge cumulative impact on the course of world history). Each discipline establishes incentives for its scholars to investigate certain questions and to employ particular methods which are more amenable to some questions than others.[4] Economists, for example, have paid relatively little attention to economic growth in recent decades because its study requires interdisciplinarity and does not lend itself to mathematical modeling. Scholars who investigate questions on the fringes of their disciplines may find that their efforts (if published!) are soon forgotten because others do not build on their insights. Later scholars, in consequence, often reinvent the wheel. An organizing schema can serve to encourage a more balanced scholarly effort, and also serve as a structure on which to hang various insights so that these are not forgotten.

Is this the right schema? I have now read hundreds of works— monographs, works of synthesis, and texts—spanning human science, and have found it straightforward to summarize the arguments contained therein as causal links among the phenomena listed in Table 1. Of course, the schema is inherently flexible, such that as new phenomena are dis- covered—by my own reading in the first instance, or more generally by human science as an enterprise—these phenomena can be added to the schema. While I believe the ten broad categories with which our schema begins are exhaustive, I cannot claim that at lower levels of aggregation I have necessarily listed all phenomena about which human scientists have or should care. I can claim, however, both that the existing schema copes with a vast amount of human science research, and that it can be extended easily to deal with advances in understanding.

Recognizing that the schema I propose is likely to be imperfect in some respects, I would hope that this book motivates scholarly discussion of how to delineate phenomena and place them within a hierarchical struc- ture. I hope and suspect that for most phenomena consensus will not be difficult to achieve. Even if consensus proves elusive in some cases, the schema will still be able to provide a useful framework for interdisciplin- ary research and teaching. And discussion along these lines would help to develop common definitions of a set of terms which will facilitate inter- disciplinary dialogue, research, and teaching.

The bulk of this book is devoted to a detailed description of hundreds of causal links among these phenomena. I will in the fifth section provide an introduction to this material. At that time I will also discuss previous attempts at delineating a list of such causal mechanisms, and the degree to which I found similarities in links across pairs of phenomena. As well, I will explore the degree to which the schema allows us to identify causal links which have received little scholarly attention.

In the sixth section, I discuss how the schema can be visualized as a massive flow chart. In section seven, I describe how my schema is related to previous scholarly suggestions regarding an organizing schema for human science. In section eight, I discuss the advantages of a schema such as this over attempts to unify human science by grand theory or ideology. In section nine, I argue that the schema fits well both with recent trends in philosophy of science and with at least one key strand of postmodernist thought. The tenth section discusses further the value of such a schema: the schema can change the world view of scholars, aid both integration and skill acquisition by students, provide answers to many modern critiques of liberal arts education, facilitate curricular change, and improve public policy.

It is necessary to devote most of the introductory chapter to justifying and describing the schema around which the rest of the book will be structured. Having done so, I can turn in section eleven to a discussion of the rationale for and advantages of the focus on links to and from cultural phenomena which characterizes most of this book. I will discuss in that section how the use of the schema in general, and its application to cultural phenomena in this book in particular, can aid both research and teaching on culture. I close the section by briefly delineating six broad lessons concerning the study of culture that the author draws from the analysis in later chapters.

The book has two broad goals. I wish to justify and establish the value of the schema by applying it to the case of culture. Yet I also wish to provide a structure which enables us to enhance our understanding of the role of culture in human society. That is, I do not just view culture as a testing ground for the schema, but as a subject of great importance whose study the schema helps to illuminate. The fact that this second goal is elucidated late in the chapter reflects only the prior necessity of acquaintance with the schema.

The final section provides an overview of the remaining chapters.

DEFINITIONAL ISSUES

The *organizing schema* consists of two components: a hierarchically structured list of the hundreds of *phenomena* of interest to human scientists, and the thousands of *causal links* which operate among these phenomena.

Kuhn's (1974) definition of the elements of his system could serve as a definition of our *phenomena:* any identifiable entities, concrete or abstract, individual or collective.[5] Kuhn speaks, though, of events. Individual events would not be considered as phenomena in my schema, for my definition of phenomena has the important caveat that I am speaking of ongoing, indeed eternal, characteristics of human society. Individuals may be unique, but our personality dimensions are always with us. Genetic evolution may change our aggressiveness, but attitude to aggression remains a phenomenon worthy of study. Economic and political institutions evolve, but our categorization schema need not change to allow us to capture this diversity (societies lacking a particular institution fit as comfortably within our schema as those who differ in the details of institutional structure).[6] Neither the French Revolution nor Michaelangelo are phenomena; nevertheless we can within our schema discuss both the causes and effects of changes in political structure and acts of artistic genius, and we can test the value of our schema by how well it allows us to understand particular events.[7]

The most precise definition of phenomena is provided by Table 1, wherein I provide a lengthy list of phenomena. What characteristics do these hundreds of phenomena share? They are, as noted above, enduring aspects of human existence. They are also of interest to human scientists and susceptible of scientific description and explanation. Indeed, they comprise the complete set of enduring aspects of human existence which are (or should be) of interest to human scientists.

This definition of phenomena has important implications for the definition of *causal link.* In examining the link between two phenomena, we are asking either how a particular realization within one phenomenon effects the realization within another, or how a change in the one realization induces a change in the other. "Attitude toward honesty" and "economic output" are both phenomena within our schema. In looking at the link between the first and the second, we would wonder whether or not greater honesty tends to facilitate economic transactions and thus a higher rate of growth in output. It is thus not the phenomena themselves which change in our schema—they are defined so that they do not change—but rather particular realizations of those phenomena which change.[8]

Scholars in different disciplines interpret the word *causal* differently. For some, to say that a change in A causes a change in B implies that only a change in A does so. Yet we have seen that all phenomena are affected by many others. As the word *influence* captures this idea of multiple causal links better than the word *cause,* I have used it here. I have, however, stuck with *causal link* because there is no obvious alternative, and I dislike creating jargon unnecessarily. To avoid excessive repetition of the word "influence," I will from time to time speak of causation in what follows. I emphasize that I never mean to imply that *only* one phenomenon influences any other; one key result of this book is that this is never the case. By cause or influence, then, I refer merely to the various ways in which a realization of one phenomenon induces a change in the realization of another.

As Barber (1993) has noted, the lack of a reliable set of definitions of what we are trying to explain is a major obstacle to interdisciplinary research. Some (e.g., Shweder and Fiske 1986) would argue that this is inevitable, that we as humans are inherently unable to define any terms objectively, that definitions depend on points of view. Certainly philosophers have long since abandoned the Platonic ideal whereby all terms could be defined precisely. Yet we need not lose hope. A word like "democracy" hardly lends itself to easy definition, but most of us nevertheless share a fairly similar view of what it means.

Kuhn (1974) recognized that defining terms so that they had the same meaning across disciplines was a first step toward unifying human science. While space alone would prevent me from attempting brief definitions of hundreds of phenomena, the very act of disaggregating serves us well. Whereas Wittgenstein suggested that words could at best be defined in terms of examples of usage, I strive for an exhaustive list of subsidiary phenomena. There are literally hundreds of definitions of the word "culture" in the literature; none is as precise as the disaggregation of the phenomenon below. Culture (as with all other phenomena) means all of the phenomena into which it is unpacked, and only that. Scholars and students from varying disciplines, if conversant with this schema, could thus share very similar definitions of the key phenomena of interest to human scientists.

Finally, I follow what seems to be common practice in using the term *human science* to refer to the social sciences plus psychology and the humanities (note that human science research is undertaken by people outside these disciplines, notably in education, law, and medical faculties). Caws (1993) defines human science as the study of processes involving human agency. This provides a handy guide to our subject matter, for all of the causal links in our schema would involve some human action (or at least a reaction, as to an earthquake); as with *phenomena,* though, the lengthy list of phenomena below provides a more precise definition of our subject matter than any single sentence could.

DEVELOPING A LIST OF PHENOMENA

In describing this project verbally to others, I have often used a convenient shorthand: my purpose is to show how the subjects of the several disciplines in the human sciences are related. While the statement is broadly true, I knew that it nevertheless gave a misleading impression of how the schema was constructed. The simple fact is that the human science disciplines have not carved up their collective subject matter according to any rules of logic. It was not logic but historical accident which decreed that sociology departments lump together criminologists, demographers, students of social divisions by family, race, gender, or class, and some of those intrigued by the idea of culture (the rest being housed in anthropology departments alongside students of human evolution). Even the earliest disciplines to emerge—economics and political science—came over time to focus on some sub-areas of what might seem logical domains, while paying scant attention to others. In the humanities, too, individual departments combine specialists in language, literature, or culture, with departmental divisions predicated on language spoken or region of concern rather than scholarly orientation.[9] Moreover, with the recent proliferation of departmental structures, there is considerable room for doubt as to what qualifies as a discipline. To have taken our modern disciplinary/departmental structure as the basis for the broadest categories would have forced me, then, into a depraved sort of intellectual gymnastics from which my project could hardly have been expected to emerge intact.

I must begin, then, by attempting to divide the subject matter of human science into logical categories.[10] These categories must cope both with individual characteristics and with societal characteristics. At the level of persons I begin with our "genetic predisposition." As a species, we share a gene pool which gives us all a set of basic abilities, motivations, and emotions. While our common gene pool guarantees a certain set of characteristics that define us as a species, differences in the precise genes which individuals possess, in concert with differences in environment, serve to guarantee that individuals differ from each other both physically and psychologically. This yields a second category of "individual differences."

All humans are necessarily part of a larger community, especially for the first few years of life (that is, one of our shared genetic characteristics is that we are born needing the help of others). I identify several distinct categories of collective behavior:

- How we interact with the nonhuman environment in order to create (and distribute) food, shelter, and other items of practical utility: "the economy."
- How we interact with the nonhuman environment to create items desired (primarily)for their aesthetic appeal rather than their utility: "art." (Note that works of art, through their aesthetic appeal, may serve further purposes, such as encouraging religious belief; such effects would be captured in causal links.)
- How the various subgroups of society interact: "social structure." (There are always at least two types of subgroup, for the family is ubiquitous, albeit in

different forms, and genders have never yet been treated in precisely the same way.)

- How power is distributed and exercised: "politics."
- It is obvious that hierarchical economic, social, and political structures evolve (or at least attempts are made by those at the top to do so) beliefs in the correctness of those structures. Such beliefs thus logically belong to those categories. Yet societies have a host of religious beliefs, customs, habits, and so on whose connection to these other realms is (at least potentially) tenuous: these I call "culture." (I will follow common usage here and treat "languages" as a subset of "culture.") The precise definition of culture will become clearer below. (Attitudes toward all categories except economy, politics, and social structure are thus part of culture.)
- We also develop knowledge of how we can best manipulate the nonhuman world to suit our various ends: "science and technology."
- The list may seem complete, but we must also perpetuate ourselves as a species, and thus must consider "population." Our ability to reproduce depends in turn on our ability to survive. We must also, then, consider the related matter of "health," which deserves more attention than it receives from human scientists.
- I have mentioned the "nonhuman environment" more than once above. Since it both shapes and is shaped by us, it deserves its own role in our schema as another category.

We now have a list of ten (eleven if we treat health and population separately) logically distinct categories. I believe them also to be exhaustive, for they seem to subsume all human activities and characteristics, and I have found it straightforward to place all subsidiary phenomena within these categories. In other words, I have used both induction and deduction: induction in the sense of reading widely and finding a place in the schema for all phenomena discussed in these works, and deduction in the sense of thinking about how phenomena could logically be broken into their constituent parts (I would note here the broad though not unanimous consensus among philosophers of science that both induction and deduction should play a role in scientific inquiry). In several cases, I must be careful to establish the boundaries between categories: for example I can distinguish "art" from certain aspects of "culture" by defining "art" as that which has an aesthetic appeal not limited to members of particular groups. These precise boundaries will become clearer as I disaggregate the categories in what follows.

Some readers may imagine a somewhat different logical division of human activity. The author himself was a little queasy about including languages within the culture category. Yet in practice the choice of major categories is less important than it might first appear. The causal links which interest human scientists are generally, though not always, to be found at lower levels of aggregation. Even scholars who talk of cultural influences usually have in mind a subset of what I will subsume under the heading "culture." Indeed, I have referred to our ten categories as "categories" rather than simply "major phenomena" or "higher-level phenomena" in part to signal the fact that they are not in general the focus of causal analysis. As we disaggregate our categories into subsidiary phenomena, we can examine how these phenomena influence other phenomena within their category as well as in other categories. In this way, we can see, for example, if language is closely linked with other cultural phenomena. This can help us to determine whether we feel comfortable including language within the "culture" category.

Despite the arbitrary nature of disciplinary boundaries, human scientists have accomplished much. As a first check on the exhaustiveness of our schema, then, it is useful to see whether it subsumes the subject matter of existing disciplines (we examine disciplines in more detail in the concluding chapter). Economists, political scientists, and linguists have the least to worry about, for three of our phenomena respectively bear their names. Only at lesser levels of aggregation need we concern ourselves with inclusiveness. The same is largely true of cultural anthropology. Physical anthropology, on the other hand, is concerned in part with human evolution and in part with how traditional societies functioned; this latter role touches on all of our phenomena. Geographers who focus on how the physical environment shapes human activity will have an obvious place in our schema; those who study the spatial element of all sorts of human activity will find their research interests strewn across a wide range of causal links. Psychologists who focus on explaining average human propensities (or developmental processes) will find their work reflected in our discussion of genetic predisposition; those who study personality or mental disorder will find that the category of individual differences covers their concerns. Sociology inevitably will find its interests distributed among various phenomena. Two of these, social structure and population, have been primarily the province of sociologists in the past. So has criminology, though properly it is a political activity. Sociological concern with norms and values will within our schema be treated as part of culture. Literature and fine arts departments will find their focus of interest represented in "art." Area studies departments will find their subject matter spread across phenomena, as will historians.

What, finally, of philosophy? In past centuries philosophers focused on questions of metaphysics (is there a god?, and so on) and ethics. Such questions lie on a plane above our present analysis. We are concerned in this work with how the world works, not with how it should work. I will, for example, discuss the relationship between certain cultural attitudes and economic growth, while leaving it to the reader to determine whether these are good or bad outcomes.[11] Such worthy debates are best left to other works.[12] One important philosophical field, the philosophy of science, will be the subject of our second chapter. This will give readers guidance as to how to evaluate the scientific evidence of later chapters. Much of modern philosophical research is concerned with questions of language and logic; I have discussed the former briefly above. As with philosophy of science, these areas of philosophical inquiry guide us in our analysis but do not form part of the subject matter. In recent decades, the boundaries between philosophy and other disciplines have weakened, and some philosophical work has focused on particular causal links: action theorists ask how belief shapes action, philosophers of mind examine how our brain functions, and philosophers of science look at how science has proceeded. Such insights will be reported as appropriate.

In disaggregating, we are identifying subsidiary phenomena which together comprise a category. For example, within our social structure category we can identify societal divisions by gender, class, and ethnicity. If we succeed in identifying all such social divisions, we will have a list which comprises (and thus defines) what I have called social structure. In most but not all cases we will wish to disaggregate further: classes for example are composites of various occupations. I have termed phenomena such as class to be second-level phenomena, and phenomena at the yet lower level of disaggregation to be third-level phenomena (and will note where further disaggregation to a fourth level is possible and desirable). This is done to identify their place in the schema; there is no value judgment in the terminology. Scholars are free to decide at which level of disaggregation they wish to focus. And note further that causal links are not constrained to act only within a particular level: second-level phenomena can influence third-level and vice versa.

A reductionist research agenda (that is, one which seeks explanation in terms of phenomena at the lowest level of aggregation) would stress *only* the ways in which lower-level phenomena influence higher-level phenomena. I wish the schema to organize human science research and teaching without constraining it. I would thus not artificially encourage the discovery of only one direction of influence. If over time it was found that "bottom-up" influences were much more important than "top-down," the reductionist research program would be advanced. But this is an empirical question on which the schema itself is silent. We will find in this book that higher-level phenomena do exert important influences on lower-level phenomena, and thus the analysis of this book is inconsistent with a reductionist approach. I would note that this finding is in accord with recent research in the natural sciences which suggests that higher-level phenomena such as living organisms cannot be entirely comprehended in terms of the analysis of lower-level phenomena such as atoms (Hodgson 1993).

A mixture of deduction and induction was used to arrive at the lists of subsidiary phenomena, just as with the ten major categories above.[13] Although the details of this disaggregation must be left to chapters 3–11 (each of these starts by introducing and disaggregating a different phenomenon), I would be cheating the reader if I did not take a first tentative step down that road here. While Kontopolous (1993) suggests that all phenomena can be analyzed in terms of four levels of social interaction (global to local), we will find it best to disaggregate different phenomena along different dimensions. Some of these are obvious. Our genetic inheritance consists of a finite number of diverse abilities, goals, and emotions. Along with gender and family, we will, under the heading of social structure, worry about occupation, class, and ethnicity. Culture comprises a particular set of beliefs, values, and customs. Psychologists have developed hierarchical typologies of personality types (though these are not the only individual differences). When we turn to the economy and politics we will find that we are primarily concerned with institutions, and will discuss how these might be categorized. We also concern ourselves with average income and income distribution (and ideology) under the economy heading. In politics, ideology, nationalism, and public opinion will also be foci. Technology, science, and the arts will all be unpacked primarily in terms of subject area. Table One (pages 329–335) in this book provides a summary of our hierarchical listing of phenomena. While the appendix does not contain the rationale for the categorization therein, the reader may find that consulting it nevertheless gives them a flavor of the overall schema.

In my introductory remarks, I provided one form of justification for the schema: that it is easy to fit all human science understanding into this. Nevertheless it is useful here to further justify the choice of phenomena. I must first respond to a philosophical complaint; as Cromer (1997) notes, human scientists are sometimes guilty of devising categorization schemes that are incapable of empirical validation. While some of our phenomena clearly do exist (income, art, technology), others, such as various cultural attitudes, are not as concrete. Nevertheless, I will ensure that all phenomena are open to some form of scientific identification.[14]

In doing so, I will naturally rely heavily on existing research. This is also the best defense against a second possible complaint: that this hierarchical list of phenomena is only one of many equally valid ways of carving up human science. We will often find in what follows that there is a fair degree of scientific consensus on how to disaggregate certain phenomena. In other cases, such as our discussion of personality dimensions, we will find that there is intense scholarly debate over the correct categorization scheme. In such cases, I will present varying points of view, and choose among these that which best facilitates cross disciplinary linkages.

I will also seek completeness: every phenomenon that meets my standard for existence should find some place in the schema (and as noted above, phenomena I may have missed can be added). The schema can thus not be accused of omitting key phenomena. Of course, scholars may disagree on where a particular phenomenon best fits within the schema. I can strive to minimize such concern by justifying each choice in terms of the existing scholarly literature.

While completeness is an important goal, we should nevertheless keep in mind that some phenomena and causal links are more important than others. I have not attempted to rank these here; this further step in scholarly debate is best postponed until the idea of a comprehensive schema has achieved wider acceptance. I should stress that there are at least three good reasons for not examining only those phenomena and links which "seem" most important. First, scholarly bias may cause us to neglect important linkages. Second, even seemingly trivial linkages can have an important cumulative effect on human history. Third, complexity theory tells us that small changes can have a huge impact within a complex system such as our schema (see Hodgson 1993).

I should stress again the flexibility of the schema. As our understanding of the strength of various causal links increases, we can decide empirically how best to place particular phenomena within a hierarchical schema. The schema itself can thus guide us toward its own improvement. And the degree of scholarly consensus available in many areas should encourage us to believe that we will not have to make too many adjustments.

Finally, let us pursue the analogy of mapmaking a bit further. We are all aware that a variety of maps can be made of any locale. Some emphasize topography, others road networks, still others variation in climate or economic activity. Yet we also recognize that maps are extremely useful. Likewise with our schema; the possibility that there *may* be other ways of providing an overview of human science should not distract us from the inherent utility of this effort to provide the first map of the region.

CAUSAL LINKS

While there is still philosophical debate about whether a cause must always precede its result (some relationships in physics may involve reverse temporal causation), this is certainly the general case. Moreover, influence (causation) does not usually occur at a distance: proximity in time and space is required. That being said, events can have a worldwide impact as long as there are worldwide communication links. Similarly in time, Plato can still affect us both because we can still read him, and because previous readings of him have shaped our culture and institutions. Thus, with recourse to a more complex chain of causation, we can have causation at a distance (see Lambert and Brittan 1992).

We are often able to define causal links in human science only in a probabilistic sense: a change in one phenomenon increases the probability of a change in the other.[15] In some instances, this reflects the limits to our understanding: if we understood cancer better, we might be able to specify under what conditions smoking will cause it, rather than just speaking of increased risk. In other instances it reflects the fact that human decisions are not perfectly predictable. We would hardly agonize so much over decisions if it was always clear which choice we would make.[16]

We cannot just assume that correlation implies causation; the observation that X and Y tend to occur together could mean that either causes the other, or that some other unobserved phenomenon causes both, or could be the result of chance (decreasingly likely as the number of observations increases). Even if X is observed to precede Y we would not be comfortable arguing that X causes Y unless there was some theoretical argument as to why this should be the case (possibly involving intervening phenomena). We would then look for various sorts of evidence by which to test whether the theory appears to approximate reality. Unfortunately, much human science research, and most descriptive history and everyday conversation, fail to make causal mechanisms clear, but merely point to an alleged cause (Elster 1989, 4).

In studying causation (influence), we can often distinguish between making a result possible, and acting on such potential. Some chemical reactions occur only in the presence of a catalyst; the catalyst can be said to cause the reaction by making it possible. Likewise a speeding car reflects both the decision of the driver and the mechanical capability of the car.

Elster (1989, 6) warns us of cases of causal preemption, such as when a bullet kills someone who would otherwise have soon died of cancer, and causal overdetermination, such as when either of two bullets would have killed someone. In the general case, though, there will only be one cause, or more accurately one set of causes which combine to bring about a particular result (though, of course, we may have trouble identifying these).

We can identify five types of causation:

STRICT CAUSATION

This is the direct action of one entity on another, such as when a bat hits a baseball, or sodium and chlorine react. In some cases, strict causation is entirely predictable, at least theoretically: if we know the acceleration of the baseball and bat, the precise nature and shape of these, the angle of impact, and air pressure, we can calculate where the ball will land. In other cases, such as quantum mechanics, only probabilistic prediction is possible.

INTENTIONAL CAUSATION

Considered by some a subset of strict causation, intentional causation occurs when some sentient being or group thereof purposely acts in a particular way. This often will involve present suffering for future gain. Humans, at least, are also capable of collective action which only aids individuals if adopted by all. For our purposes, the key characteristic of intentional acts is that they have unforeseen consequences, because none of us completely understands how the world works (see Merton 1996). If not for this, explaining human behavior would be much easier, for we could assume that people must have wanted the result that they achieved. Rather, we must try to understand action in terms of people's desires, schemas, and environment, and then analyze the effects of these actions.

According to Secord (1986), in the behavioral sciences, when talking about causation, we are really looking at an organism's capacity for action. As with strict causation, we can recognize this as only a part of the answer: we must understand both an individual's capabilities, as well as the choices they make among many feasible actions. We must be careful to avoid aping the natural sciences by downplaying the element of human choice so that intentionality becomes indistinguishable from strict causation.

SEMIOTIC OR HERMENEUTIC CAUSATION

Considered by some a subset of intentional causation, we are concerned here with the meanings we impose on the world. Many of those primarily concerned with symbolism shy away from explicit discussions of causation. In turn, Zolberg (1990) and many anthropologists worry that a focus on the symbolic meaning of cultural creations is incompatible with an effort to uncover causal links. Philosophers, too, have worried that it is impossible to scientifically analyze "meaning." Yet this need not be the case. If people create cultural symbols, and these have an impact on the behavior of others (that is, communicate some meaning to them), then scientists must examine these causal links. The variety of symbols will naturally appear daunting at first. Moreover, symbols generally have meaning only within a larger set of symbols; practitioners of hermeneutics thus argue that we must understand both the whole and the parts, which are interdependent. And the fact that some symbols affect us sublingually complicates the task of describing the effect in words. As with other aspects of our schema, though, we must endeavor to classify symbols in some fashion, and then see how certain types of symbols are created (note that we cannot assume these to carry the meaning intended by either the conscious or unconscious mind), interact with others, and in turn affect behavior. If we look at a wide range of situations, and employ diverse methods, scientific judgments should be possible (D'Andrade 1986).

FUNCTIONALIST (STRUCTURALIST) CAUSATION

A functional explanation involves arguing that X is necessary for Y to exist (e.g., one might argue that a police force or army is essential to the maintenance of a state). Functional relationships are too easily assumed (Why are police needed? What happens without them?), and are often key elements in hypotheses of stable subsystems of phenomena; we must both empirically and theoretically describe how the functional relationship came into being: for example, how do states find the resources for army/ police? (see Vromen 1995; Elster 1983). By doing so, functional explanations come to bear a strong similarity to intentional, though with an added element: those that do not create armies will not be able to create states.

EVOLUTIONARY CAUSATION

Evolutionary explanations involve a dynamic process consisting of some source(s) of variation and some sort of selection mechanism. In biological evolution, for example, genetic mutation is the source of variation, and genes are selected on the basis of whether they enhance reproductive fitness in the organism's environment. It is noteworthy that evolutionary explanations were applied to other phenomena before genes: Darwin borrowed from ideas of the evolution of state forms. Many, though not all, of our phenomena are subject to evolution, with other phenomena serving as the selection environment. We can speak of cultural, institutional, technological, scientific, and artistic evolution, in addition to genetic evolution.[17]

Genetic mutation is random (see chapter 4); genes cannot achieve some "desired" improvement purposely. All other forms of evolution of interest to us differ in this important respect: they depend for the most part on individuals or groups purposely striving to improve their institutions or technology (accidental advances are possible too, perhaps especially in the realm of culture). This allows scope for superior explanation. We can hope not only to explain why particular changes were selected for by the relevant environment, but also why people would have introduced such changes in the first place. We must be careful, though, not to assume that people always foresaw the particular effects of their innovations.

Most biologists are highly skeptical of the idea of group selection. They would argue, for example, that a genetic propensity for altruism could only have been selected for if it aided the fitness of individual organisms. That is, the fact that altruism may be a helpful attitude of a group does not explain how a genetic propensity for altruism could have originally gained a foothold. We must understand how altruistic individuals would have prospered when surrounded by the selfish. With respect to other forms of evolution, though, we can easily imagine group selection of beliefs, institutions, or techniques which are only advantageous if adopted by many.

Following Durham (1991) we can think of five key questions in the study of evolutionary mechanisms. First, what units should we use for studying evolution? In biology scholars focus on genes, and in technology on techniques. There is considerable debate over the course of cultural evolution; I would suggest that culture evolves through changes in individual cultural traits. Second, what are the sources of variation? Mutation, innovation, and cross-cultural contact are among the possibilities here. Third, what are the mechanisms of transmission? If genes, culture, or technology were not passed on from generation to generation, we could not speak of evolution, for each generation would start from scratch. If, however, transmission were perfect, then random mutation would be impossible. Fourth, what is the selection mechanism? What other phenomena are most important in determining whether a mutation survives? Fifth, what causes different groups to evolve differently? An explanation of why a particular institution or cultural trait exists in one society must include some explanation of why it does or does not exist elsewhere.

THE SCHEMA IN OPERATION

I have described the schema above in terms of one-way causal links between two phenomena. In the real world that I hope to capture, though, phenomena often combine in exerting influence on other phenomena, causal links often affect more than one phenomenon at a time, and effects in one direction often elicit some sort of feedback response (which may act to either reduce or reinforce the initial impulse; in the latter case we speak of vicious or virtuous cycles, and must appreciate that small initial changes can have a huge cumulative impact). Yet if we were to conceive of the schema as a (very messy; see next section) flow chart with arrows denoting causal links among phenomena, feedback effects could be captured with two-way arrows, and multiple causation could be captured by arrows joining and/or splitting between phenomena. In other words, the schema is flexible enough to incorporate the multiple causation and feedback effects which characterize the real world.

Often when two phenomena combine to influence another, one creates a potential for change which the other acts upon. For example, genetic inheritance creates various potentials within an infant. A variety of environmental factors then act to determine to what extent these potentials are realized. In this case there is great scope for examining the effects of genes in isolation.

Another common occurrence is for various other phenomena to affect the strength of a particular causal link between two phenomena. We may thus observe that a causal link which is strong in some times and places is weak in others.[18] In such cases, we must first analyze the link itself in detail, but also analyze how other phenomena affect it. One can think of an electronic metaphor: a causal link is like a flow of electricity along a circuit, with other phenomena affecting resistance. Rule (1997, 208–15) argues that in human science, unlike natural science, there are few universal laws but rather the strength of causal links depends on a range of other phenomena; if so then identifying these "resistors" is a key task of human science research.

Taylor (1993) suggested that all changes in culture or institutions must be mediated by individual action. Interpreted too literally, this would automatically eliminate the bulk of our proposed links from consideration. Cultural values, for example, could have no direct influence on the economy, or politics, or technology. All such effects would be filtered through individual personalities. If so, this would be unfortunate for our schema, for it would crowd all that was important onto a small subset of causal links. Yet when Taylor himself goes on to discuss the causes of revolution, his arguments for the role of individuals mostly collapse into arguments about culture or institutions. For example he talks about how the cohesiveness of the local village community is a major determinant of revolutionary potential. In such an argument the individual disappears, except for the fact that village communities are formed of individuals. If $X \to Z$, but only through the passive intermediation of Y, it is best to focus on $X \to Z$, for the links $X \to Y$ and $Y \to Z$ will be meaningless on their own. Even if the role of Y is a little less than passive, it will still be best to focus on $X \to Z$, with some mention of how different states of Y will affect the strength and direction of $X \to Z$.

In describing the links between phenomena it is often useful to discuss several links together, even when these can be logically separated. For example, a general discussion of how personality characteristics influence leadership capabilities or human creativity can be followed by more focused discussions of how leaders are chosen and act within particular institutional settings (recognizing that being chosen a leader tends to affect one's personality), or of the particular creative requirements of technological innovation, entrepreneurship, or various arts. In this way, the tremendous insights of Alfred Kuhn (1974) are easily incorporated within the schema. He proffers a detailed examination of three types of human interaction: communication, transactions, and organizations. He develops first of all some general characteristics of these three and then shows how with additional sorts of qualifications his analysis can be narrowed to particular examples of human interaction of interest to scholars in different fields. I can discuss his general observations when the phenomena of interpersonal relationships and organizations are first introduced, and relate these to more particular discussions elsewhere.

Kuhn's objective was even more ambitious than my own. He wanted to develop an axiomatic system for human science. Yet he was only able to proceed from the general to the particular in a handful of cases spanning just a couple of disciplines. Our present approach is quite different, though not necessarily incompatible. By first delineating the causal relationships we need to understand, and then noting similarities where these exist, we can at once sketch the big picture while pointing the way to further integrative research. Nevertheless, the very complexity of our schema highlights the difficulty of fully implementing Kuhn's vision.

More recently, Kontopolous (1994) has suggested a lengthy list of "logics" (causal mechanisms). Game theory, sorting rules, matching rules, fractals, cascades, and thresholds are among the logics he discusses. Many of these, such as the observation that the diffusion of any innovation tends to occur slowly at first, then more rapidly, before slowing again as saturation is approached (the S-shaped diffusion curve), do indeed have a wide applicability. In explicating the schema, it naturally pays to elucidate such mechanisms only once (though for students there are advantages in repetition). Rarely if ever, though, does discussion of how one phenomenon influences another revolve around any one single mechanism. And Kontopolous recognizes that his list is far from exhaustive.

I discussed in the third section the five major types of causation. Now we have seen some more detailed "logics" which each will operate across a range of causal links. Individual causal links generally involve more than one type of causation. Likewise, different logics are important for different links. Moreover, feedback effects and multiple causation are more important in some cases than others. While I naturally note similarities across causal links when these exist, as for example in the way that various genetic predispositions constrain variability in various cultural attributes, the overwhelming result of my research is that it is uniqueness rather than similarity which best describes individual causal links between phenomena.

Just as we need to be cognizant of the fact that small changes can, in the right circumstances, have a huge impact, we must also realize that human history is dotted with great transformations. The development of agriculture, the invention of writing, or the emergence of a new religion are examples; their occurrence changed the course of human history. More generally, Laszlo (1987) suggests that human history is best seen as periods of gradual change punctuated by crises in which large changes are observed in many phenomena. Scientific theory (and hence our schema) must be flexible enough to handle both big and little changes. I will discuss both in subsequent chapters.

VISUALIZING THE SCHEMA

We can reproduce the list of phenomena derived in the third section and later chapters in tabular form (Table 1). Remember, though, that third-level phenomena could generally be subjected to yet further disaggregation.

The causal links can be represented as arrows joining one or more phenomena in our table with one or more others. If we wished to visualize one causal link, such as the effect of a particular personality dimension on crime, this can easily be done by drawing a line between these phenomena. If we wished to visualize the "major" causes of crime, as identified by diverse scholars, we might find ourselves with a manageable set of such lines. If, however, we asked ourselves to draw in every plausible cause of crime, and especially if we allowed indirect causation via intermediate phenomena, we would find our table covered in lines. And if we moved back yet further to consider all of the causal links of interest to human scientists, even the most skilled draftsperson would drown our table in ink. While it is useful to think of our schema as a set of arrows between phenomena, we must remember that we can only actually draw in the arrows for particular narrowly defined questions.

RELATIONSHIP TO PREVIOUS SCHEMAS

My research as an economic historian and economic methodologist had caused me to explore phenomena within each of our ten major categories. Thus, when the idea of designing an organizing schema first came to me, the broad shape of that schema was already fairly clear in my mind. When I became aware of previous efforts in this area, then, these served as a scientific check on my thinking.

Talcott Parsons (1966) developed an organizing schema with four main components: the human organism (similar to our genetic predisposition), personality, culture, and social structure. Social structure for Parsons referred to the interaction among the previous three components. These interactions are what I have called causal links. Parsons recognized the nonhuman environment (in which he included the nonbehavioral elements of our genetic predisposition) as a background for his schema. Economic and technical issues arose as interactions between humans and their environment, while politics emerged from a study of personality.

As it would be fairly easy to add art and health and population to this schema, it does not differ hugely in terms of broad categories from mine, though the borders between categories are not exactly the same. Parsons differed from me, though, in positing the existence of fairly autonomous subsystems within the broader schema. It is possible, of course, that a subset of phenomena might collectively have such weak (or counteracting) links with other phenomena that they could safely be treated separately. I have felt it best to not build such subsystems in, but rather to construct one large schema and leave it to empirical investigation as to whether fairly autonomous subsystems can be identified. The ubiquity of causal links within the larger schema seems to suggest otherwise.[19] Parsons also implied that the schema itself would need to increase in complexity to describe societies of increased complexity; I have tried to define our phenomena in terms of the purpose served in the hope that the same schema can be applied to all societies.

Barber (1993) divides the human science subject matter into cultural structure, social structure, and personality structure. The latter category (which he subdivides into five personality attributes) bears the closest similarity to one of mine (note, though, that he makes no mention of genetic predisposition). His cultural category contains several elements of my culture (languages, religion, philosophy, values), as well as the arts (literature, music, architecture, and drama) and science (science, mathematics). His social structure contains prestige stratification, gender, family (kinship), and organization, as well as the economy and polity (he also speaks of power stratification). He also refers to both socialization and communication, which would be causal links rather than phenomena within my schema. Despite ignoring genes, nonhuman environment, technology, population, and health, and placing ideology with culture, at the highest level of aggregation within my schema there is much similarity. Since he did not intend, at least immediately, to put his schema to work, such omissions should not be assigned a great importance.

The most important distinction is Barber's use of three super-categories. Every human act, he notes, is conditioned by personality, the individual's social position, and the culture in which the individual operates. Thus, we might be guided always to search for three-variable multiple causation. Often, these effects will prove difficult to disentangle. At other times, though, we can advance our understanding by looking at the causal links separately. Still other times, we will find that one causal link overwhelms the effect of others. Thus while Barber is right in suggesting that we always look in these three broad directions, we should not constrain our answers to always come in that form.

Brady (1989) proposes a schema comprised of five main categories. Three of these—beliefs (culture), physical environment, and demography (population)—bear a striking resemblance to three of my categories (and notably fill a couple of the gaps in Barber's schema). His fourth category, behavior, includes art, organizations, relationships, ownership, income distribution, and a variety of other elements. These all have places in my schema. His fifth category is relationships among the first four. This will be captured by my causal links.

It is gratifying, though perhaps not that surprising, that I can find support for my broadest categories in these previous works. What I cannot find in any of these is any considerable attempt to disaggregate the major categories into their constituent phenomena. This necessarily means that any discussion of causal links must occur at a very general level. Since almost all of the action in human science occurs at lower levels of aggregation, these earlier attempts have had a limited impact on research and teaching in human science.

A group of scholars associated with the Human Relations Area Files (HRAF) project have produced a disaggregated list of human science phenomena (see Murdock et al. 1982). The list was developed for two purposes: to assist scholars in annotating and classifying their observations of diverse societies, and to aid researchers in locating material in HRAF files, which contain millions of pages of societal descriptions. It thus serves a broadly similar purpose to library classification systems: it allows not just books but individual sentences or paragraphs to be coded by content. While Murdock et al. (1982) take pains to emphasize the inter-disciplinary nature of their project, their system has primarily been used by ethnographers and generally in the study of traditional societies.

While the HRAF organization encourages causal analysis (see Ember and Ember 1988), there is nevertheless a huge difference between their classification system and my schema. I began with a set of logically distinct categories and attempted to disaggregate these into logically distinct subsidiary phenomena. Murdock et al. admit that while they attempted to group like elements together, and arrange entries in "an order not wholly without logic" (1982, xvi), their approach was essentially pragmatic in that they listed categories commonly used by ethnographers. They had from time to time experimented with more logical classifications based on theory, but found that this made coding ethnographic material more difficult. The resulting system consists of 79 major (given two-digit codes) and 637 minor (three-digit codes) divisions. The major divisions, though, are not really aggregates but catchalls for information not readily classified by minor division. Lacking the hierarchical structure of my schema, the system thus provides a limited guide to how phenomena are related (it is an address book rather than a map). Moreover, without such a structure, the authors confess that their categories are not necessarily mutually exclusive.

Ethnographers often record various aspects of an event simultaneously. The coding system thus mixes up elements of our ten categories. The several major divisions devoted to economic activity tend to include technological (how) and economic (how much) information in the same minor divisions. On the other hand, our cultural category is strewn widely: norms (code 183), attitudes (208), ethical ideals (577), taboos (784), sex (83).

I do not mean to criticize the HRAF, which I think a laudable attempt to bring some order to a vast body of research, but rather to emphasize its difference in purpose and form from the schema outlined here. It does highlight the potential of a comprehensive classification system for collating all scientific research. It also shows that a complex system can still change with experience and new information. And it allows me an opportunity to check for phenomena I may have overlooked. The differences in the HRAF list and my own reflect the fact that they disaggregate some phenomena, such as the economic and technological, much further (listing various products and processes), while not disaggregating others such as norms or personality dimensions at all (the HRAF list also includes some entries which are better thought of as causal links or evolutionary processes: cultural contact, personality development, socialization). This consistency in lists is especially noteworthy given the HRAF focus on traditional societies and the tendency of my own research to focus on modern societies.

GRAND THEORY IS NOT THE ANSWER

Attempts to unify human science have generally taken the form of grand theories rather than organizing schemas. From the time of Smith, Hume, and Marx, who naturally roamed across yet-to-be-created disciplinary boundaries, through the earliest sociologists, led by Comte and Spencer, to the postwar efforts of structuralists, system theorists, Foucault and Derrida (who, Skinner, 1985, believes decried the idea of grand theory while creating their own), and recent works of White (1992) and Barkow, Cosmides and Tooby (1992), among many many others, scientists have been tempted to believe that one great insight (or perhaps a handful of interrelated insights) held the key to understanding human science. Such theories have often captured the imagination of thousands of human scientists. The disillusionment that naturally accompanies the discovery that no theory has all the answers has arguably lessened the enthusiasm for interdisciplinarity of all types (Barber 1993), though the dream of a unified theory has not died. I would share Parsons' (1966) conclusion that "All such single factor theories belong to the kindergarten stage of social [human] science's development," and Trigg's (1985) warning that, "In our quest for the nature of reality, it can be disastrous to assume that it is less complicated than it is." I hope that the recognition that human science comprises thousands (millions) of causal links among hundreds (thousands) of phenomena will help put to rest the idea that one theory can explain all or even most of human experience.

Of course, our own everyday experience should always have guided us to understand that the world is a very complex place indeed. We do not guide our behavior by some grand theory but rather several rules of thumb (schemas) applied to different situations. And we are often surprised when these fail to guide us in novel situations. It is likely that our natural desire to oversimplify the world in order to believe that we are in control supports the dream of grand theory; perhaps a clear exposition of a unifying alternative is the necessary antidote.

The natural sciences, it might be noted, are not characterized by one grand theory but by a large number of theories focused on different causal relationships. The natural sciences appear more integrated precisely because there is widespread agreement (not necessarily deserved) on the phenomena of interest and a concerted effort to ensure that theories are compatible across disciplinary boundaries. While our schema alone cannot ensure compatibility, it can at least ensure that scholars know when they are talking about the same causal link.

One advantage of abandoning the quixotic quest for the quintessential theory of human science is that we can proceed to a more sensible debate concerning the validity of theories. It is too easy to point to circumstances where Marxism, neoclassical economics, or evolutionary psychology have little to tell us; it is too dangerous to then leap to the conclusion that these theories are somehow "wrong" and cannot illustrate any facets of human existence. A much better course is to evaluate theories link by link. In doing so my schema provides us with the advantages of a unified theory in showing how the pieces fit together, while at the same time facilitating the theoretical (and methodological) flexibility on which scientific advance depends.

This latter point deserves emphasis. Klein (1990) notes that many early interdisciplinary efforts failed due to a misguided belief that some grand theory would naturally fall out of attempts to bring interdisciplinary "data" together. Within disciplines too, scholarship has become overly fragmented, with only limited attempts to fit the pieces together (Hugill 1993, Barber 1993). It does not take too great a stretch of the imagination to suspect that the very arbitrariness of disciplinary boundaries, coupled with the repeated failure of naive grand theories, is largely responsible for this state of affairs. My schema offers us a means to tie thousands of autonomous research programs together.

PHILOSOPHICAL JUSTIFICATION

Many who do interdisciplinary work "stress the need to develop integrating frameworks in which cross-disciplinary research can proceed" (Bechtel 1986, 38–39). Dogan and Pelassy (1990) advocate the establishment of an overarching typology, followed by analysis of the dynamic relationship between pairs of phenomena. Elster (1993, 2–3) recognizes that progress will not come from grand theories, but rather from the explication of an interrelated set of specific causal patterns. Klein (1990) recognizes the advantage of searching for causal relationships within some cohesive structure. Further, she notes that this is only possible to the extent that researchers share a set of concepts.

Law (1994, 12–14) warns us of the dangers of reductionist theories which assert that only causation in certain directions is important. He is equally wary of structural arguments that leave little scope for the change which is endemic to [at least] modern societies. He concludes that we must remain open to a variety of causal links with a place for physical, technological, and environmental as well as social phenomena. He applauds Foucault, many feminists, and some others, for their willingness to look at causation in two directions. The social world is not tidy but rather the result of a "complex and messy" interaction of diverse causal links. I might make special note of the word "messy," for we must get past the idea that some tidy set of (symmetrical or similarly structured) theories will capture human diversity for us.

Wilson (1998, 298) argues that, "a united system of knowledge is the surest means of identifying the still unexplored domains of reality. It provides a clear map of what is known, and it frames the most productive questions for further inquiry." He notes that asking the right question is a greater scientific virtue than providing the right answer. Such a system does not limit creativity but encourages it, due to the complexity of natural and human science. "The greatest challenge today . . . in all of science, is the accurate and complete description of complex systems" (1998, 85). While Wilson dreams of unifying both natural and human science, he recognizes that the two key areas of interaction between these two spheres of inquiry are our genes and our natural environment; these are both prominent parts of our schema (and I draw on insights from natural science as necessary). Wilson at times speaks favorably of reduction, but at other times clearly recognizes the need to analyze the two-way interaction between simple and complex phenomena.

Brady (1989) argues that humans need conceptual structures into which they can place diverse information. These allow them to simplify information and generate new propositions. He thinks it is obscene that helping students to recognize, analyze, and describe relationships between distinct phenomena is not recognized as the primary goal of education.

REALISM

Our approach bears a close resemblance to the philosophy of "realism" as advocated with great success by Roy Bhaskar. As outlined by Cloke, Philo, and Sadler (1991) Bhaskar's realism involves the recognition that the world is made up of systems, structures[20]—more generally "things"—which exist in causal relationships with each other. The task of science is to identify these "things" and outline the causal links between them. In the human sciences both individuals and social formations are "things" with causal roles to play. Some of these "things" may be readily observable while others are not. Thus we should expect that as science advances we will find ourselves adjusting our schema. In particular, just as physicists have increasingly explored a diversity of subatomic particles, we will find that our "things" have constituent parts (and these in turn have parts). We are also likely to find that particular phenomena are joined by multiple causal mechanisms. (Some have thus recoiled at the complexity of the realist research enterprise.)

Realists use the term "unpacking" to refer to the process of examining the components which comprise "things." Although I generally eschew jargon in this book, I will borrow this phrase and often speak of unpacking in later chapters.

Realism suggests that we should not worry overmuch about the possibility of leaving out key phenomena. Most, though perhaps not all, "things" of interest in human science will already be described in the language of the day-to-day world. Rare indeed should be the life-affecting phenomenon which will have escaped notice by all of the billions of people who have inhabited this globe (though certain causal links will have received little attention). However, as we search for the constituent parts of our phenomena at lower and lower levels of aggregation, we are increasingly likely to uncover previously unremarked forces at work.

Realism has a great deal in common with other philosophical traditions; indeed, it has at times been accused of trying to embrace all other theories. To the extent that realists are willing to analyze phenomena which are not readily observable, their approach is compatible with idealism (this view, associated foremost with Plato, that human phenomena should be analyzed in terms of ideal forms, does differ from realism on many issues, however). Realism is also largely compatible with hermeneutics—the study of meaning—since realism allows for a diverse range of causal links (except to the extent that advocates of the hermeneutic approach would insist that the only relationship between things involves the communication of meaning). Bhaskar also concurs with the critical theory of Jurgen Habermas. In essence, this enjoins human scientists to eschew the belief that any theory explains all, but rather to take on each causal link afresh. This does not mean that we must turn our back on such theories. Indeed it reflects a willingness to suspect that all such views of the world likely contain some element of the truth. Our purpose as scientists is to establish such limits case by case.

POSTMODERNISM

While a precise definition of the phrase "postmodern" is impossible, Cloke, Philo, and Sadler (1991) argue that postmodernism recognizes the need to turn away from grand theory, in part in response to the ideological excesses of this century, and focus instead on humble, diverse, empirical work. It is especially sensitive to distinctions such as gender, ethnicity, and class (all of which are recognized in our schema). Postmodernism "resides in the complex collision of all manner of objects in the messy collage of contemporary people and places." While some postmodernists claim that the social world is too complex for scientific understanding, most recognize a need to deal with diversity (and employ diverse methods) rather than abandon science. Our schema can be seen as a postmodern attempt to show how science can deal with complexity. Rather than shrink from it we will in true postmodern fashion embrace diversity.

Blau (1993) emphasizes the importance of a diversity of viewpoints. It is not just important to countenance a range of theories, but to actively pursue the views of people from diverse economic, cultural, and social backgrounds. While some postmodernists suggest that there is in fact no one "reality," that we each have an equally valid reality in our minds, Blau feels that this is going too far. Nor would she accept the argument that since all "facts" are social constructs science is therefore impossible. Most postmodernists would be more concerned than Blau with the subjective nature of knowledge. They would emphasize that each observer sees the world in a different way. Some go on from this to argue that "reality," if it can be said to exist at all, is internal rather than external. However, as in the parable of the blind men touching different parts of an elephant's anatomy—tail, trunk, legs—and reaching different conclusions as to what stood before them, we should be careful of leaping from the observation that people view the world differently to a conclusion that we cannot speak of an external reality. As Haack (1998, ch. 9) notes, once we accept the existence of an external reality, we need no longer conclude that we cannot progress beyond subjective argumentation. Yet the basic observation of subjectivity is one we must deal with at many levels. When describing individual causal links, we must devote considerable attention to how people develop their world views, the biases that can creep in, and the effects these can have (while recognizing that our understanding of these processes is imperfect). In designing this schema, I have striven to ensure that it limits neither theoretical nor methodological flexibility (and the schema itself is flexible, if scholars feel that new or different categories are required).

Rust (1996) concludes that, "A postmodern approach . . . is not intended to discredit any orientation, but to see the kind of relationships which exist. Postmodernists would by and large neither seek to silence nor make invisible any of the theoretical orientations in the field, although they would challenge the claims of some that their approach is the only valid perspective." This is precisely the approach I will take in this book.

Postmodernists, it would seem, face a choice. They can give up hope of advancing our understanding so that we can aid society, and revel in subjective conversation. Or, they can strive to battle complexity and subjectivity, holding out hope that we can slowly advance our understanding (see Appleby, Hunt, and Jacob 1994). Those who choose the second path should find much to agree with in this work.

Collins (1998) argues that skeptics of the possibility of enhanced understanding have emerged many times in intellectual history when there were "too many" competing scientific theories or viewpoints. In the modern era, the division of science into diverse disciplines has encouraged this skepticism. Ironically, so has the advance of science: "We suffer from cognitive overload, from having amassed too much information to assimilate it" (1998, xvii). We can hope, then, that an attempt to integrate disciplines, to show how a diversity of theories can each have a place, and to show how a huge mass of information can be incorporated into a larger whole, will overcome the skepticism of extreme postmodernists.

Appleby, Hunt, and Jacob (1994) note that many postmodernists do not like causal explanations, as these have tended to ignore the complexity of the world. Yet they conclude that our very need to make sense of the world forces us to value causation. One value of my schema is that it allows us to simultaneously embrace causation and complexity.

A key subset of postmodernist thought is "deconstruction." With origins in literary theory—a recognition that texts are full of contradictions and thus it is impossible to find the one true meaning of a text[21]— deconstruction has evolved into a view of the world that searches for multiple meanings in all theories and events. I would argue that events are naturally composed of the intersection of a variety of causal links, and theories as generally constructed tend to be similarly composed. Thus, the search for a hierarchical ordering of phenomena and causal links would seem to be compatible with deconstruction (except, of course, for those who view deconstruction as the antithesis of science). I might note in particular that causal links can and often do involve complex feedback mechanisms, a likely source of ambiguity and contradiction. And I would stress that I have striven to define phenomena in terms of a unique purpose so as to severely limit ambiguity.[22]

Perhaps the clearest "postmodern" justification for our present work can be found in the emerging practice of "social cartography". As the title suggests, this method involves the mapping of various sorts of causal interrelationships. Various authors in Paulston (1996) discuss how this method allows the pursuit of postmodernist science. Mowat (1996) argues that while early postmodernists stressed the fragmentary nature of understanding, there are many signs of an increased interest in how these fragments fit together (such as complexity theory). Stromquist (1996) notes that mapping appeals to some postmodernists simply because highly disaggregated maps leave room for every point of view; she notes, though, that this hardly precludes the mapping of highly aggregated categories. Huff (1996) applauds the use of maps, but worries that maps are often too simplistic and urges the expansion in the number of links contained in individual maps, as well as the recognition of feedback. Our giant mapping of all human science relationships should fit the bill admirably.

DEALING WITH DIVERSITY

As noted above, one of the driving forces in postmodernist thought has been a concern with diversity. Still, we must be careful of not equating one with the other (Appleby, Hunt, and Jacob 1994). Many have worried that our modern scientific theory and method are suspect due to the past domination of scholarship by white middle-class males. They *might* thus hesitate to embrace a schema developed from the existing body of knowledge (and the author confesses to a greater acquaintance with Western than Eastern thought). The flexibility of the schema provides a powerful counterargument. And issues of race, gender, and class find a prominent place within the schema (see Szostak 2001). I have tried, moreover, to develop a schema that is applicable to all people and societies. And, as our discussion of grand theory suggested, one of the virtues of my schema is that it suggests limits to the authority of all past great thinkers.

Practitioners of interdisciplinarity have often noted that rigid disciplinary paradigms which privilege certain types of research and teaching are likely repositories of bias (Hendershott and Wright 1997). My schema, by providing scholars and students with a guide to related work in other disciplines, could help to expose such biases. Scientific advance depends on open and honest communication among scholars, and this is enhanced when they bring diverse interests and experiences to the task.

Beckwith (1999) discusses how postmodern skepticism of objective scientific understanding has influenced (and been influenced by) modern attitudes toward culture. Arguments that members of groups have a subjective understanding of themselves that cannot be obtained by others has had a self-fulfilling effect: we have little confidence that groups can understand each other, we believe that modern history and literature courses can only be taught by members of relevant groups (but still manage to teach ancient history and literature, despite all relevant group members being dead),[23] we rarely appeal to our common humanity, and we revel in incomprehensible and subjective scientific argument. If we deny the extreme postmodern premise that enhanced understanding is impossible, none of these results need follow. Beckwith argues that we would be much better served by a belief that our common humanity enables us to communicate, and that we can learn much about ourselves and others by interacting with members of different groups. Since my project rests on a belief that enhanced understanding is possible, I will argue in chapter 3 against the conjecture that "cultures" are monolithic, and emphasize instead that they are evolving and interacting amalgams of diverse cultural phenomena (with substantial within-group diversity).

THE VALUE OF AN ORGANIZING SCHEMA

I believe that an organizing schema will help us to solve many of the difficulties presently facing human science. We have already seen that the schema can ensure a more balanced scholarly effort and protect against certain types of discovery being forgotten.[24] I would also hope that acquaintance with such a schema would alter the world view of most disciplinary scholars; they may now be dimly aware that the causal links on which they focus are not the whole story, but can all too easily forget this fact in practice. I must say that while researching this project I was continually shocked by the ignorance which even the best of scholars would display toward closely related research in other disciplines. Insights from one discipline not only have to be noticed by scholars in another, but must be stated in words they understand, respecting their discipline's modes of argument and views of what is important (Salter and Hearn 1996,

140–43); the schema can help overcome terminological confusion. Scientists often talk at cross purposes simply because they are focused on different links. And scholars of a particular phenomenon are often only cognizant of a subset of the forces which influence it. They are thus in great danger of acceding to simplistic views of the universe.

Interdisciplinary scholars have long recognized these dangers. Yet not only are interdisciplinarians a minority among human scientists, but interdisciplinary research is at present as fragmented as the disciplinary research from which it has evolved. Salter and Hearn (1996, 30–37) identify three broad types of interdisciplinarity. By far the most common of these they term "instrumental": here scholars focused on a particular problem recognize the need for expertise from more than one discipline. These scholars make no effort to fuse the relevant disciplines beyond that required for the solution to the particular problem, and generally exhibit no concern with disciplinary reform. While laudable, these efforts rarely span more than two disciplines. "Very few scholars, the present one included, can pretend to expertise in more than one or two areas, and the professionalization of university disciplines and the ethic of 'publish or perish' discourage the intellectual bush pilot" (Newman 1987, 52). It is very time consuming to master (some part of) yet another discipline, and it would be churlish to condemn those who have taken the unusual step of straddling two for not having ventured further. Yet we should recognize the costs of the present situation. There is no strong sense of interdisciplinary unity. Economic sociologists have little more to do with political psychologists than economists with political scientists.[25] Fragmented as it is, interdisciplinary research may be defenseless if the pendulum were to swing back toward disciplinarity. The case that disciplines provide a limiting frame of reference cannot be made convincingly by reference to a diverse and disconnected body of interdisciplinary research efforts. Rather, these diffuse ventures must be tied together so that it becomes abundantly clear that the subject matter of human science forms a unified whole, and that one cannot fully understand the subject matter of any discipline without reference to the rest.

Salter and Hearn's other two types of interdisciplinarity are both "conceptual"; that is, they have some vision of how the pieces fit together. One of these approaches feels that disciplines have an important role to play in policing the quality of scientific work, but that they must be more willing to learn from each other. Proponents of this view fear that unified knowledge is impossible. My schema should overcome this fear. Moreover, we will see in appendix 1-B and in chapter 2 both that our disciplines provide an arbitrary division of human knowledge and that the methodological biases of particular disciplines severely limit the scope of scholarly inquiry. By recognizing the fact that we should always seek a variety of evidence for any line of argument, the hypothesis of these inter-disciplinarians that it is dangerous to forego disciplinary standards is turned on its head.

The second type of conceptual interdisciplinarity joins us in challenging the present role of disciplines. Some within this camp see the role of interdisciplinarity as criticizing the inherently conservative nature of disciplines. I have already argued that my schema should encourage scholars to break free from narrow mindsets. Others within this second camp pursue the dream of a unified realm of knowledge. Sadly this is often done through a search for grand theory. My schema moves beyond these failed theoretical attempts at unity and shows that unity is possible schematically. In doing so, I believe we put interdisciplinarity in human science on a much firmer footing.

It might be thought that any attempt to "map" human science must itself constrain scholars in some ways. While most maps do indeed focus attention on particular features, our map excludes no phenomenon or link from consideration. Scholars and students are still free to follow their curiosity in any direction. The map serves to point out the various possibilities, keeps us from getting "lost," and guards against the all too common error of thinking the route we follow is the only one.

Students would gain indirectly from any enlightenment of their teachers. More directly, the schema would provide them with a road map as they attempt to integrate material from diverse courses. This could, in the extreme, be viewed as a bad thing, if we accept that the predominant purpose of interdisciplinary education is to force students to stretch their minds.[26] Yet students develop their thinking skills best when integrating material across different courses. And there is widespread recognition that students find this almost impossible without some integrating framework to guide them. Moreover, even with this integrating framework in place, the world will still be a mysterious place where intellectual puzzles abound to stretch the minds of any student. The schema, indeed, encourages students to follow their curiosity through a web of relationships (and thus encourages lifelong learning). Lucas (1996) speaks of a debate between those who stress coherence, and those who emphasize stretching students' minds; the schema allows us to pursue both goals simultaneously.

Instructors tend naturally to teach only some of what we could about a subject. We rarely, though, confess to our students that we are communicating only a piece of the puzzle, nor tell them where they might look for more. The schema both encourages and allows us to do these things. Instructors will necessarily continue to emphasize a subset of links, but can readily communicate a sense of the full range of relevant links. Students could be encouraged to cover other links in papers or presentations. Both instructors and students should find that having the schema in front of them while studying, researching, or preparing courses or classes, would prove a useful source of inspiration.

Interdisciplinarians often stress that interdisciplinary courses impart a number of valuable skills to students. Along with critical thinking skills, they emphasize coping with complexity, appreciation of diverse viewpoints, awareness of bias, and suspicion of authority. My schema will aid students in all of these areas. In particular, it highlights the fact that all grand theories do a better job of explaining some causal links than others; it should thus encourage students to approach each new question with an open mind.

The liberal arts have come in for a great deal of criticism in recent decades. While I could hardly summarize a diverse debate here, I would note that a common complaint is that there is no longer a core set of information we feel an educated student should possess. This leads many to advocate a return to a previous emphasis on Western civilization (usually history and/or literature, often with a classical focus). Responding with a list of the cognitive skills we hope our students will attain is certainly valid, but unlikely to mollify our fiercest critics. Gaff (1991) notes that many proponents of core programs are motivated by a fear that college curricula are no longer coherent,[27] but fears there is no obvious path to achieve this goal without losing the advantages of specialization. And Lucas (1996) notes that scholars have struggled to reintroduce coherence into undergraduate education since a classical focus on Greek and Latin was replaced by electives in the nineteenth century. Wilson (1998, 269–70) finds "it hard to conceive of an adequate core curriculum in colleges and universities that avoids the cause-and-effect connections among the great branches of learning. There lies great opportunity." The schema herein may take us a step further: it allows us to argue that there is a coherent structure to understanding in the liberal arts, and to structure one or more courses which will impart this broad structure while focusing on a diversity of causal links. Each student would then gain some insight into issues of culture, gender, race, power, status, aesthetics, and so on. before choosing some subset of causal links as the focus of their studies.[28]

The schema is easily incorporated into existing curricula. Where sequences of required interdisciplinary courses already exist, it could serve as a background resource for all. At universities that rely primarily on breadth requirements to give students an extra-disciplinary perspective, introductory courses could be designed with the schema as their basis. If the schema were used in such a manner, it might over time encourage a reduction in disciplinary boundaries or at least a more logical distribution of disciplinary tasks. But such advances are not a prerequisite for its use. (We return to curricular issues in chapter 12.)

One of the forces driving the modern interest in interdisciplinarity is a recognition that public policy issues do not come in neat disciplinary packages (Klein 1990). Yet the vast majority of scholars still have a disciplinary orientation. Economists comment on trade agreements as if these only had economic effects; political scientists and sociologists match their folly by speaking as if there were only political or cultural considerations. Economists ignore the suffering of the unemployed, the role of altruism in human motivation, and cultural influences on economic activity simply because these have no place in their map of what is important. The situation is duplicated in other disciplines. If we all worked from a shared map, we could not so casually ignore diverse causal links. Scientists would still specialize, but they would be guided to a greater humility in public policy pronouncements.

Economists in giving policy advice emphasize the causal links they (think they) know much about, and simply ignore the relevant links which they know little about (see Mayer 1993). That is, if advocating policy X to achieve result W, they speak of how Y causes Z, and simply assume that X causes Y and Z causes W in the desired fashion. While Mayer does not emphasize this, they also often use "cause" in its narrowest sense, and ignore the likelihood that X (and Y,Z, and W) will have myriad effects, some of which may be undesirable. Other human scientists are surely guilty of the same behavior. Familiarity with a schema such as mine would make it much more difficult for scholars or decision-makers to simply forget about other relevant links.

I have been critical in the preceding pages both of those who attempt to oversimplify the world we live in, and those who become so overwhelmed by the complexity of our world that they give up hope of scientific understanding. My fondest hope is that the schema will cause a softening of both positions. The world is a complex place indeed, but we can reasonably expect to gradually extend our understanding of each causal link. We will never be able to predict the future in its entirety, but we can steadily enhance our ability to predict the effects of particular human actions.

A FOCUS ON CULTURE

I have devoted the first chapter so far to a discussion of the organizing schema. It is now time to turn to the book's subtitle and examine the rationale for and advantages of the second characteristic of the book: a focus on culture in succeeding chapters.

The true test of the schema comes from an exploration of causal links. It is only through the study of such links that I can establish that I have developed a fairly exhaustive list of phenomena. As well, we can only see whether it is both straightforward and useful to view all human science theories as describing one or more causal links among our phenomena by doing precisely that. In preparing this book, I read widely across all fields, and could thus speak at length here about links between phenomena in any two categories. To have reported all of these findings would, however, have resulted in a book of enormous dimensions.

It might be objected that the "test" I speak of is largely hidden from readers. The author knows that he read widely, and was able to organize all that he read in terms of the schema, but the reader has to take his word for it. However, the reader can observe in what follows that an immense diversity of scholarly argument can be understood in terms of one or more of the causal links identified in the schema. Both scholars and students can judge the degree to which the schema helps organize this vast body of material. And scholars of culture can readily speculate as to whether analyses which I may have failed to uncover might not also be comprehended in terms of the schema.

By focusing only on links to and from the cultural category, I am able to produce a book of manageable size which nevertheless serves as an extensive test of both the validity and value of the schema. It is noteworthy in this regard that culture both requires and receives more unpacking than any other category. Not coincidentally, it is also the phenomenon that is defined most ambiguously in the existing scholarly literature. If I am correct in arguing that the schema is both valid and valuable, then the book will be especially useful to both scholars and students of culture. It will provide in one place discussions of hundreds of causal links they might wish to pursue (with some introduction to the relevant literature). It will provide a very precise definition of culture and its major components. It will show that culture is both a result of and influence upon diverse other phenomena.

Interdisciplinary courses often have a cultural focus, reflecting a widespread desire to provide students with some understanding of diverse cultures. Cornwell and Stoddard (1998) critique the present state of affairs. They describe three types of such courses. The "multicultural" courses tend to ignore questions of racism, treat cultures as monolithic and unchanging, and argue that we should not try to evaluate cultural practices. The "diversity" courses are broader, but tend to reinforce the idea that other cultures are a deviation from "normal" culture. Finally, those called "global studies" privilege nations, downplay internal tensions, and lump all Africans or Native Americans together. Cornwell and Stoddard urge instead "intercultural studies" that would analyze a variety of causal links and recognize that cultures evolve. The approach of this book is clearly consonant with this recommendation. As well, I will discuss in chapter 3 the importance of unpacking culture. Only then can we understand the process of cultural evolution. By unpacking we are also able to open up the possibility of evaluating particular cultural practices, while at the same time recognizing that it is folly to argue that any entire culture is superior to any other. Our discussion of cultural evolution, and of various links, will show that it makes no sense to speak of a "normal" culture. In chapter 9 and elsewhere, we will explore the internal divisions within societies, and the question of racism.

Cornwell and Stoddard suggest that cultural education should have two goals. The first is global citizenship, an ability to understand, appreciate, and yet evaluate other cultures. This, I would argue, can only be done by unpacking culture and analyzing the causal links between cultural phenomena and other phenomena. The second goal is an enhanced understanding of how our own individual identities are constructed by the variety of groups to which we belong. We will discuss at length the links between culture and personality in chapter 5 (while noting a variety of other influences on personality). While Cornwell and Stoddard focus on teaching, many of their criticisms reflect difficulties in scholarship itself. Disciplinary boundaries limit our understanding of the linkages on which "intercultural" understanding depends. I would hope that this book provides a guide to further scholarly exploration of these linkages.

In the concluding chapter I will discuss six broad lessons for the study of culture which I draw from the material covered in the intervening chapters. I list them briefly here, so that the reader can have them in mind as they proceed, and also to provide a further justification for my focus on culture. The first lesson is that we can only comprehend the role of culture in human societies by unpacking culture into its constituent phenomena (unpacking, as we shall see in chapter 3, also allows us to sail between the twin dangers of either cultural bigotry or a fear of criticizing any cultural element in any society). The second is that a full understanding of culture requires the study of hundreds or thousands of causal links. It is folly to think that any one theory or method can guide us. I know of no other book that does or could bring this point home as forcefully. The third lesson follows from the second: while unifying theories or methods are attractive due to a false promise of simplicity, they inevitably guide us to ignore much that is crucial to our understanding. The fourth lesson is that cultural phenomena both influence and are influenced by other phenomena: the all too common practice of treating culture as only cause or effect is thus inherently misguided. The fifth is that our schema serves as a crucial antidote to the siren song of grand theory and oversimplification. And the sixth lesson is that the schema serves an important pedagogical role. While it is undoubtedly difficult to master all of the causal links discussed in this book (a task that is not necessary for an appreciation of the complexity of the subject matter), it is nevertheless possible to gain a much more accurate comprehension of the role of culture in human society in this way than through the sort of courses which Cornwell and Stoddard (1998) critique. Without the schema to guide them, it is too easy for both instructors and students to believe that some subset of links, or one theory, tells them everything they need to know. The schema allows us to fit diverse bits of understanding together, while appreciating the complexity of the whole.

OVERVIEW OF BOOK

The basic structure of most of the remaining chapters has been fore-shadowed in the preceding material. Each of chapters 3–11 begins by unpacking one of our ten categories (two of them, in the case of chapter 4). The unpacking of categories has involved a mix of deduction—asking what sorts of subsidiary phenomena should be looked for—and induction—reading widely and placing observed phenomena in the most appropriate category. When evolutionary mechanisms are important, this material is followed by a discussion of the sources of mutation and the criteria for selection. Discussion of evolutionary mechanisms naturally revolves around the five questions outlined above. The remainder of each chapter is then devoted to discussing the causal links among these un-packed phenomena and the cultural phenomena unpacked in chapter 3.

I should emphasize the importance of the opening sections of each chapter. It is here that the lists of second and third (and sometimes fourth) level phenomena are derived and justified. While both induction and deduction were used to derive these lists, the presentation is largely in terms of deduction. I argue that there are logical reasons for placing each phenomenon where it is. Whenever possible, I rely on scholarly consensus regarding the key phenomena, and how they might be best aggregated or disaggregated. Where there is debate, I seek a middle ground. Where the task of identifying key phenomena has scarcely begun, I make the best arguments I can. These early sections of chapters 3–11 thus both fill out and justify the schema that I began to develop above. And in so doing they establish the structure into which all later analysis in the chapter falls.

We will not discuss every possible causal link (remember that some link likely exists between any pair of phenomena). While I inevitably focus primarily on the links which appear most important, I also pay attention to some which appear less important in order to illustrate the ubiquity of links. My style of presentation inevitably differs by link, to reflect the differing approaches taken by academia more generally: when a link has been the subject of considerable debate I strive for an openminded and evenhanded reprise of competing views, when only isolated inquiries have been made I report what seems to be the dominant view, and when a link has been virtually ignored I speculate on relationships which might exist. Since my coverage of links is incomplete, I will necessarily unpack some phenomena that are not discussed further. This reflects my desire to be as exhaustive as possible in unpacking. Readers may wish to explore on their own how these phenomena might be causally related to culture. Note that often these phenomena are strongly linked to noncultural phenomena.

More than one link will be discussed at a time whenever it is impossible to disentangle influences, or when similarities across links make simultaneous discussion an advantageous mode of presentation. Links will sometimes be grouped together for discussion in terms of common causes, and at other times in terms of common effects. Whether links are discussed together or separately, it is often necessary or advantageous to refer to other links. In appendix 1-A I develop a simple notation to facilitate cross-referencing.

My guiding principle in discussing causal links has been openmindedness. Where I am aware of differing perspectives, I try to discuss the advantages and disadvantages of each evenhandedly. Being human, I have undoubtedly allowed my own biases to creep in on occasion. Yet one advantage of this schema is that no one "mistaken" idea—whether the "mistake" is mine or the broader scholarly community's—can have a wide impact.[29] Its impact is limited to the causal link(s) in which it appears. Moreover, even if the reader should disagree with my discussion of a particular link, they will hopefully still appreciate my illustration of the importance of that link.

I will lean heavily on the existing scholarly literature in what follows. This will decrease the incidence of authorial bias. I must inevitably discuss some links with which I have limited familiarity (though my previous research had involved many of the links which follow). My purpose here is not to put forth novel analyses of particular links, but to synthesize a diverse literature, illustrate the value of the schema in general and unpacking in particular, and show how a full understanding of cultural processes requires some familiarity with diverse causal links.

It is my belief that all grand theories—those that aspire to cover a wide range of causal links—do a much better job of explaining some links than others. Rather than engage in some vague discussion of various theories, then, I discuss their advantages and disadvantages where appropriate link by link. Sadly, this attitude is not endemic in academic circles. This approach may have a jarring effect on a reader accustomed to books which attempt to place complex material into the straitjacket of one overarching theoretical or methodological perspective. There can be no unifying theory or method here. Rather I will show that a diverse range of theories—sometimes grand theories which purport to speak to many links, sometimes mid-range theories which engage a handful of links, and sometimes link-specific theories—shed light on diverse causal links. Attempts to argue otherwise may appeal to an innate human desire for simplicity, but must inevitably give a misleading view of the terrain.

As an example, we can take the discussion of rational choice theory in Booth, James, and Meadwell (1993). Rational choice theory might seem fairly innocuous at first: it suggests that individuals will try to take all relevant information into account and then act in a way that is most likely to allow them to achieve their goals. Yet the theory has become associated with the idea that only individuals matter, and has thus been attacked by institutionalists, communitarians, Marxists, and feminists, among others. It has also been conceived in many circles as necessarily implying the primacy of the economic sphere. Yet as Taylor (1993) makes clear, rational choice theory can readily incorporate beliefs, values, and habits, both in shaping one's goals and in determining the sorts of behaviors one deems appropriate and advantageous. He thinks that in certain (repeated) situations, where both the options and goals are clear and limited and the choice clearly matters to the individual, a narrow application of rational choice theory is all that is needed to understand individual behavior. In other situations, though, we will need to understand the sociocultural pressures on the individual. Although he does not go that far, it is not much of a leap to hypothesize the possibility of situations in which the forces acting on an individual are so strong that rational choice is simply swamped as an explanation of behavior. So why the fuss? Science will be much better served if we explore the advantages and limits of rational choice theory situation by situation rather than engaging in a vague global debate about whether it is a good theory or bad. (Rule 1997, reaches a similar conclusion.)[30]

It is my belief that our understanding advances fastest when advocates of competing views engage in open and honest debate. It is my hope that by breaking down disciplinary barriers, and providing an evenhanded discussion of competing perspectives on individual links, the pursuit of understanding will be facilitated. The one case in which I do reserve the right to take sides is when scholars denigrate the importance of causal links outside their purview. To be sure, it is a legitimate scholarly activity to debate the importance of individual links. Yet all too often scholars casually assume away the importance of feedback effects, or alternative causal explanations of changes in particular phenomena, or steps in a causal chain they have little to say about (see Mayer 1993 on the latter). If this schema serves but one purpose, it should serve as a warning against such casual causal oversimplification.

We should take special note of one sort of bias which taken to extremes would divide the human sciences into two competing camps with no common ground on which to meet. I noted earlier that some scientists focus on the individual, while others focus on societal aggregates. This on its own is not a problem as long as each values what the other does. Unfortunately methodological individualists assert that society is no more than a collection of individuals and can have no independent causal status. The reaction is all too predictable: others have come to view individuals as nothing but social constructs: "it is not possible to depict a person divorced from his or her culture, society, gender, ethnicity, and, above all, economic and ecological contexts. Psychic reality and sociopolitical reality conjoin" (Samuels 1993, 201).[31] Yet, as Sartre argued, if we view individuals as mere social creations, then we are forced to view any unusual behavior as dysfunction, when it may better be viewed as a strategic means for the individual to cope with the world. Kontopolous (1994) provides a detailed analysis of the issue. He traces the evolution of thought within both extreme traditions. He then notes that many leading scholars, especially Boudon, Giddens, Bhaskar, Bourdieu, and Foucault, have since the 1970s argued forcefully for a more balanced view (we could add Kuhn 1974). Building on this work, he proposes several forms of "frustration" that prevent societies from being a mere aggregate of individual behaviors and desires: the actions of one limit the opportunities of others, actions have unexpected and/or undesirable consequences (pollution, overfishing, over-population), collective action is difficult to organize, and behavior is conditioned on expectations based on the actions of others. Societies, he argues, constrain individual behavior, but also leave considerable scope for individualism. While most scholars would likely take the common sense position that individuals both shape and are shaped by society, the currency of extreme views suggest that in their research they are likely to look only at one or the other (Kontopolous 1994, Hinde 1987, 27). Collectively, then, we are rewarded with a number of incomplete views of how both individuals and societies function and change. Needless to say, I explore various lines of causation in both directions in this book (as Kontopolous recognizes, we can value the results of extremist research while rejecting their narrow perspective), and can hope that it will serve as an antidote to methodological extremism of either type.

There has also been a debate in human science between those who believe that researchers should focus on understanding stable systems and those who feel that we need to understand the dynamics of change. Yet the two views are hardly incompatible. Societies are, at any point in time, comprised of elements of both order and disorder, or stability and change. To focus on stable structures alone is to be unable to explain the process of change that is endemic to society (see, e.g., Burk 1991, 26). Yet to focus on dynamic relationships does not necessarily mean that we cannot explain stability. Understanding how X affects Y tells us not only how some changes in X will cause changes in Y, but also how other changes in X may have no effect on Y. Moreover our schema has room for feedbacks such that Y reacts to changes in X so that it causes X to move back toward its original state. And if it is hypothesized that X→Y→Z→W→X in such a way as to ensure stability, our schema has a place for all of those lines of causation, and leaves it to empirical research as to whether the end result need always be a lack of change.[32]

Law (1994) approaches this question from a slightly different angle. The development of human societies is largely a self-governing process (both he and I can recognize a role for the physical world as an external causal agent). Thus, it is a mistake to distinguish between structure and process. Since behavior changes over time, what appears to be a stable structure at one point in time will in a longer view be part of a dynamic process.[33] We can only understand the structure if we comprehend the dynamics, yet "most theorists in the social sciences do not feel any need to understand how the structures and processes that they posit might have evolved" (Boyd and Richerson 1985, 18). Thus, again, we must remain cognizant both of feedback effects which tend toward stability, and those which would cause change.

In the face of competing explanations, how can readers evaluate these? To help them with this task, I have in chapter 2 provided an overview of the latest thinking in the philosophy of science. One key insight is that we should not privilege one methodological approach over others, but rather look for theories which are supported by various types of empirical evidence. The chapter also discusses guidelines for scholarly research, and explores how interdisciplinarity can serve to limit the role of scholarly bias in research.

I have focused above on the advantages for interdisciplinary research and teaching of my schema, and only briefly alluded to the potential advantages for public policy. I return to that question in chapter 12. Also at that time I will discuss further the degree to which the schema points the way to a superior curriculum, which may satisfy at least some recent criticisms. And as noted above I will review the six broad lessons for the study of culture that emerge from this analysis.

Appendix 1-A: Notation for Cross-Referencing

The existence of feedback loops and multiple causation guarantees that there will be times when more than one causal link will be discussed at a time. As well, when discussing Y→Z it is sometimes useful to make reference to X→Y or Z→W. To avoid unnecessary duplication, I will code our causal links so that reference can easily be made to one link while discussing another. Ideally, this coding would occur at a disaggregated level, where most causal links exist. However, this would require a complex coding scheme indeed. I will, then, code in terms of our largest categories. Individual causal links will be indicated numerically by the order in which they appear. Thus, G→C3 is the third causal link discussed between genes and culture. The codes are the first letter in the category name:

C	Culture	N	Nonhuman environment
G	Genes	I	Individual Differences
E	Economy	P	Politics
S	Social Structure	T	Technology and Science
H	Health and Population	A	Art

If I refer to another causal link in the text, the coding will appear in regular parentheses, just as if it were a reference to the literature. If, for ease of exposition, I discuss a particular causal link elsewhere, I will indicate where the discussion more properly belongs with square brackets. Thus, if a G→C link was discussed in the I→C section, I would place [G→C] there. There will be a few occasions where I will discuss simultaneously the effects that one phenomenon has on a number of other phenomena. In such cases, I will denote this collection of other phenomena by * (e.g., C→*).

Appendix 1-B
The Arbitrary Nature of Disciplinary Boundaries

I have not used existing disciplinary boundaries as the basis from which to construct the schema, although disciplinary loyalists will to varying degrees be able to discern some rough approximation between our major categories and existing disciplinary concerns. Those boundaries—and in many cases they are blurred at best—reflect a complex historical evolution rather than any logical division of scientific labor (see Messer-Davidow, Shumway, and Sylvan 1993). Topics are not divided logically between disciplines, disciplines are divided into fields which have little contact, and a variety of groups have formed in which scholars interact with other disciplines more than with other fields in their own (Salter and Hearn 1996, 21). We need not delve too deeply into this historical evolution here. Despite philosophical warnings of the dangers of specialization—from Bacon, Descartes, Kant, Hegel, and Comte among others—the growth in size of universities and the increase in range of scientific exploration (associated with increased "knowledge" and more complicated scientific "apparatus") led to first the separation of the natural from the human sciences and then the departmentalization of each. We might note that in large part the physical sciences ended up with a remarkably logical set of divisions. Certainly boundaries between natural science disciplines are more well defined than boundaries in human science (Klein 1996, 39).[34] Physicists focus on atoms and their constituents, chemists worry about how elements comprising these atoms behave in turn, and biologists ask about the complex chemical reactions which create and sustain life. While I have not captured all that each one of these sciences is concerned with in such a simple description—physicists and biologists operate at more than one level, and geologists are even harder to pigeonhole—still the broad point at issue is largely correct. The natural sciences are divided in terms of the level at which their research is focused. While this has not made them immune from disciplinary jealousies, it has served to ensure that there is a consistency in the findings of the various disciplines. Biologists take the laws of chemistry into account as they formulate their research plans, and chemists know that chemical reactions must obey the laws of physics. Even cases of disagreement, as when physicists sneered at the claims of some chemists regarding cold fusion, highlight the recognition that theories in one discipline should not ignore the theories of another. As Robert Frost said in a different context, good fences make good neighbors: the logic of disciplinary boundaries in natural science has encouraged the development of a coherent body of science. Interdisciplinarity in the natural sciences is still essential so that insights of one discipline are applied to another, and to ensure that disciplinary theories remain compatible.

In human science, alas, it is all too common for one discipline's research programs to be entirely incompatible with the research programs of another. This shocking state of affairs would hardly be tenable if human scientists were both intimately familiar with and respectful of the works of others. Safely cocooned within high disciplinary walls, human scientists can all carry on secure in the "knowledge" that within their discipline and it alone lies the key to human understanding. One can only guess at how much we might know if the human sciences worked together.[35]

The human sciences have not compartmentalized their activities as elegantly as the physical sciences. Psychologists might seem at first glance to be concerned with individuals, while the other disciplines are focused on social interaction of varying types. Psychologists have, however, devoted much of their energy to understanding how one individual is shaped by interactions with others. Other disciplines have not only haphazardly carved up the field of interpersonal interaction, but, crucially, have tended to adopt mutually incompatible visions of individual behavior.

How did the social sciences slice up the study of society? Economics was the first to appear, and has been the most consistent in focus. This is not entirely a good thing for, as I have argued elsewhere (Szostak 1999), economists have tended to emphasize a fairly narrow part of what seems their natural domain. We thus know a very great deal about how markets work, but are only beginning to understand how economic institutions evolve and the effects these have, and have a shocking lack of understanding of the causes of economic growth. To a large extent, these priorities reflect the reticence of economists to explore interdisciplinary connections. Subjects which lay too close to economists' self-defined borders were eschewed lest one be viewed by one's colleagues as the follower of some lesser god.

Within their focus on markets, economists were rewarded with the discovery of a rich vein of impersonal mechanisms which govern exchange across a range of institutional settings. Most economists took this as justification both for laissez-faire government policies and for disciplinary specialization (socialist and institutionalist economists, a minority, favored an interdisciplinary orientation). As other social sciences developed, it was perhaps only natural that practitioners search for similar mechanisms internal to their disciplines. While from afar it might seem extremely unlikely that human society would be governed by a set of independent discipline-based causal systems, the illogic of such a research program would not be apparent to anyone whose gaze extended no further than their own discipline.

Political science, long combined with economics under the term "political economy," eventually gained its independence. Here too, a choice needed to be made between those who favored the development of internally oriented "natural laws" of politics, and those who favored the exploration of the interdisciplinary influences on the evolution of political institutions. I suspect it is the subject matter rather than the people which caused the former group to fail to establish hegemony as in economics. Analysts of voting behavior, laws, or leadership (but less so international relations), not to mention students of the pragmatic practice of politics, inevitably found that their inquiries carried them into other disciplines. Indeed political science is the most willing of all social sciences to admit to the lack of a unifying theoretical structure (Bulick 1982, 43). Yet in a climate in which disciplinary independence was lauded, the political science community could not be entirely comfortable with such an interdisciplinary emphasis.

Anthropology—the study of humans, and sociology—the study of society, were denied the obvious focus of economics and political science. It was thus up to early practitioners in these fields to set the task for those who followed, though later researchers have often opened up entirely new areas of research. This evolution is reflected in the fact that introductory texts in anthropology and sociology (and also political science) almost universally begin with a history of the discipline, while economics texts reflect the confidence of the economics profession that it is following the one true path and make no reference to the history of economic thought. Both anthropology and sociology naturally looked to areas of social inter-action which seemed ignored by political economy. This area being fairly vast, especially a century ago, different scholars moved in different direc-tions. Thus to this day anthropology departments contain two fairly dis-tinct groups, loosely linked by a focus on empirical study of mainly tradi-tional or historical societies. Physical anthropologists are most noted for archaeological excavations, especially as concerned with human evolu-tion. Cultural anthropologists are justifiably famous for extensive field research with "traditional" societies. While "culture" is the unifying (if varyingly defined) theme of this latter group, practitioners of field studies could hardly be expected (nor desired) to avert their gaze from all eco-nomic, political, or social aspects of tribal society.

Sociologists took all that was left (geography having first come along and laid claim to human activities with a spatial element; since this could well apply to all human activity, research in geography has inevitably overlapped with all other disciplines). This makes sociology departments both large and diverse (some would discern a common focus on social "problems"). The largest group is concerned with the subgroups which inevitably comprise society by gender, race, class, or family. Others focus on the study of human population: births, deaths, and migration. Still others are criminologists. Many borrow from the anthropological vocabu-lary and focus on norms and values.

This is not a complete survey, for I have said nothing of the linguists or the many subdivisions of the humanities, though they are as important to my purpose as the social sciences. Yet the message should be clear: if we were to design our disciplines from scratch today we would not choose our present configuration (I will return to this issue in our concluding chapter). This does not mean that an incredible amount of valuable research has not been undertaken. It does mean that coverage has been uneven; issues with disciplinary blessing get attention while those on the borderlands are either shunned or subjected to contradictory analyses.[36]

To this point I have attempted to describe disciplines by their subject matter. Yet increasingly they became at least as distinguishable in terms of methodology (there were yet other unhelpful distinctions, as for example the tendency of economists to be more conservative in general than oth-ers). "Generally speaking boundaries are determined more by method, theory, and conceptual framework than by subject matter" (Klein 1996, 46). With only some exaggeration, one can think of economists fashioning mathematical models and analyzing data statistically, psychologists run-ning experiments, anthropologists doing field studies, sociologists survey-ing, and geographers drawing maps. Exceptions there always were, of course, but the dominant methodology in each discipline had an important effect on the type of questions which researchers asked. As students, they learned the preferred methodology, with each method taking much time to master, and then they applied what they knew as scientists. Their view of the world, plus their interest in career advancement, further steered them toward the accepted method. Moreover, different disciplines develop their own "culture" which provides members with a sense of identity not to be easily sacrificed. For some of these disciplines especially—geography foremost, then economics—methodology now defines the discipline to a greater extent than subject matter.

Inevitably, a focus on only one narrow method limits the pace of scientific advance in any discipline. While surveying is less dominant now than in the 1970s, it still forms the core of methodological training in most sociology programs; yet surveys provide little scope for description and classification, essential elements of any science, and need to be supplemented by other methods like participant observation and field experiments. In Szostak (1999), I discuss how economics has paid little attention to economic growth because this subject has not lent itself to the dominant method, and more generally how reliance on one method has severely limited the empirical base on which scientific advance depends.

A natural result of methodological orthodoxy has been disciplinary imperialism: practitioners of one method taking their tool kit to the subject matter of another (they naturally carry the theories of their own discipline with them; indeed these are generally embodied in a set of assumptions scholars apply with their favored method). Thus economists apply simple economic models to the family or voting behavior, anthropologists do field studies of racial minorities in Western cities, and geographers map the daily routine of entrepreneurs. Literary theory has also invaded other domains; advocates of deconstruction feel that not just texts but all forms of human interaction can be analyzed in a similar fashion in order to discern their hidden meanings.

Just as war eventually destroyed the Great Power system in Europe, disciplinary imperialism may yet weaken the arbitrary boundaries between disciplines. So far the signs are weak. Researchers have a considerable capacity for talking past their extra-disciplinary counterparts. Different jargon, methods, and theoretical perspectives are not easily overcome. Yet as Smelser and Swedberg (1994, 20) have noted with respect to economic sociology, the early days of economist raids and sociologist retaliation may well be giving way to a recognition on both sides that no one theory or method is best, but rather that a mixture will best elucidate those matters of mutual concern.

If true, this may spell the end of discipline by method. If, as I strongly suspect, there is no good reason why particular methods should dominate the study of particular subjects—and not only does common sense dictate otherwise, but the very act of imperialism screams this to be the case— then once one has admitted methodological plurality at one's borders it can only be a matter of time till it wins the day. The barbarians must be stopped at the gate or not at all.

2

Philosophy of Science

It is desirable before launching out upon this survey of understanding in human science to reflect somewhat on what science is, how it is best—and worst—performed, and how human science differs from natural science. Since I will often present a range of theoretical perspectives in what follows, readers should be armed with some idea of how scientists (and they) should evaluate theories. Although lack of space will prevent me from delving deeply into empirical verification in this book, I will try to touch on the sort of evidence which supports differing views, and provide readers with an introduction to the relevant literature. This book in many ways reflects the scientific judgment expressed in this chapter: I strive for a variety of points of view on many links to encourage (especially interdisciplinary) communication, and because I believe strongly in open-mindedness. I report various types of theory and evidence because I believe in both theoretical and methodological flexibility.

I should stress that it is not my intention in this chapter to provide a comprehensive overview of the present state of affairs in philosophy of science. I have read enough of the philosophical literature to understand the basic thrust of many leading lines of argument, and also to recognize the many points on which philosophers disagree. The purpose of this chapter is to emphasize a handful of points which will guide my efforts in the next chapters: that science is possible, but proof and even falsification impossible, that we can pursue but not precisely define "explanation" and "confirmation," that we should therefore be open to a range of theoretical and methodological arguments, that we should be wary of the biases that can slip into scientific research, and that interdisciplinarity is an antidote to both (some) subjective biases and to methodological or theoretical orthodoxy. The chapter should acquaint the reader with the philosophical outlook of the author. I also believe that the broad arguments presented here (subject to a range of caveats) would be accepted by many, though not all, philosophers of science. Since all scientists must accept the lack of philosophical consensus on how we should best proceed, acceptance of this belief is not essential to an appreciation of the argumentation in later chapters.

What is Science?

Decades ago, during the reign of positivism in the philosophy of science, this question was easy to answer. Positivism maintained that empirical testing could, if not prove that theories were true, at least prove that they were false. Thus science was the enterprise by which theories were exposed to reality in such a manner that the real world rather than the whims of humanity could decide on their veracity. Philosophy, astrology, and a host of other quests for knowledge could be dismissed as nonscience if they could not point to empirical tests which could potentially disprove their theories. Ah, the good old days!

Positivism has fared poorly over the last decades (though legions of both natural and human scientists are unaware of this). It is now widely recognized that "there is just no method that enables scientific theories to be proven true or even probably true" (Chalmers 1982, xii). The fact that X preceded Y a million times does not mean that it necessarily does so. Nor can theories be falsified; the fact that Y does not follow X once does not prove wrong a theory that states it should. Our very observations of "X" and "Y" are grounded in theory. As I discussed in chapter 1, definitions are only possible in context. Since our very observation thus depends on theory, any clash between observation and theory can be blamed on the former rather than the latter. That is, if we observe that X does not cause Y in a particular instance, we can simply redefine X and/or Y rather than reject our theory. Alternatively, we could search for some "problem" which prevented us from observing the true "X" and "Y." Since in practice various other assumptions have to be made external to the theory (e.g., that all other variables remain constant), an 'undesirable' empirical result can be blamed on violation of these rather than taken as a refutation of the theory at hand. Moreover, as we shall see, many key theories have a probabilistic element: X greatly increases the probability of Y. Such theories could never be falsified.

None of this is philosophical nitpicking. The history of science shows that theories have been maintained for centuries despite apparent falsification. While the Copernican revolution is rightly hailed as a major scientific advance, it is less often recognized that this system still fit poorly the observed movements of the planets. Only centuries later, with an understanding of the elliptical orbits of planets, did theory accord well with observation. Science, then, does not have recourse to some infallible external reference of right and wrong. There is always and necessarily scope left for human judgment. In some cases, such as the earth orbiting the sun, the evidence is (now) so compelling that virtually everyone accepts a particular scientific judgment. In other cases, the evidence is less 'conclusive' and thus scientific judgment can vary. In no case, though, can we say that a theory is definitely right or even definitely wrong. Science, then, might well be viewed as an attempt to approach one extreme or the other (Lambert and Brittan 1997).[1]

Philosophers have also noted that for any finite body of empirical evidence, it will always be possible to construct more than one theory that explains it. This is known as the Duhem-Quine thesis, and can be justified in two ways: by recognizing, as above, that any theory can be reconciled with inconvenient empirical results by adjusting subsidiary hypotheses, or by noting that all theories have some unobservable elements, and thus one can potentially construct theories that differ only in unobservables (Papineau 1996). Historians add a further cause for pessimism: since all past scientific theories are now believed to be incorrect at least in part, we should be doubtful that present theories are correct in all respects. Yet defenders of science argue that there are always external grounds for choosing between theories,[2] and that the finding of errors in past theories is evidence of scientific advance rather than scientific impossibility. Moreover, while it is theoretically possible, it is in fact quite rare to find two theories that fit observations equally well.

Many leading philosophers, Feyerabend, Foucault, and Derrida among them, have taken the position that there is no such thing as "science." Once we recognize that human judgment is the final arbiter of scientific truth, they argue, there is no standard by which we can claim that some forms of pursuit of knowledge are superior to others. The physicist and the mystic are playing the same game. Some justification for their position is found in the fact that most languages do not make the distinction that English does between "science" and other "knowledge-gathering" enterprises. Taken to an extreme, though, such a position suggests that scientific knowledge reflects nothing more than the whim of the scientific community; that it is an elaborate charade whose output we need hardly have faith in.[3]

Sampson (1993) pursues this logic. He says it is folly to search for reality. Rather, we should try to ensure that all social groups have had an input. He quotes favorably a Native American who says that archaeological accounts of native history are of no interest to him, since his people's myths tell him all he needs to know. It is one thing to respect an individual's beliefs. It is quite another to equate (or even prefer) myths taken at face value with an archaeological dig. While archaeologists may differ over what particular finds mean, and they will naturally tend to interpret them within their preconceptions of native history, still they are at least making some attempt to seek external evidence. And it is this willingness to expose theories to real world evidence that characterizes science.

If conclusive proof is impossible, then perhaps we are doomed to an interminable debate on major issues, with the participants having no rational basis for choosing one position or the other. Perhaps the scientific revolutions which Thomas Kuhn applauds as the basis of scientific advance are really just changes in scientific fashion; Copernicus just took the fancy of the scientific community and really gets us no closer to "truth." As Bechtel (1986) notes, it was common for decades for the sociology of knowledge literature to stress the nonrational "cultural" choices of scientific communities, while their colleagues in the history of science stressed the logical evolution of science.[4] These days it is most common for denizens of both communities to recognize that both rational and nonrational arguments have a place in understanding scientific evolution. For Freeman (1994), we must expose the influence of power and envy on scientific enterprise, "and still recognize that the laws of nature can not be bent and can not be broken by power and money." He concludes that, "the history of science is most illuminating when the frailties of human actors are put into juxtaposition with the transcendence of natural laws." The very fact that we are better able to manipulate the physical and social worlds is evidence that our understanding has improved. Our study of genetic predisposition will show that we are likely "hard-wired" with rules for both induction and deduction in order to understand and react to different situations (Hutcheon 1996). While there may be all sorts of imperfections in, for example, our sensory apparatus, it would nevertheless appear that we are endowed with an ability for scientific advance.[5]

If we can avoid the extreme of rejecting the possibility of science, then sociologists of knowledge do a valuable service in warning us of the biases that inevitably creep into scientific enterprise in the absence of conclusive empirical tests. Feminists also have correctly taken the demise of positivism as a reason to fear that the theories inherited from a male-dominated past may be misleading. Here again, there is a tendency in some writers to go to the extreme and suggest that all knowledge is entirely subjective (e.g., G. Rose 1993). They can draw on the writings of Foucault for both conclusions. In his studies of mental institutions, prisons, and sex he stressed that scientific theories in these areas were inseparable from the interests of the powerful in maintaining social order. To save humanity, he urged the destruction of the social sciences. Yet in his later writings he softened this position considerably, perhaps as he recognized that himself was positing a theory of social interaction or that in the absence of science we could have no basis for objecting to the abuse of power. The existence of bias need not mean that science is impossible.

Derrida approached this debate from a different perspective. His focus was on the analysis of texts, and he has left us with one of the key analytical tools in human science today: deconstruction.[6] The essence of deconstruction is easily grasped. Due to the inherent ambiguity of language, texts can be interpreted in an infinite variety of ways. No one way is superior to the other. Since scientific writings could be subject to various interpretations, the scientific enterprise was doomed from the outset. The only task for scholars was to show this over and over with a variety of interpretations. When first exposed to deconstruction my reaction was harsh. As the writer of this text, I know what I am saying, and can thus settle any interpretive debate by providing the "right" interpretation. As I have become more aware of the subconscious and cultural influences that act on any author, I have been forced to recognize that others can indeed find implications of my text that are "correct" interpretations even though I neither consciously intended nor agree with them. Thus I have come to view the deconstructionist research program as a potentially very useful enterprise.[7] Ironically, though, I do so while rejecting the philosophical conclusion that Derrida reached. This particular text puts across the idea of an organizing schema in the human sciences. While every argument may not have quite the effect on the reader I intended, and may have quite different effects on different readers, there is still a fairly obvious argument being made. The same can be said of (all?) other scientific texts (we should note that Derrida first focused on fiction, and many deconstructionists feel the method is more appropriate to fiction than non-fiction). Wilson (1998) is hostile to Derrida on the grounds that he must have thought his own text had a particular message (despite his deliberately obscure style) and can thus not deny this attribute to texts in general. Again, the mere fact that knowledge is not perfect—in this case that we cannot entirely agree on what this or any other book is about—does not necessarily imply that science is impossible.

And let us all be thankful for that. As Heidegger and others have argued, if we accept the extreme positions of Foucault or Derrida, then we are left with no alternative but to blindly accept authority (Hey 1985). Without a belief in science, we are each open to the preaching of any demagogue. Foucault may succeed in prying us from the grip of present elites only to deliver us to the service of another. We would have no basis for insisting on any rights or obligation.

So what is science? I will follow Law (1994) here and speak of the pursuit of rigorous ways of knowing. That is, while perfection is beyond our grasp, there are ways of exposing our theories to the evidence which yield more "reliable" results than others. My purpose in the remaining sections of this chapter is to discuss how science is best pursued. This is not a precise definition of science, with which we can always be sure when an activity qualifies for the title or not.[8] As we have seen, though, definitions need not be precise to be useful.

SCIENTIFIC EXPLANATION AND CONFIRMATION

Philosophers have struggled to provide definitions which would allow us to judge whether a particular argument qualified as a legitimate scientific explanation, and a particular piece of evidence qualified as scientific confirmation. Having seen that we can neither prove nor disprove scientific theories, we should welcome limits on what qualified as a legitimate theory, and what sorts of evidence should increase our confidence in the accuracy of a theory. We should not be surprised, though, that precise definitions have so far eluded philosophers.

The classical definition of a scientific explanation can be traced to Aristotle. It calls for a combination of scientific law(s) (if X, then Y) and other arguments (M is X, L is Y). It is often called the "covering law" approach because of its insistence on an appeal to laws. The covering law approach could deal with stochastic relationships (if X, then Y will probably happen), but only if a resulting probability of more than 50% was involved (if X causes Y with less than 50% probability, one would require further explanation of any observation of Y). While a reasonable starting point, philosophers have shown that the covering law definition excludes apparently legitimate scientific explanations (such as attributing tides to the moon on the basis of empirical observation before Newton's laws of gravity) and can include irrelevant scientific explanations (the birth control pill decreases the probability of pregnancy by 95%; therefore Fred is not pregnant because he took the pill).

The causal-statistical definition also requires a law, and insists that this be a causal law. It is willing to countenance any explanation of Y in terms of X, as long as the probability of Y given X is higher than the probability of Y without X. It can thus deal with unlikely results, without requiring further explanation as with the classical approach. The causal-statistical approach provides a useful guideline for much scientific activity: scientists should search for statistically relevant factors and explain these relations causally (not necessarily in that order). However, it is criticized for not overcoming some of the weaknesses of the classical approach, such as the pre-Newtonian explanation of tides.

To overcome the perceived narrowness of the two law-based definitions, philosophers have developed a pragmatic approach (which can subsume all explanations embraced by the previous two).[9] Its focus is on giving answers to "why?" questions, by analyzing what "why?" means in terms of what else might have happened. Unfortunately, this approach too can be criticized both for errors of inclusion and exclusion. It is criticized for being so broad as to allow, say, astrological explanations. On the other hand, it has difficulty with stochastic relations where the resulting probability is less than 50%. And some philosophers wonder if all "how?" questions can necessarily be reduced to "why?" questions.

One response to the fear that all of these definitions can encompass "nonscientific" explanations is to focus instead on confirmation. We could then distinguish theories according to their empical validity rather than some *a priori* judgment of their scientific credentials. There are three main definitions of scientific confirmation. Hempel posited that confirmation occurred in any instance in which a suggested relationship was observed. The Bayesian approach speaks of any evidence which raises the probability that the hypothesized relationship is true. One problem with this approach is that it has no place for evidence that predates the hypothesis, whereas most theories are developed to explain a range of existing evidence. The bootstrap hypothesis starts from the recognition that no empirical test can falsify a theory; it thus speaks of confirmation in terms of a wide variety of empirical tests which approach variables differently, and allow for separate estimation of each variable (I have borrowed heavily from Lambert and Brittan 1992, in this section).

The lack of philosophical consensus on definitions of either explanation or confirmation should not distress us. We have seen in chapter 1 that precise definition is generally impossible. And note that philosophical debate over these definitions has generally involved pointing to examples which discredit the definition. Yet if we can (generally) agree that a certain type of explanation or confirmation is legitimate (or not), then we can safely rely on scientific judgement. We may not be able to precisely define explanation or confirmation, but that does not prevent us from recognizing these when we see them.

OPENMINDEDNESS

The only way in which a human being can make some approach to knowing the whole of a subject is by hearing what can be said about it by persons of every variety of opinion and studying all modes in which it can be looked at by every character of mind. No wise man ever acquired his wisdom in any mode but this.—John Stuart Mill

We have seen above that scientific theories cannot objectively be proven or falsified. Yet the majority of philosophers have not therefore given up on the pursuit of science. Rather, they have recognized that scientific advance depends crucially on the integrity of the scientific community. Scientists must rise above their subjective biases and try to evaluate competing theories according to their accordance with reality. "Science works as a collaborative community because that is the only way it can work" (Hatton and Plouffe 1997, iv; they note that most practicing scientists are unaware of the importance of communal judgment).

Openmindedness would seem to be a virtue whose advantages are so obvious that one should hardly need to exhort anyone to its pursuit. Yet elements of both our personalities and our environment turn all of us away from this idea. Among scientists, Bruno Latour has noted that academic incentives push scientists to be committed and assertive;[10] he feels that both the sins of absolutism (only my view is right) and reductionism (oversimplification) are in large part a result of these incentives (in Barber 1993, 10). Yankelovich (1991, 212) bemoans the fact that both English and American philosophers (the same could be said for others in human science) tend to behave like trial lawyers and maliciously attack the weak points of others' arguments. He applauds continental philosophers such as Gadamer and Habermas for adhering to the Socratic tradition of listening carefully to opponents, under the assumption that the other likely has a useful point to make.[11] Habermas urges us all to pursue the "ideal speech situation" in which we try to explain to others why we disagree, so that in the end we can agree; he blames power relations for causing us instead to use conversation to manipulate others (Potter 2000, 15).

This regrettable state of affairs in the sciences parallels the situation in the non-scientific world. People seem genetically programmed to dislike uncertainty, and thus like to believe one world view wholeheartedly. Our very definition of ourselves, our self-esteem, tends to depend on some set of strongly held beliefs.[12] Moreover, in conversation we tend to be more impressed by the forceful than the evenhanded. We disdain politicians who cannot answer questions about complex issues without caveats. We may praise openmindedness, but in our everyday behavior we often act to undermine it.

The implications for science are huge. Scientific progress depends on innovation, after all, and innovators will inevitably find their task more difficult if their peers all have fixed views. This does not bring science to a halt: it is indeed geared to make small advances which do not threaten the hegemony of a particular theoretical viewpoint. As historians of science have long recognized, however, science in the long run advances through occasionally overthrowing the dominant theoretical apparatus (paradigm). This force for change can be delayed significantly if the scientific community lacks the requisite degree of openmindedness. Centuries thus passed between when it was first suggested that the Earth orbited the sun, and when this became widely accepted.

Moreover, if, as I suggest, the "true" theory of human science is a composite of many smaller theories, then scientific advance will be severely hobbled if each individual scientist is tightly wedded to a particular theory. In Kelly's (1991) words, every theory has its "range of convenience"; therefore even the most ardent supporter should be able to recognize a theory's limits. Sadly, though, science is often viewed as a battleground where only one theory can survive, and scientists are thus tempted to be less than honest with their arguments. This only rarely (I hope) involves the deliberate falsification of results, but more commonly involves emphasizing or reporting only the evidence consistent with one's preconceptions (see La Follette 1992).[13] McCloskey (1987) has delineated the various rhetorical devices by which scientists can make other scientists believe that their evidence is more convincing than it is; he concludes that scientific advance depends on us arguing openly and honestly with each other.

The last point deserves emphasis. Science will advance fastest when scientists openly and honestly compare the ability of competing theories to answer particular questions. Scientists who ignore competing explanations or inconvenient empirical results may have some success, but will not be advancing the cause of science as they should. It is regrettable that I will in writing this book likely be criticized by some for my inclusion of the views of others. But if Habermas is right that there is some kernel of truth in almost all theories, we can hardly expect to identify this kernel with our eyes closed.

METHODOLOGICAL FLEXIBILITY

There is no one best methodology. There are many ways in which we can "test" our theories. Common sense tells us that if experiments, statistical analyses, surveys, historical examinations, ethnographic observations, and textual analyses all yield the same conclusion, we can be many times more confident of the result than if we relied only on one form of verification. Yet we have seen (app 1-B) that most human science disciplines elevate one method above the rest. To be sure, not all methods are equally applicable to all questions, but it is equally true that no question is best served by only one method.[14]

The desirability of methodological pluralism is widely recognized by philosophers if not by scientists. Charles Sanders Peirce perhaps said it best: truth is the confluence of independent streams of good evidence. Thomas Kuhn was also notable for demolishing the idea that there was one truth criterion. Nor has this advice gone entirely unheeded. Fraser and Gaskell (1990, 13), for example, exult in the range of methods employed by social psychologists: interviews, observations, group discussions, content analysis, statistical analysis (though Himmelweit in the same volume feels that even social psychologists do not avail themselves of some research methods as they could). And Pervin (1990) concludes his handbook on personality theory by celebrating the fact that, "At least for the present, however (and, we may hope, for the future) the time of dismissal of some phenomena as not legitimate for investigation and of hegemony of some research methods over others has passed." Not all areas have shown such healthy signs, though, and as Pervin himself makes clear the future of flexibility is nowhere assured.

Interdisciplinarity suffers from this state of affairs. The suspicion with which human scientists greet the methods of other disciplines is redoubled when faced with the novelty of interdisciplinary research. In the never-ending battle over limited university resources, interdisciplinary work is often dismissed as shallow and lacking in standards and expertise. Even Frey, who takes pains to distinguish himself from those economists who view other disciplines as merely new playgrounds for economic methodology, fears that methodological flexibility will easily yield to the lowest common denominator. It is alright for sociologists to apply their methods to the subject matter of economists, but the intermingling of methods should be avoided (1992, 15–16). Only as it is fully recognized that methodological flexibility is desirable within disciplines will it cease to be a barrier to interdisciplinarity.

Methods differ in the degree to which they are deductive (certain hypotheses are applied to novel situations) or inductive (a variety of observations are taken together to generate new hypotheses). It should be obvious that science will advance fastest when there is a two-way interchange between theory and data, deduction and induction. Both Kuhn and Lakatos argued forcefully that neither theory nor evidence have priority; each benefits from the other. Snooks (1993) surveys the case of economic history. Economists are primarily deductive—most papers in top journals provide "theoretical minutiae." History, on the other hand, tends to be largely inductive. Economic history, rather than blending the two, has swung from inductive to deductive extremes in recent decades. Where once the field was characterized as facts without theory, it is now the reverse. The pull of methodological purity is so strong that the happy medium is difficult to achieve (though not impossible—Snooks recognizes that some schools of economic history have combined the two).

I will in this book focus on theory, and thus might mistakenly appear to favor a deductive approach. Yet I must emphasize that theories should be developed through an interchange between deduction and induction. Moreover, when there are observations that fit poorly with existing theory, I will report these to encourage further theoretical development. Note, though, that my ability to do so depends on the degree to which scientists have been willing to study/report real world occurrences which fit poorly with their theory. Advances in natural science over the last centuries have often been driven by technological exploration: scientists were thus forced to confront real world events which their theories could not explain. Human scientists have recourse to an even larger set of observations, but only if they choose to look (see Cronbach 1986, Rule 1997). Salter and Hearn (1996) worry that human scientists spend too much time developing competing theories, and too little on empirical work; their answer is to search for a variety of evidence.

Some philosophers worry about the process of induction: how exactly do scholars move from a body of empirical observation to a theory? One concern is that they may too readily confuse correlation with causation. This danger can be minimized by subjecting new theories to a range of further empirical tests. A second concern is with our mental capacity to recognize complex relationships. We will see, though, that we are genetically "programmed" to develop complex world views (chapter 4). Still, Hodgson (1993) notes that we cannot fully comprehend the inductive process without reference to human creativity (I→C3).

BIASES IN HUMAN SCIENCE

While many distinctions between natural and human science are overdrawn, it is certainly true that human scientists should worry more about the biases which they bring to their research. In looking at either individuals or societies, after all, we are studying ourselves. It would be ridiculous to assume that researchers could be neutral in their attitude toward society; such an attitude would in fact be psychologically unnatural (Heilbroner 1990). In order for us to function daily in a complex world, we have to devise—consciously or subconsciously—some rules of thumb (schemas; see chapter 4) to guide us. These naturally embody implicit views of how the world works, and thus guide our attempts as researchers to comprehend that world. This is especially the case when we are engaged in the important task of induction: moving from observation to generalization. Establishing a plausible set of causal factors naturally depends on one's prior convictions, and thus people from similar backgrounds will tend to reach similar conclusions (Jaspars and Hewstone 1986).

Two characteristics of human science facilitate the exercise of bias. First, we are rarely able to replicate, whereas *some* natural scientists can run the same experiment over and over. This reflects both the fact that we generally deal with complex causal interactions,[15] and the fact that people behave differently in laboratories and real life (Secord 1986). Second, we must worry about intentionality, which is not directly observable. Neither of these is an insurmountable obstacle to science, but both should encourage our vigilance against bias.

Less innocuously, we all know that theory in human science has public policy implications. Can we doubt that scientists will be tempted to develop theories which support their favored policies? The danger of the abuse of science in the interest of power was the focus of Foucault. Economists especially are often accused of (unknowingly) pursuing ideological goals. Thus, Eichner suggests that, "to those who constitute the 'establishment' within the profession, it is more important to limit the power of the state than to understand how the economic system works" (1983, 4). While we can certainly debate whether biases are as strong as Eichner suggests, we should recognize that it would be unscientific to rule out the possibility of substantial bias.

We have seen above that attempts by positivists to claim that one methodology could immunize the scientific enterprise against bias are no longer tenable. Yet we need not go overboard in the opposite direction and deny that science is possible. Rather, we should pursue the middle course of trying to face up to our biases (see Trigg 1985, 203–4). Note that individuals are generally not aware of their biases. It is generally a mistake to think that any group purposely pushes a narrow view of the world; most scientists genuinely think they are pursuing truth.

Ethnographers have been forced to come to grips with this fact earlier than other human scientists. The focus of their study has, after all, been the belief systems which guide the behavior of people in other cultures. Once one has recognized that people there infer (sometimes illogical) causal connections based on their prior beliefs, it is not too great a leap to suspect that members of one's own culture—even oneself—do the same. This has caused ethnographers to question the time-honored practice of talking to traditional tribespeople, but only putting on paper the ethnographer's interpretations. They have long worried that they would thus impose their own theoretical categories on other societies: an in-joke in anthropology was that ethnographers should receive no formal training (Agar 1981). One result is "social constructionist analysis," which aims at clarifying responses from individuals in foreign cultures in order to avoid ethnocentricity (see below).

There is a lesson for us all in this. If a diversity of perspectives is essential to one area in human science, we should hardly be surprised that such diversity is invaluable in uncovering and overcoming bias throughout human science. This is not a novel thought: feminist scholars have long argued that white males might unknowingly bias their interpretation of events.[16] Gender is not the only issue: race, ethnicity, and class, as well as the psychological attributes of those prone to enter academia, are other sources of potential bias. Yet still these are not the only sources of bias, and arguably not even the most important. The sociology of knowledge literature stresses the belief sets which characterize communities of scientists.

That is, whatever our backgrounds we are further socialized to a particular way of solving problems as we are trained as academics. This involves the sorts of questions which we are expected to ask and the methodology and theory we are expected to employ.

Interdisciplinarity can serve as a (partial) antidote to bias. The different disciplines, as we have seen, tend to emphasize different theories and methods. Bringing them together must inevitably expose individual scholars to a diversity of viewpoints. In the short run this should serve to soften the ideological differences which separate disciplines. In the longer run, the recognition of an overarching schema should militate against approaching particular questions from one narrow perspective. Finally, let us not forget that the best protection against subconscious bias is to expose our theories to real world tests.[17] The methodological flexibility that comes with interdisciplinarity is our greatest ally.

SOCIAL CONSTRUCTION AND INTERSUBJECTIVITY

Rather than survey a vast literature on social construction and intersubjectivity, I focus here on Prus (1996); Prus himself recognizes that he takes an extreme view of intersubjectivity, which allows no scope for compromise with either postmodern or more mainstream approaches to science. I can, by focusing on Prus, show why compromise is necessary, and identify some of the strengths and weaknesses of the research program identified by Prus. Prus begins his book by stating that, "At the heart of the sociological enterprise is the idea that human behavior is the product of community life, that people's behavior cannot be reduced to individual properties" (1996, 2). I argued in chapter 1, though, that we should be open to a recognition of both how social aggregates affect individuals and in turn how individuals affect social aggregates. I can thus welcome Prus' elucidation of the first sort of effect, while rejecting his dismissal of the second (which should at the very least be considered an empirical question). An essential element of Prus' approach is the recognition that different groups will achieve different attitudes; he also notes that groups learn and adjust their views, and that individuals negotiate in various ways with other group members. Yet he stops short of a recognition that every individual necessarily develops a unique set of attitudes and beliefs, and that the group learning process he speaks of results from individuals choosing to change. I will discuss this and many other influences of individuals on culture in what follows. And we will see that our genes (and numerous other phenomena), join the cultural milieu emphasized by Prus in shaping who we are.

Prus defines the scientific mainstream as believing that we can study humans in a similar fashion to physical objects (and thus ape the natural sciences). The minority he champions are "interpretivists"; their starting point is the belief that we cannot speak of an objective reality but only of the subjective perceptions of reality by different groups. While such a belief might seem to challenge the very existence of enduring phenomena on which our schema is based, Prus does not deny that there are objects "out there" which resist our efforts to control them.[18] Rather he emphasizes that our awareness of these, our views of these (including our efforts to categorize), and our behavior toward them, are "problematic in scope, emphasis, and particulars" (1996, 12). Prus suggests that it will be difficult or impossible to fairly objectively identify the realizations of particular phenomena, or how phenomena are related to each other. This is, I would suggest, a conclusion open to empirical evaluation phenomenon by phenomenon. I would argue that we can fairly objectively establish realizations of most of the phenomena in our schema, especially those in the nonhuman environment, health and population, technology and science, and institutions (though "measurement" problems sometimes arise). In other cases, Prus is quite right. I will note, in our discussion of classes and mental disorders in particular, that realizations here depend crucially on societal attitudes: do workers see themselves as a distinct class?; how erratic does behavior have to be before we diagnose a disorder? But in such cases I can still strive to establish how particular attitudes influence particular realizations, and how these realizations influence other phenomena. Prus' pessimism is unnecessary; he speaks of how we cannot assume that different groups will judge color in a similar manner, despite a vast body of evidence suggesting that different groups do indeed divide the color spectrum in quite similar fashion. Group differences in perception of realizations of phenomena are at times important, but should not simply be assumed.

Prus argues that in order to understand human society we must learn how people make sense of their experiences and construct meaningful activities. He feels that mainstream scientists ignore this insight. Since individuals are social actors, and scientists are individuals, we cannot study others without participating in their lives and they in ours. Only then can we gain an intersubjective understanding. Attempts to observe behavior from a distance cannot tell us how people come to make sense of their world (Prus ignores the opposite danger, identified by Woolgar, 1988, of "going native" and thus taking for granted the attitudes of the group under study). I wholeheartedly agree that we should strive to put ourselves in the place of others and try to comprehend how they come to the attitudes and behaviors they exhibit (though I would examine both individuals and groups). But Prus again goes too far when he claims that there is no given nor predictable reality but just collectively developed attitudes. We will see in what follows that there are a wide range of "cultural universals" or things that virtually all groups agree on. This suggests that we can indeed speak of an external reality with respect to a wide range of phenomena. Moreover, casual empiricism suggests that outsiders can often form useful insights about our society; why should we assume that immersion is the only way we can gain insight into other groups?

Prus argues that the postmodern critique of the mainstream is misguided. Postmodernists focus on phenomena such as gender and class, without recognizing that these are subject to change. Note, though, that my schema allows us both to appreciate the importance of gender and class, and to recognize that our perceptions of particular genders and classes and their relationship to other phenomena are ever-changing (and we can strive to identify these relationships). Prus is critical of the postmodern antipathy to the ethnographic research he favors (which they see as voyeurism and imperialistic); he counters that *only* by immersing ourselves in a group can we achieve understanding. (He criticizes social constructivists for not identifying this one methodological path.) He notes that many "optimists" would like to see a synthesis of mainstream, postmodern, and intersubjective approaches, but concludes that this is impossible (1996, 26). I have argued above that we should not arbitrarily constrain the methods which scientists can employ. I can see advantages and limitations to the favored research methods of each of the three groups identified by Prus (we discussed postmodernism in chapter 1). We should be aware of the dangers identified by Prus in the methods of others, as well as the dangers identified by others in the methods of Prus. And I would maintain that the best evidence for any conjecture comes from diverse methods. We may find that some methods are better suited to certain questions (though I think the best starting assumption is that all methods can shed some light on each question). There is room in what follows for the arguments and evidence of all types of science. These can be compared and contrasted link by link. By openminded exchange among scholars from differing perspectives, we can hope to gradually enhance our understanding of each link.

In sum, I think Prus, and the many authors he builds upon, have something important to tell us. But I decry his desire to limit the methods we pursue to only one, to deny the very possibility of an objective reality, and to denigrate links from individuals to societal aggregates. The approach of this book is to synthesize the best of diverse approaches, and not place arbitrary limits on scientific practice.

THE ADVANTAGES OF INTERDISCIPLINARITY

The role of interdisciplinarity in combatting bias deserves repetition. Each human science discipline has its own "culture," which tends to include

favored theories, phenomena, and methods, and also standards of col-
laboration, cooperation, and publication, preferences for quantitative
versus qualitative analysis, an emphasis on empirics versus theory, and
mechanisms for encouraging scholarly adherence to disciplinary culture
(Klein 1990; Salter and Hearn 1996). Interaction of scholars across
disciplinary boundaries must of necessity serve as an antidote to at least
some of the biases which afflict the human sciences.

Such biases lead groups of scientists to ascribe greater authority to
certain theories than the evidence would warrant. Biases also limit the
exploration of new ideas. As Kenneth Burke has noted, "A way of seeing is
also a way of not seeing" (Simons and Melia 1989). Discipline-based
researchers operate within a narrow mindset. As Foucault emphasized,
disciplines discipline (and thus serve the interests of the powerful by
limiting scholars' ability to evaluate the status quo; Salter and Hearn
1996). Much that should be of interest to practitioners is unknown. Even if
they are dimly aware of activities in other disciplines, that information is
rarely made a central part of their mental processes. In common parlance,
they do not feel it in their bones. They are thus limited in the type of
research they pursue.[19]

The cross-fertilization of ideas between groups of scholars can be especially valuable. At present, different scholarly approaches to particular
questions are only rarely juxtaposed. When I discuss scientific/
technological evolution in chapter 9, I will show that the key to advance is
the synthesis of diverse bodies of knowledge into something new. Moreover, in chapter 5 we will see that inspiration tends to come during rest
following a lengthy period of thinking about an issue (I→C2). If we focus
our thoughts narrowly, we must necessarily limit severely the types of
syntheses possible.

Bechtel (1986) defends interdisciplinarity in terms of the arguments
above, as well as the concern that disciplines have not covered all of the
questions of interest in human science (a concern which I discussed in the
first chapter).[20] He notes that skeptics point first to the advantages of
specialization. But the argument for interdisciplinarity is not that we all
pursue the big picture all the time. Most scholars will always be focused on
narrowly defined questions. The advantage of interdisciplinarity is that it
gives these scholars a wider array of theory and method to apply. And an
interdisciplinary organizing schema would allow them to readily place
their research in a broader context.

Gaff (1997) argues that interdisciplinarity should appeal not just to
scholars and students but to the wider public. University research serves
two goals: supporting university teaching and expanding our understanding of the real world. Society will judge human science by how well it can
provide solutions to pressing social problems. Many have suggested that

recent interest in interdisciplinary research is primarily a result of a desire to cope with the real world (Klein 1990, 42; Davis 1995; Walshok 1995). Postwar social problems—war, housing, crime, or welfare—do not fit conveniently into the bailiwick of any one discipline. Rustom Roy speaks of an "inexorable logic that the problems of society do not come in discipline-shaped blocks" (in Klein 1990, 35). While some may wish to avoid facing this logic,[21] the cost of such a strategy is huge. If our experts only comprehend small pieces of the puzzle (but speak as if they know all), it is an easy step for the public to decide that they know nothing of use. The solution of real world problems requires research of an interdisciplinary nature and students trained to appreciate complex interactions.[22]

Gaff (1997) feels he can speak for the 57 authors in his volume in saying that specialization "has often led to disconnected bits of information, fragmentation of the learning experience of students, and disintegration of the academic community. We are in the midst of a historical reversal of this trend because it is not conducive to good education for students, academic communication for faculty or campuses, or continued financial support from the public." Gaff is notably unsure, though, of the shape interdisciplinarity will take in future. As noted in chapter 1, my organizing schema serves to highlight the importance of interdisciplinarity, unifies the work of interdisciplinary scholars, and points the way to further developments in both interdisciplinary research and teaching. It thus greatly enhances the probability of an interdisciplinary future.

Rules of the Game

I have striven above to detail the importance of both theoretical and methodological flexibility, while yet asserting that there is a thing called "science" which can be identified by a dedication to "testing" theory through real world observation and/or manipulation. It is useful to note some guidelines which should guide the evaluation of scientific theories:

- We should insist on logical consistency of the theory itself. If it claims that X causes Y sometimes and Y causes X other times it needs to be clear as to what other conditions must have changed in order for the opposite result to occur.
- It is important to insist that theories be spelled out clearly. This does not mean that they need to be reduced to mathematical equations. However, theories that are presented only in the densest of prose are open to too wide a range of interpretation. While jargon may facilitate advance within a discipline, theories should be expressed in a language accessible to nonexperts.
- Theories should be compatible with collateral theories (or alternatives to these at least suggested). As Bartley suggests, we must be willing to accept

some theories even while we proceed to attack others. A theory that is inconsistent with related theories should be subjected to greater criticism.

- Evidence should be sought of diverse types and from many times and places. Reliance on only one form of evidence or one time period or place is simply bad science. We should be especially suspicious of theories which rely exclusively on some appeal to authority.
- Whenever possible theories should be broken into their subsidiary conjectures and each of them evaluated on their merits according to the criteria above.[23] Theories that are composed of illogical or unrealistic components should be highly suspect.

3

Culture Unpacked

THE DEFINITION OF "CULTURE"

THE WORD "CULTURE" IS BOTH ONE OF THE MORE COMMONLY USED OF MY category titles and likely the most imprecisely defined term we will have to deal with in this entire volume. This is quite unfortunate for, as we will see, cultural elements influence our lives in myriad ways. When authors do define what they mean by culture, it is clear that they view the term as encompassing quite different sets of phenomena. How then are we to interpret that large body of work in which culture is never defined but viewed as central? Or, on the wider stage, when culture becomes a focus of political debate, how can human scientists provide useful input if we all use the word differently?[1]

The solution to this conundrum is to unpack the term "culture" into its constituent parts. We will find that there is a wide range of phenomena that deserves to be viewed as cultural (there are also phenomena that are viewed as cultural by other writers, but are better viewed as social ideology or art within my schema). We will also find that causal links are best understood at the level of these phenomena rather than at the aggregated level of "culture." This is no surprise: the fact that scholars have chosen to define culture in diverse ways was an indication that they had found different subsets of phenomena to be of particular importance for the questions with which they were most concerned.

Nevertheless, some scholars—and countless politicians—will be opposed to the idea of unpacking the concept of culture. They view culture as an integral whole, even if they can not concur on a definition. To be sure, there are strong links between the phenomena that comprise culture: religious beliefs, for example, influence a variety of social practices. If not for these links, the utility of the word "culture" would be questionable. Yet we should not exaggerate the degree to which one element of culture will determine the rest (see below).

PREVIOUS DEFINITIONS

Already in 1952, Kroeber and Kluckhohn found 164 distinct definitions of culture in the literature. I make no pretense of being exhaustive here, but merely provide a sample of the definitions that I encountered as I researched this book. These can be placed in two categories. First, there are those that define culture in terms of some broad generality: "the common way that a community of persons makes sense of the world" (Gross 1985, 1); "Culture consists of the conventional patterns of thought, activity, and artifact that are passed on from generation to generation in a manner that is generally assumed to involve learning rather than specific genetic programming" (Brown 1991, 40); "the total pattern of human behavior and its products embodied in thought, speech, action, and artifacts, and depending upon man's capacity for learning and transmitting knowledge to succeeding generations" (Cavalli-Sforza 1981, 1, from Webster's dictionary); "collective programming of the mind which distinguishes the members of one group from another" (Smith and Bond 1993); "inherited ethical habit" (Fukuyama 1995, 34). As attempts to describe a complex concept in a few words, these can hardly be faulted. And it is worth noting the common emphasis on how culture is transmitted; this will be a major concern below. Yet if I were forced to establish the boundaries between my major categories on the basis of these definitions alone, I would have little guidance indeed. These definitions are so broad that much—indeed, all—of what we will term economic, political, technological, or artistic, could be subsumed under the word "culture." A term that is stretched to embrace everything tells us nothing about the causal forces at work. Thus, Durham (1991) applauds attempts to redefine culture "so that it includes less and reveals more." And Smith and Bond (1993), recognizing that traditional concepts of culture are too imprecise for scientific use, urge unpacking so that cultures can be compared and contrasted along various dimensions.

The second category of definitions involves attempts to list the constituent phenomena. Tooby and Cosmides (1992) note that definitions of culture have variously included behavior, tradition, significant symbols, social facts, control programs, semiotic systems, information, social organization, social relations, economic relations, intentional worlds, and socially constructed reality (nor is this list exhaustive). Some individual definitions are themselves very broad. Milner (1991) speaks of the entire range of institutions, artifacts, and practices which make up our symbolic universe. While his emphasis on symbolism does provide a basis for distinguishing the cultural from the noncultural, what of art, political insignia, or even money? And what about beliefs?; these need not be symbolic but would be included in many definitions of culture. Indeed, Namenwirth and Weber (1987, 8) believe that culture is only a system of ideas (but all ideas: art, morals, laws, customs, knowledge, memories, goals); they exclude institutions and behavior from consideration. Alternatively, Boyd and Richerson (1985, 2) speak of "knowledge, values, and other factors that influence behavior," which again risks widening the definition so that it includes everything.

The wide scope of many definitions of culture is no accident. The word was utilized by anthropologists in the nineteenth century to describe traditional societies. Since those societies differed in economic, political, social, technological, and artistic ways from Western societies, it was only natural that these differences were included in anthropological accounts. As the word "culture" came to be applied to "modern" societies, and utilized by non-anthropologists, many clung to this holistic sense of the word.[2] Thus, Milner (1991) is critical of attempts to treat culture as a residual shorn of economic, political, and other aspects, and feels that only Western society would attempt such a distinction. Milner is correct, of course, in suggesting that economic and political activity both influence and are influenced by this cultural residual. This book is based on the premise that such links are likely to be important. Yet we cannot hope to understand any society unless we can understand the causal relations among its constituent phenomena. To that end, viewing culture as all-encompassing serves no purpose.[3]

I will attempt no precise definition of culture here, but proceed in the next section to outline the constituent phenomena that comprise "culture" within my schema. In doing so I will naturally exclude elements that rightfully belong in other categories, and thus my "definition" is the sort of residual that Milner decries. Yet the mere fact that culture is not easily defined in a few words does not mean that the word has no meaning. Readers can ascertain for themselves that the constituent phenomena that comprise culture have much in common. As discussed in chapter 1, this is all we need or should ask of a definition.

UNPACKING CULTURE

"The most pressing challenge to students of culture is taxonomy: clarifying the objects of study and the boundaries between them" (DiMaggio 1994, 27). I begin by looking at the efforts of previous scholars to compile lists of the components of culture. I then eliminate those elements that clearly belong elsewhere in the schema. Barber (1993, 16) has attempted a provisional model of a social system, with phenomena gathered under three headings: culture (which for Barber involves diverse symbolic systems), social structure, and personality structure. His cultural variables are languages, law, science, religion, ideology, values, literature, music, architecture, philosophy, and mathematics. I would assign many of these to the categories of politics, art, and science. This leaves languages, religion, values, philosophy, and perhaps some elements of ideology. With the (partial) exception of languages, these fit within the emphasis on "ideas," which characterize many definitions of culture.

Brown (1991) reproduces Wissler's (1923) suggested "universal pattern" for ethnographic reporting (which inspired the Human Relations Area Files [HRAF] discussed in the first chapter), and applauds his attempt to describe a set of categories in which all societies could be analyzed. Wissler's first of nine categories dealt with languages (including literacy). Second was "material traits." Some of the components here are clearly technological or economic in nature (tools, weapons, industries). When we think of ornamentation in attire, however, then there is clearly something other than economic motives at work. Wissler's third category is art. His fourth comprises both myth and science. Religion (including treatment of the sick) is fifth. Family and social systems come sixth, property seventh, government eighth, and war ninth. These last categories are best assigned elsewhere in the schema, except that "sports and games" is included by Wissler within the sixth category. Removing art and science from consideration leaves us with language, "ornamentation," mythology, religion, and sports and games. This list is similar to that extracted from Barber, but includes a couple of elements with which we move beyond ideas to actions. Durham (1991) and others would prefer to limit "culture" to the realm of ideas, in order to emphasize that behaviors have multiple causes. I can applaud this motive while recognizing an overarching goal of trying to categorize like with like to the greatest degree possible. If the distinctive dress of Mayan villagers or the rules of Irish hurling are not (primarily) expressions of culture, what are they?

Languages and religion are two elements of culture that need little exposition. Beyond these, however, we would need to know more about what sorts of ideas and practices are to be considered cultural, and how these should be organized schematically. Talcott Parsons (1966) advocated distinguishing between cognitive (beliefs about the world), expressive (emotionally charged symbols), and valuative elements. Tilly urged the separation of beliefs about desirable goals from those about acceptable means. DiMaggio (1994) felt that those elements taken for granted should be distinguished from those more accessible consciously. All of these distinctions have their uses, but our purposes will best be served by a functional taxonomy.

We might start with "norms," a concept used much by both sociologists and anthropologists. Bethlehem (1990) defines these as ways of thinking or behaving that are considered correct. He distinguishes between "mores" (e.g., hitting others is bad) and folkways (customs; e.g., how to hold one's fork when eating). Thus, some norms involve definitions of behaviors as good or bad. Other norms involve no such ethical judgments, though there may nevertheless be great social pressure to conform.

The term "value" is similar to "norm" but can cover a somewhat wider range of circumstances. For example, while norms might govern the means an individual utilizes to achieve their goals, values would be a better descriptor of how a community shapes the choices of individuals about which goals they shall strive for. Since human societies are very complex, the norms or values of a community are not easily codified. As DiMaggio (1994) stresses, values are context dependent. For example, a particular community may expect its members to behave self-interestedly when engaged in economic activity, according to some code of justice in the legal/political arena, and in terms of a sense of collective responsibility within the family. Since not all communities will have well-defined values for every contingency, there can be confusion when context is unclear—for example on how religious objects or art should be marketed. Note, though, that while context-dependence makes the task of identifying a society's values difficult, it does not render the task impossible, and indeed shows us how to proceed. I will in this book outline the set of attitudes and behaviors that comprise culture; students of a particular society must allow for these attitudes to differ by context.

Stories are an embodiment of a community's values and/or religious beliefs, generally involving some real or imagined event concerning the group's ancestors. Thus a group that values honesty may tell tales in which the honesty of some forbear had benefitted the group. Almost inevitably the evolution of stories is untraceable. Yet by looking at a story's content we can hope to deduce the role it plays in a particular society. However, as modern literary theory makes clear, any story contains innumerable and often conflicting messages. This is, if anything, even more true for a story shaped by considerable retelling than for a novel with one author. Stories may thus have a variety of subtle influences, and these may be at odds with the central theme.

The mention of literary theory alerts us to the fact that we have moved close to the border with another of our categories, art. Stories indeed possess elements of both culture and art. Yet this is not a grave problem. While art will prove to be no easier to define than culture (in chapter 11), we can think of it here as creations that appeal to an aesthetic sense which transcends cultural boundaries (thus it would be a mistake to view art as a subset of culture). One does not have to be Greek to take pleasure in Greek myths. Yet those who appreciate these myths as works of art alone are not affected by them in the same fashion as the audience for which they were intended. The makers of stories—consciously or not—aimed for an aesthetically pleasing tale that contained a message.[4] I will treat stories here as a component of culture: a component whose main function is to support other components such as values. Yet I recognize that stories can only serve that function if they are appealing. Otherwise, one would just tell people the rules, rather than bury them in a story. Stories will inevitably be much influenced by the world of art. Nor are stories the only area in which artistic influences will interact with culture. In matters of attire, ritual, and even food preparation, cultural practices will be greatly influenced by aesthetic sensibility. Later (C→A), we will find that works of art are strongly influenced by culture in return.

I must also carefully delineate the boundary between culture and politics. Politics involves the exercise of power, and must rely in the end on the threat of physical force. A cultural value can be distinguished from a law, then, by whether officially sanctioned force will be used to enforce it. Laws should, and often do, reflect community standards, and thus should be substantially shaped by cultural values. Yet if a community finds it desirable to enshrine some of its values in law, it has explicitly decided that force rather than more subtle forms of community pressure are necessary (C→P3).

I can now proceed to unpack culture into its constituent parts. Although languages are classified by historical antecedents (Jahr 1993, complains that this practice ignores the fact that each language borrows heavily from a diversity of other languages), and can be distinguished by grammatical structure, tonality, and so on, such distinctions do not appear to have great causal significance and can be ignored for now. However, terms such as "expressions of culture," "values," "norms," "stories," and "religion" require a further exercise in unpacking for their meanings to be clear.

The phenomenon of story can be subdivided into myths, fairy tales, legends, family sagas, fables, and (some) jokes and riddles. All of these share the common elements of a message(s) and aesthetics, but differ in how they are constructed.[5] We can also speak of several "expressions of culture": rituals, dances, songs, cuisine, attire (including fashion and symbols like wedding rings), ornamentation of buildings, and games. Some of these serve a similar role to stories; all serve as expressions of cultural "identity."

Values can be categorized as follows:

i)   values concerning goals:
   • ambition (achievement motivation); is one person's gain viewed as another's loss?
   • rate of time preference (live for today or for future)
   • attitude toward wealth, power, knowledge, prestige, honor, recognition, love, friendship, beauty, sex, incest, marriage, physical or psychological well-being
   • optimistic versus pessimistic

ii) values concerning means:
- honesty
- ethics (sense of fairness, and so on)
- sense of righteousness, ethical superiority
- is work just a means to an end, or are skill and craftsmanship valued for themselves?
- belief in fate versus individual achievement (sense of justice)
- openness to innovation; inquisitiveness
- mastery of nature versus living in harmony with it
- attitudes toward violence and vengeance

iii) attitudes toward community:
- strength of sense of identity
- loyalty to family versus wider community
- openness to those outside the community (including intermarriage)
- attitudes toward young and old
- egalitarian versus competitive outlook
- sense of responsibility for others (e.g., the sick)
- trust
- authoritarian versus cooperative (note overlap with attitude toward prestige)
- respect for individual

iv) everyday norms (folkways, customs):
- manners, courtesy
- "proxemics" (physical distance maintained, tolerance of odors, degree of eye contact)
- tidiness, cleanliness
- punctuality
- conversation rules (propriety of interrupting, shouting, eye contact)
- driving, walking on right, facing front in elevator
- tipping

This list, by its nature, is unlikely to be exhaustive. It does include all of the cultural elements that will prove to be important in the causal links of this and later chapters. The list was developed by reading widely and attempting to group common elements together. It thus reflects both inductive and deductive activity, as did my original list of categories.

The reader may note the absence of words such as "freedom," "truth," and "mercy" from the above list, and the parenthetical mention of justice. I have purposely eschewed words that tend to have diverse meanings. With respect to justice, I can think of two main sorts of question: do I think the world is just? (captured by attitudes to fate), and will I behave justly? (captured under ethics). Mercy is captured by righteousness and vengeance, and truth by honesty and the search for knowledge. Freedom means countless things. Attitude to fate captures part of it. So does attitude to individuals.

There is (surprise!) no scholarly consensus on how best to categorize the religions of the world. Some scholars advocate classification along geographical or ethnic lines. Others trace how particular religions evolved in relation to others (e.g., what elements of Judaism and Christianity are maintained in Islam).[6] We could compare religions on the basis of how many assumptions they need to make, or how coherent they are. Some would prefer a philosophical scheme: theism versus polytheism, universalizing (Christianity, Islam, Buddhism) versus ethnic (Judaism, Hinduism, tribal). Yet all of these proposals run into difficulties due to the fact that there is great diversity within all major religions. The most popular approach, then, is one which fits nicely with the approach of this book: to focus on particular beliefs and practices and classify these (that is, to unpack).

This also spares me from trying to define religion in a few words.[7] Already in 1912, Leuba could identify 48 distinct definitions of the word, none of which were entirely satisfactory (Batson, Schoenrade, and Ventes 1993). As with culture itself, I can identify the constituent phenomena I would wish to subsume under the heading "religion":

1. Providence. All religions have some concept of providence. The greatest distinction to be made is between an emphasis on god(s) intervening on our behalf versus a sense of some cosmic order to which humanity should attune itself. Most religions have elements of both, despite the fact that a complete cosmic order leaves no room for godly intervention. While some religions have capricious gods, which help them reconcile the ideal of providence with the existence of evil, it is noteworthy that all have benevolent gods.[8]
2. Revelation. All religions must be based on some idea of past or present revelation. Revelation can come from nature, personal insight, or the acts of god(s). It may, but need not, involve prophecy concerning the future course of human affairs.
3. Salvation. Many would view this as the key element in all religions (though some would claim that early Judaism and some other faiths did not promise an afterlife). Does the body get resurrected, or does the soul separate from the body? Do we return to a golden age, or enter a better world? (where evil disappears?). Does it happen due to magic, personal beliefs, personal acts, or divine whim? Do we only speak of salvation from death or from disease and other calamities too? Is life a test or a learning experience?
   Many religions have visions of the end of the world (eschatology). These serve to encourage belief in a future, better world. However, some religions, notably Hinduism and Buddhism, contain no eschatology.
4. Miracles. These are not quite universal, but nearly enough so that the absence of miracles from a religion is noteworthy. They serve as both evidence of the correctness of a particular religion, and a sign of hope.
5. Definition of the sacred and profane. While not quite universal, such distinctions are integral parts of the vast majority of religions. Many Eastern

religions have no concept of "sacred." Those who fear that the decline of the sacred in Western societies signals a decline in religion itself may therefore be misguided. Sociologists view the concept as primarily a justification for various cultural values. One cannot have the sacred without the profane, and it is then an easy step to taboos.

6. Doctrine. The phenomena above could be subsumed under the heading "dogma," for they deal with the essential tenets of a religion. Doctrine refers to the rational arguments used to support dogma, whether by an organization or an individual. Due to the ongoing efforts of theologians, doctrine evolves over time (in large part in reaction to other changes in society). One important concern here is the degree to which individuals and communities are open to ecumenicism, which focuses on the common elements of all religions. I should emphasize that religions with similar dogma can have quite different doctrines, and that these can both create barriers between communities and have myriad effects on members of those communities.

Scholars of religion speak of two other religious phenomena: the organization of religion, and rites and ceremonies. The former is a political phenomenon, though greatly influenced by doctrine and dogma. The second is best subsumed under "cultural expressions" to avoid duplication. Rituals can serve to establish times, people, and places which a group thinks sacred, imbue the key transitions in life with religious significance, and provide evidence of faith. Yet as Adams (1993) emphasizes, like national flags such rituals only maintain meaning to the extent that they express beliefs valued by the community.

The Unity of Culture

It is clear that the constituent elements of culture have much in common. The various values, customs, and beliefs provide answers to questions about the purpose of life, and provide guidance on how to behave toward other people in all sorts of situations. Stories embody some of these ideas in a form that encourages cross-generational transmission. Languages alone appear to be a bit of an outlier. To be sure, languages are the primary medium by which culture is passed from one individual to another. However, it is an empirical question as to whether the form of language used by a group is related in any significant way to the group's beliefs, values, or customs.

We would naturally expect that there should be some high degree of consistency among at least the values of a particular society. This will probably not be perfect: I have discussed above how situations are likely to arise in which values clash. Debates about abortion or capital punishment provide examples in which not all of a society's values point in the same direction. Still, for culture to be meaningful at all, much of daily activity must occur without such value conflicts coming into play. The society cannot value both honesty and an "anything goes" mentality. The requirement of this degree of consistency is no problem within my schema. It merely suggests that there will be strong causal links among some elements of culture. If, for example, a society adheres to a religion which preaches that people will be justly rewarded in this life, then we might expect that society to look more favorably on, say, ambition, than a society whose religion states that justice comes only in the next life.

The sociologist James Coleman has suggested the existence of what he terms "social capital," which represents the ability of group members to cooperate. This in turn depends on the degree to which group members share norms and values, as well as whether those values favor individual sacrifice for the sake of the group (Fukuyama 1995, 10). Such a concept is easily dealt with in the schema, first by ascertaining whether there is coherence between, say, group identity, honesty, and trust, and second by seeing whether such values combine to have the effects Coleman suggests in the economic and political realms.

The potential problem arises only when scholars go beyond demanding consistency to claiming that culture is something more, that there is some bond between all elements of culture such that constituent parts can only truly be understood in terms of the whole:

> Culture is more than the mere aggregate of institutional or individual behavior patterns. Strictly speaking, culture is a coherent world view, a universe of discourse giving meaning to institutions, rituals, and networks, and making it possible for members of the culture to interpret reality in terms of a shared set of values and meaningful categories (Staudenmaier 1985, 122).

Since most authors have not faced this question head on, it is not clear how widespread this view is. Namenwirth and Weber (1987, 8) aver that culture is more than just the sum of beliefs, but rather a design for living. Later, though, they suggest that it is best viewed as a combination of blueprints. Durham, likewise, describes culture as a system of behavior standards or a system of knowledge. He then notes that it "strains toward consistency" and suggests both that some elements are more important than others and that consistency between some elements is more important than consistency between others.[9] I could take an empirical stance here and wait to see to what extent causal links appear to operate at the level of culture as a whole versus its constituent parts. However (looking ahead), the fact is that almost all causal links will operate at the disaggregated level. DiMaggio (1994, 28) argues from the fact that important causal links occur at the disaggregated level that it is nonsense to speak of the effect of culture as a whole.

Milner (1991) provides a description of structuralism: beliefs and so on are organized in a structure which must be understood as a whole, and individuals absorb this entire structure of knowledge from their society. Structuralists suggest that the hidden structure of a society may be quite different from its surface indicators. As Milner makes clear, such a view (not all "structuralists" would necessarily accede to Milner's definition) is incompatible with an attempt to understand how cultures evolve over time. If culture truly is absorbed *en masse* by individuals, how could cultures ever change? (Moreover, how could complex cultures ever emerge in the first place?) Structuralists could at best understand cultural change as a sudden, revolutionary step; this, Milner argues, accords poorly with the historical record. Moreover, our understanding of child development (chapter 4) suggests that children must learn about their culture one element at a time.

It is certainly much easier to understand how cultures would evolve if we only require them to be imperfectly consistent rather than coherently unified. Durham, indeed, has argued that even individual values or beliefs are too large a unit for analyzing cultural evolution; he proposes that individual symbols or "memes" be the subject of inquiry. In this, he attempts to mimic the approach of those who study biological evolution. They recognize that change (usually) occurs gradually. Moreover, they recognize that change is made difficult but not impossible by the complementarity of different elements of an ecosystem. When change does occur, it naturally changes the selection environment for other elements of the ecosystem. Changes in other elements are then likely so that consistency is restored. Similar arguments can be found in the works of others who focus on how cultures evolve. Cavalli-Sforza (1981) is adamant that, like geneticists, students of cultural evolution focus on particular traits rather than culture as a whole. Boyer (1990, 3–4) notes that individuals are not taught coherent world views but are gradually exposed to different elements of the surrounding culture as they mature. While each individual strives to achieve consistency, cultures evolve as community members put the pieces together in a novel fashion (including modifying some of the pieces).

Alternatively, Turner surveys attempts to comprehend entire cultures as causal objects; "The problems about causality are overwhelming; if a culture is a causal object, how does it work, and what kind of object is it?" (1994, 6). He concludes that one cannot in fact treat entire cultures causally, precisely because they are not monolithic, and because transmission is imperfect. While he does not mention it, this leaves us a choice of ignoring culture in causal explanations or of unpacking culture (he is skeptical of our ability to observe and measure particular traits, an issue I turn to below).

Nor does the study of cultural change provide the only rationale for eschewing the view of culture as indivisible. There is the fact that ethnographers have always found the disaggregated approach congenial: "anthropologists have commonly presented culture as the sum of customs, usages, traditions, myths, and rituals to be found among a discrete people, tribe, class, or nation" (Gross and Rayser 1985, 1). Also, casual empiricism suggests that the connections among some elements of culture are weak indeed. One could point to a number of values shared widely by citizens of the European Union; this does not prevent Europe from being characterized by diverse languages and customs. Likewise, Barth (1987) discusses how neighboring tribes in Papua New Guinea often show great similarity in language and some cultural attributes, while at the same time betraying great diversity in religion and ritual.

These observations raise the possibility, indeed, that different aspects of culture might best be studied at different levels: regions, countries, neighborhoods.[10] I have so far in this work adopted the common usage of "a culture" to define a group of people commonly presumed to share a set of cultural attributes. Yet clearly we should not expect that a society will be distinguishable from its neighbors in terms of all characteristics. Only as much greater efforts are made to classify societies in terms of each characteristic can we hope to answer the empirical question of how useful for scientific investigation is the common division of the world into distinct "cultures."

Can We Classify Cultures?

If we accept that "cultures" are collections of a number of imperfectly related characteristics, then we could hope to classify and compare cultures. Scientists have virtually never turned their gaze to questions such as: "Is culture A more like culture B than culture C?" Since any pair of cultures is likely to diverge along more than one dimension, there must always be some degree of subjectivity to such an answer. If A differs from B in religion, and from C in language, who is to say which difference is greater? While our answer to such a question can never be perfect, scientists could hope to serve two functions. First, we can at least develop measures such that we can state each culture's position in terms of each individual cultural characteristic. Second, by examining the causal links between these characteristics and other phenomena (including, it might be noted, how dependent these are on the economic and political environment), we can greatly inform decisions as to which characteristics should be viewed as most important.

Daniel (1978, 14) feels that a taxonomy of culture is impossible due to the infinity of possible classification schemes,[11] as well as because cultures are ever-changing and internally heterogenous. Note, though, that the attempts of zoologists to classify species face the same difficulties. As long as differences within cultures are smaller than differences between cultures, and change not so rapid that a snapshot at a point in time is meaningless, we can hope to classify. We might wish to place greatest emphasis on those characteristics that change most slowly. We should also be open to the possibility that our answer to questions about which other culture A most resembles are likely to change over time.

The concern with internal heterogeneity raises another key question: how do we define the boundaries of a particular culture? In other words, perhaps internal differences would best be handled by defining a set of subcultures. Individual cultures are presently delineated by historical circumstances. Geography is the most common determinant of cultural boundaries. Where history has bequeathed a situation in which more than one ethnic group inhabits a particular territory (and these have not developed a shared culture), then ethnicity is used. Effectively, this means that languages, among our cultural variables, has become the key determinant of cultural boundaries. It will thus inevitably loom large when scientists measure differences across cultures, even though differences in language may have extremely little effect on other elements of culture. Ideally, we would wish to establish cultural boundaries scientifically in accord with our schema.[12] If any group differs from the wider society in terms of a large number of cultural phenomena, it would be treated as a distinct cultural group.

How well can we measure any community's position with respect to individual cultural elements? Our ability to do so varies across phenomena. It is fairly easy to classify languages along various dimensions, but much harder to determine the importance of observed differences. In the case of religion, we need to recognize that "official" religious dogma (especially written texts) may be only loosely related to the everyday beliefs of adherents. Since people may be wary of appearing unorthodox it can be difficult to accurately ascertain the belief set of the population. Values of all sorts are largely subconscious, and thus simplistic surveying techniques can easily reach mistaken conclusions. And we must be wary of inferring cultural attitudes from behavior, for behavior will reflect other influences (see I→*). While difficulties of various sorts naturally abound, it is not these but the belief in the inherent unity of cultures which has prevented attempts to classify cultures in the past. Most, if not all, characteristics would seem amenable to a considerable degree of measurement.

Namenwirth and Weber (1987, 14–15) note that (most) values are described in terms of opposing pairs: individualism versus collectivism, optimism versus pessimism. These extremes are rarely realized; most cultures will fall on some continuum between them. There is thus an obvious scale on which we can attempt to rank different groups (we might in some cases need separate measures for type of belief and intensity). As for cultural symbols (e.g., attire), Barber (1993, 299) has suggested that these could be measured in terms of abstraction, systematization, and exhaustiveness. As we examine causal links throughout this volume, we will gain insight into the sorts of differences which previous scholars have found to be important, and this can inform future attempts at measurement.

One technique for measuring cultural attributes is discourse analysis. This involves the application of quantitative techniques to written texts (including transcriptions of speeches). Texts are read and scores assigned for the number of statements that express a certain opinion (the word "attitude" is shunned by discourse analysts). As might be expected of a technique embraced by several disciplines, there are many definitions of discourse analysis, but they all refer to an emphasis on analyzing more than a sentence at a time and recognizing social and cognitive contexts (Potter and Wetherell 1987). The advantage and disadvantage of discourse analysis is that it does not depend on any theory of mental processes. How individuals develop particular opinions is irrelevant; their statement of those opinions is all that matters. Discourse analysis even skirts the entire issue of whether people's description of their thoughts is accurate (whether they mislead themselves or purposely mislead others). In Potter and Wetherell's words, it does not take for granted that statements reflect underlying beliefs (1987, 49). Nor does discourse analysis require any particular position on the question raised above of the unity of culture. Inevitably (as deconstruction predicts) analysis of particular texts exposes contradictory viewpoints. These can be attributed to deception. Or, they could be taken as evidence that an individual's belief set need not be consistent. A more common view is that, since norms are situation-dependent, contradictory statements in different contexts need not imply that the belief set is incoherent. This, Potter and Wetherell (1987) recognize, means that discourse analysts must be extremely careful in defining the belief set associated with particular texts. Groups may differ not so much in terms of the interpretive schemes they use, but which they choose to apply to a particular event.[13]

Our final concern must be with the degree of agreement among members of a cultural community. Rare indeed is the case where every member of a community accepts community values without question. More commonly, one can discern a strong majority view, and this will likely be supported by some sort of community pressure to induce conformity from those with different views.[14] Not all communities need have standards with respect to all values, however. Thus, we would have to classify some cultures as being open with respect to certain questions (we might still measure opinion on these issues and compare different groups).

CULTURAL RELATIVISM

"Every man should be proud of his own culture, but should not believe it must be better than others" (Daniel 1978, 194). A century ago, ethnographers commonly assumed that Western cultures were 'superior' to other cultures. Racist explanations were often proffered for this state of affairs. Alternatively, simplistic evolutionary arguments were utilized where it was taken for granted that Western culture was the form toward which others would evolve (as times changed, evolutionary theory therefore gained a negative reputation among anthropologists). It is no longer politically correct to make such judgments. Each culture is to be appreciated for its uniqueness (with ethnographers often being accused of opposition to modernization in the Third World as a result).[15] We are warned that we cannot objectively evaluate other cultures because we are embedded in our own. This at times places scholars in ethical dilemmas. If a particular group favors cannibalism or wifebeating, must we eschew attempts to transform that culture into something "better"?

We will see in the next chapter that there is likely little genetic difference across human groups. Thus, Hutcheon (1996) concludes that there are likely also common ethics that apply to all of humanity. While anthropologists do valuable work in showing how values differ across societies, this should not blind us to the fact that some values are better than others. Refusing to recognize universal values not only blunts our ability to criticize offensive practices, but turns us away from recognition of our common humanity (Wilson 1998). While it is good to preach respect, to argue that all beliefs deserve respect prevents us from recognizing flaws in our own beliefs by comparing these to others (Haack 1998).

This conflict between the desire to recognize the legitimacy and advantages of cultural diversity on one hand, and to pursue ethical objections to particular cultural attributes on the other, ceases to be severe once we recognize that cultures are a collection of diverse elements. One can advocate that a group turn away from wifebeating while still appreciating its religion or ritual or cuisine. Just as importantly, one can treat critiques by others of one's own group's characteristics with healthy respect. One would want to be cognizant that change in one element will have some effect on some other elements (as we increase our understanding of the relationship between cultural elements, we will be better able to predict such effects). It is possible, though perhaps not likely, that a reprehensible practice or belief is supportive of one or more positive cultural traits. But we need not view change as inherently undesirable.

At the same time scholars can feel free to denounce claims made by political leaders that their culture is somehow better or that the people they represent are more "cultured" than those they oppose. Human culture, after all, guides our behavior in a host of different circumstances; and we cannot rationally evaluate the best path in every possible situation (Gellner 1989). Given the number of cultural elements, and the fact that each must be evaluated according to separate standards, comparisons can only meaningfully be made at the level of individual cultural elements.[16]

William Sumner and others in the 1930s applied the idea that changing one cultural attitude could upset the entire "social fabric" to the case of the United States. Many seized on an obvious policy implication: racism, no matter how much people disliked it, could be eradicated slowly at best, or American society would collapse. We cannot know how many people of good heart may have reduced their opposition to racism as a result. Generations later, most Americans would likely conclude that it was possible to fight racism—and other social ills—without destroying American culture (see Rule 1997, 218–19). [C → S].

Still, there are a couple of very good reasons for being careful in making value judgments even at the level of particular phenomena. First, as we shall see, cultures are to a significant degree adaptations to particular environments. Values or customs that are admirably suited to one group may not meet the needs of another (I think here of attempts by missionaries to convince inhabitants of the tropics to dress in a more civilized manner). Let us be careful, though, not to err in the other direction and assume this result. Many scholars, especially functionalists, have implicitly or explicitly assumed that the values observed in any society are somehow the only, or at least the ideal, reaction to environmental pressures (Knight 1992). Yet evolution need not yield ideal solutions. We will uncover diverse influences on cultural evolution in what follows; culture is not simply an ideal adaptation to local circumstances. Especially given the imperfect foresight of human actors, we should suspect that values may often be far from ideal.

Second, we should recognize that there are advantages to cultural diversity. Seasoned travelers can well appreciate that such diversity is the source of much frustration but also much fascination (if other cultures were as unintelligible as extreme relativists claim, the ratio of frustration to fascination would be much higher). It is now widely appreciated that the interaction of people with diverse technical backgrounds is a key ingredient in technological advance [I→T]. We should not be surprised then if cultural diversity is conducive to progress. Fukuyama (1995) argues that cultural differences can be a source of creative change, and points to the two-way borrowing between Japan and the West. And, since we live in a changing world, we have to expect that cultures will continue to evolve, and diversity gives us more options for adaptation. Moreover, cultural diversity creates some potential for individuals to "choose" a society to their liking, though the tendency to define cultures by ethnicity severely limits this.

MECHANISMS OF CULTURAL TRANSMISSION AND CHANGE

Before proceeding to a discussion of particular causal links, it is worthwhile to discuss in general how culture is transmitted from one generation to another. Transmission can be considered in two parts: the communication of values, beliefs, or customs, and their adoption by the receiver. Cultural change can occur either because communication is imperfect or because the recipient decides (consciously or not) not to adopt some of these cultural practices, at least in their original form. Rejection may occur at the time of communication or later (Cavalli-Sforza speculates that adoption rates may be almost complete for very young children but fall with age). As the French sociologist Tarde noted at the turn of the century, invention and imitation are the distinguishing features of human life. These two conflicting tendencies ensure that culture is passed on from generation to generation (imitation), but that it changes in the process. Readers can note the basic similarity between cultural transmission and genetic inheritance. Culture, like genes, is reproduced and suffers mutations. However, we must be careful to note differences as well as similarities between the two evolutionary processes.

Certainly we would expect natural selection to play a role in cultural evolution. That is, practices which enhance genetic fitness (reproductive potential) should be selected for. Cultural practices that enhance fitness (like the Yoruba village cleaning ritual of exposing shady areas to firebrands, which decreases the incidence of malaria; Durham 1991, 151) should be maintained. Cultural practices that serve to limit a group's reproductive capability will in the extreme cause the culture to disappear as the group which carries it disappears (as with the Shakers, a religious sect which preached celibacy, and could not attract new members to compensate for the absence of children). Before this happens, we might expect pressures within the group to change the culture so as to avoid this calamity. Once we allow for this purposeful (if not necessarily conscious) decision to change—something genes are incapable of—then we must recognize that selection pressures will be different than in the genetic case. Maximizing population growth has rarely been the sole aim of any group; cultural elements may thus be selected which enhance, for example, economic well-being at the price of fitness. Note, though, that a group's cultural values now play a role in determining the selection process governing its own cultural evolution.

Practices which serve the community well will tend to be maintained while characteristics with negative consequences will face pressure for change. Boyer (1990, 5) notes the common scientific sentiment that adherence to tradition is undesirable; this misses the point that traditions will in most cases be adhered to because they have brought the community success in the past. Only if we ignore the likelihood that harmful traditions will be selected against can we maintain a negative predisposition toward tradition. Boyer also recognizes that traditions that are "maintained" may nevertheless have changed in many subtle ways through time. Of course, if the selection environment changes more rapidly than culture, groups at any point in time may possess some undesirable traditions. Elster (1989) stresses this as a crucial problem in applying evolutionary theory to social science: given that the environment changes much more rapidly than with respect to genetic evolution, we can be much less confident that selection will have generated an outcome suitable to the environment.

Moreover, biases in transmission could severely constrain the operation of selection criteria. Boyd and Richerson (1985, 9) suggest a couple such possibilities. People might tend to support the majority view ($G{\rightarrow}C10$), even if this flies in the face of personal experience. This would severely weaken selection processes. Or, people may be willing to follow particular leaders ($P{\rightarrow}C$), in which case personal idiosyncrasies can have a major influence on the course of cultural evolution. Barkow (1989, 290) reminds us that small—even undetectable—biases in transmission can have a huge cumulative effect over time.

Random mutation must be an important factor in any evolutionary process. This inevitably limits our ability to explain the results of evolution. In the case of cultural evolution, we have noted the possibility of purposeful intervention in the evolutionary process. This should not blind us to the fact that not all cultural change is by design. Merton (1996, ch. 7) emphasizes the unforeseen effects of human actions, and notes in particular that attempts to satisfy particular human needs may unintentionally become cultural practices, and these can easily outlive their usefulness.[17] Given our limited ability to predict the full impact of any change, the results of purposeful change may well be little different from random mutation (Cavelli-Sforza 1981, 61–62). The fact that much of culture is subconscious further limits our ability to direct cultural evolution (Lemonnier 1992, 100; Namenwirth and Weber 1987).

Durham (1991, 199–200) takes a slightly more optimistic view of purposive cultural change. He feels that the human brain has the capacity to imagine the effect of different decisions and choose the best (he downplays the role of subconscious decisionmaking). Given that unforeseen effects are commonly observed in the areas of scientific and technological innovation, we could question how well we are likely to evaluate the impacts of cultural innovations. We can only poorly visualize that which has never happened. Durham is aware that these decisions will be "imperfect," and that this imperfection will likely increase with the size of the innovation.

Cultural mutations, like their genetic counterparts, are at greatest risk in the early stages. The longer a mutation survives, the greater its influence on the surrounding environment. For both genes and culture, one danger is that mutations which are advantageous if widely distributed may be disadvantageous to their carriers if these are a minority. Honesty is an obvious example: a society imbued with honesty *may* fare well, but an honest person in a den of thieves may suffer. Politics may provide a possible solution: punishing dishonesty until (if) honesty becomes a cultural norm. On the whole, though, this problem serves to further highlight the difficulty of culture by design.

Cultural evolution is likely characterized by path dependence. Any purposive efforts to alter a group's values will be seriously constrained by the preexisting culture. Likewise, the transmission of cultural attributes between groups will be mediated by the recipient group's culture. A culture at any point in time comprises the surviving variant of all previous cultural attributes of that group (Durham 1991). Note in particular that in cultural evolution, unlike genetic evolution, acquired characteristics are passed on. If economic or political changes cause members of a group to adjust their values or customs, these members will indeed transmit these characteristics to others (Dunbar et al. 1999).

With genetic evolution we expect the result to be homogeneous populations; but significant differences will occur between groups if there is minimal migration from one to the other. Given the possibility with respect to cultural evolution that different selection mechanisms might operate in different populations, we could anticipate even greater cultural diversity across groups. What about homogeneity within groups? Here we must recognize how different the transmission mechanisms are. Compared to genetic inheritance, they are weaker but more dense. Genetic mutation is rare, but imperfect communication of values an everyday occurrence. However, while we inherit genes from our parents alone, we absorb cultural influences from a variety of sources. Thus culture can be transmitted within generations, backwards, or forward more than one generation. If we get the same message from all, we will likely adopt it (especially if we have previously absorbed the value of learning from elders or people in authority). If, however, our culture is characterized by internal diversity, our exposure to different viewpoints is likely to encourage even more free thinking. Thus either homogeneity or diversity can be reinforced by the density of transmission linkages.

The relative importance of different transmission links can also have a major impact on the rate of innovation. Societies in which peer groups from one's own generation are a major source of influence will likely be more open to change than societies in which parent to child transmission is dominant.[18] Similarly, the degree to which transmission across social boundaries (families, classes, and so on) is possible and important affects the likelihood of community-wide consensus. The rate of innovation will also be influenced by the strength of penalties for nonconformity. Wright (1994) argues that for cultural norms to be effective they must be supported by "metanorms." It must be clear not only that those who transgress will be punished in some way, but also that those who approve of the transgression will suffer. If such metanorms are weak, innovation will be more likely.

As with interspecies genetic evolution, there is a 'creationist' alternative. This is to assume that all cultures have existed in fixed fashion since the dawn of time. While clearly ridiculous when stated thus, one can discern elements of this creationist perspective in ethnographic treatments of other cultures in which they are viewed as completely static, or in the lack of scholarly interest in tracing common historical antecedents of modern cultures (Durham 1991). Concerns about the 'death' of particular cultures often ignore the fact that in an evolutionary sense cultures (defined as the set of attributes at any point in time) are always dying; we might otherwise focus on particular elements we would like to preserve.[19]

The previous discussion can be summarized in terms of the factors which can affect the proportion of people in a particular group which "carry" a particular cultural element. Strict natural selection works to the extent that those who transmit element "X" have more (or less) descendants and these also transmit X (natural selection also affects the survival of the group as a whole). If transmitters of X communicate with many potential receivers, this could enhance the frequency of X within the group. Alternatively, outmigration, death, or memory lapses among transmitters will reduce frequency (of course immigration of X has the opposite effect). New ideas—whether random mutations or purposive—may win favor for a variety of reasons. Even alternative "old" ideas may do so. Those in positions of influence may be able to exert a powerful influence on the direction of cultural evolution (perhaps resorting to coercion; P→C). Changes in mechanisms of transmission—such as the media, educational systems, or childrearing practices—may also influence the probability of a recipient absorbing a particular message. Finally, certain cultural values—such as respect for authority or religious orthodoxy—will influence the likelihood of values being transmitted flawlessly.

I close by noting that there have been a handful of attempts to model the process of cultural evolution in recent decades (e.g., Cavalli-Sforza 1981; Boyd and Richerson 1985). These have naturally borrowed from the models of geneticists but taken pains to reflect the difference between the two forms of evolution. At present these are not well integrated in the literature with the case studies which provide the basis for most of our further discussion. That is, these models outline what the mechanisms of cultural change might be but tell us little about the causes of change. Thus Cavalli-Sforza shows that an S-shaped diffusion curve is likely for cultural innovation: at first adoption will be slow (as the advantages are not clear, and people tend to side with the majority), but at some point the advantages of the innovation will become widely apparent and adoption more rapid; adoption rates inevitably fall off again as the remainder of the population clings to tradition. But what sets the process in motion? And what selection criteria separate the successful innovations from the losers? Durham (1991) has criticized these mathematical modeling attempts for not telling us more. Yet his own approach to modeling cultural evolution has been questioned on similar grounds. His focus on "memes" as the unit of evolution tells us little about how complex ideas evolve; research in the discipline still focuses on much larger units of analysis. And Durham's emphasis on person-to-person transmission leaves no clear place for group dynamics. Finally, while Durham strives to identify one central mechanism of cultural evolution as Darwin did for genes, we must face the likelihood that a variety of mechanisms may be at work (as these other works suggest).[20]

What is the unit of cultural change? Should we urge scholars to focus on Durham's 'memes' or rather on particular values or attitudes? Evolutionary theory pulls in the first direction, by suggesting that change will usually happen in small steps (and I have stressed the value of unpacking). Difficulties of observation pull in the latter direction. A compromise seems possible. In the case of values and attitudes, we have seen that these are highly situation dependent. Change will likely occur in terms of the expansion or contraction in the set of circumstances in which a particular interpretive schema is employed. Thus we have identified a very small yet observable change in culture. We can strive to do likewise for all cultural characteristics along all dimensions of possible change.[21]

C → C: CULTURE → CULTURE

There are two broad areas of concern here. First, when contact occurs between groups, does this encourage cultural change and if so how? Second, within a particular group, how do changes in one cultural phenomenon affect other cultural phenomena?

I. CROSS-CULTURAL CONTACT

Durham (1991) feels that the degree of cultural diversity in the world has decreased markedly in the last decades. This sentiment is echoed by numerous ethnographers; indeed there is a common sense among anthropologists that they must urgently document diverse cultural practices before these disappear. While the rate of cultural convergence has likely increased in recent times, the phenomenon is hardly novel. The spread of major world religions from group to group is well documented. So also is the spread of what I have called stories: hundreds of variants of the Cinderella story can be found in the world. Stories, handed down orally from generation to generation, are perhaps ideally suited to cross-cultural fertilization. Story elements which appeal to audiences will be incorporated into the tales of other groups (convergence is aided here by similar aesthetic "tastes," which might be traced to genetics; G→C).

While Durham bemoans the modern rate of convergence, he suggests that convergence has been a key force in human history. All cultures are related by descent: even the most isolated of groups share cultural elements with their neighbors. Thus, it is only the limits on cross-cultural contact in past times that prevented cultural homogeneity from occurring (in concert, of course, with some process of cultural transformation internal to groups). Yet he may well overstate his case here: one can still find important cultural differences between societies which have been in close contact for centuries.

That the degree of contact is an important determinant of the degree of convergence can hardly be doubted. While communication of ideas does not ensure their adoption it is a necessary first step.[22] Thus, Park (1994) notes how both Christianity and Islam spread along established trade routes. A mere century ago, leisure travel (as opposed to migration) was still a prerogative of the rich (though those of high status can play a disproportionate role in transmission; religious conversion of a king has often meant conversion of an entire society), and mass media a limited and generally local force. Today even the poorest ghettoes and most remote villages are linked.

Even within cultures transmission is imperfect. This must lead us to suspect that not all cultural elements will take root when communicated to a new group. There must be some selection criteria, after all, which allows individuals/groups to choose the 'best' cultural elements (see Tooby and Cosmides 1992, 119–20). If these criteria were/are the same everywhere, then we would expect convergence toward the superior cultural trait. Selection processes need not be identical, however. Particular cultural traits (layered clothing) may be advantageous in some environments (cold climate) but not others. One major goal of this book is to illustrate the causal relationships between particular cultural elements and all other phenomena. We can anticipate that some cultural elements are highly influenced by economic considerations, others by climate, still others by social structure or technology.[23] Only as we understand these relationships can we hope to comprehend why convergence may be more common in terms of some cultural elements than others.

A group's attitude toward other groups is of special importance. On the receiving end, groups that feel threatened by foreign contact will strive to avoid convergence. When Europeans arrived in parts of the Americas, the South Pacific, and Africa, locals (especially those whose social status was challenged) responded with messianic cults that promised some sort of deliverance from this new evil. Overt rebellion is another option sometimes pursued in preference to acceptance (see Barber 1993). Attitudes of the sending group can also be important.[24] Durham, for example, blames much of modern convergence on Western intolerance. He urges an increased understanding and appreciation of diversity.

We should emphasize that cultural transmission does not only work from advanced and powerful to weaker societies. Indeed, most of the world's major religions emerged in areas on the fringes of great civilizations. Still, Mukherjee (1991) is undoubtedly correct that culture generally flows from advanced to backward, at least with respect to cultural elements influenced largely by economic circumstances [E→C]. Nevertheless, synthesis is a likely result of cultural contact. Each group borrows from the other. We can hope that selection pressures work so that the best of what each group has to offer is transmitted.

Even within a particular cultural element, I have suggested above that change usually occurs in small steps. Thus the rate of convergence, and perhaps even its feasibility, will depend on the size of the original cultural gap between two groups. Nor is only the gap with respect to that phenomenon important. The interdependence of phenomena also limits convergence: borrowing any one cultural element will be limited to the extent this 'fits' poorly with other elements. "They enter as alien fragments into a complete way of life that has no holes, no institutional niches left unoccupied. For this reason, one might expect such civilizational encounters to result in changes, but not a complete change" (Hamilton 1994, 197). Moreover, as noted above, convergence in some elements is unlikely in the absence of convergence in economic, social, and other realms. Since convergence is not possible everywhere—due to climate variation for example, some degree of cultural diversity is perhaps assured. The likely result is that the rate of cultural convergence (has and) will vary considerably by phenomenon. We should not ignore another possibility here: perhaps some cultural elements are so 'weakly' connected with other phenomena that there is no selection pressure for conformity. It could, for example, be very important that groups develop dances, songs, and Cinderella stories, but the exact form these take may be of no great consequence for the group's wellbeing.

A final (if unlikely?) possibility is that there may be "multiple equilibria." Think of how species have evolved to occupy certain ecological niches. If giraffes had not developed, the niche for tall leafy trees in the African savanna would be quite different—and vice versa. In stable ecological situations there is no reason (except genetic mutation) for the numbers of any species to change over time. Yet one could not have predicted in advance the exact form such an ecological equilibrium would take. It will have depended on the course of evolution of each species and the interactions which resulted from and affected that course of evolution. One can imagine a few identical ecological zones (soil and climate and topography the same) each with quite different equilibria. It is entirely possible that little migration will occur if one brings them into contact. The giraffe may find no place in another homeland. The same could hold for cultures: there may be no optimal solution, and thus no necessary convergence.

2. VALUE CONSISTENCY

I have discussed above the fact that we should expect imperfect value consistency within any group. That is, values should not blatantly contradict each other. However, situations will arise in which different values suggest different courses of action. Changes in any one value, then, may or may not force changes in other values. Increased appreciation of honesty may have no impact on a group's view of ambition. A likely outcome when values do conflict is that decision rules that determine which value has preeminence in particular situations will change over time. Thus, one value will come to guide behavior more often, and an 'opposing' value less often.

Although my method of categorizing values was rough indeed, it still seems likely that in general a value change is most likely to induce changes in similarly classified values. Our view of ambition must be compatible with our view of wealth or prestige. Yet I should not exaggerate this insight; we should also expect some compatibility between such values and, say, our sense of the value of work, or sense of responsibility for others. We could expect weaker links between such values and our fourth category of everyday norms. Table manners should be unaffected by changes in attitudes toward honesty. Yet strong links are still possible here: table manners may reflect an authoritarian bent.

3. LANGUAGES

In a sense the links between languages and other elements of culture are strong: languages are social creations and therefore cannot exist without culture; much of culture depends in turn on a facility with language. But what of the links between particular languages and particular cultures? The fact that cultural groups are often demarcated along linguistic lines suggests that these links are strong. Yet we must separate two sorts of effect here: languages as a barrier to communication versus languages as an element of culture. Linguistic differences may serve to distinguish groups culturally entirely by limiting the flow of information between them. For linguistic reasons, English Canadians and French Canadians tend to read different magazines, watch different television shows, and listen to different performers: cultural practices may thus spread very slowly from one to the other.

Stories are one cultural variable whose transmission is likely to be impeded. Storytellers in any language will avail themselves of various techniques to enhance their appeal: rhyming or alliteration are but two examples. Their stories will inevitably lose something in translation. In the case of stories passed orally over many generations, such barriers are likely not impregnable. Good stories will be translated, and generations of storytellers will embellish these within the confines of their language. Proverbs may present a greater problem: a catchy phrase in one language may have no attractive counterpart in another. In our literate modern world, translation problems are enhanced. Our stories are now written down, and connoisseurs of the written word will forcefully argue that translations are never as good as the original (due partly to matters such as rhythm, but mostly to the fact that words have ambiguous meanings). This judgment necessarily applies to all written works, whether they be art, science, or philosophy. To the extent that these tracts embody values explicitly or implicitly, different linguistic groups will be exposed to a different value "mix." If Sartre or Foucault are a better read in the original French, then their world views will fare better in French-speaking societies (other things being equal). The works of Shakespeare, in contrast, will work their influence primarily in the English-speaking world.

A group's literary inheritance (and its language itself) is often a key token of identity. Language barriers dictate that each group will have special access to their own authors. Not surprisingly, in places like Ireland, Scotland, and Wales, where English has made large inroads, defenders of cultural autonomy often bemoan the loss of privileged access to the literary tradition of their group. They will likely take little solace in the fact that linguistic evolution makes all of us outsiders with respect to literary classics: Shakespeare seems stilted to the modern English-speaker, Chaucer (fourteenth century) is difficult, and Beowulf (eighth century) unintelligible (Fellman, Getis and Getis, 1990).

Do languages exert any influence beyond their role as barrier? Certainly it is clear that linguistic divisions are not essential to cultural diversity. I have lived in four different English-speaking countries and two French-speaking, and can attest to the fact that the same language need not imply other cultural similarities. Breton (1991) provides numerous examples of different linguistic groups sharing other cultural attributes, and vice versa.[25] Ireland provides an interesting case study: the common use of English has not caused (at least not complete) cultural convergence. The fact that English was the official language in India hardly made Indian culture more similar to English than is German to English culture.

Still, one commonly hears French referred to as the language of love, Italian as emotional, German stern, and so on. This might simply reflect the projection of perceived cultural qualities onto a group's language: the Japanese think of their language as descending from the culturally advanced Chinese when in fact it is more closely related to Korean and Turkic. Jahr (1993) bemoans the unnecessary conflict which has resulted from misguided beliefs that one language is superior to another. The fact that the Inuit have seventeen words for snow is taken as evidence that language reflects and reinforces what is important to the group. Yet I think it is safe to say that there is extremely little scientific evidence at this point that supports the idea that the nature of particular languages has any significant influence on other cultural variables.[26] English also has a number of words for snow (slush, sleet), and there is no Inuit word for snow that cannot be translated into English with the use of one or two adjectives. Some philosophers have stressed the imprecision of language and thus suggested that language shapes our view of reality. Yet we saw in chapter 1 that we can still define terms precisely enough that we can all speak of the same thing (Trigg 1985, 192). While hermeneutics has correctly alerted us to the existence of hidden meaning in our utterances, it has failed to show that different languages convey different meanings. Anthropologists (with the notable exception of Levi-Strauss) had long tried to argue that language shaped our view of the world. Most famously, Whorf had argued that the Hopi of Arizona had a vastly different conception of time because of their language These and similar claims have not stood the test of time well.[27] As Brown (1991, 27–31) notes, even Whorf late in his career recognized that language "is in some sense a superficial embroidery upon deeper processes of consciousness which are necessary before any communication, signalling, or symbolism whatsoever can occur." German culture may be different from its neighbors (due in large part to linguistic barriers) but the characteristics of German culture are not (apparently) causally related in any important fashion to the nature of the German language.

4. STORIES AND VALUES

I should note, first of all, that there is an infinite variety of stories that could be devised to support any particular attitude (Bethlehem 1990). Conversely, particular stories will likely reinforce more than one attitude. Gellner (1989) has argued that 'primitive' man was especially prone to attaching diverse meanings to particular statements. A simple phrase like "It is raining" might communicate the speaker's faith in the priest who had predicted rain, rather than being simply an observation of fact. (Likewise one ritual may serve as right of passage, marker of time of year, and guide to mate selection.) He suggests that it may thus be difficult for stories to evolve so as to reflect changes in values. People would not be conscious of the diverse roles played by particular statements, and could not revise them as the situation required.[28]

Durham (1991) emphasizes the importance of symbolism in cultural transmission, and notes that even simple symbols can stand for a variety of concepts. This enhances the information density of transmission; one simple story may communicate many values. He also recognizes that this form of transmission encourages creativity; the story may change in subtle ways so that the treatment of certain values is altered. Durham allows for a more conscious role in this process than Gellner: symbolic information has value because it makes sense, holds value, has a point. Thus recipients can adjust the story to make the point they like. This accords well with the view of other scholars that people do indeed think about the significance of their stories (and rituals; Trigg 1985, 98).

Scholars of myths recognize that it is impossible to know how any myth began (it is commonly hypothesized that they were components of early religions). They are cognizant of the fact that myths have generally changed so much during intergenerational transmission that their original purpose is no longer clear (we might also question to what degree even the first author of a myth would have been aware of its multiple purposes).

Where does this leave us? Although scholars disagree on particulars— especially the degree to which groups can purposely change their stories— there is still an overarching sense that we cannot expect a perfect fit between stories and values at any point in time. Popular stories may well contain messages that are at odds with dominant values (deconstruction, discussed in chapter 1, suggests this conclusion as well). Other values may be ignored by the existing body of story. Yet there is still a connection. Whether consciously or not a group's values will both shape and be shaped by its stories.

5. RELIGION

Religious beliefs affect other cultural elements in myriad ways: they can encourage fatalism or ambition, free thinking or authoritarianism (Gellner suspects that in early agrarian societies authoritarian religion was essential to the maintenance of social order), a high or low value of human life, a perception of sexual intercourse as sacred or profane, and so on (see Park 1994, ch.5). Indeed, Adams (1993) worries that due to the central role of religions in the formation of personal identity (C→I1), there has been a (declining) danger of religious domination of culture. Certainly, religions must have rituals, myths, and other strong ties to the wider culture. The effects are not always obvious. Many suggest that Christian eschatology is largely responsible for a pervasive Western belief in human progress (a pressure the author readily confesses he has not been immune to).

Yet the wider culture also shapes religions, especially in their formative stages. "Every religion develops within a cultural context . . . It embraces its basic metaphysics, much of its value system, and many of its beliefs about human history and the factual structure of the world" (Adams 1993, 55). Once part of religious doctrine, these cultural elements become harder but not impossible to change. Adams himself recognizes that when inconsistencies arise between culture, science, or religion, the latter must adapt or risk becoming obsolete. If this were not possible, the major world religions would hardly have been able to diffuse so readily across cultural boundaries.

C → *: CULTURE → ALL FORMS OF BEHAVIOR

To avoid repetition later, I note here how culture will shape all forms of behavior. The social psychology literature refers to social representations: schemas that guide action, are created through interaction, facilitate communication between members of a group, and provide a unifying force within a community (Potter and Wetherell 1987). Such a definition applies to most elements of our category "culture" (and some of what we will call "public opinion" later). Social psychologists and anthropologists bemoan the fact that little connection has been drawn between social representations and the personal representations (schemas; see chapter 5) used by individuals to guide behavior (e.g., Lemonnier 1992, 79–80). Yet clearly social representations will guide schema formation of individuals within the group. These individual schemas will determine how we analyze incoming data and the conclusions we draw. Whether we blame others, ourselves, or fate for our misfortune, and therefore how we react, depends on our social representations.[29]

4

The Nonhuman Environment and Our Genetic Predisposition

KEY ELEMENTS OF THE NONHUMAN ENVIRONMENT

LITTLE JUSTIFICATION NEED BE PROVIDED FOR INCLUDING NONHUMAN elements within a schema concerned with human activities of all sorts. The Inuit cannot frolic on the beach in January, whaling fleets depend on whales, and no history of battle is complete without a detailed analysis of the battleground itself. "The physical environments nurturing or afflicting societies, play a large role in historical speculations about the rise and fall of civilizations, cultures, and nations. These factors are often thought to determine individual proclivities as well, as mountain men are said to be different from south sea islanders" (Books and Prysby 1991, 1–2). Still, human science has tended to focus on individuals and societies, and has paid little heed to the role of location in affecting human behavior. Even many geographers have downplayed the causal role of our physical environment, in fear that to stress this would seem deterministic (Hugill 1993). Yet one can recognize that location constrains and even shapes behavior without having to conclude that humans are not still left with a wide freedom of choice.

Most phenomena of concern here are fairly obvious: topography, soil (and water), climate, flora, and fauna. Both some omissions and additions are worthy of note, however. Neither "time" nor "space" have a place in the organizing schema, though it is clear that human activity is profoundly influenced by both. Pred (1990, esp. 3–5), following numerous other geographers, decries the fact that most social scientists give lip service to the importance of space but do not fully recognize its importance. He favorably cites Giddens as the scholar most notable for emphasizing the importance of space. Giddens' key point, though, was that all activity takes place in a physical (and temporal) context and will inevitably be shaped by that context. It is due to this very ubiquity of time and space that no special categories are allocated to these concepts in the schema. Rather, as we saw in chapter 1, causation requires proximity in time and space, and thus both are implicitly represented in each causal link.

While the nonhuman environment has some claim to causal priority—it was, by most accounts, here before humanity emerged—it is nevertheless clear that humans have had a dramatic impact on our environment. Hardly any newscast is complete these days without some report on how humanity is changing some nonhuman phenomenon. Thus, we must be open to causal links *→N. Given the complexity of human life, our shaping of the nonhuman environment will reflect a variety of forces, and these in turn will have conflicting and unintended effects on human behavior (Pred 1990). I can thus feel free to add human effects on the environment to the schema. Three of these effects are poorly captured by the five phenomena outlined above, and thus encourage the addition of new phenomena. The first of these is transport (and communications): geography and human effort together shape the ability of one human to interact with others; we shall see that the impact of this phenomenon is great. So also is the effect of "population density." While in a global sense density is merely population divided by the earth's surface area, population is very unevenly spread across that surface. The causes and effects of this unequal distribution are diverse. Our third new phenomenon is "built environments" (buildings, fences, and so on).

N→C: Nonhuman Environment → Culture

When I discuss nationalism (C→P6), I will note that cultural identity is generally associated with an attachment to a particular geographical area (see also Hufford 1994). Humanistic geographers examine emotional and practical attachments to place by studying literary descriptions, reviewing history, and interviewing individuals. Yet very little work has been done that identifies causal links from geographical differences to cultural differences. The small field of cultural ecology in geography focuses predominantly on causation in the other direction. Geographers as a whole have long avoided any hint of environmental determinism, and stressed that people, not environments, are the source of dynamism in cultural development (Fellman, Getis and Getis, 1990; they later discuss the role of different geographic settings in various stages of civilization). Does geography serve a similar role to languages, providing a barrier between groups (and privileged access to the group's history if it has inhabited the same place for some time and built monuments, shrines, and so on) but with little or no separate causal influence? The answer would seem to be negative. Some links are fairly obvious, such as the effect of climate on attire, and soil and climate on cuisine. The question remains of whether values can be similarly explained. There are extremely few indications of such links in the literature, and those are generally indirect, but perhaps future research will be more illuminating.

1. CLIMATE → MYTH

One of the more specific links is outlined by Durham (1991). The ability of adults to absorb lactose (fresh milk) varies with latitude. In northern latitudes, with decreased exposure to ultraviolet radiation, milk serves to compensate in the absorption of vitamin D into the body. Durham feels that as a result we observe within Indo-European cultures a change away from a focus on male animals and sacrifice toward female animals and nurturance. Note that genetics plays an intermediary role in this causal chain: N→G→C.

2. TERRAIN → EGALITARIANISM (N→P→C)

Farmers inhabiting difficult terrain such as mountain valleys or inhospitable deserts are generally able to escape consolidation into large political units (Gellner 1989, ch. 6). The small autonomous communities in such situations tend therefore to develop an egalitarian perspective.

3. SOIL/CLIMATE → RITUALS, ATTITUDE TO OTHERS (N→E→C)

Cashdan (1989) notes that within hunting-gathering societies the density of edible material and its seasonal variation determines how large a community gathers at one place and for how long. The type of rituals that are feasible clearly depends on these two variables. Since they also determine how widely the group must range, and how often they move, it will also affect their relations with neighboring groups. If group boundaries fluctuate, hostility toward foreigners is likely.

4. URBANIZATION → VALUE FLEXIBILITY (N→S→C)

Rather than interacting intimately in many ways with a small number of people, residents of large cities interact with many people in specialized roles. This provides a degree of anonymity to individuals, freeing them from much social pressure to obey norms. We would thus expect to see greater variability in values within urban populations than rural. The increased social and geographic mobility of individuals further weakens the hold that small groups can have on them: thus "social norms lose their hold on people because people spend a larger proportion of their life with strangers who are not enforcing the norms with the same efficacy" (Elster

1993). [*→C] Johnson and Earle (1989) note, however, that our very need for culture expands with urbanization. When hunter-gatherer communities of 25 or less were the norm, one's personal knowledge of all others could guide behavior. Cultural guidelines become increasingly important as density increases.

5. URBANIZATION → RELIGION

Gellner (1989, 81–82) suggests that urbanization, by cutting individuals off from a supportive local community, was of great importance in fomenting universal religions (generally adaptations of pastoralist religions, shorn of their ethnic identity). Both he and Park (1994) are perhaps guilty of downplaying the human need for religion even in the best of circumstances (G→C9).

6. CLIMATE → RELIGION

Park (1994) suggests that harsh and uncertain climates are more likely to bring forth religion. This is a partial explanation, perhaps, of why all world religions originated in southwest or south Asia. Others suggest particular links: the desert contribution to Islam, or the monsoon and Hinduism. With respect to the latter religion, I might note that recent studies have suggested an economic rationale for veneration of the cow in the Indian environment. The cow was a valuable source of manure, power, flooring material, milk, butter, and fuel, whereas only 20% of the cow was edible. The taboo against killing cows thus served to overcome the temptation to slaughter a valuable capital asset in times of food shortage (see Haskell 1993; G→C13).

7. TRANSPORT → ECUMENICISM

Who can doubt that closer contact between the people of the world has been an important encouragement to the ecumenical movement? More generally, Irwin and Kasarda (1994) argue that just as transport improvements lower the cost of economic trade they also encourage cross-cultural transmission and convergence.

8. ECONOMIC DEVELOPMENT (N→E→C)

Diamond (1997) has detailed how the nonhuman environment, and especially the types of flora and fauna available, played a major role in determining which societies were able to develop economically. As we shall see later, economic development in turn has a huge impact on culture.

9. DAY AND NIGHT

Various cultural practices are associated with particular times of day.

C→N: CULTURE → NONHUMAN ENVIRONMENT

Culture clearly affects the way that we shape our environment. Climatic and technical considerations may loom larger in determining the crops that we grow and the types of houses that we build; politics may have the predominant influence on defensive structures; and transport links may be mostly influenced by political and economic considerations [N,T,P,E→N]. Yet even here cultural considerations play a role: religion and culinary preferences influence crop and livestock choice (with feedbacks needless to say), we ornament our buildings and public works in all sorts of ways (especially religious structures; see Park 1994, ch. 7; Fellman, Getis, and Getis 1990), and our attitude to outsiders will influence our desire to build roads. I might also mention the obvious cultural influence on place names (see Fellman, Getis, and Getis 1990).[1]

All societies recognize their dependence on nature to some degree. Thus, values that limit environmental degradation are common. When water is in short supply, frivolous use is frowned upon. Hunter-gatherers had norms to limit overhunting, such as the Iroquois prohibition against taking female animals during the breeding season.

The clearest expression of this causal link is in landscaping and particularly public gardens. During the Renaissance, the formal composition of such spaces reflected the sense of (and desire for) order in the wider society. In seventeenth-century France, gardens combined aristocratic and bourgeois values: their organization reflected the increased power of the king, while the fountains and foreign plants exalted technology and trade (see Haskell 1993). Since that time, while all gardens have some focal point(s) (likely because that is the way our brain processes information; G→N),[2] European gardens have become less formal, reflecting a cultural appreciation of diversity.

Still, gardens in the Western tradition are less "natural" than their Japanese counterparts. The former reflect a culture predisposed to mastery of nature, while the latter reflect a desire to live in harmony with nature (Ponting 1992, attributes this difference to religion). Smith and Bond (1993) feel that this difference in attitude toward nature is one of the key cultural differences in the modern world, and wonder if increased environmental concern will diminish it. Western culture has changed in this regard of late: Hufford (1994) speaks of how westerners once destroyed wolves as predators but now bring them back as an integral part of the ecosystem.

One can differentiate societies by the attention they pay to landscaping. Sadly, many urban spaces in many parts of the world have received only perfunctory landscaping, despite evidence that humans are happier when in pleasing natural surroundings (Kaplan and Kaplan 1989; N → I).

OUR GENES

At some point in the not too distant future, scientists will likely understand the main properties of all human genes. Even then, we will not wish to sketch all causal links at the level of individual genes, for we already know that genes generally work in concert. We will thus always wish to speak of certain genetic predispositions that result from the interaction of several genes. I will identify many such mechanisms in this book and discuss their causal role. At times, particularly when discussing genetic diseases, I will also speak of individual genes. At other times, I can only refer more vaguely to the entire human gene pool.

As a species, we spend perhaps too much time focusing on our differences. Yet our similarities are neglected at our peril: upright stance, two legs, two arms, two eyes, biological capability to mate with any fertile member of the opposing gender. All of these similarities are coded in our genes. So also are some of our differences: pigmentation, eye color, hair. What is obvious at the physical level has been the subject of intense debate at the psychological level. Some recoil in horror at the very thought that our genes might shape our psychology. As with geography, there is a fear that to do so is to invite determinism. This fear is joined by another which stems from past and present abuses of genetic arguments: the eugenics movement of the early twentieth century which sought to improve the human race by selective breeding, or the claims of racists that one group is "better" than another.

Our very schema is the best response to the first complaint. If genes determined everything, I could have saved myself the trouble of writing the next several chapters. Just as the nonhuman environment is limited in its causal role, so also are our genes. In Barkow's words, "the social sciences are not to be replaced by biology but made compatible with it" (1989, 225). We cannot as scientists turn our back on the role of genes, but must leave to empirical investigation the questions of how and how much our genes influence our behavior. For those who are still wary, I can perhaps leap ahead a bit and admit that at least at present science does not suggest that our genes are too overpowering. Thus, Hinde (1987) suspects that understanding our genes will tell us much (but far from all) about individual propensities, less about human relationships, and very little about societal level interaction (see also Gordon 1991, 536–45).

What of racism? The same logic applies. We can be reassured by the fact that even those scientists who suggest important racial differences in terms of characteristics such as intelligence (e.g., Herrnstein and Murray 1994) find small enough differentials that one would be misguided to apply them at the individual level. Even if there were a difference of a few percentage points in average IQ scores across races, you would not if interviewing for a job be wise to choose the Asian candidate on this basis. Differences in IQ within races swamp the alleged differences between. Moreover, there are compelling arguments that environmental influences (such as poor schooling, and family environments which discourage self-confidence) rather than genes can explain the observed differentials. It is extremely unlikely, therefore, that exploration of our genetic disposition will serve to buttress the cause of racism. Indeed, we can be optimistic that the reverse is true. Wright (1994) in fact feels that the guiding assumption of evolutionary psychology is that the largest differences between people are unlikely to be due to genes. And Cromer (1997) suggests that 99 percent of our genes may be identical across individuals; we are thus much more the same than different.

Small differences may well be observed. We already know that certain genetic diseases affect different groups. The gene that causes sickle-cell anemia is found primarily in blacks. Rather than a sign of genetic inferiority, however, this gene provides resistance against malaria, and was thus advantageous in the sub-Saharan environment. While it appears that there has been enough contact across human groups through history that we share pretty much the same gene pool (otherwise mating would not be possible), some differences in gene frequency across groups will inevitably be found. Still, the genetic testing techniques presently used in criminal trials and paternity tests show that the degree of difference found within any ethnic group is many times greater than the difference across groups.

If differences in the environments in which human groups live(d) encouraged some slight genetic differences, large or important differences are unlikely. As Konner (1982, 399–401) notes, intelligence is a broad concept that encompasses a variety of intellectual talents. It is highly unlikely that any environment selected less strenuously for all sorts of intelligence. This is especially the case if we accept the arguments of Byrne (1988) and many others that it was the need for social interaction rather than manipulation of the physical environment that encouraged selection for ever-greater intelligence. If intergroup differences do exist, they are likely in terms of visual, spatial, logical, linguistic or a host of other particular skills. Given the diversity of modern occupations, it would be silly to imply that any group was even marginally better prepared on average for modern life.

To pursue only those research programs whose results we think we will like is not only unscientific, but serves humanity poorly.[3] "If a given perspective has social implications we must pursue it: If there are biological factors mitigating against our building the sort of world we would like to build, it is urgent for us to know about them, understand them, and learn how to circumvent them" (Hinde 1987, vii). Our genes influence us but do not control us completely: only by understanding them can we hope to overcome any undesirable influences they may have. Only by recognizing that whites are highly susceptible to sunburn have we developed sun lotion to protect them (Cromer 1997); we should be open to further discoveries of this type.

While politicians may potentially abuse genetic analysis, the same is true of all theories. Konner (1982) notes that the antithesis of genetic theory, the belief that humans can be shaped to any form, has proven even more dangerous: he refers to the efforts to create a "New Soviet Man" as these played out in Russia, China, and Cambodia. He lists our tendency to violence and to insatiable material wants as the sorts of genetic facts we have to recognize before we can combat them. Marxists, in contrast, have tended to oppose evolutionary psychology because of its emphasis on individuals and a (misguided) fear that it inevitably supports a dog-eat-dog orientation (Trigg 1985). Wenegrat (1990, 5), after reviewing the literature for and against, concurs that it is both ethically and politically superior to explore our genetic composition.

We will find in what follows that our genes bequeath to us a number of competing drives rather than one comprehensive "program": this raises the possibility that we can choose to emphasize some drives over others. The fact that our genetic predispositions were likely shaped by selection processes over the millennia spent by humanity as hunters and gatherers suggests that these may no longer be ideal for the quite different lives which most humans lead. Fortunately, hunters and gatherers had to adapt to environmental change, and thus we have most likely been "programmed" for flexibility.

One notable aspect of this flexible programming is what we call consciousness. This, arguably, more than anything else, separates humanity from the animals. Every complex organism must develop a "map" of the important characteristics of their environment to guide decision-making; if this "map" includes a representation of the self the organism experiences consciousness, and at some level of complexity this becomes self-awareness (Barkow 1989, 103–4). Why did consciousness evolve in humans?[4] A necessity for human hunting (and other activities) is complex cooperation. In order to be able to accurately assess the dependability of potential collaborators, we need to be self-aware. This, at least, is Crook's (1980) explanation of the emergence of human consciousness. While not without its drawbacks—the source of psychological trauma is to be found in the relationship between our conscious and subconscious minds—this self-awareness is the key to our being able to potentially rise above genetic urges.

A further criticism of the genetic approach is methodological: are genetic hypotheses subject to scientific analysis? The answer is yes. Though we cannot as yet identify the particular characteristics of our genes, there are many paths by which we can try to identify our genetic predispositions. The continued research in the laboratory by geneticists is one such path, though its greatest insights likely will fall some decades in the future. Geneticists have naturally begun by looking for "big mutations," and have identified single genes that induce color blindness, cystic fibrosis, hemophilia, sickle-cell anemia, and a host of other diseases; the complex genetic interaction that produces common characteristics like altruism will be much harder to identify (Wilson 1998, 145). At present, a more profitable endeavor for our purposes is evolutionary psychology. This pursues the hypothesis, hinted at above, that humanity's genes would have been selected over the millennia in which humanity operated as hunters and gatherers. Despite the recent dramatic expansion in human population, it is nevertheless true that 90 percent of all humans who have ever lived were hunter-gatherers. Given the very slow pace of genetic evolution, little change will have occurred in the mere few thousand years since humanity first turned to settled agriculture.

Since genetic evolution must rely on random mutation, knowing the selection criteria can not allow us to perfectly predict our genetic tendencies (Symons 1992, 149, seems to suggest otherwise). And since modern hunter-gatherer societies have all been "tainted" to some degree by outside contact, we cannot be sure that we fully comprehend the selection environment. Still, evolutionary psychology provides us with a source of many useful hypotheses. We must then seek corroboration in observations of modern human behavior. Sometimes, indeed, scientific exploration works in the opposite direction, from some observation of a common element in human behavior to hypotheses about how such a trait might have been selected for. If so, we must be careful of assuming our result. As we saw in the case of sickle-cell anemia, a gene that aids one goal may have deleterious side effects. Just because a genetic tendency exists does not mean that it ever served a purpose.

I have been careful in the above to speak of genetic tendencies rather than simply genes. One can find in the literature loose references to, for example, a gene for altruism. This, strictly speaking, is wrong. Our genes combine to shape our behavior. We are only beginning to understand the characteristics of individual genes. Eventually, we will hopefully be able to say that a particular gene strengthens a particular tendency, or increases its probability, or will do so in combination with some other gene. Our exploration of genetic tendencies can both inform that research effort while providing invaluable insight into human behavior.

A final distinction needs to be drawn between genetic tendencies and behavior. We may all have a tendency toward aggression, but some may never display this if always surrounded by stronger opponents (I→*). Our tendencies interact with our environment to shape our behavior. Observed similarities in behavior may reflect environmental rather than genetic similarity. One common approach to the nature/nurture debate is to calculate the proportion of variability in a particular characteristic that can be attributed to one or the other. This can be useful information, but in most cases we can hope to do better. By understanding how our genes have predisposed us to act in certain circumstances, we can then hope to comprehend how particular environmental influences shape our behavior within these genetic constraints.

Evolutionary Mechanisms

Since the best known of evolutionary theories is that regarding genetic evolution, I will be brief here. I might first note that one does not have to accept the evolution of species to recognize the importance of evolution within species. The mechanisms, though, are the same: random mutations will inevitably occur and those that enhance "fitness"—defined as the ability to reproduce and of one's heirs to do so—will tend naturally to expand in importance within the gene pool. Unless one invokes godly intervention, mutation must be random, for no organism can (yet) design its own genes. Successful mutations will almost always be small, since any large deviation is unlikely to be fitness enhancing. Thus, genetic evolution occurs very slowly, though some brief periods of rapid change are possible.[5]

MENDELIAN GENETICS

How exactly do genes work? Gregor Mendel's long forgotten experiments with flowers still provide some of the most important insights. When a purple and white flower were mated, the resulting offspring were all purple. This result leads to the idea of a dominant gene: the gene that causes purple coloration dominated the other. Yet when the offspring were in turn mated, one quarter of the resulting grandchildren were white. Mendel hypothesized—correctly—that each organism is guided by gene pairs where one of each pair is inherited from each parent. In turn, one of each pair is passed on to any children. If we look at the grandchildren generation, we see that they have a 50 percent chance of receiving a purple or white gene from each parent (since each parent will have one of each). Probability theory suggests that one quarter of the grandchildren will receive two white genes. The fact that one quarter of the generation was white is due to the action of a recessive gene—a gene that is not activated unless paired with itself. We know of many recessive genes in humans: hemophilia and blue eyes are among the traits that are only activated when an identical pair of the relevant genes is inherited.

Not all gene pairs follow a dominant/recessive rule. Breeding red and white flowers may yield pink offspring (one-quarter red, one-half pink, and one-quarter white in the next generation). The pink color results from the blending of the genes' influence.

In general, it is much more difficult to trace Mendelian mechanisms in humans because of the fact that several gene pairs (out of a hundred thousand) interact in determining most human traits. There are at least four pairs of genes that influence skin pigmentation in humans, for example. Some pairs appear to "blend" while others are dominant/recessive. Thus children usually, but not always, have a skin color intermediate to that of their parents. One final note: some genes can inhibit others; thus a gene for albinism inhibits all pigment-producing genes.

SPECIFIC RATHER THAN GENERAL MECHANISMS

As mentioned above, our focus is generally not on specific genes but on genetic tendencies embodied in our genes. The most important point to be made here is that our genes have not endowed us with a master program that governs all of our actions. Rather, we appear to have a substantial number of fairly independent mental mechanisms that guide us in different aspects of our lives. This fact is borne out in the observation of people suffering from brain damage: generally some functions are unimpaired while others are severely hampered. It is also consistent with the logic of genetic evolution. Think of the diverse goals hunter-gatherers needed to pursue: food, shelter, mating, protection of offspring, reputation for fairness, aiding group members, keeping abreast of group activities, understanding the nonhuman environment (Barkow 1989, 132). Random mutations that serve to enhance one goal without severely restricting the achievement of others would be selected for. The likely result: a set of distinct mechanisms for the achievement of various goals.

Nor does each goal necessarily have only one dedicated mechanism. Fodor (1983) notes that perception skills such as sight and language are governed by separate mechanisms. Jackendoff (1992) extends Fodor's analysis by arguing that even at the level of data processing different inputs are handled differently. He identifies at least three distinct mechanisms, one for language, another spatial, and a third for governing our own bodies. His main conjecture that different types of information will be processed in different "modules" or according to different "languages of the mind" (other scholars use a variety of terms) leaves open the possibility of a large number of distinct mechanisms.

While scholars disagree on the precise definition of these separate mechanisms, there is great consensus that some separate mechanisms exist (Jackendoff 1992, speaks of this as a robust result). These deal with different sorts of information and/or with different goals. "On this view, the human mind would more closely resemble an intricate network of functionally dedicated computers than a single general-purpose computer" (Tooby and Cosmides 1992, 221). In many situations it will be clear which computer should govern behavior. There is still room for debate as to how loose the coordination mechanisms are that determine which computer runs the show, or whether they somehow cooperate, when goals conflict.[6]

The computer analogy is a powerful one. I will often speak of mental "programs," though I should emphasize that natural selection is unlikely to lead to very tidy programming, and that some strands of neurophysiological research suggest that the brain is much more than a collection of computer-like junctions transmitting electrical impulses. The analogy has encouraged many scholars to pursue the idea of a master program. It is noteworthy in this regard that one of the latest trends in computer programming has been "fuzzy logic," whereby a number of fairly simple but distinct decision rules are employed in place of a complex master program. The rules themselves are based on "fuzzy" inputs like "hot" and "cold" rather than precise mathematical measures; helicopters and air conditioners are among the mechanisms that can be managed more efficiently by fuzzy programming. The key to fuzzy logic is to employ lots of rules for situations in which small changes in inputs should yield big changes in output, and much vaguer guidelines elsewhere. Given the number of decisions that humans have to make, and the limited size of the human brain, it could be that our distinct processing systems may not just be an evolutionary accident but the best way for our brains to be organized.

The computer analogy may lead some to expect that each mental mechanism will be housed in separate parts of the brain. I do not advocate a return to the phrenology of a century ago whereby each bump on the brain was presumed to signify some characteristic of an individual's psychology. Nevertheless, the experience with brain damaged patients does indicate that certain functions are located in different parts of the brain (though other parts of the brain will sometimes attempt imperfectly to compensate). We are far from being able to precisely map where in the brain most mechanisms would be centered, though fairly good estimates are possible in some cases. Some mechanisms, especially any coordinating systems, may have no "home."[7]

We are least advanced in our understanding of the links that might exist across mechanisms. Jackendoff suggests that the strength of these is highly variable. Those that we can talk about easily are presumably linked fairly strongly to our language faculty. Others, such as mechanisms of bodily control (including our sense of touch) seem much less connected to our language faculty. Jackendoff hypothesizes further that these particular mechanisms may be related closely to our musical appreciation faculty: we have trouble verbalizing our appreciation of music but we dance in tune to it and our bodies seem naturally to tense or relax when music is played. Further research is indicated.

CONSCIOUS AND SUBCONSCIOUS

The most powerful evidence that our mind contains loosely connected modules is the existence of conscious and subconscious minds. We all know that mental processes occur, particularly those involving emotions, of which we are poorly if at all "aware." Psychological therapy is generally designed at least in part to put people "in touch" with their subconscious. It might seem that the existence of a subconscious is a regrettable barrier to mental health. Yet both psychology and evolutionary psychology suggest that its existence enhances fitness in a number of ways.

In the course of our daily lives, it is much easier to respond "instinctively" to diverse stimuli, rather than logically plan every simple action that we undertake (Crook 1980; Epstein 1990). I argued above that it was advantageous for the mind to be composed of separate mechanisms; with a minor extension we can see the advantage of some of these mechanisms having little contact with our conscious thought processes (the conscious mind is thus more aware of some goals than others; Barkow 1989, 134). This would slow us down too much. In Fodor's words we sacrifice accuracy for speed. It is noteworthy that many scholars (e.g., Jackendoff 1992) think that the dividing line between conscious and unconscious depends entirely on how well a particular mechanism is linked to the language faculty. Consistent with this is the contention of many scholars that (most of?) our subconscious and particularly our emotions are located in the older part of our brain, while our conscious thoughts (and language capability) are centred in the evolutionary newer neocortex. Barkow (1989) describes a reptilian brain (stem) that monitors and controls other body organs, a mammalian brain that is connected to the limbic system and is responsible for emotions, and the "new mammalian brain" or neocortex that is responsible for cognition.

We have seen above that there would be selection pressure to develop some mechanisms to deal with situations in which our goals conflict. To do so consciously must cause some pain (see below). If, however, we can subconsciously repress some goals in these situations, we can deal with conflict without experiencing pain (Nesse and Lloyd 1992). Moreover, since humans need to cooperate but individual interests conflict (see below), fitness would be enhanced by our ability to detect the emotions of others. If so, then individual fitness would be enhanced by an ability to fool others. If, though, others can read our emotional state, we can only achieve this by fooling ourselves (Barkow 1989, 77; Nesse and Lloyd 1992).

Such a capacity for self-deception may be especially important during childhood. The reproductive interests of parents and children diverge. Children deceive their parents in order to achieve autonomy. Many feel that neuroses reflect a carryover into adulthood of this tendency to obey rules deceptively. Children face an incentive to be dependent and/or manipulative in order to gain parental attention. To be effective, though, such strategies cannot be conscious; there is thus a danger that these too will be carried into adulthood (Nesse and Lloyd 1992). There are times in childhood—weaning, the birth of a younger sibling—when some sense of rejection is almost inevitable. The twin strategies of repressing these memories and changing one's behavior to reduce future rejection help the child to cope (Crook 1980). As well, children often feel angry but learn that expressing that anger may cause a decrease in parental interest. They thus would wish to repress anger-inducing information. To do so runs the risk of interfering with the childhood task of learning from experience. Thus, such information is placed in the subconscious (Crook 1980, 279–84; he makes a similar argument with respect to curiosity). It is noteworthy that one has to deal with many of these issues at a time when the neocortex is poorly developed, and thus one is heavily reliant on more primitive brain structures.

Adult relationships can be aided by the existence of our subconscious as well. Most of us have endured the breakup of close relationships at some point in our lives, and are aware of how our attitude toward the other changes. One compelling explanation is that while in a relationship we repress some of our negative feelings toward the other; once we are sure it is over we instead repress some of our more positive feelings. This saves us from having constantly to face the fact that the goals of any two people will always be partly in conflict, partly in accord.

Analyses of the subconscious are inherently tentative. All we can ever observe, even of our own subconscious, is its effects. Like looking at a computer printout, we can then try to guess at the processes that might have gone on between input (and even here we may not be aware of all relevant sensory inputs; Fodor 1983) and output: why did that make me angry? why am I depressed today? Slips of the tongue, dreams,[8] and physiological reactions give us clues to the programs buried in our subconscious, but we can never hope to completely catalogue them (Dennett 1981). Still, Jackendoff (1992, 94–95) is optimistic that we may uncover some rules that regulate subconscious processes: perhaps the logical twist that governs displacement of attitudes toward one person onto another obeys the same rules as that governing slips of the tongue. This would not tell us why particular displacements occur, but would tell us which are possible. Frank (1988) discusses the value of recognizing that our subconscious may be attracted disproportionately to physical beauty in people because that is all it can "see," or more generally just realizing that our emotions are affected by stimuli of which we are not consciously aware. He even suggests that we can learn to trick our subconscious. Some people find that setting their watch five minutes ahead makes them more punctual. If we all were governed by one rational master-program such a strategy could not work, for we would simply subtract five minutes every time we looked at our watch. Our subconscious, though, is not in on the game, and guides us accordingly.

A final note: while I have spoken here of a subconscious mind, there are likely diverse subconscious mechanisms. While by definition there must be some links between the conscious parts of our mind, there is no requirement that this occurs in the subconscious. Indeed, Jackendoff (1992) recognizes that our knowledge of many linguistic rules is subconscious; this subconscious mechanism (and other "computational" mechanisms) must necessarily be separate from the bulk of subconscious processes that operate sublingually. And Fodor (1983) feels that any subconscious mechanism which guides our perceptual apparatus (including our language faculty) would be completely cut off from other elements of our conscious or subconscious minds. He notes in this regard that we cannot mentally shut off our perceptual apparatus but must physically close our eyes or cover our ears.

THE SURVIVAL OF FITNESS-REDUCING TENDENCIES

Why have millennia of selection not eliminated all genes with fitness-reducing effects? We know that there are serious genetic diseases in the world.[9] Moreover, there is strong evidence that there is a genetic basis for homosexuality, and yet this tends to strongly reduce the probability of reproduction (I hasten to point out that I am making no ethical judgment nor implying that homosexuality is a disease; I merely observe that homosexuality as fitness reducing should have been selected against).

One partial answer is that over the last centuries the environment in which we live has changed more quickly than our genes could be selected. Our sweet tooth developed in a world with fruit but no candy (Wright 1994; he suggests back trouble as another sign of sluggish adaptation). We saw above that the sickle-cell gene was (is) likely fitness-enhancing in an environment where malaria was endemic.[10] Likewise, recent research suggests that the gene responsible for cystic fibrosis provides protection against typhoid fever. And left-handedness, which is today fitness-reducing because most devices are made for right-handers, likely had advantages as a minority characteristic in a past where physical battles were more important; among modern fencers and boxers, left handers are highly overrepresented, presumably because this difference gives them an advantage.

This argument is especially important with respect to recessive genes like sickle-cell. If a gene only has negative effects when paired with itself, then it can survive within a small percentage of the population almost indefinitely. If, say, only one in a thousand people have a "bad" recessive gene, then anyone who possesses this gene only faces a one in a thousand chance of mating with another carrier (assuming monogamy for convenience). Moreover, if both are mere carriers (the bad gene is paired with a dominant gene), any child of theirs has only a one in four chance of inheriting the bad gene from each.

The sickle-cell example leads us to a second explanation: since genes serve more than one purpose, it is quite possible for fitness-enhancing genes to have severe side effects. In our present state of understanding, where we usually speak of genetic mechanisms rather than the particular characteristics of individual genes, we may be unaware of such tradeoffs. Geneticists have only recently isolated the five genes that they think are the most important genetic causes of juvenile diabetes; we do not know all of the many other roles these genes play. Some suggest that a gene that enhances female fertility may play a role in encouraging male homosexuality.

A third explanation involves the possibility of negative dynamic reinforcement. The peacock's tail, by exposing the bird to predators, reduces fitness. Yet once peahens come to choose mates on the basis of tail feathers, selection at the individual level ensures that peacock tails become ever longer. Some limit on this process would exist wherein the long tail interfered too much with peacock mobility (Dawkins 1986, 195). One might hypothesize that a similar process occurred in human males with respect to aggression.

GENETIC TENDENCIES

Genetic tendencies are of three types. I consider in order abilities, emotions, and motivations. I will here discuss some of the more important tendencies; a complete list can be found in Table One.

PERCEPTION

Perception has long been a subject of philosophical inquiry. Is the world real, or is it all a dream? I have in this book adopted the assumption that the world does exist. In that case, the question becomes one of how accurately we perceive the world around us. This question has in recent decades become primarily the province of psychologists.

We are all familiar with illusions: line drawings that will seem to represent one thing to our minds at one time and yet something different seconds later. This is the clearest indication that our minds attempt to order our perceptual inputs before we are "aware" of them. We do not "perceive" lines drawn on a page but rather what we "think" those lines represent. Drawing on this insight, Gestalt theorists have emphasized that we perceive wholes rather than parts. We see a cloud, not the individual dots of color that comprise a cloud. If a line drawing of a circle has a gap in it, we see the circle anyway. If a drawing suggests a rectangular block lying on top of but perpendicular to another we fill in the unobservable parts of the bottom block.

Jackendoff (1992) argues that our perceptual apparatus would have been selected to allow speedy and accurate responses. It was thus important to perceive wholes rather than parts. It was also desirable to focus on the key elements of what we perceived. We could expect that biases would exist in our perceptual apparatus: stimuli that suggest the presence of a hungry lion in the vicinity would be recognized, while other elements of the landscape would be ignored. With limited computing capacity, the efficient mind processes only the most vital information. Note that, unlike some organisms, we do not perceive ultraviolet or infrared light; either the advantage to hunter-gatherers of such perceptions was outweighed by the mental apparatus required, or the necessary mutation(s) never occurred.

We have seen that humans were selected for flexibility. If the perceptual guidelines outlined above were entirely hardwired, then in changing environments humans would be in danger of ignoring important stimuli. There is evidence from people born with cataracts that were surgically removed in adulthood that learning does play a role in perception. They were unable, for example, to differentiate squares from triangles. More generally, age, intelligence, and practice with certain stimuli all affect individual abilities to organize perceptions. Finally, we should recognize that our expectations affect our perceptions: place a hand in cold water for a while and then put it in warm water, and you will find that the latter seems warmer than it is.

We have focused on our perception of external stimuli above (and primarily through sight), but should emphasize that these arguments apply to internal perceptions as well. Amputees will often perceive pain in the severed limb because their minds have processed the available inputs from the body in that way. Some suggest that sudden infant death syndrome results when the mind mistakenly feels that the body is drowning and stops breathing.

LANGUAGE ABILITY

We know of no human society, no matter how primitive, that does not use language. Moreover, there is no significant difference in complexity between the languages of industrialized nations and isolated (even illiterate) hunter-gatherer societies. Within societies, too, even people who score poorly on intelligence tests are able to master the local language. It would appear, then, that the ability to learn language is inherent in humans.

Many have suggested that it is this facility with language that separates humans from animals. This is not strictly true, for chimpanzees, among others, can master hundreds of words. While language was at one time conceived as a means for expressing our thoughts, it is now recognized that conscious thinking itself requires language (Gauker 1994). Thus, while language itself may not be the dividing line, our ability to master complex languages and then to engage in complex thought processes is essential to many tasks—Konner (1982) speaks of our ability to imagine and be artistic—which do distinguish us from other animals.

But what form does this universal facility with language take? Perhaps the universality of language merely reflects superior brainpower and the obvious utility of language? Alternatively, since language is clearly important in hunter-gatherer societies, particular linguistic mechanisms might have been selected for. Noam Chomsky revolutionized the field of linguistics in 1957 by arguing that the speed with which children were able to master language, and the similar structure of all world languages, could only be explained in terms of specific mental mechanisms. Yet Chomsky suggested that these might not be the result of selection but rather unknown laws of organization within the brain. Most who have followed in his footsteps, however, have accepted that these language acquisition mechanisms were selected for. Pinker (1994) provides a detailed argument for this position, noting in particular that the development of our vocal-auditory capabilities (vocal cords and ears), which are highly efficient organs for communication, is itself strong evidence of evolutionary selection for language capability.

The evidence for universal linguistic mechanisms is certainly compelling. Jackendoff (1992, 71) speaks of four key strands of evidence: how languages are structured, how they change, how children master them (even "baby talk" obeys the same structural rules—Pinker 1994), and the language problems associated with certain types of brain damage. This latter evidence strongly suggests that we are in fact dealing with a collection of mechanisms; Jackendoff (4–9) suggests that we have different "structures" for translating sounds into words, dealing with syntax (nouns, verbs, and so on), and understanding meaning, and that these in turn are divisible into task-oriented substructures. Although Jackendoff does not mention it, the fact that children pick up languages more readily than adults, and that adult language acquisition is "processed" in a different part of the brain, provides further evidence of special mechanisms. Hunter-gatherers had little cause to master second languages as adults (Barkow 1989).

Pinker (1994) lists ten distinct universal grammatical rules. These include the fact that all languages are built around symbols for major lexical categories (nouns, verbs), all languages have rules of word order, and pronouns are ubiquitous. While we all struggle to consciously master such rules in elementary school, we display a remarkable talent for employing them from an early age. To be sure, different languages rely more on some rules than others. Yet there is abundant evidence of universal constraints on structure and function (Croft 1990). Why, then, was some one language not hardwired into the brain? The answer in part is likely just that it was much "easier" to hardwire a few rules than thousands of words. Moreover, there is no inherent advantage to applying a particular sound to a particular concept; any advantage flows only from the number of others who do the same. And we are programmed for flexibility: people need to be able to coin new words for new experiences. Therefore, while all people share the same mental mechanisms,[11] and thus children learn any language at the same speed, there is scope for some grammatical variation and almost infinite scope for vocabulary differences (though each language relies on a repertoire of 10–70 distinct phonemes or sounds).

Similarities in structure across languages both reflect (through selection pressures) and reinforce similarities in function. Brown (1991) discusses many functional universals. All languages allow for humor and insults. All use metaphor, metonymy, and onomatopoeia, and all are employed in poetry. All have kinship terms, though the categorizations differ. All allow for measurement, contrasts, continua, and the distinction between general and particular. All provide for the concept of the individual in a psychological sense, including descriptors of character and normality. Prestige comes from skill with language.[12] In all languages different speech patterns are used on different occasions. (We could add to Brown's list the fact that all languages serve three distinct functions: communicating information, transmitting emotion, and facilitating persuasion.) Also, all languages appear to be about half redundant. That is, you can take out over half of the words in a paragraph and still comprehend its meaning; this redundancy serves to overcome the inevitable noise in transmission.

Jackendoff (1992) points out that there are more words in every language to describe what an object is than where it is. He suggests that this reflects limitations in both universal language and our perceptual apparatus. Without debating the merits of this particular case, I could emphasize again that evolution need not yield efficiency, and limits in one aspect of our functioning will likely be associated with limits in correlated functions.

ORGANIZING SCHEMAS

I have stressed above that humanity was selected to cope with a complex and changing environment. Despite the expansion in size of the human brain, it does not have the capacity to evaluate each new situation in detail in order to determine the appropriate course of action. Yet since the environment changes it would be inefficient to "hardwire" programs for how to deal with a variety of situations. Rather, we inherit an ability to learn from experience and develop schemas that guide our future behavior.[13] These schemas contain judgments of people (he is a jerk; ignore him), rules of conduct (slow down on slippery roads, don't insult drunks, and more complex guidelines such as how to initiate or respond to seduction), and views of self (I am no good at poker). With such schemas (or "maps of reality"; Braddon-Mitchell and Jackson 1996) in place, we are able to cope almost automatically with the vast majority of experiences in our daily life.

We likely first develop our schemas through trial and error. Since schemas are our guides to behavior, though, at some point they will become fairly entrenched in our minds, such that conflicting evidence—which we will tend to ignore—will not cause us to revise a schema. Psychologists use the phrase "cognitive dissonance" to describe those uncomfortable moments when some new bit of information is inconsistent with previous thoughts: you see a friend you trusted lying, or are helped by someone you did not respect. We dislike moments of dissonance for they pressure us to change schemas we have long relied on. It can hardly be surprising that people will avoid, ignore, or rationalize new information which threatens to cause cognitive dissonance.

The disadvantage of this approach is obvious. If we develop misguided schemas, then we will react poorly to a range of situations. We might have an unduly negative (or positive) view of others (including groups of people), or, more seriously, of ourselves. We might "learn" to ignore warnings of ice on the roads, or that arrogance is an endearing quality. As important, our schemas guide us as to which stimuli to pay attention to, and we may thus ignore the most important. Since we will develop most of our schemas while young (some feel that we lose our earliest memories because these are "filed" in terms of superseded schemas), our families will play a major role in shaping them. So also will the culture in which we are raised (C→I); more emphasis could be placed in ethnographic studies on the degree to which children learn different ways of organizing their thoughts.

While our first schemas must be developed inductively, it would be incredibly inefficient for us to follow this path for each marginally novel situation that we encounter. Instead, we also possess deductive capabilities which allow us to apply the insights of particular schemas to other situations. These capabilities are reflected in the popularity of metaphor and analogy worldwide. Indeed, one can think of our schemas as a system of analogies. What more powerful rhetorical device could there be, then, than to convince another that a novel situation can be viewed in terms of a schema they already possess?

LEARNING

The fancy word for the process by which we develop schemas is "learning." Learning in turn can be broken into two "simple" components. First, disparate thoughts are thrown together. Second, we make a judgment as to whether the resulting combination is worthy of remembering and incorporating into our world view (Dennett 1981). At the first step, we will not wish to rely always on accidental juxtaposition, and will thus seek means of choosing which thoughts to put together (aided often by others). At the second, we will need some mechanism for choosing combinations. In both these respects, note that one of the things we must learn is how to learn itself. But not, of necessity, at the beginning: we must be endowed with some natural ability to learn, or we could never learn how to. Nor is this surprising: if we were selected to rely on schemas (and thus get pleasure from learning; Konner 1982), we are likely endowed with specific learning mechanisms for their development. In other words, while it was not "desirable" for us to be hardwired for all contingencies, we were selected to be able to softwire ourselves with some degree of accuracy, at least with respect to the hunting-gathering environment.

When we think about learning, we generally think of a conscious act. Yet we are capable of both conscious and subconscious learning. As with other animals, we have been selected to repeat behaviors that are rewarded and avoid behaviors that are punished (this was the starting point of behaviorism, which we shall discuss in chapter 5). We thus learn without being aware of it. But consciousness allows us to go a step further and choose the best course in novel situations. We should have been selected, then, for mechanisms that help us to determine which cause-effect relationships adequately reflect outer reality (Dennett 1982). This would help us as individuals in our daily lives, and prepare us as scientists to comprehend the world around us.[14]

Jean Piaget and Noam Chomsky sparked a huge debate concerning the degree to which guidelines for learning were hardwired in the human brain. Piaget marvelled at human creativity, and thus favored the idea of limitless flexibility (though noting that not everyone acquired the ability for abstract thought). Chomsky argued that humans would struggle forever to master complex subjects like language without innate guidelines. Jackendoff (1992, ch. 3) sketches a middle ground: a few rules for making combinations, aided by a few primitive concepts (e.g., language structure), would overcome Chomsky's objections, while still providing for the creativity (I→C2) that Piaget treasured. Each individual learns only a small subset of the virtually infinite potential they possess.

We were selected to both learn from others and investigate our environment on our own. Others will urge us to make certain combinations. Many, but not all, of these we will accept on authority: we believe the theory of relativity, for example, even if we have no idea how Einstein established the relationship. While relying on authority provides a powerful means for learning a lot of material quickly, it inevitably exposes us to bias. Ironically, beliefs based on authority may be harder to change than those based on our own investigations. In the latter case, we tend to adjust our schema if faced with contradictory information (I thought the dog ate my plants, but know he was inside the last time it happened). Since we do not fully understand the logic behind beliefs accepted on authority, it is hard to overturn them. If a physicist approaches you at a cocktail party and tells you Einstein was wrong, what can you do (unless you know enough physics)? This adherence to authority allows people to continue to believe myths that appear to outsiders to violate their everyday experience (Sperber 1990).

Learning from experience is subject to biases as well. We do not in fact learn directly from experience but rather from what we think has happened. Since each event in our life is unique, we can only learn anything useful by discerning causal links. We note that we get sick every time we get up early and make pancakes. What is the cause? Trial and error will sometimes, but not always, lead us to the right conclusion. In particular, we may not have noticed some key elements of the puzzle (the germs in the pantry). This is especially likely because of inherent biases in our perceptual apparatus: for example, we tend to like stimuli we are exposed to most (Smith and Bond 1993) and tend to exaggerate both our role in events and those events themselves. We are thus likely to misattribute causes (most of us have a tendency to attribute good outcomes to our own efforts, while blaming others for bad outcomes). If we then ignore further information, we never achieve the right answer. Our first few observations may thus be crucial. Another source of bias is the fact that we will try to place all information within a coherent schema structure. If this is mistaken, when we apply it to new situations it will often guide us to focus on the wrong "facts." As Goethe long since recognized, every fact is already a theory, for our schemas tell us how to categorize everything.

This analysis has important implications for the task of teaching. Each student will of necessity bring a different set of schemas to the classroom. Some may find it easy to incorporate new knowledge into existing schemas, while others will find the new information completely alien. One of the advantages of one-on-one time with pupils is that teachers may gain some insight into the student's schemas, and thus be better able to show the student how new information fits. Even when lecturing, though, teachers can, by being clear on the cognitive framework behind course material, and providing a diversity of examples and other connections, increase the probability of all students finding some way of integrating the new information.

Repetition is very important for many sorts of learning. If we are to establish causal links from everyday experience, we need to experience similar outcomes enough times to deduce a cause. Behaviorists took the argument a step further and stressed that with limited memory capability the brain needs an incentive to store particular information. Thus, reinforcement of certain behaviors would cause the individual to learn the desired behavior. More generally, repetition would act as a signal to the brain that this is worth remembering (say the twentieth time your teacher asks you what eight times seven is). This "investment" of brain space would be more than rewarded by future occasions in which the information could be recalled easily rather than the problem solved from scratch.

An interesting example of the value of repetition is when we purposely practice some physical act: playing the piano or swinging a golf club. What we are doing in such cases is trying to deliberately program mental pathways that will allow accurate repetition and lesser mental computation. That is, the first time we swing a golf club we have to consciously think about stance, grip, clubface, and a host of other variables. The goal is to program our brain so that instead of drawing on general information it simply accesses the subprogram "golf swing." Repetitive learning of multiplication tables likely works in much the same way.

Thus, it is hardly surprising that studies show a large impact of homework time on learning. Poring over tedious math or spelling problems may not yield the sort of reinforcement that behaviorists emphasized, but does signal the brain that this stuff must be important (homework also extends the total amount of time devoted to learning, instills discipline, and may encourage parental involvement; it does, though, take time away from learning through play). While homework helps people from all social backgrounds and of all ability levels, it appears to help those of lower ability the most, perhaps because these students have more difficulty drawing links in the first place. And practice over long periods is best: cramming for exams has been shown to be a very poor way of learning.

Yet repetition is not the whole story. We cannot understand complex human behaviors in terms of simple repetitive or associative mechanisms. While the goal of piano playing may be flawless repetition, in most aspects of our life we are constantly faced with the novel. We rely on schemas to guide us, but they cannot do so perfectly. Much of the time, they will tell us which subprogram is best applied in certain situations, based on what past experience our present situation most resembles. We go beyond learning through repetition every time we expand our knowledge to cope with a new situation. Note that novelty and failure will both stimulate the brain to remember. Those who are persistent in the face of failure will learn much from eventual success (Sternberg 1994).

We are at the very early stages of understanding the neurochemical bases of memory. We do know that different types of memory are located in different parts of the brain. Psychologists still debate some of the basics, such as whether there is a distinction between short- and long-term memory, though most accept this distinction as well as a third type of immediate memory. Why do we forget? With the exception of traumatic events for which there may be an advantage to repression, the only reason we would have been selected to forget is that there is limited storage capacity in the brain. We thus have a greater tendency to remember events or information that were unusual. One problem with this hypothesis is that hypnosis and electrical stimulation are able to recover "lost" memories. In the case of repression this is easy to understand. In the more general case we can look to the computer analogy for guidance. Hypnosis is like recovering information from a disk when the file name is lost. Perhaps, the brain has limited random-access-memory space, and stores less valuable information in a deeper and harder to access type of memory. The rules the brain uses in these allocations are as yet poorly understood.[15] One common hypothesis, though, is that the more links we establish between one bit of information and others the more likely we will be able to retrieve it. In other words, the key to memory is organization. This provides yet another advantage of schemas (including the one in this book); we are much better able to remember disparate pieces of information if we can tie them together. It also provides yet another advantage of studying and/or applying what has been learned.

GENDER DIFFERENCES

Various aspects of hunter-gatherer life may have caused there to be different selection pressures operating on males and females. These would be represented genetically by genes that have different effects when operating in conjunction with X or Y chromosomes, or by the character of those chromosomes themselves. Neurological studies verify that there are some gender differences, though these are usually overwhelmed by within-gender variation.

While it is easy to exaggerate the degree of specialization of men as hunters and women as gatherers, some division of labor along gender lines is observed in all modern hunter-gatherer societies. This likely reflects the fact that women were less mobile than men due to pregnancy and breast-feeding, and any other advantages women possessed in childrearing (Cashdan 1989). It may also be that societies were less willing to risk women due to their extended role in reproduction. Whatever the cause of specialization, one result may have been a greater selection pressure for size and strength among men. Women seem to have greater finger dexterity, and men faster reaction times. Women appear to be better at remembering the spatial configuration of objects (and thus at finding lost objects). They may also be more prone to perceiving wholes rather than parts (hunters must recognize signs of danger), and thus to illusion. While hunting requires cooperation, women may nevertheless have had more occasion to interact; this might explain superior verbal abilities.

The different roles of men and women in reproduction may account for even greater differences. If males compete for mates, they will be selected for strength. The gender difference in strength and size in humans is much smaller than in early humanoids and many other species; one explanation of this is that the lengthy childhood of humans encourages monogamy and thus reduces competitive pressure for mates. Along with size and strength, there may have been selection for penis size and sperm count, while the female hymen may have served as a signal of chastity (Barkow 1989, 371).

LOVE

Crook (1980) suggests that while bipedalism offers humans many advantages, including increased ability to use tools, it makes giving birth much more difficult, and thus imposes severe constraints on infant size. Whether or not his analysis is correct, it is true that human infants require a much longer period of dependence on parents than is the case for any other species. Since parents who care for their children will thereby enhance fitness, we would expect strong selection forces to have operated over the millennia to ensure parental concern.

What mechanisms would have been selected for? The most obvious is commitment (note that commitment also provides benefits outside childrearing in terms of long-term arrangements to share the output of hunting and gathering pursuits). Commitment is achieved through the human emotion of love. Love in turn induces feelings of guilt if one acts against the interests of one's family (e.g., by having an affair). Love causes people to stick with relationships through the bad times. As Frank (1988) notes, couples who view their relationship in an exchange framework—I give this and get that—are much less happy and their relationships less likely to survive. He cites the poet Yates who wrote that people who are sensible about love are incapable of it. One hotly debated topic is the degree to which these pressures will have operated differentially by gender.[16] Breastfeeding provides a clear physiological argument that motherly love is more important. There is also the fact that males cannot be sure of paternity; this too would act to weaken the selection pressure for caring fathers. If a differential does occur in attitudes toward children, does it carry over to the capacity for love in general? (Remember that observed behavior is conditioned by culture as well as genes.)

I should not exaggerate the degree to which selection has ensured proper child support. In particular, I should note that the interests of parent and child inevitably diverge. The needy child wishes the parent to lavish all of their attention on it. The parent, though, wishes to enhance the fitness of all offspring. First children will therefore receive more parental attention as infants than their younger siblings. Last children may receive more attention over their lifespan than others (Hinde 1987, 116). Sibling rivalry is to be expected, then, for children must compete for a very scarce resource. Children who are especially weak or sickly will demand even more attention, yet fitness-maximizing parents may be motivated to cut their losses and focus their efforts on the children with a higher chance of survival (parental love may thus be conditioned by available medical technology). Love will act to mitigate such seeming cold-heartedness, but we are guided to expect some limits to the scope of parental affection.[17]

AESTHETIC SENSE

Hunters and gatherers had to choose which environment would provide the most positive outcomes for their efforts. We would expect selection for aesthetic preferences that encouraged the exploration of environments rich in resources and limited in dangers. Such an aesthetic sense would allow hunter-gatherer groups to quickly and accurately make location and exploration decisions. What sorts of scenes should we prefer? Kaplan and Kaplan (1992) suggest that we should, and do, prefer scenes that are clear, contain the possibility of new information, provide for an escape route, and can be surveyed from safety. They note further that young children tend to prefer savanna scenes, while older children are more likely to prefer the environment that they have become accustomed to.

Such an aesthetic sense would affect not only our appreciation of natural landscapes but of built environments. There is thus a strong feedback effect as humans have increasingly tried to shape their world to fit these preferences (see C→N). It is noteworthy that one of the key elements in landscape architecture is the provision of free-flowing walkways that define the movement of the observer through the space; this accords well with the guidelines suggested by the Kaplans above. So, too, does the theory of interior design which stresses such characteristics as honesty (do not make plastic look like wood), harmony within and with the surrounding environment, variety and change (but avoidance of being too busy; note that we can only process so much information at a time), and good illumination.

EMOTIONS AND THEIR DISPLAY

Love, guilt, and aesthetic appreciation: I have already had cause to discuss the role of some emotions. It might seem at first glance, nevertheless, that we should have been selected to be coldly logical maximizers of our reproductive potential. Happily, this has not been the case. The predominant reason for this is that human cooperation is facilitated by the display of emotions. The problem is simple. If we were all selfishly logical, we would cheat all of the time. We might agree to aid our compatriots if they were, say, charged by an elephant, but could hardly be expected to do so when the crunch came. Yet if we cannot count on others to aid us when it is not to their personal benefit, then the cooperation required for activities as diverse as hunting or mating will not occur. Caring facilitates cooperation.

We thus have a rationale for the existence of emotion. We still have a limited knowledge of exactly how emotions are triggered within our brains. It appears that emotions are centered in the oldest part of our brain, the limbic system. Their existence thus likely dates from the very dawn of humanity, though the precise mechanisms by which emotions are triggered could have been shaped over subsequent millennia. Konner (1982) sketches one possible path of development. We begin with fear: primitive humans would have needed the rush of adrenalin which spurs action in dangerous situations. Pleasurable emotions, Konner suggests, may reflect the passing of a fearful situation. Thus children enjoy hide-and-seek due to the continuing triumph over the possibility that they or others might disappear. Later we enjoy roller coasters, and perhaps nature walks, for the same reason.

Having emotions, though, solves only part of our problem. A comrade may attest their love and devotion, and yet still abandon us to the elephants. We need some way of detecting each other's emotions. Thus, we get the ironic result that our inability to conceal emotions from others is in fact a fitness-enhancing characteristic. Frank (1988, 121–30) discusses the range of involuntary body signals that communicate emotion: eye dilation, bright eyes, blushing, perspiration, lack of saliva, change in voice pitch, intake of breath. He notes that some facial muscles respond more to involuntary control than others: we draw down the corners of our mouth when sad, and furrow our forehead in grief, and narrow our lips in anger. Most of us are unable to fake these movements. Even those who are good at covering their emotions will usually evince some involuntary reaction when faced with a sudden stimuli.

We need not be consciously aware of all of the emotional signals we receive. I have heard that right-handed people tend to look up to the left when recalling an event but to the right when making something up. I may well have been reacting to such signals subconsciously my whole life; one often gets a sense that one is being lied to but cannot say how one knows. There is certainly strong evidence that we pick up on some cues. Indeed, one of the first "skills" displayed by infants is to discriminate between facial expressions. Adults have universal perceptions of others' emotional states (Wenegrat 1990, 18–19). Small children are sensitive to both visual and auditory clues to emotion (Jackendoff 1992). Experiments show that people are very competent at gauging the trustworthiness of others from such clues alone.[18]

As Jackendoff (1992) recognizes, the existence of specialized mechanisms to both send and receive emotional signals only makes sense if the mind possesses other faculties that can build upon this information and form complex relationships with others. Along these lines, Crook (1980) asserts that the cognitive capacity necessary to handle these interpersonal relations is great. Indeed, though many think it was humanity's use of tools that caused selection in favor of increased brain size, it seems more likely that it was the demands of being a social animal that caused human brains to far exceed the capabilities of other species (Byrne 1988). This is especially ironic given the modern feeling that we are much better at mastering nature than managing human society—and thus further evidence that cognitive capacity can be put to uses other than those nature selected for. The ability to detect others' emotions itself required a significant expansion in cognitive capacity. Once this ability was extant, an evolutionary advantage would exist for those better able to cheat. This in turn would cause selection for those even better at detecting cheating. Pinker (1994, 483), following many others, discusses the cognitive arms race that would likely ensue, and notes that some have suggested that this was the biggest single cause of the rapid growth in size of the human brain.

Having provided an evolutionary explanation for the existence and display of emotions, I must now proceed to the difficult tasks of defining and disaggregating. It should not surprise us that psychologists tend to eschew the idea of a simple definition in favor of a recognition of a family of resemblances. Four characteristics are emphasized. Emotions require some trigger, with emotion generally (always?) following immediately (e.g., a charging lion triggers fear; note that sometimes we have difficulty identifying the trigger). Since emotion thus depends on our perception of our world and ourselves, there is an important cognitive element (are lions dangerous?). Emotions are registered physiologically (fear raises the heart rate). Finally, emotions have an object (we are fearful of the lion) (Solomon 1993). Many would add to this list a fifth characteristic: emotions involve a tendency to action (run!), and note that this is a key to their evolutionary importance.

While cognitive elements are important, I should emphasize that—with rare exceptions such as when we are acting—we can not consciously choose which emotion to feel. The charging lion elicits fear, even if we are fully aware that the lion can not leap the fence between us. We can learn over time that lions in zoos are not a threat, and reduce our fear response. And we can plan our lives so that we avoid situations that elicit emotions that we dislike (e.g., avoiding the poor lest we feel guilt). But the link between certain triggers and certain emotions is buried deep in our subconscious.

Several attempts at disaggregating the phenomenon of emotion have been made. Plutchik (1993) posits a circular continuum broken into eight emotions (with opposites in the circle being emotional opposites): adoration, ecstasy, vigilance, rage, loathing, grief, amazement, and terror. He posits that many of our common terms for emotions refer to less severe instances of these emotions; fear and apprehension for terror, surprise and distraction for amazement, anger and annoyance for rage, and so on. All other emotions are hybrids: hostility from anger and disgust (a mild form of loathing), sociability from joy and acceptance, guilt from joy and fear.

Shweder (1993), in an effort to show the cultural embeddedness of emotional categorization, provides a list of the eight principal emotions generated by Hindu scholars between the third and eleventh centuries: love/passion/delight, amusement/laughter/humor, sorrow, anger, fear, perseverance/heroism/energy, disgust/disillusionment, and wonder/astonishment (some scholars add a ninth, serenity/calm). He then provides the list of nine basic emotions compiled by Paul Ekman in the 1980s: anger, fear, sadness, happiness, surprise, disgust, interest, shame, and contempt. While some have noted the similarities between these lists, Shweder argues that in many cases accidents of translation make them appear more similar than they are.

Our definition of emotion can help us determine the "best" categorization. Ekman focused on the physiological aspect, and identified facial expressions that accompanied each of his nine basic emotions (Shweder suggests that he exaggerated cross-cultural similarities in identification). Others have focused on the triggers or objects of emotion, identifying emotions focused on others (anger, fear, and so on), ourselves (guilt, pride, and so on), the past (regret, elation, and so on), or possessions of others (jealousy, and so on). If we accept that emotions are the result of selection pressures, though, our best guideline may be the fifth element of our definition, which looks at the purpose served by emotion. Izard (1993) provides this sort of justification for a nonexhaustive list of six emotions [G → I, C, S]. Joy encourages social cohesion as it allows us to gain pleasure from the company of others, recover from stress, and form supportive relationships (Izard subsumes much of what we have called "love" within the joy category). Sadness also supports societal bonds but through our ability to share grief: it encourages empathy in others, and at least sometimes encourages deep thought in individuals by decreasing their activity level. Anger increases our activity level and serves (sometimes excessively) to decrease others' hostile actions toward us.[19] Disgust steers us away from dangerous substances and practices.[20] Shame encourages social conformity, group cohesion, and personal responsibility, while driving individuals to self-examination and self-improvement (Lewis 1993, emphasizes how we compare our actions with our sense of what we should have done; other scholars stress the difference between self-oriented "guilt" and other-oriented "shame"). Finally, fear encourages both escape from danger and attempts to alleviate dangerous situations (see also Ohman 1993). I should emphasize though, as Izard does, that while each emotion serves a purpose, glitches in either our neural pathways or our cognitions about the world and ourselves can cause emotions to lead us astray.

Where does this leave us? Obviously, unpacking would be easier if there was greater scholarly consensus here. Since I strive for completeness, I would prefer to err if necessary on the side of including overlapping emotions, rather than leaving out some type of emotional experience. Izard's six emotions are not only well-justified, but appear in most other lists. I can follow Plutchik in recognizing that many of our words for emotion refer to more or less intense versions of these six. I have already suggested that love deserves special treatment. It could be that empathy also deserves separate treatment from "joy." Other elements that appear on other lists and do not appear to be closely linked to any of Izard's emotions are amazement/anxiety, humor, perseverance/heroism/energy/interest/ vigilance, fatigue, and jealousy. Of these, interest and perseverance are better viewed as motivational than emotional. Ignoring these, we are left with a list of twelve emotions: joy, grief, love, anger, jealousy, fear, guilt, empathy, anxiety, fatigue, disgust, and humor. To this, I add aesthetic sense, for we do react emotionally to nature and art in ways that do not appear to be captured by any of these emotions.

What of Shweder's suggestion that our categorizations of emotion are mere cultural constructs with no universal applicability? We cannot doubt that words for emotions sometimes translate poorly across languages. And there appear to be some societies in which guilt and love are hardly recognized. Yet these observations alone do not establish the impossibility of defining universal emotions. White (1993) also stresses cultural differences in the perception of emotion. He nevertheless advocates comparative research of how people respond to various situations in order to identify common cross-cultural emotional reactions. And even Shweder speaks of decomposing the emotions of each society into what he terms "narrative slots"; as these would be universal we could then translate flawlessly any emotional experiences. He also marvels at our ability to understand emotions cross-culturally.

HUMOR

I have suggested above that most of our emotions have/had some evolutionary advantage. But what of laughter? It, like these other emotions, is a spontaneous reflex. Yet it is harder to see the fitness-enhancing role of laughter. One might try to view it as a side effect of more advantageous emotions. However, laughter is triggered by very complex stimuli different from those that trigger other emotions.

Humor has troubled philosophers for some time. Bergson characterized laughter as rebellion against the mechanization of human behavior and nature, Freud viewed it as the expression of repressed sexual feeling, and Koestler saw in it individual enlightenment or revelation. A fair degree of consensus exists today that humor reflects the dissipation of tension. Storytellers create a sense of apprehension which is in turn released with the punchline. The humor of children (and hunter-gatherer tribes) tends to focus on release from aggression (e.g., tickling). Sometimes, the tension can be stored for a long time; thus we can laugh when reminded of a previous laughter-inducing incident.

A related explanation is that the key to humor lies in unexpectedly moving from one plane of logic to another. For example, in puns we switch quickly from one definition of a word to another. More generally, we describe a situation in terms of two self-consistent but mutually incompatible frames of reference (schemas). What is the connection between the two explanations? The logical jolt stimulates our laughter response. We laugh because our emotions cannot adjust to the new train of thought as quickly as our thoughts. This causes emotional tension and its dissipation. One of the interesting characteristics of humor is that the pleasure from the release of tension far exceeds any discomfort from the tension itself.

What good is it? It could be a reward for creativity. Many feel that the creativity of the comedian is very similar to that of the scientist or artist. All involve an ability to stretch analogies to new territory. A more compelling explanation is that humor provides a much-needed release valve. It is often observed that we are programmed with more aggression than is ideal for the modern world. Hunter-gatherers needed to be able to respond to danger quickly and energetically. Yet even they needed to be able to relax when among friends and family. We all can identify with the difficulty of bouncing back from a tense situation. I have already noted that our emotions change much more slowly than our thoughts. How often have each of us recognized that we had misunderstood an anger-inducing action of another, but been unable to quickly shake the feeling of anger? Laughing at the situation can serve as a signal from the conscious to subconscious mind that all is well.

Willeband (1993) argues that humor serves to decrease tension, anger, fear, stress, discomfort, and pain. This not only provides a direct benefit to individuals but aids social cohesion. Most obviously, by overcoming fear and anger, it facilitates peaceful interaction. As well, the ability of people to share intense enjoyment in the form of laughter provides an incentive to interaction and a sense of belonging.

ALTRUISM, FAIRNESS

I have suggested above that it was humanity's need to cooperate that was the primary cause of increased mental capacity. Yet the arguments I have made all fit nicely within the vision of individuals as inherently selfish. We are selected, in essence, for our ability to get others to act in our interest. How then to deal with altruism? We are all familiar with stories of people rushing into burning buildings to save complete strangers. If humanity has been selected for selfishness, why would anyone ever behave in a selfless way?

There are four possible arguments. One follows naturally from our previous discussion. Since we need to cooperate with others, and tend to communicate our emotions to them, it is advantageous to think that we wish to help others, even if subconsciously we are only out for number one. On its own, though, this would not propel us into burning buildings. Our subconscious mind should be able to overwhelm us with fear at such moments. Our desire to help must be more than a conscious icing on a selfish cake.

The most obvious rationale for helping others is the possibility of reciprocity (thus the elderly are the most likely to act and promote altruism; Crook 1980). The hunter who abandoned his companions in a time of need would find it impossible to enlist their help in future. Selection being an imperfect process, it is possible that a general desire to aid others in need was selected for. This is especially the case given that hunter-gatherer groups tend to be small and thus one could anticipate reciprocal aid from all members of one's group (and we will see that there was a strong tendency toward group identity; G→C2). Our modern willingness to aid strangers may simply reflect the fact that selection occurred in a stranger-less environment.

A similar argument can be made with respect to our third rationale: we would have been selected for willingness to aid close relatives. Other things equal, a family that is mutually supportive will be able to rear many more children. My willingness to aid my nephew or cousin may slightly reduce my fitness, but will serve to enhance the number of carriers of my grandparents' genes. Perhaps in small hunter-gatherer societies all are relatives and it may not be necessary to discriminate among those worthy of aid. Again, we may be altruistic because we were not selected for success in the modern world.

However, these arguments rely on a simplistic view of hunter-gatherer societies. To avoid inbreeding, then and now, several groups would need to gather together from time to time for mate selection. Thus, people would have faced situations in which they interacted with non-kin who they would not reasonably expect to need the aid of in the future. Over the course of millennia one would think that any desire to help someone like that would be selected out.

This raises the fourth possibility: perhaps selection occurred in terms of a group rather than an individual. The selection forces I have discussed to this point operated at the level of the individual. The one exception occurred just above where I discussed the possibility of selection at the level of the kin group. Some scholars believe that selection could occur at the level of a much larger group (this group would have to be small, or frequently exchange members with other groups). In a tribal war, the tribe that hangs together will likely win. They will also hunt and gather better. If true, then we might well be "programmed" to help everyone we come in contact with (with the possible exception of members of outgroups who we disdain). While attractive philosophically, we must remember that the case for selection at the level of large groups is far from firmly established. Wright (1994), for example, argues that group selection of altruism would have been overwhelmed by the rewards to individuals of cheating their gullible colleagues. Yet perhaps the group could "achieve" selflessness if cheaters were detected and punished.

A related concept to altruism is "fairness." If we did not care about others' well-being, we would not concern ourselves with whether others were treated fairly. Yet we feel guilty if we do not leave a tip at a roadside diner we expect never to revisit (Frank 1988, 18–19). In experimental situations, participants will generally eschew a strategy that would maximize their income in favor of one in which all participants receive a "fair" share. Just as with altruism, we appear to be programmed to pursue fairness. Again, it is not entirely clear why we pursue these goals even in situations where they are not fitness-enhancing.

TIME PREFERENCE

It is well known that people value the present more than the future. Our whole financial system rests on the simple fact that people prefer a dollar today to a dollar tomorrow, and therefore need to be rewarded for putting off expenditures. Yet we do not totally discount the future; we plan for it, dream about it, and save for it. Hunter-gatherers operated in an environment where a mistake could easily end their life, and thus needed to have their mind focused on the present. Yet they also had to save food from one kill to the next, and plan their travels with an eye to the seasons. They were likely selected, then, for the fitness-maximizing attitude toward time in that environment. Frank (1988, 89) suggests that in the modern world of long-term investments and career planning (and dieting and drug abuse), we might be better off with a more forward-looking orientation than that which we have inherited.[21]

AGING

I have spoken above of genetic mechanisms that affect all people. I have recognized that some of these *may* operate differently in men and women. I close by noting that our genes cause us to behave differently at different ages. Indeed our lifespan itself was undoubtedly selected for. We require well over a decade as children to both grow physically and learn how to hunt and/or gather. We then become fertile, able to have children of our own. Once we have raised a family, our fitness-enhancing role in society decreases rapidly. Cruelly, we would be selected to die shortly after fulfilling our childrearing responsibilities (cushioned by the fact that grandparents aid in childrearing). One might ask why we do not remain fertile for a longer period. Many answers are possible. Some are complex biological analyses of the "costs" of longevity. Others focus on the advantage to the community of being able to devote substantial parental resources to all children. It has been suggested that menopause may have been selected to limit family size (male fertility, while not eliminated, does fall with age).

We would expect selection for different skills/goals at different ages. Put simply, children should be focused on learning, adolescents on mating, and adults on nurturing. Ethically, children may be programmed for selfishness, but need to learn reciprocity in time to mate. Midlife crises may reflect to a large extent these gene-induced changes. In particular, we should recognize that there would have been little selection pressure for elderly characteristics; as we live longer we need to consciously put meaning into a period of life with limited fitness-enhancing programming.[22]

G→C: Genes → Culture

This causal link has experienced more than its share of exaggerated scholarly dispute over the years. While cultural anthropologists would in a crunch have to admit some role for genes (you cannot dance without legs, say), there was a long-standing tradition of treating the human mind as a blank slate (tabula rasa)[23] on which (almost) any cultural practices could be imprinted. Thus Tooby and Cosmides (1992, 32) complain of a widespread belief that we have evolved to a point where innate psychology has a negligible impact on culture. Evolutionary psychologists reacted to this assignment of causal priority to culture by asserting the predominant role of genes—in a pinch, they too might recognize some evidence of cultural variability. Barkow (1989, 154–55) takes a firm position: "Culture . . . is not a cause of anything. To describe behavior as "cultural" tells us only that the action and its meaning are shared and not an individual idiosyncrasy."

Like many debates, this one has eased somewhat with the passage of time. Yet Smith and Bond (1993, 74) are still able to decry a methodological chasm between those who favor looking at cross-cultural similarities (e.g., we all wear clothes), and those who look at cross-cultural differences (we wear different types of clothes). We should strive to bring these two points of view together (see also Brown 1991). Our genes put some limits on the range of cultural diversity, but do not fully determine the shape of culture (if they did, several other causal links in my schema would be empty).

Symons (1992) reacts negatively to the idea that genes and culture affect each other, because he is uncomfortable with the idea that culture could act to limit genetic fitness. Yet casual observation tells us that cultural elements can be powerful enough to cause individuals to shun sex and/or food and even embrace death. Especially as we observed above that cultural transmission is subject to random mutation and diverse selection pressures, we should not leap to the conclusion that cultures will always and everywhere be compatible with genetic fitness (Boyd and Richerson 1985, 13–14).[24] Moreover, to the extent that one group imposes some cultural elements on another (P→C), it is only the fitness of the imposers which would be important (Durham 1991, 209).

Yet we should be equally surprised if genes do not exert some influence. While cultural diversity exists, casual observation suggests that differences are much less than would be expected if culture was completely unrestrained (Brown 1991, 148). Evolutionary psychologists have devoted much effort to debunking particular "tabula rasa" claims of ethnographers. Margaret Mead had claimed that adolescents in Samoa were untouched by sexual jealousy.[25] Others had suggested that there were no universal patterns for dividing the color spectrum linguistically. Malinowski had argued that the Oedipus complex did not exist everywhere. Further research has shown all to be wrong. As Brown (1991) has suggested, we cannot blindly subscribe to the credo that there is an exception to every cultural regularity.

One point often emphasized by evolutionary psychologists is that if there were not considerable similarity across cultures we would have much greater difficulty communicating cross-culturally. The very fact that we can "make sense" of another culture indicates that there is a fair degree of common ground. This is as true for scholars as travelers. Anthropologists can only do their research because in crucial ways the differences between them and the people they study are not very great (Brown 1991, 5). Tooby and Cosmides (1992, 91–93) refer to a genetically programmed metaculture that allows both scholars and infants to comprehend any particular culture.

The emphasis on unlimited cultural diversity leaves anthropologists with little ability to explain their observations. If anything is possible, then all cultures can appear to be the result of historical accident (Tooby and Cosmides 1992). If we were to attempt to explain the diversity in the world's stream beds without reference to fluid dynamics, we would achieve little; understanding culture without reference to genes is similarly difficult (Brown 1991, 147). Still, we must be open to the likelihood that genes restrict some aspects of culture more than others. Durham (1991) justly criticizes those who push for genetic explanations of all social behavior. Egalitarianism *may* be much less determined by genes than loyalty to family.

The major danger in analyzing any causal link is to confuse correlation with causation. If we have identified a universal then we must proceed to explain both how and why our genes would have caused this universal. (It is not enough to make some vague plea on behalf of a particular predisposition; one must also outline how selection would have occurred; Barkow 1989, 291–92). Since we all have fairly similar genes, we could otherwise all too easily attribute all cultural similarities to genes. Anthropologists, alternatively, had long presumed that cultural similarities were evidence of common cultural descent (thus, inevitably, some scholars looked for links between Egyptian pyramid-builders and Mayan pyramid-builders). Cross-cultural diffusion must always be viewed as a possibility (though even here genes could play a dominant role in the selection mechanism which causes various groups to choose the same cultural attribute). This is increasingly important in our modern world, where cross-cultural transmission is common. Economic or technological pressures which cause similar selection mechanisms across cultures could also be responsible for cultural similarities (E, T→C).

We must also be careful of semantics. Some anthropologists have claimed that "evidence" of universal cultural traits merely reflects definitional errors (Brown 1991, ch. 3). For example, if we define breathing—or even raising our eyebrows in surprise—as cultural, then it is all too easy to find cultural universals. This problem is largely solved by the logical structure of the organizing schema. Characteristics shared by all humans would correctly be viewed as genetic. We are looking here for likenesses, not identities (that everybody raises eyebrows in surprise is genetic—Hinde 1987, 108; the degree to which people try to mask the facial expressions of emotions is cultural—Brown 1991, 23–27). I have earlier defined the components of culture. There is still room for quibbling about the focus of attention: should we be more excited that everybody wears clothes or that groups wear different clothes? But once we move away from extreme positions and try to define the exact scope of genetic influence, it is clear that both results are important.

I. GENETIC DIFFERENCES → CULTURAL DIFFERENCES

It should be emphasized that the argument above—that our genes constrain the range of variability in culture—is quite distinct from the suggestion that genetic differences between ethnic groups might cause some of the observed differences in culture. Yet one argument does not necessarily preclude the other. The scholarly literature has less to say about this link than the popular. Cultural leaders commonly use ethnic and cultural identity interchangeably. While it is possible to ascribe such analysis to the effect of a common upbringing, one can often detect more than a hint of genetic predisposition in these pronouncements. Delisle (1993) has examined the case of French Canadian nationalism. While her work has been controversial, a couple of facts seem clear. Earlier writers, notably Lionel Groulx in the 1930s, were quite explicit in the connection drawn between "blood" and culture. One of his novels focuses on a French Canadian who realizes the error of his ways in marrying and "mixing blood" with an English-speaking woman. Redemption through "converting" her to French culture is not an option. Thankfully, more recent nationalist literature does not draw such a connection. Yet there is still a tension between those who advocate the assimilation of the non-French speaking population of

Quebec and those who fear that these can never be the same as the French Canadian "pure laine," the descendants of the pre-Conquest population. Similar connections between genes and culture can be discerned in most if not all debates about the cultural identity of a particular group.

Does it make sense to posit such a connection? I argued above that between-group genetic differences are likely very small, but not necessarily nonexistent. I have already discussed one small way in which environmental conditions could have affected genetic makeup ($N{\rightarrow}C1$). We can think of ways in which genetic differences could drive cultural differences: basketball may be unattractive to pygmies, for example, or proxemics be affected by the propensity to halitosis. Yet links to values are harder to imagine.

There are several reasons to suspect that such links are small at best. First, cultural traits are regularly transmitted across ethnic boundaries. Second, the very idea of ethnic purity is ludicrous. Human history is full of invasions and mass migrations; breeding across ethnic lines has been inevitable. This both limits the degree of genetic difference between groups, and indicates that people of diverse genetic backgrounds can cohabit culturally. Third, children from one group that are adopted by another appear to absorb culture as readily as indigenous adoptees. Notably, this is not true if the child is self-conscious of a "different" identity; a belief that genes determine culture can have a self-fulfilling character.

While all of these arguments are powerful, they all lack conviction in the absence of an alternative explanation of cultural diversity. As Tooby and Cosmides (1992, 9) note, denying the possibility that genes constrain culture globally ironically opens up the possibility that racial differences are greater than they are and that these cause cultural differences. Convincing arguments as to how common genetic traits lead to cultural diversity must render arguments from genetic differences less compelling.

2. GENES $\rightarrow$ CULTURAL IDENTITY

One way in which our genes encourage cultural diversity is that they guide us to identify with small groups. "Xenophobia, which divides people in fact, unites them notionally, because it is the common weakness of the human race" (Daniel 1978, 12). Hunter-gatherer groups were often in conflict with other groups. Internal cohesion was necessary both to fight these external enemies and to hunt animals in the absence of modern weaponry. Thus, both a capacity for culture and for ethnocentrism should have been selected for (Barkow 1989; he notes that capacity for culture would also have been selected for internally if the culturally adept were more successful at mating).

As Brown (1991) notes, all human groups are conscious that their group has unique patterns of doing and thinking, and that these patterns are passed from generation to generation. Woolfson defines cultural identity as "commonly shared attitudes, emotions, and ideas forming a psychological membrane that separates those within from those without" (1982, 393). Thus, the human tendency to aid kin is enhanced by a sense of cultural identity.[26] The word "culture" might have been coined by anthropologists, but groups were always aware of and proud of their differences. Moreover, they, like anthropologists, could recognize, at least subconsciously, that the various cultural constraints on individual behavior were necessary in order for their group to function in an orderly fashion (see Barber 1993; he argues in particular for the importance of trust for group cohesion).

Individuals were likely selected for more than just a propensity to identify with their group. There is evidence of a strong individual tendency toward conformity. Solomon Asch's experiments in the 1940s are justifiably famous. Subjects were asked to say which of a series of lines was the shortest. When in a group situation in which all other group members gave the wrong answer, a third of participants went along with this clear error (though note that two thirds went against the crowd). In matters on which independent assessment of the "right" decision is more difficult, there would likely be a much greater degree of conformity. This tendency logically follows from the fact that we are "programmed" to learn from others (see above). This would help groups develop common cultures; those groups that succeeded in developing a sense of identity would be most likely to survive.

Asch's experiments have since been duplicated in many countries, and there has always been a significant number of participants who have conformed. Yet there were substantial cross-cultural differences: groups that stressed individualism were less likely to display conformity. While some tendency to conform may be essential for group coherence, cultures can act to further enhance this tendency.

3. ADAPTABILITY → NECESSITY OF CULTURE

If genes are so important, why do we need culture at all? That is, why did natural selection not serve to hardwire all of the beliefs, attitudes, and customs that facilitate interpersonal cooperation? We have seen the answer above; the human brain was selected for adaptability to changing circumstances. Ironically, the fact that evolution has stressed the development of human flexibility has served to make humanity less aware of our inherent genetic predisposition (Crook 1980, 187). Yet it is the twin facts that humans need to cooperate and that these cooperative mechanisms could not be hardwired genetically that make culture necessary. Note also that if culture itself did not evolve much more rapidly than genes in response to changing circumstances, it would have no evolutionary advantage over hardwiring.

Of course, if culture changes too rapidly it ceases to serve its purpose in coordinating human activity. Many fear that, in our modern ever-changing world, culture is in too great a state of flux, and individuals thus find themselves in many situations in which they do not know how to behave. Yet even today culture still guides us in much of our daily activity. To serve us well, then, culture must be flexible enough to change, but not so flexible that it ceases to provide behavioral guidance.

Culture would also be unnecessary if we had the computational capacity to evaluate each situation we faced. Yet in the absence of some rules of thumb to guide us, the computing capability required to cope with complex personal interactions would be simply enormous. "Cultural norms are [in part] schemata that are invented to help overcome cognitive overload" (Harvey 1981, 36). How would our capacity for culture have been shaped by selection? We have seen that culture is not an indivisible whole. We appear to be programmed to learn a number of distinct cultural elements. Yet since every human event has some element of novelty we must be able to extrapolate our cultural knowledge beyond the particular circumstances in which it was acquired. Our brains must then strive to achieve consistency when conflicting cultural rules appear to apply to the same situation.

4. GENES → MODELS OF HUMAN INTERACTION

As we will see below, our genes constrain culture in a variety of ways. This raises the possibility that there is some genetic mechanism that does more than just allow extrapolation and strive for consistency. Culture must be learned, after all, and it is certainly possible that our genes make some cultural variants much easier to learn than others (Barkow 1989, 90). Perhaps there are some basic guidelines that have been hardwired and which provide a structure into which much of what we term culture must fit (recall our discussion of language acquisition above).

For example, all human societies are observed to bring order to their world in terms of dichotomies: good versus evil, in versus out, male versus female. Levi-Strauss and other "structuralists" argued that such dichotomies were based on inherent contradictions in the mind which had to be faced and conquered. Thus, the contradiction between life and death would commonly be overcome by a belief that death was a gateway to eternal life (Wilson 1998, 153–54). This hypothesis remains controversial.

Fiske (1991), following others (notably Polanyi), has suggested a set of guidelines that have a great deal of intuitive appeal. He proposes that there are four models of human interaction: communal sharing, authoritarian, equality-matching, and market.[27] Both cultural rules and individual behavior will reflect the application of all four models. Yet both cultures and individuals will differ in the range of situations for which they apply different models. Evidence of hardwiring of these models is found in studies of human development. Infants have no concept of ownership and thus apply the communal sharing model universally (though they do not immediately appreciate the need to work together and achieve consensus). Efforts to teach some other model fail miserably. At about the age of three, however, the authoritarian model comes to play a role; children recognize situations in which others can and should tell them what to do. A year later, equality matching (all people are equals; if given apples I should reciprocate with apples) emerges. Finally, by nine, market valuation is recognized as an alternative (but try telling a two-year-old of the market value of his teddy bear). Fiske also recognizes a null or asocial possibility; Jackendoff (1992) builds on this and posits "social hostility" (e.g., stealing) as a fifth model.

While these models seem most directly applicable to the realm of exchange, Fiske devotes much of his book to showing their applicability to attitudes toward work, ownership, inequality, decision-making, self-definition, ethical judgments, and interpretation of misfortune (see Chai and Swedlow 1998 for a similar analysis). Take goals for example: the communal sharing model suggests intimacy as a goal, the authoritarian model suggests power, and markets imply a focus on achievement and accumulation of money. Even our attitude toward time is shaped by these models: communal sharing implies a reliance on tradition and eternal relations (how else can the community always achieve consensus?), authority generally also requires a reverence for past decisions, equality means reciprocation as quickly as possible, and markets capture the passage of time in terms of rates of interest.

Different models can be applied to different situations. Even within models there is much flexibility. Authority relationships can be based on—and justified with reference to—birth or ability or luck. This flexibility, coupled with the fact that we are generally not conscious of these models even as we apply them, acts to obscure the role of this cognitive structure in culture formation.

How would these models constrain cultural evolution? Most clearly, they will affect transmission mechanisms. We cannot teach our children particular rules until they have matured enough to possess the relevant model. Fiske (1991, 400–407) raises the possibility that the cultural rules to which a child is exposed immediately after developing the relevant model may have a strong and lasting effect on the child's cultural outlook. We might also wonder if the child development process does not introduce some bias into model choice (e.g., infants are most impressionable and thus communal sharing rules are absorbed more strongly). Certainly, analyses of cultural change need to look at age-specific changes in transmission.

Compared to the "tabula rasa" hypothesis, the hardwiring of four models should decrease the likelihood of any group relying exclusively on one model. Still, Fiske hypothesizes that each society will have a preferred model which is most likely to be invoked in novel situations.[28] In terms of our previous analysis, we could speak of an inferential mechanism which allows extrapolation and consistency. Since life is full of novelty the dominant model could exert a powerful influence indeed. If we observe, say, communal sharing in one context, this increases the probability that we will observe communal sharing among that group in other contexts. We should not expect complete dominance, though. Casual empiricism suggests that even in our market oriented society there are still areas in which we invoke other models: communal sharing in the family (with more than a dash of authority), or equality before the law. We could stand to know much more about cross-cultural similarities in such choices.

The preference of a particular group will be reflected in its symbolism. An emphasis on communal sharing will be marked by a reverence for tradition. Authority will be denoted by symbols of rank. If we observe people exchanging exactly the same gifts, or matching labor stroke for stroke, then equality is likely the guiding model. Markets are symbolized by prices. These symbols will serve to reinforce the group's choice of a dominant model.

I should note that the four models are not equally responsive to change. Communal sharing, grounded in tradition, is very slow to evolve (those who break the rules, even inadvertently as in the case of rape victims, are often ejected from the community). The market model is extremely flexible, as changing technical and economic reality can instantly be reflected in individual behavior and community values. The degree of change in the surrounding environment will likely influence the choice of dominant model.

5. GENETIC MECHANISMS → CONSTRAINED CULTURAL VARIATION (E.G., HONESTY, AGGRESSION, INCEST, VENGEANCE)

Barkow (1989, 177) suggests that some cultural elements may have a very strong genetic basis (do not eat excrement) while others are entirely culturally determined. More generally, though, our genes provide us with a certain predisposition but culture significantly enhances or detracts from this.

We know that societies differ in their attitude toward honesty, though all societies seem to have some rules requiring honesty in at least some situations (especially when dealing with other members of the group). This observation alone provides some indication of a common genetic element. This we would reasonably expect, given the need of hunter-gatherers to cooperate. Frank (1988, 64) takes us a step further. He notes that honesty only serves individuals if it is generally reciprocated. Being honest in a dishonest society will lead to disaster for the individual. Yet what are the incentives toward honesty even in an honest society? Cheaters will prosper there, for nobody will expect cheating. As more and more people cheat, the cost of honesty will rise and even more people will be induced to cheat. Thus, Frank concludes, honesty could never be sustained as a cultural value in the long run if it was only culturally determined. The fact that we blush when we lie is further evidence of a genetic predisposition to honesty. (We discussed above the barriers to selection for a genetic predisposition toward honesty, and how these might have been overcome).

If the genetic urge to honesty were overwhelming, then we would hardly need cultural norms to support it. Yet we can easily imagine the disadvantage of hardwiring an honesty-only rule. We have all faced some circumstances in our life in which we thought dishonesty the best policy, not just for selfish reasons but to help others. Little white lies can be good. So also can the ability to obfuscate when others apply illegitimate force. In cases like this, the urge to honesty conflicts with other guiding principles. Culture, then, can be seen as providing us with necessary guidelines as to which principle takes precedence in particular situations. One question which remains is whether we reduce our tendency to blush in circumstances where our culture sanctions dishonesty.

Along these lines, Fiske (1991) discusses how our aggressive nature can be channeled by culture. A culture that stressed the communal sharing model (G→C4) would focus aggression outward in racism or even genocide. The authoritarian model would sanction the use of physical force by the powerful over the powerless. Adherence to the equality model would support revenge and retaliation. Finally, the market model would channel aggressive tendencies toward the economic realm: slavery and crime.

Incest taboos have been the focus of considerable debate. Some scholars have asked why we would need cultural taboos if there was a genetic predisposition that opposed incest. Others have pointed to the hundreds of thousands of cases of incest in the United States every year as evidence that such a predisposition could not exist (Trigg 1985). We can now see that such critiques miss the mark: genetic predispositions would not entirely determine such a result. Although incest has negative effects on genetic fitness in general, there are situations that arise in small groups where non-incestual mating options may be nonexistent. It is also worth asking how in practice an incest avoidance mechanism would operate. Wenegrat (1990, 101–3) suggests that the taboo operates through programming a lack of sexual attraction to those we grow up with: he suggests—and finds—that incest taboos are strongest in societies in which close relatives are not raised together. Of course, incest taboos are often extended beyond blood relatives; such extensions can be explained in terms of preventing concentration of power, limiting opportunities for extramarital affairs, or avoiding battles over inheritance.[29]

Frank argues that while culture tends to enhance the genetic tendency toward honesty, it restricts other tendencies such as vengeance (see also Hinde 1987, ch. 8). In a sense this is a misnomer: there is no default determination of which principles take precedence in particular situations. If we use universal primacy in application as our benchmark, culture acts to limit all genetic tendencies. Frank's (and my) values are creeping into his analysis here: we think of honesty as good and vengeance as bad. Yet it could well be that as societies have become more complex since hunter-gatherer days the benefits of honesty and the costs of vengeance have increased. Or, if our genetic programming guides us to treat close associates well and others with hostility, again culture should strive to extend our tendency toward honesty and restrict our urge to revenge, to aid us in coping with modern urban society.

I could extend the analysis here almost endlessly. Culture will act to determine which genetic tendencies dominate in particular circumstances. As Barkow, Cosmides, and Tooby (1992) have noted, it is the large number of genetic predispositions that provides for the existing variety in culture.

6. GENETIC DRIVES → CULTURAL GOALS AND MEANS

(Note the similarities to [5]). While adaptability is central to human genetic makeup, there are some elements of the human environment that were (are) stable enough that very strong genetic predispositions could come into place. Our body needs sugar, and thus humans everywhere have a taste for sweetness. Only very recently in human history have humans had to worry about ingesting too much sugar: note that our ability to adjust to change may be severely hampered if hunter-gatherers never faced the possibility of maladaptation. Even here, though, culture still has a role to play in shaping our goals (in what form we prefer our sugar) and the accepted means of achieving them (see Symons 1992, 138–39).

Barkow (1989) develops this idea at great length, positing a hierarchy of goals, subgoals, and plans. The lower in his hierarchy a subgoal is, the greater the cultural as opposed to genetic influence. Subgoals may serve more than one goal: we may value wealth both because it allows us to buy food and attract sexual partners. Multipurpose subgoals are the most likely to survive from generation to generation. Alternatively, cultural traits with little or no connection to genetic drives will be very susceptible to errors in transmission.

Cultural elements that do not seem at first glance to have much to do with genes may nevertheless serve an important fitness-enhancing role. Take gossip, for example. It appears that gossip of some form can be observed in all human societies. It is only natural that people would be interested in gossip about, say, sexual promiscuity concerning people that they or their families might interact with (Barkow 1992, 627).[30] Yet gossip can be harmful: it often spreads misinformation, and can serve to undercut the social cohesion of a group. Inevitably, then, groups develop guidelines on gossiping.

One of the most basic genetic drives is for food. Yet even among hunter-gatherer societies the environmental conditions under which food needed to be procured varied greatly. In environments in which individual food acquisition was characterized by high variance (some days one kills a large animal, other days one gets nothing) sharing would be beneficial. Yet sharing suffers from the same problem as honesty (G→C5); culture alone may not be able to discipline cheaters. Thus Tooby and Cosmides (1992) posit a genetic predisposition for sharing which is evoked culturally in some situations but not others (if any isolated human group had always lived in a no-variance environment, they would not have developed such a predisposition, of course). This predisposition should ideally possess certain rules: we are more willing to share high-variance food than low variance, we are more willing to give to the unfortunate than to the lazy. These elements do seem common to cultural sharing rules, and are thus further evidence of a genetic predisposition at work.

How are "selfish" desires turned into cooperation? Kagan's (see Frank 1988) studies of children suggest that while cultures try to instill a varied and complex set of social norms in their young, these efforts all rely on a basic human desire to avoid shame or guilt. Our genes, then, program us not just to want some things but to want to avoid others. It is these negative goals that provide the base for the inculcation of ethical sentiments. We inherently feel guilt—and show it—but culture determines what we feel guilty about (with much scope for individual differences). If this were not the case, we would not devote so much time and effort to teaching our children right and wrong (Frank 1988). I would note that some scholars would emphasize a distinction between societies that stress personal guilt and those which emphasize shaming one's family.

7. ORGANIZING SCHEMAS → CULTURAL COHERENCE

Barkow (1989, 177) speaks of a "mazeway" or series of cognitive maps (schemas) of the physical and social worlds and our place in them. We could think of the individual "choosing" which map to utilize in a particular situation. Since there is a limit to the number of maps that any brain can contain, similar maps (or parts thereof) are used in very different contexts. This is evidenced by the human predilection for metaphor. If we have programmed ourselves to catalogue an event in a certain way, then we will both process the information we take in and react accordingly (Jaspars and Hewstone 1986).

Since we will develop our cataloguing system by interacting with others, there will inevitably be considerable consistency in this system across individuals within a particular cultural group. Anthropologists have proffered many examples of such cultural metaphors: Firth in 1936 suggested that Tekopia concepts of the soul were a recreation of their social structure; Douglas in 1966 hypothesized that attitudes toward the body might parallel attitudes to society, and Barnett in 1969 followed up and found that groups that drew a large distinction between a safe village and a dangerous outer world also tended to be controlled and shameful in their attitude toward their bodies (see Hinde 1987, 147–49).

As Hinde notes, maintaining coherence among cognitive domains must become increasingly difficult as societies become more complex. Remember, though, that cultures are not unified wholes; there is still scope for a series of maps to be used so that some elements of culture are hardly connected to others at all. Still, any requirement for coherence among a number of elements raises questions about the ability of cultures to evolve smoothly over time. As Barkow (1989, 177) recognizes, if rapid change causes existing maps to be proven inaccurate, a mass cultural "conversion" or revolution in which many elements change simultaneously may be unleashed.

8. SEXUAL PREFERENCES → VALUE OF AMBITION, YOUTH, CHASTITY

Genetic fitness depends primarily on one's ability to reproduce and of one's heirs to reproduce. Thus, the most likely of hardwired genetic mechanisms are those concerned with our choice of mates. Such mechanisms inevitably affect gender relations, but also have diverse effects on culture. Not surprisingly, suggesting genetic determinants of gender-specific cultural behavior can be controversial. This is regrettable. I will take special pains in what follows to note how genetic tendencies can be counterbalanced as the society evolves. That is, while we should be cognizant of our genes, we should be equally aware of the scope for cultural diversity, especially as the environment becomes markedly different from that of hunter-gatherers.

Across species, the gender with the greatest reproductive potential competes for access to the other gender (Wenegrat 1990, 88–89). In most species physical aggression is the major form of competition. While this arguably still plays a significant role among humans[31] —women prefer men who possess physical strength and broad shoulders—other forms of competition are more important. Women should seek mates who are best able to provide for their young: thus males should be driven to compete on the basis of status, power, and wealth. Symons (1992, 153) argues that the only possible psychological explanation for the pursuit of status by men is that this would have enhanced reproductive potential in ancient times (he recognizes that status—and power and wealth—also serve to enhance one's own chances at survival; it is thus not "unnatural" that women might seek such goals). Hinde (1987, 165–67) concurs that it is generally observed that men compete for resources that enhance fitness, but recognizes that a variety of genetic processes could be at work. Women, even those of high status themselves, are observed to prefer decisive, self-assured, and ambitious men.

In modern Western societies, the link between achievement and fitness is weak at best. Men who could easily afford hundreds of children do not pursue this goal (a weak argument can be made that they are able to enhance child quality through education and so on, but again this does not appear to enhance reproduction in the next generation). Indeed there is only the slightest positive correlation between income and number of children. It is easy in such an environment to doubt the genetic basis for ambition. Remember, though, that our genes evolved in an environment with little or no access to birth control. Thus, genes were selected that enhanced male access to fertile females. This, money, status, and power likely still do. It is the connection between sex and reproduction, which did not require genetic hardwiring, that has been broken. The fact that men may not choose to use the fruits of their ambition for reproduction does not diminish the fact that they have been selected for ambition.

We might also note that modern Western societies are historically unusual in breaking the link between achievement and fitness. In polygamous societies, it is common for the most "successful" males to have many wives, while poor males have none. Even where polygamy is not sanctioned, having and impregnating mistresses is often acceptable behavior for elite males (as attested by the illegitimate children who populated European courts mere centuries ago). This may reflect some weak urge toward reproduction, or more simply the fact that with poor birth control sex translates into children. In either case, polygamy (or concubinage) may be a predictable cultural response to an environment in which wealth, power, and status are very unequally distributed (see Hinde 1987, 161–62).

Wright (1994) takes this argument a step further. He suspects that the choice of monogamy despite great inequality in society reflects a desire of powerful males not to alienate poor males (P→C). Note that Western market-oriented societies thus use a different one of Fiske's four models (the egalitarian) in deciding on acceptable marriage forms. While Westerners generally find the idea of polygamy distasteful, Wright suggests that women on average do better under such a system. Many might well be willing to trade their present role in order to be second or third wife to a high status male. Those who are presently sole mate of high status males will thus lose, but all other women would gain by access to better mates. Most men would in turn suffer from reduced access to desirable mates.

Perhaps our society has moved to an appreciable degree beyond the hierarchical ordering of mates at the heart of Wright's analysis. Wenegrat (1990) suggests that as women become more economically independent, they no longer need to align themselves with rich or powerful men to assure the support of their children. Some attraction may survive—few women earn so much that they can be oblivious to their spouse's earning potential—but male success need no longer dominate other considerations. To the extent that women are able to overcome a gene-based appreciation of ambition and/or success, men will find that ambition no longer even increases their access to sexual intercourse.

There are also pressures that affect men's genetic programming with respect to women. Men have no way of judging female fertility, and were thus likely selected for their appreciation of the physical and behavioral features associated with women of prime childbearing age (Buss 1992; Symons 1992, 143). However, preference for young (looking) women ceases to enhance fitness as women come to use only a small part of their childbearing years for that purpose, as plastic surgery makes age deception easier, and as women cease to be especially attracted to (richer, more powerful) older men. Still, the effects of the preference for youth can be subtle: male preference for large eyes and small noses likely reflects the fact that eyes shrink and noses expand with age (Wright 1994, 65). The preference for long legs may likewise reflect the fact that the ratio of leg length to total height peaks at puberty (Morris 1994). Studies with adult males also show strong cross-cultural preferences for certain facial types, with "masculine" features being widely disliked. Recently, it has been suggested that bodily, and especially facial, symmetry, which is preferred by both men and women, acts as a signal of genetic quality (studies show that symmetry is positively correlated with both health and intelligence; Morris 1994). Mates are apparently also judged by smell; some hypothesize that odor may signal the degree of genetic compatibility.[32]

Birth control technology acts to decrease male emphasis on female chastity (and genetic testing could overcome lingering male concerns over paternity). If so, one of the more subtle effects of evolution may become redundant: babies and small children have a much greater tendency to resemble their fathers than they display later in life. Selection for paternal resemblance would increase the probability that fathers would care for their young.

The double standard by which women are expected to be less sexually active than men is often ascribed a genetic base. It is certainly observed across a wide range of cultures. And we can see how women might compete for men on the basis of chastity if men are worried about the risk of supporting another man's child (as they would be selected to be; Buss 250). Note, though, that male jealousy would be selected for only if female infidelity was common enough to worry about (perhaps because women in a dangerous environment would be guided to have a backup mate or two, or might seek better genes for their children than those of their official mate) but not so common that supporting one's mate's offspring was misguided (Wright 1994). Males should not be hardwired to insist on virginity, therefore, and thus culture can influence the male definition of chastity.[33] On the other hand, women should also have some preference for chastity among men: this establishes that her man will support her family alone. This provides at least some antidote to the presumed male urge to have many partners. It also suggests that cultural opposition to male adultery—and to the male tendency to mislead women during seduction— would enhance the average quality of childrearing (Wright 1994). As well, as women come to play a larger role in child support, men's fears should diminish. Wenegrat (1990, 97–98) finds that in societies in which women control resources the double standard often virtually disappears (see also Buss 254). Finally, we should note that since chastity is largely unobservable the selection pressure in its favor may be much less strong than is often presumed (Buss 262).

The double standard illustrates the difficulty cultures can face in prescribing different behaviors for different people. Especially as gender equality emerges as an ideal, it is natural that cultural values lose their gender attachment. Ambitious women gain favor (among Zulus, where women do much of the work, Buss found that men value ambition in women more than the reverse; this was the only such case he found), and youth is applauded among men, even while these attributes lose their hold on the gender of origin. In such an environment, other qualities such as kindness and intelligence (which have always been valued by both genders—Buss 254) can come to play a larger role in the preferences of each gender and thus the behavior of the other.

Hinde (1987) notes that women competing on the basis of chastity have an incentive to emphasize its cultural importance. Likewise assertive men will exaggerate the value of assertiveness. Thus genetic tendencies are buttressed by cultural guidelines. Still, the losers will have an opposite incentive to mock these rules. And as the fitness advantage weakens, the cultural guidelines will likely follow.

A final note: we have discussed here only how men and women value each other as sexual objects. This does not preclude us from valuing each other in myriad other ways (see Wenegrat 1990, 6–7). Those who view genetic programming as a justification for traditional gender roles abuse the analysis. Yet those who ignore the role of genes limit our ability to understand (and change) human society.

9. RELIGION

Evolutionary psychologists have not devoted a vast amount of attention to religion. Brown (1991) recognizes that the human tendency both to be curious and to develop organizing schemas encourages the development of supernatural explanations of, for example, the vagaries of climate. Wenegrat (1990), drawing on his book on the subject, notes that since our mind has been selected for social interaction, it is only natural that we "personalize" our relationship with nature and develop the idea that some entity can both reward and punish us. Even atheists, when interviewed, display ambiguous feelings toward the supernatural; Wenegrat wonders if we are incapable of rationally evaluating religious questions.

One could make a deeper claim of an inherent need for religion. Humanity alone has a sense of its own mortality; religion may be a natural "side effect" of such a cognitive capability. To be self-conscious is to wonder about the scheme of things (Adams 1993, 1). Psychologists have long contemplated the ubiquity of religious belief: while Freud thought of religion as a fantasy which we must rise above, Jung viewed it as an aspect of a collective subconscious. It is certainly noteworthy that all major historical religions share a set of basic beliefs (Adams 176); we based our unpacking of religion on these. Adams feels that we are all driven to make our lives meaningful and worthy, and need some religious belief (broadly defined) to do so. Particular elements of religion may express other genetic drives; the ubiquity of demons in religion may reflect our need to assuage feelings of guilt (by blaming demons for temptation).

I should make special mention of how age affects religious belief. Young children are incapable of abstract reasoning and formal logic (they also only slowly come to appreciate mortality). They thus interpret religious stories either magically or literally (e.g., holy is a substance that flows from a man-like god). They may later translate these beliefs into a more appropriate abstract schema, or instead come to view religion as childish (Batson, Schoenrade, and Ventes 1993). Eric Ericson, the noted psychologist, posited that individuals go through eight stages in life, each characterized by an important question to be answered. The last four of these have religious overtones. While this typology seems a bit over-simplified —people cope with the meaning of life long before the eighth stage — it is suggestive of the fact that religious questions grow in importance as we age (at least to some point). This trend is far from even, however; many experience a crisis of identity in early adulthood which can serve to set the basic religious parameters for the rest of their lives.

Religions serve also to support various cultural values: they preach both love and control of our basic urges (C→C5). In these respects, we can see the operation of our genetic propensity to feelings of guilt, and more broadly the various genetic programs which allow us to overcome selfishness in the interests of cooperation. Note, though, that many religions emphasize brotherly love only toward others of the same faith; this serves to harness our desire for a sense of community/identity to the service of a particular religion.

10. LEARNING → FADS AND FASHION

Most elements of culture change only slowly due to imperfect transmission between generations. Yet others—such as taste in clothes—can change almost overnight. How is it possible that so many people can change their minds so quickly? The answer is to be found in the fact that we are programmed to learn by mimicking the behavior of others. Yet a simple appeal to such a mechanism would raise the concern that all of our cherished beliefs could be subject to sudden reversals: like lemmings we would follow the latest fashion in religious beliefs or interpersonal ethics. However, our programming is more complex than that: we imitate others when situations are novel or when being in tune with others is a predominant concern (as in ensuring one's clothes are fashionable). While imitation still plays a role in the development of, say, religious beliefs, these are justified by a series of learned arguments, and therefore will not change simply because we are exposed to people with different beliefs. Cognition places some limits on fashion too: we are aware that some clothes signal sexual availability or group membership, and only wear these if that is the message we wish to send. Within these constraints (which change over time as other elements of culture do), though, we have freedom to imitate.

How does a fashion trend get launched (or a fad like hula hoops or pogs)? It is too simple to blame the entrepreneurs who launch these crazes: they fail more often than they succeed, and would be thrilled if they could better separate the winners from the losers. The first people to adopt a new fashion or fad may do so for no particular reason (they may have flipped a coin on what outfit to buy) but once they have made their choice they become the best signal to others as to which way the wind is blowing. Their status can be very important in determining the size of the effect [S→C]. It is noteworthy that our propensity to imitate can dominate even when there are important qualitative differences in the choices we make. What movie should we watch? What drug should we take for a headache? One could pore over a host of critical reviews or medical studies. In all such matters, the individual consumer faces a choice between doing substantial market research on their own or simply doing what they observe others doing. This is why film companies care so much about how their film does in the first week; without word of mouth the best film becomes a loser.

11. TIME PREFERENCE → CULTURAL ATTITUDES TOWARD TIME

I have suggested that hunter-gatherers likely had a greater incentive to focus on the present than is optimal today. I can also recognize that, since their environment was not unchanging, some flexibility in programming is likely. Certainly, we can readily discern great differences in the attitude toward time across modern cultures. There is much speculation as to the environmental causes of these differences: did colder weather in northern Europe reward foresight more than in the Mediterranean [N→C]? If so, is it possible that there is some difference in genetic programming (remember, though, that there has been a lot of migration over the last millennia)?

Some would say that many modern Western societies are guilty of devoting too much time to introspection: What is the meaning of life? Where am I going? They suggest that the advantage of Eastern philosophy is that meditation is not focused on such potentially esteem-destroying questions (Crook 1980). If our lifestyle is conducive to a much greater degree of self-contemplation than in hunter-gatherer days (which is far from certain; many ethnographic studies suggest that hunter-gatherers have more leisure time than us), it could be that our mental mechanisms are poorly equipped for the strain.

12. GENES → VARIOUS CULTURAL "UNIVERSALS"

To this point I have developed our causal links primarily by thinking of genetic programming and asking what effects this would likely have on culture, followed by searching for the expected cultural commonality. There is another way of uncovering causal links. Taking the vast ethnographic record as a starting point we can first look for "universals" or cultural traits shared by all groups. We can then ask what sort of genetic tendencies would generate these (Brown 1991, 142). The mere existence of many universals is powerful evidence of genetic constraints on culture. We must, though, be careful to establish that a particular genetic tendency would have enhanced hunter-gatherer fitness (or possibly was a side effect of a fitness-enhancing mechanism; Brown 117), and that cultural diffusion is not a more plausible explanation. In this latter regard note that in our modern world we can increasingly expect diffusion-based universals; we should thus be very interested in historical descriptions of cultures when proffering a genetic explanation.

Can we still speak of a universal if there is one group that provides an exception? According to Brown (1991, 42–49), and Tooby and Cosmides (1992), the answer is yes. First we should not rule out the possibility of scholarly error. We have seen that for decades the focus of many anthropologists was on providing exceptions to any cultural rule; subsequent research has found many findings in this vein to have been erroneous. Second, we have seen that culture can work against genetic tendencies. Thus, if a particular characteristic is shared by the vast bulk of human groups, we would not be misguided in thinking that there might well be a genetic mechanism at work that is blocked or counteracted in some circumstances. If some cult were to collectively outlaw game-playing, and were successful in coercing their children to eschew games, would game-playing be any less a universal? By granting this point we of course make it impossible to disprove the existence of a universal. We have seen in chapter 2 that this is no barrier to scientific analysis.

Brown (1991, ch. 6) surveys the ethnographic literature and provides an extensive list of universals, which he nevertheless recognizes as incomplete. Some of these I have discussed before. Novel elements on his list (with my brief parenthetical commentary) include:

- the importance of nonverbal communication (our genes cause us to display our emotions in order to enhance communication)
- a sense of time: past, future, seasons, day versus night (a reflection of the world we live in; [N→C])
- fear of strangers in children of about one year old (in safe environments, this fitness-enhancing fear can ebb as the child matures)
- artisanship; a tendency to decorate items of utility [G→A]
- living in groups (some hermits aside, we are programmed to be social animals, though the type of group differs widely)
- territoriality (N→C, C→P6)
- marriage (human children require extensive parental support) (rising incomes may decrease the necessity for marriage (E→C))
- close family valued above others (a fitness-enhancing predisposition)
- existence of laws; willing to use physical force to enforce some rules (C→P)
- conflict, rules which attempt to deal with it (our programming for cooperation is flexible so that we can adapt to change)

- ethics, sense of right and wrong, personal responsibility (human need to cooperate, and thus cannot be entirely selfish)
- etiquette, greetings, rules of hospitality (to smooth in-group cooperation)
- feasts, celebrations (to enhance the sense of attachment to the group)
- modesty concerning sex, urination (concerns regarding reproduction, disease)
- attempts to interpret dreams
- concern about personal appearance (to attract mates; perhaps other motives)
- playing of games, especially by children (a key form of learning; also group identity)

Wilson (1998) adds to this list:

- bodily adornment; hair styling (related to concern with appearance)
- rules governing cleanliness, hygiene (concern with disease)
- cuisine, food taboos, mealtimes (in part serves cultural identity)
- funeral rites (concern with mortality)
- personal names
- puberty customs

Note that in most of these cases it is very easy to posit a genetic mechanism that would explain the observed universal. Modesty and game-playing are a bit trickier, though the former might be attributed to sexual jealousy and the latter to enhancing both learning and group cohesion. Since these universals appear to apply to cultures of the past as well as present we can rule out diffusion as an explanation. In one case—our sense of time—our physical environment may be a more important cause than our genes, but in other cases genetic tendencies must be at least the prime suspect.

13. GENES → STORIES

One leading anthropologist who went against the grain and searched for universals decades ago was Claude Levi-Strauss. His starting point was the accepted wisdom that every language is a variation on certain abstract principles. He then applied the same analysis to stories and rituals (and social structure). He examined stories from different groups and found that, though they appear quite different on the surface, in fact they had a similar structure and represented similar concepts (see Boon 1985).

C→G: CULTURE → GENES

Acquired characteristics cannot be passed on through genes. You may be proud of your skill as a salesperson or of your deep integrity, or even your success as a bodybuilder, but you cannot transmit these to your genes (of course, these acquired characteristics may be shaped by characteristics of the genes you inherited and will pass on). It has not always been recognized that this is the case. Indeed, the nineteenth-century evolutionary theorist Lamarck had argued quite the opposite, and some would point out that his case is not disproved.

We have seen that we are designed for flexibility. It would defeat the purpose of flexible programming if that which was learned in one generation became hardwired for the next. Moreover, we would hardly want negative acquired characteristics such as injuries to be passed on. Even if it were advantageous, it is not clear how genetic imprinting of acquired characteristics could occur. Our genes do not provide us with a blueprint of all of our potential behaviors so that a conscious decision to act in a certain way could be reflected in a simple adjustment in genetic structure. Rather, our genes provide us with a recipe; thus working out cannot instruct our genes to bequeath larger muscles to our offspring (Dawkins 1986, 292–300).

We may be only a generation or two from the day when we can design our genetic makeup, and could well begin to puzzle over the ethical implications of designer children (Szostak 2002). Direct genetic manipulations are not the only way that human activity can alter our genes, however. Any act that alters the selection environment will affect the frequency of genes within succeeding generations. Such changes must inevitably be slow. Boyd and Richerdson (1985) believe in relatively "fast" genetic transformation, feeling that cultural rules could become embodied in genes in as little as fifty generations (a thousand years); most scholars feel that the process would take several thousand years. Barkow, Cosmides, and Tooby (1992) argue that there are no psychological differences between modern hunter-gatherers and those whose ancestors turned to agriculture millennia ago. The debate may be academic, since no culture is stable for anywhere near a thousand years. Still, if we can identify certain long-standing characteristics of the human environment in historical times, it is possible that some changes in gene frequency will have occurred as a result. In other words (most of) humanity may have begun to adapt to the practice of settled agriculture or the existence of large civilizations.

Durham (1991) provides one such example. Those sub-Saharan groups that long ago turned from hunting-gathering to slash and burn agriculture, and thus reduced their exposure to malaria, are observed to have a much lower (but not nonexistent) incidence of the sickle cell gene (see N→C1 for another example, lactose tolerance).

It is also possible that if the French value "joie de vivre" and the Germans military formality, then fun-lovers may be able to have more children in the former society than the latter. Given the glacial pace of genetic evolution, any significant change in the gene pool would require that such cultural differences be maintained for centuries if not millennia. Cultural change and migration both work to limit the strength of such a link.

In the hunter-gatherer era, though, this link was likely quite strong. There undoubtedly was a feedback from the earliest elements of culture to our genes. Indeed, I argued above that infants are programmed to learn language; this could only have occurred after (along with) the development of language. Likewise our propensity to display emotions serves to aid cooperation and can be viewed as a feedback effect from culture (Wilson 1998, 158).

5

Individual Differences

Personality Types

Physical differences among humans — in height, weight, and appearance—affect various other phenomena (and differences in skin pigmentation will receive special attention in chapter 8), as do differences in mental ability or "intelligence." Yet the main focus here will be on psychological differences, and thus I must first develop a classification of human personality. I am aided greatly in this by the fact that personality psychologists have long worked on such a system. They have, however, not achieved consensus.

One common element in the typologies of personality theorists is a recognition that personality must be defined along continua. That is, it would be foolhardy to say that a person is either introverted or not. Rather, we differ by degree, and thus can think of an introversion-extroversion continuum on which we could try to place particular individuals. How many such continua can be identified, and how exactly can these be defined? Most personality researchers speak of five main personality dimensions. Some add a sixth. Eysenck (1990) has argued for three. Yet he would be the first to recognize that his typology bears strong similarities to other formulations. I start with his three continua—extroversion/introversion, emotional stability/neuroticism, and superego control/psychoticism—and see what adjustments others make. As he recognizes, the vast majority of scholars would accept the first two of these (often called "sociability" and "emotionality").

One leading version of the "big five" personality dimensions would substitute for Eysenck's third category the following three: conscientiousness/impulsiveness, reasonableness, and openness to experiment. Yet John (1990) slices the pie differently to arrive at these five categories: outgoing/shy, happy/moody, kind/selfish, active/lazy, and intellectual orientation. There are strong similarities here: conscientious and lazy could be viewed as opposing ends of similar continua, as could reasonable and selfish, and one could even see a connection between types of intelligence and openness to experiment. Still, we are some way from the precision of definition that scholars aspire to.

For our purposes, though, we have a good starting point. I will certainly accept Eysenck's first two categories: sociability (that is, extrovert/ introvert or outgoing/shy), and emotionality (stability versus moody). I can also embrace a personality dimension that captures conscientiousness. It also seems worthwhile to capture one's degree of selfishness/ agreeableness; this continuum is commonly referred to as "affection."

To move beyond this, it is useful to briefly examine where these personality dimensions come from. All scholars agree that in attempting to understand personality dimensions we should look at three elements of psychological functioning: cognition (how we think), motivation (or conation), and affectation (our feelings). Our personality must be determined by these three elementary mental functions. Note that these all reflect our basic genetic predispositions; I discussed in chapter 4 the various competing drives that could be subsumed under the heading of motivation, as well as evolutionary explanations for our cognitive powers and emotions. [G→I].[1]

The four dimensions I have accepted so far emphasize motivational and emotional elements. Greater attention to the cognitive aspect would thus be desirable. Miller (1991) notes that interest in cognitive styles was great in the 1970s, waned thereafter, and is apparently in a resurgence. He stresses a distinction between focusing on details versus seeing the big picture (and recognizes the advantage of a third cognitive style which is able to move freely from the one to the other as appropriate). He argues that this analytical/holistic distinction can be discussed in terms of all mental operations: perception, memory, thinking. Miller (1990)—who refers to personality types as "cognitive styles"—argues that additional distinctions can be made: speed versus accuracy, seeing similarities versus differences, being flexible versus routinized, and memory hazy versus sharp. Sternberg and Ruzgis (1994) suggest further distinctions: do we focus on one goal at a time, prioritize goals, or juggle diverse goals, and do we have an internal or external focus?

I thus accept intellectual orientation as a fifth category (with openness to experiment as a subset). I should stress that we are not dealing here with intellectual capability, but with how we prefer to think. The one naturally influences the other, but we need not wish to follow our strengths (as Miller [1990] recognizes, a problem arises if our goals are inconsistent with our abilities). For example, Eysenck posits that those with very high affect intensity will be very easily conditioned when young and are thus likely to become cognitively inflexible no matter how "smart" they are.

What of John's laziness dimension? Are there elements of this that have not been captured by "conscientiousness?" It would seem so. It is noteworthy in this regard that Miller (1991), following others, titled the sociability dimension "energy." My own casual empiricism suggests that some people are simply more energetic than others across all domains. And investigations of those suffering from severe depression suggest that differences in energy level are attributable to the levels of particular neurotransmitters in the brain. Should this be added as a further personality dimension, or does it more accurately reflect basic physiological forces? Relatively few scholars have worried about this concept. But my hunch is that it is both physiological and worthy of much greater attention.[2]

In sum I propose five personality dimensions: sociability, emotionality, conscientiousness, kindness/selfishness, and intellectual orientation. These join differences in physical appearance, physical and mental ability, and energy level as major individual difference phenomena. To these I will add sexual orientation below. We have seen in chapter 4 that we are programmed to develop schemas; individual differences in schema formation also deserve a place in our organizing schema. I will discuss below (I→I1,2) their relation to personality.

UNPACKING PERSONALITY DIMENSIONS

Consensus exists that the 3 to 5 key personality dimensions can be unpacked into a hierarchy of subtraits (Zuckerman 1991), and that different levels of aggregation are appropriate for different enquiries (John 1990). Eysenck recommends that below the level of key dimensions, we speak of a large number of traits, which in turn can be subdivided into habits (such as punctuality), and these in turn into individual thoughts. I will deal here mostly with the level of traits, though occasional reference will be made to habits (the correctness of disaggregating to the level of thoughts is debatable in any case). Once we recognize the value of unpacking, then the only difference between our typology and Eysenck's revolves around the question of whether some of our dimensions can usefully be combined in his superego control/psychoticism dimension. As this is an empirical question, it need not interfere with our explanation of causal links at the most appropriate level of disaggregation. Eysenck himself recognizes that Cattell's popular typology of 16 personality types is best understood at the trait level, and can easily be subsumed within his 3—or other's 5—dimensions.

In fact, unpacking is in a sense the wrong word, for scholars have long attempted to derive their typologies empirically: if strong correlations existed between a number of traits, these were gathered into a larger dimension. Only the observation that talkative people tend also to be assertive, outgoing, adventurous and enthusiastic (but not reserved, withdrawn, or shy) makes the extroversion dimension meaningful. Evidence that we can meaningfully speak of a handful of trait clusters has now been compiled in many different countries (Smith and Bond 1993). Yet trait correlations are not perfect; otherwise unpacking would be unnecessary. Note then that the "big five" personality dimensions are actually collections of related (trait-level) dimensions; the same can be said of traits.

Traits associated with emotional stability are contentment and composure, while instability is reflected in tenseness, anxiety, nervousness, moodiness, worry, and self-pity. Conscientiousness embraces thoroughness, foresight, organization, perseverance, and precision (but not carelessness or disorder or frivolity). Kindness/selfishness subsumes sympathy, affection, appreciation, and generosity versus fault-finding, quarrelsomeness, cruelty, and negativity. Intellectual orientation embodies such traits as imagination, originality, curiosity, and artistic sensitivity.

Still, some traits appear to fit more than one dimension (and John, among others, recognizes that the borders between dimensions are a bit fuzzy). Thus, some have suggested that new dimensions be added to deal with traits such as dominant/submissive, independent/dependent, or strong-willed/weak. Future research may allow these to be viewed as components of other personality dimensions.

What of our sense of humor? This is certainly one of our most important characteristics if one judges by personal ads. Miller (1990) feels that humor requires an ability to take a broad view, and know what is really important in life; also those who are altruistic tend to have a well-developed sense of humor. If he is right on both counts, humor reflects a combination of at least two of our dimensions: holistic thinking and selflessness. If this is true for humor, it is likely the case that other key aspects of human personality, including aggression and happiness, depend on more than one personality dimension.

Personality Integrity

It might be objected that the very act of unpacking individual personalities is somehow wrong: that we should appreciate people as a whole rather than as combinations of traits. I would recognize the danger of reducing those we interact with to a couple of readily observable traits, without wondering why they are angry or moody or devious. As scientists, though, we can hardly understand individuals without unpacking. Many scholars thus bemoan the absence of the person from personality theory, yet recognize the value of analyzing the effects of particular personality traits. After all, we are each unique, and thus examining behavior in terms of the whole individual would lead us nowhere. Still, a complete understanding of personality (and behavior) can only come as we understand how personality characteristics interact within the individual. There has been some statistical work on how particular outcomes like alcoholism are correlated with certain personality mixes; this needs to be buttressed by individual-level analysis (John 1990).

In ancient Greece, personality analysis focused on four body fluids, and posited that their relative strength in particular bodies determined stable personality types. We have advanced considerably since then, and not only in terms of deemphasizing the psychological role of phlegm. As seen above, we now recognize that particular traits are distributed (normally, it appears) along continua, and that traits combine to form personality dimensions. Thus, these dimensions and traits are not artificial categories; we need to understand both how they operate and how they interact.

One final distinction should be made. Some personality characteristics are very stable, while others can be changed relatively easily. Our analysis is made more complex by the fact that people vary in which are the flexible traits. In a sense, we all "choose" some self-defining characteristics, and will not change these in any but the most extreme circumstances. [I→I]

PERSONALITY DISORDERS

"I am a man. I consider nothing to be alien from me"; Apter (1992, xii) uses this quote (out of context) from the Roman writer Terence to illustrate his argument that we should not view psychological disorders (for the most part) as alien and incomprehensible phenomena. Some may indeed reflect severe mental "malfunction" (at least from our perspective)—or disease or demon. We can think of Alzheimer's disease here, or of the erratic behavior of those whose brains are injured in accidents. Most disorders, however, should be seen merely as extremes of personality attributes shared by us all. Over the years this point of view has been reflected in the American Psychiatric Association's (APA) directory of mental illness. Reacting in part to accusations that previous definitions of particular illnesses were merely ad hoc compilations of symptoms (a complaint which our discussion of definitions in chapter 1 would do much to counter), the Association's 1980 manual tried to relate disorders to personality attributes. The feeling was that disorders represented a failure of personality to cope with the environment in which the individual lived. More recent revisions to the manual have returned to an atheoretical basis: disorders are defined in terms of clusters of symptoms which practitioners observe to occur together.

Yet both therapists and academic psychologists would like to be able to move beyond discussions of symptom clusters to the causes of mental disorder. Most practicing therapists are eclectic: while they may have a favorite theory they are willing to try others if their favorite does not work.[3] They are even flexible in their use of the APA's manual of disorders: some patients fit poorly into any of those categories and are thus dealt with in terms of individual symptoms (some therapists prefer to focus only at this level, though for most it leaves an unmanageably large set of possibilities to deal with).

One can distinguish the intensity of disorders in terms of how frequently they induce maladaptive behavior, how severe these episodes are, and whether they need be triggered by external stimuli. Therapists use the word "syndrome" to refer to irregular bouts of extreme behavior. It is now widely accepted that syndromes result from disorders: these cause the individual to face constant stress while also making them vulnerable to additional symptom formation. As the stress builds beyond some point, explosions occur. Yet not all who are diagnosed with disorders go this extra step into abnormal behavior. If our hypothesis that disorder reflects extremes of personality is correct, then the degree of personality extremism is likely correlated with susceptibility to syndromes. Milder cases of disorder have often been labeled "neurotic," though this term (and "psychotic") has fallen into disfavor in some circles. Mild cases present special therapeutic difficulties, for the patient will generally try to ignore the problem by repressing the cause of the disorder. They will thus find their behavior not entirely satisfactory, and will feel guilty about their failures (Johnson 1994).

Many have attempted to integrate the APA's categorization of disorders with some classification system of personality characteristics. One of the more comprehensive of such efforts is that of Miller (1991). One advantage of his approach is that previous scholars had tended to ignore the Intellectual Orientation dimension. Miller suggests that those who are too analytic will tend to be "obsessive" since they can see only details. Alternatively, those who tend to the holistic extreme will be prone to "hysteria": they overreact to events and others' opinions, their memories are fused, and details are lost. Most personality disorders likely reflect unfortunate combinations of extremes along more than one dimension. Those who combine emotional instability with a holistic orientation may become "histrionic" or "narcissistic/antisocial." Emotionally stable individuals may lean toward "dependence" if holistic in orientation or toward "avoidance" if analytical (note that Miller's preferred personality typology differs from my own; I have adjusted his analysis here).

Miller is not able to define all of the APA's major disorders in terms of personality dimensions. He shares with many others a concern that their "borderline" category may be just that: an interval of low-level disruption with respect to many disorders (associated with high levels of emotional instability),[4] rather than a disorder in its own right. "Passive-aggressive" and "schizoid/schizotypal" are the other major disorders which he has difficulty explaining, though the former does seem associated with emotional instability and the latter with emotional stability. These disorders may reflect a severe brain malfunction with genetic roots.

We will not go into great detail in describing the various mental illnesses here. Pervin, 1990, provides precise definitions of the characteristics of all APA disorders; or one can refer to the APA manual itself. I will at times in what follows make reference to particular disorders (notably schizophrenia and others that are hard to reduce to personality categories), and provide necessary detail at that time. For the most part, though, I will accept that disorders reflect personality extremes, and focus on understanding the links between our personality dimensions and other phenomena.

A final point: it should be clear that the decision as to exactly where along a personality dimension(s) we start to speak of disorder is arbitrary (this is true even if we try to define the breakpoint statistically). It is influenced by culture to a large degree (C→I3). Behavior that earns one esteem as a shaman in one society may have one locked up in another. Societies differ both in their definition of what is normal, and how much eccentricity they are willing to countenance. Remember that the APA defines disorders as failure to cope with the environment. Hostile cultural environments will thus tend to induce more disorders. Further, if, as some suspect, one symptom encourages others, suffering rejection in terms of one personality dimension may drive the person to unacceptable behavior in terms of others. Finally, it is not just culture that determines the break point: individual variables such as our own self-esteem and the rapacity of our therapist will influence particular diagnoses.

MEASURING PERSONALITY

There are two concerns here. First, how accurately can we identify the true hierarchy of personality dimensions? Miller (1991) recognizes that the statistical analysis of correlations among traits has not solved this problem, though it may narrow the range of possibilities over time. Despite this, as we have seen, there has been a considerable degree of convergence in scholarly views of personality dimensions (and much convergence also on traits and habits lower in the hierarchy). In a post-positivist world, this is all we can hope for. Is there a danger that we have missed important characteristics? Here especially we can rely on the fact that all personality traits should have been noticed by some human observer over the years. Since personality theorists start from traits identified in common parlance, we can be reasonably confident of completeness.

The second concern must be with how well we can rank people within a particular personality typology. The MMPI (Minnesota Multiphasic Personality Inventory) personality survey allows individuals to be scored on literally hundreds of scales, depending on the analysts' typological preferences. Yet debate rages as to how reliable scores within these scales are. No one questionnaire can plumb all areas of the psyche (the Myers-Briggs questionnaire is often criticized for ignoring emotions). And people may purposely or otherwise give misleading answers. Most analysts place a greater confidence in more open-ended sorts of inquiry such as the Thematic Apperception test (people are shown pictures, and asked to tell a story) Rorschach ink blots, interviews, and extended observations. None of these methods is perfect, needless to say, and once again our best chance of accuracy lies with methodological flexibility.[5] It should be emphasized, though, that use of these formal measurements provides much better predictions of behavior than the casual judgments of experts. Further consensus on what we should actually be trying to measure can only act to improve our ability to measure it.

I→*: Personality and Behavior

Early in this century, when behaviorism was the dominant methodology in psychology departments, it was argued that psychologists should only focus on observable behavior. Thus, since personality could only be inferred from observable behavior, it should be ignored. This false positivism has been overcome in the postwar era (Miller 1991). It is now recognized that our understanding will be limited indeed unless we attempt to comprehend the internal working of the mind. While we cannot see how a person thinks, we can observe what they say, how they act, how they seem to think, their moods, their apparent self-image, and their memories, among other signs. And advances in neurological research allow us to see how brain activity is correlated with behavior.

What is the relationship between personality and behavior? Personality theorists naturally focus on differences across people in orientation and responses to particular situations. Social psychologists, alternatively, focus on how the same people behave differently in different situations.[6] Common sense—and, increasingly, scholarly consensus (Zuckerman 1991)—dictates that we combine these two perspectives and recognize that personality and situation interact in determining behavior (Higgins 1990). Due to this interaction, it is foolhardy to try to quantify the importance of each, or expect to be able to predict behavior flawlessly.[7]

Sampson (1993, 181) speaks of a small girl who behaves aggressively with other girls but passively with boys, and wonders it if makes sense to speak of personality at all. But we can easily conceive of this girl as being less aggressive than another girl who beats up boys and more aggressive than one who is passive among girls. Then we can proceed to analyze how and why these basic predispositions are influenced by (perceptions of) the situation, in this case the gender of those we interact with. We can then strive to categorize situations in terms of their tendency to bring out certain dispositions (in some people at least; Higgins 1990).

This leads us to understand personality as a process. People begin with certain genetic predispositions. As we interact with our environment we learn what "works." This feeds back into both our basic personality and our evaluation of particular situations. Note that this feedback need not require any rational calculation of goals or means, but simply a sub-conscious tendency to repeat behaviors for which we have previously been rewarded (Elster 1989). We are likely to choose a lifestyle that puts us in situations in which we can "be ourselves" (this causes difficulties for researchers trying to untangle whether observations of differences in be-havior are due to personalities or the situations people tend to face).

Since we are limited in our ability to choose the situations we must face, we will also try to adjust our personality (which involves both the goals we aim for, and the means to achieve them). It is relatively easy for us to alter lower-level situation-specific rules of conduct (I like to push people around, but will not if the other guy is bigger). We can thus react to unpromising situations without having to alter our basic higher-level ori-entation on which our self-image rests. For the personality researcher, this means that for each individual some traits will be very stable over time, while those judged less central will be adjusted with experience.

Some situations are both unavoidable and of great importance to our existence. In such cases, changes to our most basic dispositions may be necessary [*→I] This is certainly the case in early childhood, when the attitude of our caregivers toward our basic needs can have an enormous influence on our personality. We likely think here first of negative conse-quences: people becoming angry or depressed in response to miserable lives. There is evidence of more beneficial effects, though. How many of us, when thrust into roles where we doubted our competence, have then succeeded and adjusted our self-image accordingly?

As with cultures, the greatest differences between people may well not be different views on acceptable behavior in a global sense, but rather in which situations they think particular behaviors are appropriate. Almost all of us will condone violence in some circumstances (e.g., self-defense), but differ greatly on where to draw the line. In any given situation, a number of different goals will likely be in competition (making it even harder to infer personality from behavior). How do we decide what sort of situation we are facing so that we will know which if any personality attributes to suppress? This is the role of the organizing schemas discussed in chapter 4. In evaluating an individual's reaction to a particular situation, we must be concerned with their previous exposure to similar situations, and thus their ability to identify, interpret, and react to it (Higgins 1990). If we try to include people's schemas in our attempts to predict their behavior, we must also worry about how confident they are of the schema: how much information it is based on, how they learned it, and how important it is to their self-esteem (Ajzen 1988, ch. 4).

There are thus many more ways to change behavior than the stimuli-response conditioning favored by behaviorists (or the classical conditioning of physiological responses pioneered by Pavlov). We can try to change schemas through learning. We can try to reward existing behavior, so that people will expand the range of situations in which they act that way. We can pursue habituation, recognizing that people's fears generally decrease with exposure to fear-inducing situations. Practice and imitation are other possible sources of behavioral change (Konner 1982, 382).

Kuhn (1974) models what he terms the "human behavioral system." He speaks of three key mechanisms: the detector which gathers relevant information, the selector which chooses the best action, and the effector which performs that action (we could conceive of these as necessary stages). These each have three parts, devoted in turn to detection, selection (e.g., what information to gather), and effectuation. Kuhn recognizes that each mechanism reflects a mixture of genetic elements and what we would term schema formation (and also a mixture of conscious and subconscious). Kuhn notes several of the difficulties we face in decisionmaking. While we try at each stage to estimate the (subjective) costs and benefits, we cannot know in advance whether the benefits of obtaining particular information will outweigh the cost of gathering it. We will avoid information that threatens existing schemas (I→I 1). In evaluating options, we must cope with both conflict between goals and the multiple effects which any action will likely have. If a decision is divisible (e.g., how much do we do?), we need to estimate the marginal cost and benefit of each increment in activity. Since our understanding of any situation will be incomplete, we must attempt the best combination of rational calculation and intuition. If our behavior seems inconsistent with our personality, it may be because we have incorrectly evaluated a situation.

As Kuhn recognized, culture also influences behavior. Jurgen Habermas has suggested that we engage in four different types of behavior: strategic, instrumental (following rules), communicative, and symbolic (these can be mixed in practice). We should expect that personality will have the greatest influence on the first (choosing goals and how to achieve them) and third of these. Culture looms large in the second and fourth especially, though mediated by an individual's tendency to follow cultural norms. A similar result comes from Tajfel's conjecture that all behavior can be placed on a continuum from interperson to intergroup; the former is guided by individual characteristics and the latter by group membership. Personality will also affect our propensity to pursue different types of behavior: Kontopolous (1993) emphasizes that strategic behavior is inherently antagonistic while communication is cooperative. [C→*]

One final clarification is in order. As we saw before, individuals embody a number of competing mental mechanisms. When I speak of an individual's personality, I am discussing, among other things, their likelihood of choosing one goal over another. The reader must avoid slipping into the mindset of viewing us as having one master program. For researchers, of course, this fact makes their task more difficult, for slight changes in situations may cause people to bring quite different mental mechanisms to the fore.

I→I: INDIVIDUAL DIFFERENCES → INDIVIDUAL DIFFERENCES

1. ORGANIZING SCHEMAS

Psychologists in explaining behavior tend to focus on how particular stimuli interact with an individual's needs. Yet as phenomenology and Gestalt theory have long suggested, we need also to understand the schemas that individuals use to guide behavior (Kelly 1991). To some extent, this was done under a different name, for when therapy delves into a person's past it exposes how that person conceives of the world and may even encourage a desirable readjustment in schemas. Still, it is fair to say that schemas deserve greater attention.

We can conceive of three broad types of schemas. The most obvious, "guides to behavior," are our understandings of causal relationships: these range from our comprehension of natural forces like gravity and heat to our perception of how strangers will respond to various actions. We also have schemas about other people. These are arranged in hierarchies, so that we will have schemas (stereotypes) about groups of people, and sub-schemas about subgroups and individuals. Finally, we have schemas concerning ourselves: our abilities and characteristics, and the attitudes of others toward us.

We should not underestimate the difficulty we face in revising schemas that we may have learned as a child. We may, first of all, simply repress stimuli which suggest that a schema is mistaken. If we have decided that members of a certain group are stupid, we can ignore evidence to the contrary.[8] Or, we can develop subsidiary schemas which explain away any anomaly (that smart guy is not really a member of that group). Our schemas also guide us as to how to interpret situations. We may thus never admit to ourselves that we have come across conflicting information. It is a common human failing to attribute "bad" events to some external factor while crediting "good" events to our own actions. People with overly lofty views of themselves or overly negative views of others need never sense a challenge to these schemas (one symptom of this may be an urge to gamble, and feel that only bad luck prevents you from winning). We can also avoid situations in which we might gain contradictory information (it is easier to remain disdainful of others if we refuse to interact with them). People who wish to enhance their sense of understanding have two strategies: they can either restrict their experience and understand a few situations well, or expand their horizons and revise their system of schemas to deal with diverse situations (Kelly 1991). However, if placed in a situation that threatens existing schemas, we can act in such a way as to reinforce our schemas (ask questions designed to make people look stupid). We need not be aware that we are doing this: in a situation in which we expect conflict we will be anxious or belligerent to an extent that encourages hostility from others.

Such defense mechanisms do have their advantages (otherwise we would wonder why they were not selected out). Reevaluating all of our schemas in the face of each new piece of information would cripple our ability to cope with the world. We do not have the computational capability. Moreover, it is often best to keep a schema even when conflicting information is received. Your self-confidence should not be shattered simply because you do poorly in a particular test or job interview. Your belief that the world has meaning should not be shattered because a loved one dies. People differ greatly, though, in their ability to separate particular experiences from their general outlook, and this ability seems to be associated with their tendency to anxiety, depression, and self-esteem.

As with genetic predispositions, we need to develop some ordering of schemas—or perhaps a superschema—to guide us in situations in which different schemas suggest different behavior (this may still allow considerable inconsistency between particular schemas). If our schemas are somehow integrated into an overall world view, then it will be especially difficult to change any (important) schema, for we will risk bringing the whole edifice down. While psychologists have often explained this result in terms of a need to protect our image of self (I am what I believe), Kelly (1991) emphasizes the fact that we need some structure to guide behavior. People have good reason to fear the destruction of their world view. Much of the trauma associated with major life changes likely reflects the need to develop new behavioral guidelines (and not knowing how people will react). Thus, even faced with fairly clear evidence that existing schemas and behavior are disadvantageous, a person may cling to them: they at least then "know" how to behave, and can predict the results from past experience.

How is schema formation related to our major personality dimensions? The most obvious links are with Intellectual Orientation. Those who are able to maintain a looseness within their superschema will be those who are open to experiment, curious and imaginative. Links to other dimensions also exist. Indeed, all of these behavioral proclivities must depend to a great extent on what our schemas tell us "works." If my schemas tell me that perseverance or kindness or composure is rewarded in most circumstances, I am likely to try to behave in those ways. And Miller (1990) argues that personality types are reflections of our self-schemas: one who feels they are poor at socializing will not be an extrovert; one who views others as malevolent will be naturally selfish. L'Abate (1994) feels we cannot conceive of personality without some reference to our view of self.

Personality disorders can also be related to schemas. Compulsive personalities are those where the structure of schemas is very limited: individuals thus do not know how to behave outside a very narrow set of behaviors (Kelly 1991). Epstein (1990) suggests that we each have four key schemas concerned with whether the world is benign or malevolent, life is just or not, others are good or bad, and we ourselves are worthy. Extremes in any of these could be associated with disorder: paranoia, for example, is defined as an exaggerated fear that others are a threat. Since schemas are often subconscious, many disorders may reflect misguided schemas we developed as children (Wenegrat 1990, 106); this is a key way in which dysfunctional family settings can interfere with success as an adult.

We have in the preceding paragraphs noted correlations. One could conclude from these that the schemas we develop—influenced by both genes and environment—play a large role in determining our personality. Perhaps personality is merely the sum total of schemas. Or maybe personality—at least those characteristics established early in life—shapes our schemas to fit. If either conjecture is entirely correct, then I have an unnecessary duplication of phenomena in my organizing schema. Certainly at our present stage of understanding, we could not do without either schemas or personality dimensions. Moreover our proclivity to do things our schemas tell us is bad for us suggests that one does not entirely determine the other.

2. PERSONAL IDENTITY → VARIOUS DIFFERENCES

While our view of our self has at times been viewed by scholars as an attitude or even a personality dimension, it is currently viewed as one of the key schemas (Linville and Carlston 1994). While behaviorist psychology had paid little attention to the concept, psychologists have in recent decades returned to the nineteenth-century concern with the role of our self-image in our personality. The emerging field of social cognition in social psychology starts from the premise that we construct our view of self in much the same way as our other schemas; indeed it is now recognized that our view of self comprises a number of separable self-concepts, with us relying on different ones in different situations. It may thus be misleading to refer to a person as "self-confident"; more likely what one is describing is a person who sees him or herself as competent in a wider range of (observed) situations than others. Note that our view of our competence may differ from our view of how others see us.[9] Also, not all of our self-image is conscious. We may think we are optimistic, while certain subconscious schemas cause us to be pessimists in practice.

How stable is our self-image? Particular schemas may be fairly flexible. You may think that you would be a pitiful public speaker, but if forced to speak a number of times will likely upgrade your self-image on this score. Many—scholars and others—have remarked over time that exposure to certain tasks is the best way of changing one's self-view. And cross-schema spillovers are likely as well. Success at public speaking may raise one's view of self in other contexts. Managing well in any one position of responsibility may induce one to confidence on a wide scale (especially perhaps in novel situations for which one has no well-defined schema). More generally, spending most of your time in situations in which you do well is likely to increase self-esteem. Comments of others will also have an effect, though scholars debate how great this is and how it might vary across personality types.

People differ in the number of separate schemas that comprise their self-image (we can easily conceive of a number of elements: worth, goodness, health, appearance, skill, social competence). There is likely an advantage to complexity here. While some spillovers will occur, possessing a wide range of context specific schemas limits the potential for one's entire self-image to rise and fall dramatically with the inevitable ups and downs of life. It may also be best to have a balanced view of self across many contexts; otherwise one will be buffeted by radical changes in self-image as context changes. Perhaps most important is the advantage of reasonably accurate self-schemas to avoid disappointment (Linville and Carlston 1994), although some scholars suspect that a slight exaggerated optimism may be beneficial.

Miller (1990) recognizes that a sense of identity is a basic human need. If so, then it would seem likely that people would try to differentiate themselves from others. There are many ways of doing so. We may dress differently or wear unusual jewelery. We may assert a desire for anchovies on pizza to the dismay of our friends. We will be deeply attached to such habits, and greatly exaggerate their importance. Note that by definition we can only differentiate ourselves relative to our reference group: as Simone Weil has remarked, we can only achieve self-actualization as part of a living community (even hermits assert their individuality relative to the group they left). Since we also wish a sense of group identity (G→C2), we will differentiate ourselves within limits.

Most people will wish to assert their individuality in matters more weighty than food and clothing (but if you have ever been frustrated by how long it takes some to decide on pizza toppings, take solace in the fact that you are observing self-actualization at work). This provides us with an answer to a question raised by Fraser and Gaskell (1990): why do people waste time forming opinions on major issues of the day when they are unlikely to have a major impact on those decisions? The answer reflects both our desire to belong and to be different (and to understand): "Views on such matters are taken because they help make sense of the world. Equally, holding and expressing views on contemporary issues of moment is more or less a requirement of civil social discourse. Furthermore, such views may fulfill an expressive function giving the holder rights to some self-defining characteristics" (1990, 12).

If all this is possible, can we doubt that individuals may purposely strive to be selfless or disorganized for no greater reason than to assert their individuality?

3. PURPOSIVE ATTEMPTS TO SHAPE BEHAVIOR

Within a chapter that focuses on the genetic and environmental causes of personality, it is of crucial importance that I emphasize that we as individuals can purposively work to change our personalities. We are, after all, endowed with cognitive powers that allow us to grapple with complex questions such as "why did I just do that?" While we can never answer that question precisely, we can always know part of our motivation. And we can ask ourselves what our goals are, and whether our present behavior pattern seems likely to achieve those goals. We may accomplish most in this regard on a day to day basis by focusing on subgoals (passing that exam, getting that promotion, buying that stereo), but must make sure that we look from time to time at the big picture—or our life can become nothing more than a stumble from one consumer durable purchase to the next. We should strive for flexibility in subgoals; there may be many paths to happiness. And we need to strive for self-verification: it is too easy to delude ourselves that we are following the best path. At the same time, though, we have to avoid being so introspective that we become completely indecisive (see Cantor and Zerkel 1990).

Various cultural values affect this process in two ways. Most obviously they have an enormous effect on the goals we choose. Second, they will shape our attitudes toward time and self and thus our very willingness to gaze inwardly [C→I].

C→I: CULTURE → INDIVIDUAL DIFFERENCES

Cultures, we have seen, evolve through the interaction of their members. Despite this, anthropologists and sociologists have devoted very little attention to cultural effects on individuals. In general, human scientists have devoted much more attention to the effects on individuals of economic and political circumstances (Gross and Rayser 1985). Still, social psychologists in particular have illuminated several important cultural influences on the individual.

I should first emphasize that cultures do not entirely determine individual behavior (though both Cavalli-Sforza 1981, and Boyd and Richerson 1985, imply otherwise). As we have seen, cultural change only occurs as one or more members of a group "decide" to turn away from (or amplify the importance of) particular values or customs. Inevitably, then, not all individuals within a group will accept all cultural elements (Woods 1978). Indeed, individuals are never perfectly socialized, and thus deviance is the norm rather than the exception (Namenwirth and Weber 1987, 12). Just as importantly, however, we cannot sensibly speak of a person choosing their goals (or the means to achieve them) without reference to some group (Tamir 1993; Layton 1991). The most common form of within-group differences occurs when individuals put different emphases on particular cultural attributes. Barkow (1989, 176) suggests that people select from the set of cultural goals and plans at a disaggregated—situation-specific— level; the resulting mix defines their personality. At times, though, individuals may consciously find some of their groups' values unappealing or even repugnant.

Burk (1991) looks at the C→I link in terms of the ability and willingness of an individual to behave in accordance with a society's values. The "best" case is where the person accepts social values but only after critically evaluating these. If they merely follow societal values without much thought, they may be unable to resist temptation. Those who follow their conscience may also give in to temptation occasionally; this is less likely if they fear social sanction. In Burk's "best case," social and personal pressures work in harness. Burk worries that a society without clear values will encourage a lack of individual self-control.

I. RELIGION → MENTAL HEALTH

The literature on the psychological effects of religion tends, unfortunately, to focus on a vague concept of mental health, rather than on more specific personality dimensions. We can hardly be surprised that it generates mixed results. Batson, Schoenrade, and Ventes (1993) suggest that religion has diverse effects on personality, and it is best to examine these separately (I, naturally, applaud this initiative).

The major "positive" effects of religion, they say, reflect the facts that religious people are more likely to display appropriate behavior, and are thus much less likely to be considered mentally ill. In other words, religious people, by internalizing key values of their society (they are, for example, at least in the United States, less likely to engage in premarital sex), naturally find themselves facing less conflict. While these authors do not discuss it, one would wonder to what extent a similar positive effect could be observed among religious minorities, if that minority's values differed significantly from the wider society [S→I]. It is noteworthy in this regard that clergy, who are often expected to behave quite differently from others, do experience a greater propensity to mental illness. And Wenegrat (1990) worries about those who reject the beliefs of their group's religion. These are often afflicted with feelings of guilt as a result. Moreover, Wenegrat feels that therapists often fulfill the important function previously played by priests in suggesting appropriate behavior patterns to individuals.

Batson, Schoenrade, and Ventes (1993) suggest that religion has an ambiguous effect on an individual's anxiety level. The elderly appear to benefit from a reduced fear of death, but empirical studies show no significant effect among the wider population (despite the potential benefits which might accrue from a reduced interest in worldly goods or sex). Batson et al suggest that the positive effects of religion are counterbalanced by negative effects on self-actualization, personal competence, and openmindedness. These effects are especially likely if one views god(s) as vindictive, and follows religious rules only out of fear. They note in particular that if an individual comes to depend on a set of narrowly defined religious beliefs, and these are challenged by events, the individual will resort to whatever mental gymnastics are necessary to avoid renouncing their beliefs (even those who predict the end of the world tend to adjust only the date when faced with predictive failure).[10]

Many scholars (e.g., Trigg 1985) would fault these authors for emphasizing the role of religion in encouraging social cohesion. They would argue that the main role of religion is in giving meaning to life. People must, it is said, believe that life in general is worthwhile in order to believe that their own life is worth living; lack of belief invites doubt or despair (Adams 1993). Carl Jung ascribed mental disorder to a failure to achieve spiritual growth. Lasch (1991) concurs that the value of religion is not to be found in its ethical code but in the fact that it makes life worth living. And one can find empirical support for the argument that religion has a positive effect on both self-esteem and life satisfaction. It is noteworthy in this regard that suicide rates are much lower among the very religious (though this may reflect concerns about entry into the afterlife rather than contentment with this life).

Batson, Schoenrade, and Ventes (1993) feel that it is important to distinguish between types of religion here. They recognize that humans have a natural desire to put meaning in their lives. This can be done by adhering to a religion that provides fixed answers to our most important questions. Or, we can view religion as a quest in which we hope that there are answers but recognize that these may be unattainable. They advocate the pursuit of the second strategy, for it allows one to put some meaning in life without feeling constrained by a variety of religious rules. Others would argue that they exaggerate both the satisfaction that the average person gains from individual religious exploration and the constraints imposed by organized religion.

Thomas Carlyle once remarked, "It is well said, in every sense, that a man's religion is the chief fact with regard to him" (in Park 1994). What can be said about religion's effect on particular personality attributes? Very little. Batson, Schoenrade, and Ventes (1993) explore effects on such variables as compassion, prejudice, and authoritarianism. These variables reflect a mix of psychological, cultural, and social influences. It is not surprising, then, that the results of empirical research depend strongly on the type of religious belief and the particular groups involved. Those who view religion as a means to an end (and thus accept beliefs without question) tend to be authoritarian and hostile to outsiders. Religions that preach compassion can induce compassionate behavior. But it is an open question as to how well this injunction is internalized; hostility toward homosexuals may represent an "accepted" outlet for repressed hostility in many religions. Batson, Schoenrade, and Ventes (1993) conclude that those who follow religions blindly score "worse" than the general population in terms of attitudes toward others. Again they feel that openminded pursuit of religion for the purpose of personal enlightenment is the best strategy, this time from the point of view of society rather than the individual.

2. CULTURAL GOALS → ACHIEVEMENT MOTIVATION

While we have all been programmed to try to achieve status, cultures will naturally influence which behaviors are most likely to be rewarded in this way. McClelland is justly famous for his concept of achievement motivation. He believes that people have a natural tendency to pursue what he calls "competence" goals (i.e., they wish to develop and inform others of their skills), but that this will be actualized to a greater degree in conditions that foster feelings of challenge, competence, and self-determination. Barkow (1989), though, provides an important critique of McClelland's attempts to measure achievement motivation. The Hausa of Nigeria view loyalty to a patron as a key source of prestige, while the Ibo emphasize wealth accumulation. It is a mistake to think the Hausa are low in achievement motivation; rather the measures that McClelland uses are not able to capture all of the ways in which people may achieve status. However we choose to define and measure achievement motivation, though, the Hausa/Ibo case provides a stark illustration of the way culture can influence the goals we choose to pursue. Koestner and McClelland (1990) emphasize a distinction between intrinsic and extrinsic motivation; we may improve our skills either to impress ourselves (enhance self-esteem) or others. Both, however, will be shaped by our cultural environment.

Wright (1994) takes this argument a step further. If an individual lacks the good looks, physical strength, or other qualities that would cause them to readily gain status in their society, they can pursue other strategies. One such strategy—at least in Western society—is to be excessively kind to others (obsequious) in the hope of reciprocal respect. This strategy is not always successful, but is likely preferable to wallowing in self-doubt throughout one's life. The lesson here is that behavior that we judge as undesirable may well represent the individual's best strategy (Wright, regrettably, does not recognize that we may as children underestimate our life chances). Note that both the behavior itself and society's reaction to it will be culturally conditioned.

3. CULTURAL VALUES → PERSONALITY DISORDER

I have suggested above both that personality can be evaluated along a handful of dimensions, and that mental illnesses for the most part represent extremes along one or more dimensions. Our culture will determine how far along any dimension one can travel before being diagnosed as ill.[11] Davis and Stasz (1990) develop this point at great length. The purpose of their book is to show that we cannot understand deviance without reference to a society's pressures to conform. It is important, therefore, that values (and laws) represent a group's true feelings rather than manipulation by a dominant elite. While suspicious of the possibility that conformity may serve the powerful, Davis and Stasz are all too conscious that societies need values [P→C]. Students attending the first class of the semester all benefit from knowing that they need not fear being shot for their seat. Yet values can change quickly: think of the differing views Western society has taken of alcoholism over the last century.

De Swaan (1990) also points out that all societies must exert some pressure to conform to societal values. Inevitably, this will include some mechanism for coping with the abnormal. He provides a powerful example of how changing values can affect our views of illness. As women gained increased freedom of movement, the incidence of agoraphobia rose dramatically; that which would have previously been interpreted as an admirable sign of feminine restraint was now considered a disease.

Maslow (1968) is justly famous for emphasizing the importance for human happiness of self-actualization. He thus approaches this question from a slightly different angle. Those who appear to have personality problems may be fighting against the crushing of their inner nature. In most cultures certain sorts of creativity will be proscribed, and individuals may face an unfortunate choice between pursuing self-expression or being considered normal. Deviance, then, may be essential to self-discovery.

4. LEADERSHIP STYLE

Culture will inevitably influence both our goals and means. If I wish to be a leader, I will be well advised to look about me for the type of leaders that my compatriots are disposed to follow, and then—consciously or not—try to follow in their footsteps. Looking at clubs, Lewis (1990) found that while club members tend to prefer democratic leaders, more is accomplished with authoritarian leaders. Studies in Japan and Germany did not find that authoritarians were liked any more than in the United States. Indeed in Japan it seems that the simplest tasks were actually performed best for democratic leaders. Smith and Bond (1993) wonder if a much greater dispersion in leadership styles would be found if more academic research was undertaken in less developed countries (and also note that it is hard to accurately measure the effects of culture without a theory to explain cultural differences). Other studies focused on the degree of leader consultation and found great differences across both situations and groups in whether this was advisable. At times it served to convince the groups to push in a new direction; at others it had the effect of signaling that leaders did not know what they were doing.

5. INDEPENDENCE

Societies differ significantly in the degree to which members see themselves as independent rather than interdependent.[12] The former tend to define themselves in terms of personality traits, while the latter are much more likely to do so in terms of their role in society (though all of us perhaps have too great a tendency to define ourselves and others in terms of our jobs; S→I). The former will thus take responsibility for their own behavior, rather than attribute it to context. While this is laudable to some extent, they could benefit from a greater attention to the reactions of others. A balance between the extremes of independence and interdependence would seem desirable.

We would expect that cultures which value independence will be less monolithic: they will countenance a fair degree of deviation from at least some values. Those who value independence are also likely to stand a bit further away when in conversation, attribute the actions of others to personality rather than situation, and believe that ability is the predominant reason for success (Smith and Bond 1993, ch. 6).

6. EMOTION

In cross-cultural comparisons of behavior, willingness to display emotion emerges as the characteristic most affected by culture. When shown distasteful pictures in groups, Japanese students were much less likely to display emotion than American students. However, when they thought nobody was watching, they reacted the same. In this case at least, it would seem that culture has had a much greater effect on behavior than personality. Japanese students would display emotion if not for a concern that they would lose face (Smith and Bond 1993).

In other cases, though, culture appears to affect not just display but the actual emotion we experience. Oatley (1993) thus suggests that Westerners raised in societies that value individualism are more likely to feel anger at a threat to their autonomy than are those raised in societies that stress a collective identity. Oatley stresses, though, that he recognizes (unlike a small minority of scholars) that there are universal emotions; since these are triggered in part by our cognitions, though, our society can easily influence our propensity to feel a particular emotion in a particular situation.

Anthropologists emphasize the unpleasant emotion of guilt that properly socialized members will feel if they violate a cultural value. Necessarily, then, guilt will be triggered in different societies by different values. Moreover, societies or subgroups often expect different behavior from different individuals; priests are to be chaste, mothers self-sacrificing, service employees ever-friendly. Individuals will feel guilty if they fail to live up to these social expectations. (They may therefore strive to repress other emotions: the priest's love, the mother's joy, the worker's anger). Since each of us fulfills various social roles, we are unlikely to be entirely comfortable with our performance in each. Times of role change—marriage, parenthood, graduation—may be especially challenging [S → I].

We saw in chapter 4 that emotions were selected primarily to aid social cooperation. We should not be surprised, then, if different societies encourage emotional experiences that will in turn support that society's way of life. Heise and O'Brien (1993) discuss the social constructivist approach to emotion, where emotional display is interpreted as a sophisticated intercourse intended (perhaps subconsciously) to influence others. They illustrate how in particular tribes anger and grief are used to entreat others, or shaming others serves to prevent them from demanding help. Thus, not only does our society influence how we respond emotionally to particular stimuli, but it affects how we will feel and display emotions so as to influence others.

7. AGGRESSION

While we are all hardwired for aggression, there are enormous differences across both societies and individuals in our willingness to follow this impulse. Our childhood learning experiences shape individual differences in "styles of interpretation" (likelihood of taking offense at the acts of another), goals, values, emotionality, and aggression inhibitors. I have discussed the cultural and genetic (including physical size) determinants of most of these above. Mummendy (1984) notes that individuals will always try to justify acts of aggression. Since the vast majority of acts of aggression are responses to the perceived violation of cultural values by another, the first step in attempting to justify aggression involves arguing that "they had it coming." Thus, cultural values not directly related to aggression play a key role in affecting its incidence. The second step in justification seeks to reconcile the action with the reaction. For some groups and people, the slightest transgression is to be dealt with harshly. For others, aggression is considered a last resort at best. Individuals in justifying their acts will appeal to the normative support of the largest group possible. Few (excepting psychopaths) will engage in acts of aggression unless these are accepted by at least some friends and family. Note, though, that those with a need to vent hostility can choose a lifestyle that puts them in situations where aggression is accepted.

I should make special note of the role of self-esteem. We will react to events which lower our self-valuation, or reduce our sense of controlling our destiny. If we convince ourselves that the event was another's fault, an aggressive act can serve to re-inflate our ego (a more constructive response may be to prove our ability at the original task). But we can only do this if our society will approve of our behavior; if it will only earn us more disfavor we will try to focus our energies elsewhere.

It is dangerous for either a group or individual to eschew aggression entirely. While it is observed everywhere that transgressions of rules are much more common than aggressive retaliation, the threat of retaliation serves to keep people from breaking the rules (I→C1). The occasional act of aggression may prevent a host of others from giving offense.[13] And we all know some people who pursue the strategy of reacting harshly to any imagined slight; to their minds at least the cost in offense given to others is justified by decreasing their likelihood of receiving offense.

Note that aggression need not mean violence. One very common form is the contingent threat: "If you ever do that again. . . ." If convincing, this can have a substantial effect on the behavior of others. But aggression is most often entirely verbal, with no reference to physical force. When looked at in this broader light, a number of misconceptions about aggression disappear. Women are as likely as men to engage in verbal aggression. And how many gifted children have viewed the schoolyard bully as subhuman while being completely oblivious to the verbal abuse they habitually heap upon those around them? This attitude gains cultural reinforcement: Western middle-class society places few limits on verbal aggression but saves physical aggression for extreme circumstances.

Even the definition of aggression is culturally determined. Is an insult aggressive? A pat on the back? A cold stare? Within cultures, there will be misunderstandings over intent, with occasionally disastrous consequences. Between cultures (and especially subcultures, where participants may not be wary of misunderstanding) it is much more likely. One can think of a person moving from a society in which insults are considered good-natured to a society in which they are seen as an attack on honor.

8. CROSS-CULTURAL CONTACT → CHOICES, ANXIETY, OPENNESS

While within any one group there may be enormous pressures to conform, when quite different cultures come in contact individuals face a greater freedom to choose goals and behaviors. This freedom comes at a heavy cost, for the very benefits that flow to society from widely shared values can be lost. The classic case is when hunter-gatherer groups develop trading relations with settled communities. While some cling to the ideology of sharing associated with the former, others adopt the wealth accumulation motive common to the latter.

There have been a plethora of studies that have looked at the effects on personality of cultural contact, and particularly migration across cultural boundaries. Unfortunately, most of these studies could have been better focused on our major personality dimensions. A couple of (unsurprising) results have received a considerable degree of verification. Both living within a different culture and returning to one's own after a long absence are sources of stress. The degree of anxiety depends on one's emotionality, extroversion, and communication skills. Those from individualistic cultures fare better. Those of higher status tend to have more positive attitudes [S→I], and thus fare better as well. One big advantage of cross-cultural contact is that it forces people to think about their own culture and personality as they are exposed to different behavior. T. Smith (1992) concurs with millions of travelers in suggesting this as a key source of personal growth.

Smith and Bond (1993, ch. 10) survey the difficulties of cross-cultural contact. Simple differences, such as a tendency to stand too close, arrive late, display too much or the wrong type of emotion, or talk too fast, can cause enormous misunderstanding. When surprised by the actions of another, we will tend to evaluate them through the lens of our own culture: if we have been taught punctuality, we will view the tardy negatively. The main implication of Smith and Bond's analysis is that the only "cure" is greater exposure to cultural diversity; we could hope to reduce people's anxiety level by teaching them about diversity.

I→C: INDIVIDUAL DIFFERENCES → CULTURE

Sperber (1990) decries the "old" epidemiological approach to culture. For cultural traits to spread like disease, one had to assume that replication of cultural norms from one person to the next was typical, and any mutation an accident. This view—still common in mathematical models of cultural change—rests on two misconceptions, that there are no differences in cultural traits across individuals, and that a communicator's thoughts are perfectly replicated in the mind of the receiver. Instead, we should recognize that communication is naturally imperfect. Rather than replication, we should speak of transformation whereby any message is mangled by anywhere from 0 to 100% in each retelling. Only ideas that are repeatedly communicated and minimally transformed will become cultural traits in the first place. Various psychological variables determine the likelihood of an individual absorbing a particular idea: their ability to learn and remember it, their motivation to do so, and the degree to which the idea accords with existing schemas. These schemas are themselves shaped in part by previous cultural transmission (C→I): thus Kelly (1991) notes that cultural similarities in a group may reflect either accurate transmissions or simply similar upbringing so that individuals employ similar schemas. Message frequency is affected by institutions (e.g., schools), technology (media, writing), group cohesion, and the appropriateness of the idea for their environment (with feedback to the extent culture shapes the wider environment). Some messages are transmitted subconsciously, but it would be a mistake to assume that people do not consciously evaluate not only values but myths and rituals (Trigg 1985).

There has been a longstanding debate concerning the precise relationship between individual mental representations (schemas) and the "social representations" of a society as evidenced in public utterances. Anthropologists have generally argued that the latter are primary: children learn mental representations from observation of social representations. Philosophers such as Wittgenstein have concurred. Geertz pursues an ontological argument: since social representations can be seen they must cause the unseen mental representations. Not only is it unclear that the seen must cause the unseen (most world religions would dispute this), but many psychologists would argue that mental representations do exist in the brain; we just cannot see them with present technology. Further, psychologists argue for the primacy of mental representations, since children need to develop a mental framework (super-schema) in order to comprehend and interpret social representations. Sperber sides with the psychologists, arguing that social representations only have meaning as interpreted by individuals. I strongly suspect that here as elsewhere causation in both directions is important.[14] In terms of understanding cultural change, though, Sperber is most certainly right: change will occur when one or more individuals transform an existing value in their minds (perhaps accidentally) and successfully transmit this change to others.

Since the 1980s there has been a marked increase in the focus on the cognitive underpinnings of social representations within the field of social psychology. A prime example is the social cognition approach, which looks at how we process information and assumes that similar cognitive processes are involved in our attempts to comprehend both the physical and human worlds (see Devine, Hamilton, and Ostrom 1994).

Once we have recognized that we must understand cultural change at the level of the individual, it is a small step to recognize that some individuals are more likely to effect change than others. "If there had been no troublemakers, no dissent, we should still be living in caves" (historian A. J. P. Taylor, cited in Apter 1992). Individuals differ markedly, as we have seen, in their willingness/ability to conform (and see my discussion of creativity and leadership below). Some individuals may try to push culture in a variety of directions. Or they may be more sensitive to pressures of, say, economic and political change. Tooby and Cosmides (1992) note that we should all be programmed to react to change by adjusting our schemas. But since we are also programmed to pursue community membership, we must inevitably differ in our willingness to change.

I. PERSONALITY → IMPORTANCE OF VALUES

Conformity is not the only personality characteristic that influences an individual's propensity to accept particular cultural values. It is commonly believed that rites of passage help to allay the anxiety associated with taking on a new role and help individuals break the bonds (e.g., mother-child) of their previous state. Individuals with low levels of anxiety and/or weak attachments should be expected to value such rituals less. More generally, for values and especially myths to be retained they must strike the individual as interesting enough to be committed to memory. A variety of personality characteristics, then, will influence the degree to which a particular individual absorbs a particular cultural trait.

One major distinction often made in the literature is between people who adhere to values only due to fear of punishment and those who come to value them intrinsically (C→I). Inevitably, small children first come to appreciate the punishments associated with violation. They then try to work out the logic of the system of values being presented to them. Only in adolescence do they come (or not) to evaluate values in their own terms. It is impossible for a society to perfectly regulate behavior through punishment alone. A value can only be maintained—and could only become established in the first place—if a substantial portion of society believes in it; otherwise it would be violated so often that it would not be worthwhile for anyone to adhere to it (Gellner 1989). Moreover, values will always be open to interpretation on the edges, and society will have difficulty maintaining a value which its members constantly abuse (Potter and Wetherell 1987).

Different personalities will exhibit different attitudes toward values: the selfish and nonconscientious will be more likely to obey only for fear of punishment. Since culture in turn affects personality, some groups will have more of these. Such individuals may push for value change out of self-interest, or they may find that they are better off violating values such as honesty than they would be if such values did not exist. Those who believe in values will be a force for change to the extent that they think different values could serve society better.

2. CREATIVITY

We have no trouble thinking of those who develop our myths or rituals as exercising a creative impulse. Yet we might not so readily apply the term creative to those who suggest changes in values. But what is creativity? Batson, Schoenrade, and Ventes (1993) provide a useful definition: creativity is an improvement in our cognitive organization (superschema). It can thus be readily distinguished from more mundane cognitive functions. When we act logically, we are simply applying existing schemas to a situation. Whenever we are faced with novelty (and do not ignore it) we act in a creative fashion by revising our schemas. Therefore, any time one of us rejects certain values, we are by definition creating a new view of how the world works.

With this definition, we can see that there will inevitably be a similarity in creative acts in different domains: culture, art, science, technology, business (see Fiske 1991). In all cases, to be creative is to develop new connections in one's mental view of the world. The following comments, then, apply to creativity in general rather than simply cultural creativity.

How does creativity work? It is best to think of it in four stages (see chapter 9). First, the individual must become aware of some problem that is not dealt with properly within existing structures of thought. This may be a problem that others have grappled with for centuries (how could we fly?) or a new problem. The individual will likely struggle with the problem for a while at first. Since by definition existing schemas cannot dictate an answer, immediate success is unlikely. The individual likely pulls back a bit from their quest, then, but continues to gather relevant information. There are several important characteristics of this second stage. While we tend to focus on the novelty of a creative act, we should not lose sight of the fact that any creation is but a combination of preexisting ideas. Analogy tends to be utilized: Fodor (1983) speaks of how scientists conceived of the flow of electricity being like the flow of water and the structure of the atom being like the structure of the solar system, and concludes that the history of science is full of such examples. It seems only sensible that the creative would explore the possibility that a schema that works in one domain may have applicability elsewhere. Another common approach is trial and error experimentation. The artist at the easel, the tinkerer in the workshop, and the religious fanatic seeking followers all make use of this process in deciding how best to organize their views. Breaking a large problem into tractable pieces is a third useful strategy.

The key point, though, is that none of these means to attack a problem can guarantee a solution (or we would not be talking about creativity). Failure to find creative solutions to problems is a key source of frustration in many lives. The act of inspiration—the third stage in the process—is elusive. Indeed, it is more likely to come to those who are able to push the problem out of their conscious thoughts. We all have experienced this: a problem vexes us for a while and we can think of nothing, then later in the bath or bed or while walking in the woods the answer suddenly comes to us. While we cannot ignore the importance of conscious attempts to gather information, we must also recognize the key role of subconscious processes that work best when the mind is at rest. Since we could not be sure that we could ever solve the problem, we inevitably greet the solution with a feeling of elation.

We must be careful, though, not to let our feelings carry us away. Despite our elation, our solution may in fact be no improvement over our preceding cognitive structure. Or, if it is, this will likely only be the case after a number of details and modifications are worked out. Moreover, a successful cultural or technical innovation must be compatible with other cultural and technical elements in order to survive (and we will find that artists too can only innovate so far if they hope to be understood and appreciated). This is the fourth stage of critical revision. The impetuous forget this to their detriment. We must be careful of falsely convincing ourselves that we have the answer. Fiske (1991), indeed, suggests that it is in the working out of what may have been a vague inspiration that real creativity occurs.

Creative acts thus require the cooperation of different parts of the brain. Memory retrieval, synthesis, transformation, interpretation, inference, and hypothesis testing are among the mental processes involved (Fiske 1991). Cooperation between the conscious and subconscious likely reflects the fact that the former specializes in logical, disciplined thought while the latter is more open to intuitive and imaginative thought. Both are necessary. Batson, Schoenrade, and Ventes (1993) suggest further that the left hemisphere of the brain dominates the first stage, but the right takes over in the third. They also make much of the fact that inspiration usually occurs in terms of a visual image.

Maslow (1968) argued that very few of us live up to our creative potential, and further that our psychological well-being is largely dependent on our doing so. We all have a hierarchy of needs: once we satisfy basic needs for food and shelter we look for fulfillment. To achieve this we must face up to the uncertainty of life, and recognize that we should attempt to adjust our schemas to deal with novelty. While major transformations in life cause pain and grief they can also lead to greater insight: in general we must be open to the pain that comes with change. Maslow hoped that if people came to recognize their need for growth (i.e., creativity) they would find the process pleasurable rather than frightening (they should also accept that they cannot solve all problems).[15] Maslow also emphasized our need to discover our intrinsic nature (genetic endowment). Some people might be naturally artistic, and could get only limited fulfillment from life unless they discovered this. He was thus open to the idea that different people might have quite different creative potential [G→I].

Amabile's (1996) major finding is that we are all much more likely to be creative when working on a problem of intrinsic interest to us. Naturally, individuals differ markedly in the degree of intrinsic satisfaction they gain from various tasks. Noting that history shows that some times and places are more creative than others, Amabile suggests that cultural, social, and political variables affect the likelihood of creativity [C, S, P→I]. Societies that value individuality and creativity in various domains will tend to have more members working on problems they value. Rewards can be helpful too, but remember that intrinsic motivation is generally superior to extrinsic. And too much success can be dangerous: on receiving the Nobel Prize in literature, T. S. Eliot bemoaned the fact that nobody ever accomplished much after such an award.

Amabile's research uncovered more negative than positive influences on creativity. This accords well with Maslow's conjecture that we are on average far below our creative potential. Naturally, pursuit of a narrow goal—such as when your employer makes a specific request, or you contract for a specific outcome—stands in the way of the free-ranging exploration essential to creativity. Being watched, or evaluated according to narrow criteria, are similarly negative. Pressure to conform is an inevitable antidote to creativity. Amabile suggests, however, a number of ways in which creativity can be enhanced. Open classrooms, access to a variety of materials, and individual attention from instructors stimulates student creativity. Play is very important, for children at least. Every child should feel special. Creative role models are also valuable up to a point ($I_R \rightarrow C$). Giving employees independence and responsibility is useful. Access to materials and equipment is essential. A recognition that one can learn from failure encourages individuals and groups to persevere in the face of inevitable setbacks. And environments which themselves are cognitively and perceptually stimulating encourage creativity [P, E, N$\rightarrow$I].

A number of scholars have looked at the question of the personality characteristics conducive to creativity. They have done so using biographies of creative people, laboratory studies, and the correlation of results from personality questionnaires. Individuality and openness are obvious candidates. Independence, sensitivity, and a preference for complexity have been suggested (Amabile 1996). An ability to concentrate is a key attribute, but this can be taken too far—obsessive behavior is rarely creative. One also needs flexibility in thought, but again this can be taken too far in the direction of impulsiveness. As noted above, creativity requires cooperation between conscious and subconscious. Miller (1990) builds on this analysis to suggest that frontal lobe development may be the key, and that creativity is likely related to intelligence and myopia.

More interesting, perhaps, are the oft-hypothesized links between mental disorder and creativity. Aristotle himself mused: "Why is it that all men who are outstanding in philosophy, poetry, or the arts are melancholic?" Those with disorders may have a greater reliance on the subconscious (or different links to it), and thus be creative. Or, the misguided schemas in their heads may cause them to suggest connections that would never have occurred to others. Miller follows Anthony in suggesting that a strong connection between internal and external worlds (perhaps neurologically captured by stronger links between the two hemispheres) may be conducive to both creativity and disorder.

Like Maslow, many feel that creativity can be an antidote to disorder. It certainly can be an avenue to achievement for people who might otherwise have trouble fitting in to society. Leading artists and scientists are not only financially rewarded but often applauded for "eccentricities" which would earn lesser mortals nothing but contempt. But Kavaler-Adler (1993) notes that while creativity may help them in terms of self-esteem, it does not solve their basic psychological difficulties. Even with respect to their self-image, she feels that creativity encourages narcissism: they only value one aspect of their selves. Nevertheless, therapists may find clues to these problems in the creative output. She feels that therapy might have helped many of the authors she studied overcome their compulsive attitude to writing, and thus increase the quality if not quantity of their writing.

Given the diversity of disorders, it is unlikely that all would have the same effect on creativity. Compulsive disorder may indeed be bad. On the other hand, Frye (1991) suggests that paranoia may be the key to creativity. To truly open ourselves up to the uncertainty of the universe is to come face to face with the fact that that universe cares little for our welfare. A much more common observation is that creative people tend to be depressive. Jamison (1994) lists Byron, Shelley, Melville, Coleridge, and Virginia Woolf among the famous authors with that affliction. Studies show that depression is 10 to 30 times as common among distinguished artists as among the general population—though similar differentials are not found with respect to other forms of creativity. But these artists seem capable of lengthy periods of either normal or manic activity interspersed with depression. One explanation of their creativity is that mood swings require a more elastic wiring of the brain with more connections. Different parts of the brain seem to dominate during manic and depressive phases. Moreover, manic phases may throw up lots of ideas that can be evaluated at other times. The self-worth and ambition of manic phases thus feeds ideas to the introspection, isolation, and compulsion of depressed periods (Fiske 1991). Some researchers are so impressed by the connection that they wonder if the common (and heritable) tendency toward depression might have been selected for because it enhanced creativity.

There is also a strong genetic component to schizophrenia, which is also felt by many to be connected to creativity. Wenegrat (1990) notes that both are characterized by a lack of boundaries, and wonders if creativity serves to limit symptoms. On the other hand, Miller (1990) argues that schizophrenia, characterized by an inability to apply internal models to the real world (and thus a reliance on fantasy), is antithetical to creativity which requires the opposite. Again there may be a happy medium: the individual who is marginalized but still loosely connected to society such that communication is possible (thus, Crook 1980, suggests that both Newton and Einstein may have been schizoid).

3. LEADERSHIP

The field of social psychology was once almost entirely concerned with conformity. Asch's experiments (G→C2) were interpreted by many—though not Asch himself—as showing that people would conform on the surface while maintaining their own beliefs internally. But others noted that conformity more generally involved internalization of values. In recent years, there has been an increased interest in the topic of persuasion in the field, though unfortunately the two matters tend to be dealt with separately (Mackie and Skelly 1994). Yet both endeavors must start with a recognition of our innate tendency to mimic others, and to accept advice on authority when it would be too time-consuming to investigate the issue on our own. In the latter case, we must be careful to recognize that the trust we place in another (or the degree to which we feel a common group identity) will affect whether we think personal verification necessary. We should also note the possibility of the reverse effect: we may believe the opposite of what is espoused by people we do not like.

Gardner (1995) argues that there are common elements to leadership across a range of domains: cultural, political, economic (he also suspects a strong link with creativity). These are of course buttressed by domain-specific abilities.[16] Gardner does note that leadership exists along a continuum from direct leadership, in which one tells or shows others what to do, to indirect, exemplified by a scientist like Einstein who leads by promulgating new ideas.

Persuading a group to a new idea will go slowly at first. Once a few "disciples" have been converted, however, the situation is transformed. Others, observing many people now espousing the same view, will tend to assume that they arrived at it independently (G→C10; unless those with the same view are members of an out-group, in which case they will be suspected of bias). This will be viewed as a powerful indication that the idea has merit. If you observe many people going for seconds on the peach pie, while avoiding the apple, you have good reason to think the peach pie is better (Mackie and Skelly 1994).

By a similar logic, it is also true that persuasion is most successful when repeated (remember too the role of repetition in learning; chapter 4). There is also evidence that the status of the persuader is positively related to the perception of validity by the receiver. All want to be correct, but many will be most concerned with avoiding contradiction; the safest path will be to stick with the majority view as espoused by group leaders. This can also increase the individual's sense of belonging, in which case the view is extremely difficult to change. The importance of the issue to the receiver also matters. If the issue is important, people will pay attention to the transmitter; otherwise the transmitter may have almost no chance of being heard. Note that an issue may be deemed important by individuals only because it allows them to display group solidarity.

The social cognition approach emphasizes the fact that the receiver must incorporate any new view into their existing schemas. Thus the way an idea is first presented to them can have an enormous effect (abortion as murder versus abortion as choice). Further accretions of information will tend to be integrated in a manner that supports the original hypothesis, while contradictory information tends to be ignored. The view is thus likely to be applied to a wider range of situations, and become even harder to change.

Many scholars have examined the qualities of leadership. One of the more fruitful modes of inquiry is to examine the personalities of former leaders for common elements. Gardner (1995) makes the key distinction between ordinary leaders who say what others think, innovative leaders who emphasize a message latent in their group (e.g., as some recent politicians push "family values" or "personal responsibility"), and visionary leaders who create a new message. His focus, like mine, is on the last two types. Despite emphasizing cognitive elements, he finds much in common with previous practitioners of this methodology. Leaders tend to assert their own views even as children. They are usually good with words. They are almost always energetic. They take an interest in and display an understanding of others. They are competitive, but pursue power as a means to an end rather than an end in itself (unlike ordinary leaders). They betray a fondness for travel, which likely reflects a willingness to test themselves against the unknown. They also possess an unusual ability to bounce back from failure, and indeed tend to see opportunities where others see problems. Most, though far from all, are also physically attractive and/or distinctive.

Since we all have different schema systems, leaders will have to be able to tailor their message to different audiences. Gardner (1995) points to one important distinction. Some people see the world as black and white: it is a battleground between good and evil. Others see good in everyone. In between, people are able to see both good and evil in the same situation/ person (he feels these different attitudes are learned in the order presented as we age; not all of us progress to an evenhanded outlook). A political leader attempting welfare reform might then try to convince some people that welfare recipients are evil, while telling others that reform is in the interests of the poor. People also differ in their willingness to accept inconsistency, such as when leaders speak of decreasing taxes and deficits while increasing services. Our schemas are not the only differences leaders need to contend with: our emotions are likely more important than rational evaluation in choosing who to follow (Gardner 1995), and thus all of our characteristics come in to play. The easiest appeal, needless to say, will therefore be to a group's sense of identity, including reverence for particular past leaders, or to very strongly held values.

For Gardner, the key to leadership is to tell "stories" which others find compelling. In other words, leaders must speak of schemas that others already possess but think about little (innovative leaders) or can be incorporated within their body of schemas (visionary leaders). This places limits on how much change any leader can effect. Yet Gardner is careful to avoid leaping from this insight to the misguided belief that leaders are unimportant because they only embody "natural" developments in schema formation. Germany was ripe for a new order in the 1930s, he notes, but in the absence of Hitler history would have taken a quite different turn.

Finally, Gardner suggests that leaders must always find time for personal reflection. This is not easy to do, for any leader will find that others have almost infinite demands on their time. This suggests that introverts may make the best leaders (especially if conscientious, emotionally stable, selfless, and cognitively flexible). Yet particularly in the way we select modern political leaders we may have made it very difficult for introverts to rise to the top. Gardner worries that our emphasis on egalitarianism has caused us to not prepare any of our society for leadership (when society needs many leaders dedicated to the common good). He may be right in identifying the disease but not its cause.

4. PERSONALITY → RELIGION

Marx famously claimed that religion is the opiate of the masses. Other thinkers concentrated on whether certain types of people were more prone to religious belief. For Freud, religion was attractive to all as a fulfillment of primal wishes, but especially those who were neurotic or compulsive and therefore unable to deal with uncertainty. Brown (1994) attempts to update Freud by substituting depression for neurosis. Doing this, he feels, puts religion in a more positive light: an aid to those who feel lost, rather than a focus for illness.

As Brown recognizes, this causal link is one in which the biases of scholars can easily affect results. Those who view religion favorably tend to look for and see reverence, humility, and constructive obedience among adherents; those with a negative view are likely to seek and find self-abasing behavior. Thus, while Wulff in 1991 had argued that "without question the mentally disturbed are frequently attracted by religion," the contributors to Brown's volume all stress the positive aspects of (mainstream) religious belief. Other scholars would go further and question the widespread perception that members of cults are either suffering from disorders or victims of brainwashing. They would note that what appear to be "weird" practices with respect to food, dress, or sex, serve a valuable function of weeding out the nondedicated who might be tempted to "free ride" on the efforts of other cult members.

There does appear to be some correlation between religion and introversion. A likely explanation is that introspective people are more likely to face questions of the meaning of life, and thus feel a need for religion. Batson, Schoenrade, and Ventes (1993) note that the Buddha, St. Augustine, Tolstoy, and numerous other key historical figures found religion at times in their life when they had little else to worry about. If so, then existential angst need not be inevitable, even for introverts. Perhaps what happened to the figures mentioned by Batson et al is that during their periods of restful reflection they were unable to find meaning in their past (material?) exploits. In this interpretation, it is not just enough to keep busy but one must also put enough meaning in one's life that it can survive periods of reflection.

Critics of religion have suggested that it is wishful thinking, an infantile reaction to fear, and even sublimation of sexual desire. A continuing, and inconclusive, debate focuses on the connection between intelligence (and cognitive style) and belief. Attempts to measure whether religion is correlated with either happiness or optimism/pessimism have also been inconclusive (note that causation in both directions would be possible here).

Many of Brown's contributors make the point that we cannot evaluate this causal link without reference to other cultural elements. If these are strongly linked to a religion, then adhering may be part of one's cultural identity. On the other hand, if other cultural elements are providing much of the meaning that people need in life (e.g., through devotion to family or community) then religious belief may be unnecessary (and even unhealthy). This may explain why religious belief is much more subdued in many parts of Asia than in the West.

Many scholars strive for a middle ground: some religions are unhealthy while others (their own included) are beneficial. Within this group, it is common to point favorably to ecumenicism. Religions evolve but maintain core beliefs concerning the existence of god and certain ethical principles. Even nonreligions can evolve in this direction: while Sartre was an atheist later existentialists have accepted at least the possibility of god.

5. LANGUAGES

I noted in chapter 1 that no two people (or subgroups; S→C) will define a word in precisely the same way. We can nevertheless attempt to provide rough definitions of words, which capture some commonalities in how people define them. Such definitions evolve over time precisely because individuals can not transmit precise definitions.

APPENDIX 5-A: INTERPERSONAL RELATIONSHIPS

You meet a friend for lunch and they say something which offends. A stranger on the street winks at you. Your mother was a bit overzealous during toilet training. All of these events can have a powerful influence on your behavior and even your personality. But where do they fit in our schema? They require a new phenomenon of interpersonal relationships. Note that the word "relationships" is to be interpreted broadly to include casual encounters with strangers; we might, for example, be very interested in the causes and effects of sudden infatuation as strangers' eyes meet across a crowded room (T. Smith 1992). I will deal with this phenomenon here both because the personality of the participants will naturally be a major influence on any relationship (but culture, social structure, politics, and economics will also matter) and because relationships will in turn have powerful effects on the individuals involved. The phenomenon can be unpacked in terms of type of relationship: family, romance, friendship, employment, casual, business, and so on.

C→I_R: CULTURE → INTERPERSONAL RELATIONSHIPS

Our cultural values will influence our relationships in many ways. A distrust of foreigners may preclude us from engaging in a range of relationships. Cultural stereotypes may influence our attitudes toward a variety of people. Cultures prescribe acceptable levels of openness for different types of relationship. If we think that the boys (or girls) at the club will lower their opinion of us if we speak of marital difficulties, we will avoid such topics. Various cultural ceremonies, such as initiation, marriage, or sharing peace pipes, serve to define relationships. Relationships crossing cultural boundaries will be impeded by cultural differences: innocent "details" like proxemics can cause misunderstanding and even offense. And all groups have a tendency to rate themselves higher than outsiders in terms of honesty, kindness, and loyalty, which inevitably limits our desire to interact. We may, of course, overcome our culturally induced preconceptions through experience. But note the difficulty here: our schemas shape how we evaluate experience. If we expect a certain behavior from certain people we may "see" it regardless of their actual behavior.

And our schemas have advantages. The key aspect of any relationship is how confident we can be of others' behavior. When meeting someone from the same or similar cultural background, we share expectations of roles to be played, norms to be observed, and even subconscious theories of personality. We will look for clues like accent and gestures to guide us in developing expectations. Stereotypes can even have advantages in cross-cultural contact: American students at Hong Kong University are more willing to initiate conversation because of a perception that Chinese students are introverts (Smith and Bond 1993).

I have noted that language is inevitably ambiguous, though not so much that scientific precision in definition is impossible. In any conversation, there will be some difference between what the speaker intended to communicate and what the listener(s) perceive. This difference will depend first of all on the listener's familiarity with the speaker's language (including dialect and accent). It will also depend, though, on the listener's familiarity with and understanding of the speaker. Sabel (1994) speaks of how people through repeated interaction can jointly elaborate a common framework for understanding. Again, sharing various cultural traits will give them a head start.

For a relationship to continue, all participants must feel that they are better off within than outside the relationship. Nevertheless, some may benefit much more from a relationship than others. Since we are imbued with a sense of fairness, people may sometimes exit beneficial relationships because they think they are being taken advantage of. A key element in any relationship, therefore, will be the participants' sense of its fairness. To evaluate a particular relationship, we could begin with Fiske's (1991) four models of human interaction and ask which model is best applied. A similar approach is resource theory (Foa 1993). Its starting point is an argument that there are six resources that can be exchanged in a relationship: money, goods, services, love, status, and information [I$\rightarrow$E]. Fairness will be easiest to judge if participants exchange the same resource. There is no market mechanism that can determine the value of love, status, or information: cultural values must thus play a role in evaluating relationships in which different resources are traded[C$\rightarrow$I$_R$].

I$_R$$\rightarrow$C: INTERPERSONAL RELATIONSHIPS $\rightarrow$ CULTURE

A disproportionate number of leaders (and creators) lost their father when very young. While only 8% of the general population in the modern West loses a parent before the age of 18, 26% of eminent scientists, 55% of English poets and writers, and 34% of American presidents did (and 22% of prisoners; Amabile 1996). While the links are not entirely clear, biographies often emphasize how early experiences encouraged self-reliance and ambition. Getting along very well with one parent (usually the mother) but not the other often serves to heighten interpersonal skills. Also, as Winston Churchill suggested, a troubled childhood encourages tenacity. Outside the family, leaders betray a tendency to steadily widen their network of contacts as they grow older.

Relationships are also important with respect to religion. Wenegrat (1990) cites a number of studies that indicate a link between childrearing practices and later religious belief. Batson, Schoenrade, and Ventes (1993) concur: children with a close attachment to their mothers tend to copy their mothers's religion, but the most likely to become religious later in life are those with no close attachment to either parent. This latter result goes against previous hypotheses of Ericson and others that belief in god was an extension of the attitude of the helpless child toward parents; instead it suggests that religion may serve to compensate for a lack of support elsewhere. Later relationships are also important: the clearest evidence of this is the fact that charismatic prophets have throughout history attracted followers such that they could either create or transform a particular religion (see Storr 1996).

Similar arguments can be made with respect to values. We are all too aware of adolescents who hang out with the "wrong crowd" and show disdain for societal values. And obviously our family upbringing affects our acceptance of values. Did our parents enforce these? Did we respect them? Did sibling jealousy encourage intransigence?

Amabile (1996) has stressed the role of relationships in generating creativity. He feels that nonconformist parents who are nonauthoritarian but emotionally cool are most likely to stimulate creativity. Attentive teachers and creative role models outside the family also encourage creativity. As Szostak (1991) emphasizes, the second and fourth stages of the creative process generally involve a number of people working together. This depends on a conducive institutional setup and also a willingness of participants to share with others. Diversity in skills and outlook among participants is valuable. When people gather to discuss a problem, there is an optimal number of participants: enough for a range of views but small enough that intelligent conversation is possible. Brainstorming, in which a group is brought together and encouraged to think freely without criticism, often produces results. Competition between one group and another can also serve to focus the collective minds.

6

The Economy

THE PHENOMENA

Despite being an economist, when I began this project I first attended to the phenomena which comprised other categories such as culture or social structure. When I returned my gaze to the category closest to my home discipline, I realized that it was not immediately obvious what the appropriate subjects of interest were. To be sure, merely listening to the news would guide one to include the total income (output) of any group (GDP). Thus, we can deal with economic growth (a change in per capita income), business cycles (fluctuations in income), and therefore inflation and unemployment.[1] At a disaggregated level, we could also examine how much of each good or service the group produces, and why. We can even disaggregate to the level of individual artifacts; Schiffer (1999) discusses how artifacts can and should be integrated into an analysis of causal links. We would also be interested in the distribution of income or goods among group members. And, as mentioned in chapter 1, we must also concern ourselves with the economic ideology that justifies this distribution.

But is that all there is? A glance at major economics texts might leave one with the impression that the economy—at least the modern market economy—was an autonomous machine whose understanding requires little if any reference to other phenomena. Yet the "market" is not the same everywhere; it is most obviously extremely constrained in communist nations, but even the so-called market economies are quite different, with Germany much more willing to countenance collusion than the United States, and businesspeople in many less developed countries having to bribe government officials daily in order to survive. The market, in other words, is an institution, and joins a number of other institutions in shaping how much and of what we produce and consume.

The word "institution" is often defined so broadly in the literature (especially in sociology) that it would comprise most or all of what I have called culture. I will limit its use here to (sets of) rules which have been formalized, such that there are explicit sanctions for breaking them.[2] Laws, corporate charters, banking regulations, zoning rules, and employment contracts are all institutions then, but a group tendency to honesty is still culture. Note that institutions need not be written down, as long as the people concerned are aware of the penalties (organized crime is surely an institution, after all). Many but far from all key institutions will be sanctioned by government [P→E]. Many institutions are predominantly political in nature and will thus be dealt with in the next chapter. I can identify a number of important types of economic institution (note that the list is not exhaustive):

> those governing ownership (especially of land, labor, capital)
> those governing exchange: markets (types of), command economy
> those governing finance
> those governing labor relations
> those governing production (safety, pollution, standards)

I emphasize that these broad institutional types can be found in all societies.[3] Wilson (1998) provides a lengthy list of "universals," which includes property rights and inheritance rules, trade and gift-giving (the latter often substituting for the former; both require rules), and cooperative labor (which again requires rules to prevent shirking). Financial institutions *may* be a little less than universal, though some scholars would argue that we can find these even in barter societies.

Institutions are often embodied in organizations such as firms, unions, manufacturer's associations, government bureaucracies, and nonprofit organizations. Kuhn (1974) defines an organization as any interaction of two or more people in which attention is focused on overall process or effect, and distinguishes four types of organization by purpose: profit, cooperative, service, and pressure (lobbying). As with institutions in general, some of these are political in nature.[4] The internal cohesion of these organizations will have a major impact on how well the institutions they embody will work. Firms with bloated (or anemic) middle managements will not take full advantage of market opportunities. Incompetent government bureaucracies will fail to enforce regulations. Organizations, in sum, are institutions (bodies of rules) which serve to affect the strength of other institutions (see Ahrne 1994, Di Maggio 1994).

Smelser and Swedberg (1994) celebrate the many promising signs that the economics profession is once again concerned with institutions; the mainstream of the profession had (with a handful of exceptions) been ignoring these since the nineteenth century. How could economists leave out of their analysis some of the key phenomena within the economic domain? The answer here also serves to explain why economics has been the least interdisciplinary of the human sciences. As Krugman (1994) recognizes, "The marketplace is special among social interactions in that it is subject to certain logical regularities." In a free market, one does not need to know much about culture, psychology, or social structure in order to understand most price movements. An unexpected frost in Brazil will push up the price of coffee, other things equal. The regularities of which Krugman speaks fostered the development of mathematical models. Thousands of economists have been kept busy deriving models from different assumptions regarding the degree of market power possessed by buyers or sellers, their access to information, their expectations, and the existence of undesirable side-effects like pollution or congestion. Institutions appeared only in stylized form: the typical firm or union, the faceless regulator. Culture was absent, and psychology entered only in the form of rational consumers assumed to know what they wanted. "Although economic activity is intrinsically linked with social and political life, there is a mistaken tendency, encouraged by contemporary economic discourse, to regard the economy as a facet of life with its own laws, separate from the rest of society" (Fukuyama 1996, 6). These mathematical models were not without practical utility, as in explaining/predicting changes in coffee prices. Valuable insight was provided on the costs and benefits of trade restriction or government regulation. The models were less successful, though still far from useless, in understanding or dealing with business cycles. And as for understanding why some countries grow faster than others, models with no place for institutional diversity, much less culture or psychology or politics, not surprisingly provided little insight (see North 1990).[5]

MECHANISMS OF INSTITUTIONAL CHANGE

Both economic and political institutions evolve over time. Unlike the case of cultural evolution, in which imperfect transmission is a major source of change, the formal nature of institutions requires that some purposive action be undertaken to change them. Economists had often been guilty of assuming that people would naturally reform institutions in an efficient manner. That is, institutions would become better and better at achieving the goals of the society as a whole, and would be changed as culture, polity, or technology evolved in order to best reflect the new reality in these other spheres. This was for economists a natural extension of what may be the key result in economics: in free markets competition will yield the socially optimal price and amount of production.

Institutions, however, evolve in an environment quite different from that of market exchange. As with the case of culture, we must expect that individuals cannot foresee the full ramifications of the changes they propose (see Thelen and Steinmo 1992). Institutions "serve various purposes or interests in a society independent of any individual's or group's understanding of that purpose or interest" (Chalmers 1982, 135). Rendering them more effective in one direction may make them much worse in another. In particular, there are often though not always tradeoffs between enhancing growth and reducing income inequality. And if we are designing institutions to enhance economic growth, and even the experts are far from sure of the causes of growth, how can we presume that these institutions are steadily improving? Thus it is a mistake to assume—as economists and politicians all too readily do—that the institutions we like (even our market institutions) must be the best simply because they are the end result (to our shortsighted eyes) of a lengthy evolutionary process (see Schelling 1978, 37; Dosi 1988).

Hodgson (1993) suggests that we are likely to see lengthy periods in which particular institutions are unchanged, punctuated by periods of change. Given that institutions serve multiple purposes and change is unpredictable, there will be a natural conservatism in (many) people such that they do not try to change institutions that appear to function reasonably well. (Thus those sociologists who stress the stability of institutions and those who emphasize change are both partially correct.) Moreover, when change does occur it will tend to be incremental. Rather than sweeping aside the old institution, we amend it. Along with a recognition that change is unpredictable, this reflects the fact that institutions often support and are supported by values (see below) and/or other institutions; we do not wish to endanger this positive reinforcement if possible. In times of revolution—as in present day Eastern Europe—the dangers of sweeping institutional change are all too obvious. But gradual change is necessarily path dependant: institutions today are the children of yesterday's institutions (even in Eastern Europe, countries which had allowed the greatest amount of private activity under communist regimes have tended to adjust more quickly). This almost guarantees that different societies, even though they may face similar technological and other pressures today, will have quite different institutions. We should be suspicious that any of these will be perfect (especially if the environment is changing faster than institutions can evolve). In the case of Eastern Europe, this means that attempts at wholesale copying of institutions from any Western country cannot be entirely successful nor entirely desirable.

Knight (1992) reviews the history of theories of institutional change. Locke's view that institutions reflected natural rights comes close to the assumption that institutions would always be optimal. Hobbes' emphasis on a social contract also tended to assume that people knew what they were doing when they developed institutions. Hume was more conscious of the unintended effects. Spencer emphasized natural selection among states as a source of institutional advance This insight should not be lost. While we should not embrace the assumption of optimality, we should recognize that there are rewards for good institutions and penalties for bad, and thus some tendency for improvement over time (again limited by the speed of change in the surrounding environment).

Knight emphasizes a further problem, however. As Adam Smith had hinted, and Marx and Weber argued at length, those designing institutions need not have the interests of the entire society in mind. Individuals do not have equal input into decisions about institutional form, and we can expect political and economic leaders, and even experts, to pursue institutional changes in their own interest. Knight feels that it is best to think of a bargaining process among special interests.[6] In such a world, institutions will only approach the social optimum if the masses are well represented, or their interests coincide with those in power, or selection pressure from inter-state (or inter-firm, and so on) competition is strong. Recognizing that none of the bargainers knows the full effect of any change complicates the story; history is full of figures who accomplished the opposite of what they intended by pushing too far and inciting others to react. Moreover, the process of institutional change is slowed by the need to negotiate with those who benefit from the status quo. Unlike reformers, these will know precisely how they benefit from the existing rules.

I should not leave the impression that all institutions are affected by the above forces to the same degree. Some institutions are routinely fought over in the political arena, others haggled over in the back room, and still others so complex that experts have the predominant influence on their form. It may thus be a blessing rather than a curse that there are a number of competing theories of institutional change. These can be distinguished by the degree to which they suggest institutions are optimal and/or reflect the will of the whole society, and by whether they see change as intentional or accidental, subject to selection, or a natural progression (Knight 1992). Different theories may each be suited to a subset of institutions.[7]

Since institutions need not automatically reflect the (farsighted) will of the society, they deserve their own place in the organizing schema. Since they impose penalties on those who break the rules, institutions constrain our behavior (Knight, indeed, defines institutions as efforts by some to constrain the activities of others). Hodgson (1994) goes so far as to suggest that institutions should replace individuals as the basic units of economic analysis. This is a road I only follow part way in this book, for I do not wish to lose sight of the role of the individual. Certainly, though, our institutions will affect both the goals we choose to pursue, and the means we employ to achieve them (see Thelen and Steinmo 1992).

C → E: Culture — Economy

Culture has two main types of effect on the economy: it shapes institutions, and it shapes personal behavior and through this economic activity. I will deal with the latter effect first. Economists tend to assume that individuals are both rational and selfish; we have seen in the previous two chapters that this is an overly simplistic view. It should not be surprising, then, if culture also has major influences on the economy via individual behavior.

"All economic behavior is equally social in character" (Ayres 1978, 95). Just as sitting is both a physical and social act, we cannot ignore the social overtones of commercial exchange. Even in our modern impersonal world, I still greet clerks in stores, and may choose where to shop on the basis of the treatment I receive. Business people doing deals are even more likely to care about the attitudes of those they interact with (are they honest? hardworking? easy to deal with?).

John Stuart Mill, the nineteenth-century writer often viewed as the father of the rational selfish *homo economicus* of economic theory, in fact advocated the study of economic "ethology" to see how character (he referred specifically to such attributes as attitude to work, time preference, and risk aversion) differed across time and place. He felt that we could only understand differences in income levels and distribution across countries with reference to what I have called culture and institutions. With few exceptions, economists have not followed the path described by Mill. Those concerned with economic growth—the economic historians and development economists (one of the leading journals is titled "Economic Development and Cultural Change")—were marginally more open to cultural influences. Yet those who delved too deeply into the cultural realm risked damaging their reputation as real economists. Among anthropologists, a subfield of economic anthropology emerged to focus on the links between culture and economy. This was a natural outgrowth of the tendency of ethnographers to study the "whole society" while on field trips (Plattner 1989). While economic anthropologists have done much in terms of showing how economic behavior varied with cultural milieu, their holistic focus and tendency to define culture in various different ways limited their ability to identify particular causal links.

Harrison (1992) warns us that not all cultural attributes have significant implications for the economy. While certainly true, we cannot immediately leap to the opposing conclusion that only a couple of cultural attributes matter. John Stuart Mill urged parsimony, but we can hardly as scientists limit our attention to a couple of cultural elements just for convenience. Harrison himself provides a lengthy list: "Who prospers? Societies committed to the future, to education, to achievement and excellence, to a better life for all, to community, as well as to freedom and justice" (1992, 247).

I. TRUST

While all humans (except those we define as psychopaths) have a tendency to altruism and fairness, culture can act to enhance or restrict the operation of this motive. Experiments show that students from different cultural backgrounds differ significantly, for example, in their (average) willing-ness to raise prices well above costs when demand conditions allow. Some cultures stress the value of helping others, while others urge members to achievement for their own sake. Even among hunter-gatherers this can have enormous effects: in some societies the best hunters take lots of leisure during which they enjoy the proceeds of others' efforts, while in others they work hard and accumulate more wives and children (Plattner 1989).

It is often suggested that societies that value honesty and trust should and do fare better than others. If true, then we should be aware that pushing the belief that market systems function best when every person pursues only their self-interest may actually serve to undermine the effectiveness of market systems. We cannot simply rely on the natural tendency of people to behave honorably (Trigg 1985, 135–36). Adam Smith himself, while confident that selfish greed would get us 90% of the way to market efficiency, knew that "moral sentiments" were also necessary.[8] Empirical studies have indeed found a positive correlation between measures of trust and economic growth.

While business people in their everyday lives are conscious of the importance of trust, and devote much of their time to meetings whose primary purpose is to establish trust, economists have spent little effort exploring the issue. They often speak of prisoner's dilemma problems: two thiefs are arrested and questioned separately. They are told that they will serve one year in jail if both confess, two years if only the other confesses (and goes free), and only two months if neither confess. They are both better off if neither confesses than if both confess. But each of them has an incentive to confess, whether they believe their partner will confess (in which case they spend one year rather than two in jail) or not (in which case they go free rather than spending two months in jail). So selfish individuals confess and each spends a year in jail. Only if they expect to end up in similar situations with the same partner in future will they consider not confessing.

In the real world, though, thiefs may "trust" each other not to confess. Nor does this trust necessarily depend on the relationship between the two individuals. If in their society they will face ostracism for confessing (or have internalized those values, and would feel enormous guilt for confess-ing) then they can trust each other regardless of whether their partnership has a future. Business deals often hinge on the same elements: the accep-tance of a number of unwritten rules and the confidence that others will obey those rules both to protect their reputation and salve their conscience. Both the rules themselves and the strength with which they are held are elements of culture.

It is, quite simply, prohibitively expensive to negotiate contracts that provide for all possible contingencies; it is much easier to reach agreement if one can assume a shared set of values in evaluating how unforeseen developments affect the obligations of all parties (DiMaggio 1994; he notes that writers as diverse as Foucault, Talcott Parsons, Frank, and Thaler have made this point). Sabel, in the same volume, expands on DiMaggio's argument by stressing that these parties will be much more sure of the other if they can be confident that third parties will share their values. These third parties can be institutional in nature (courts, tribunals), but can also just be the shared reaction of friends or members of the business community. In the first case we look to laws, in the second to values shared by networks of contacts. If these networks are under-developed, there will be too little consensus on values for dealmaking to be easy. There is an opposite danger of values becoming so rigid that the group is unable to react to changing conditions. Still, Fukuyama (1996, 27) notes that trust will facilitate institutional evolution in response to changed circumstances.

Closely knit ethnic minorities—Jews in Europe, Armenians in the Middle East, Chinese and Indians in Southeast Asia—have often played a disproportionate role in commerce (see Brezis and Temin 1999). While restrictions on their access to other forms of livelihood were often important in encouraging a commercial orientation, the success of these groups is likely owed for the most part to the trust which existed among members. Trading over large distances in an era when transport was slow and expensive depended crucially on trust, and minority groups time and again proved to have an advantage. Yet trust is still important today (recent estimates suggest that 25% of GNP is devoted to "talk") in any business deal, whether local or global in extent. Fukuyama (1996, 9–10) suggests that both hostile industrial relations in France and the lack of black-owned inner city businesses in the United States are largely due to the lack of trust within the relevant communities. Trust may become even more important in the future, if the trend whereby large firms subcontract to networks of small firms continues.

Trust depends crucially, but not entirely, on attitudes toward honesty. Fukuyama (1996, 10–11) refers to Coleman's concept of "social capital," the ability of group members to cooperate, which depends on the degree of shared values and the willingness of individuals to subordinate individual to group interests (Fukuyama suggests that social capital is declining in the United States). He emphasizes that these beneficial cultural attitudes can not be achieved by rational calculations alone: "Law, contract, and economic rationality provides a necessary but not sufficient basis for both the stability and prosperity of postindustrial societies; they must as well be leavened with reciprocity, moral obligation, duty toward community, and trust, which are based in habit rather than rational calculation."

Trust is not the only key to a business deal, of course. Both sides will bargain, attempting to reach an agreement that benefits them the most. Deals may be easier to reach in societies with highly developed standards of fairness. Otherwise our inherent tendency to exaggerate what we deserve might cause many mutually beneficial agreements to remain stubbornly un-consummated [G→E]. Experiments have certainly shown that participants from different societies pursue different strategies in bargaining situations.

Economists try to analyze the bargaining process in terms of mathematical game theory. Unfortunately, for most real world situations we are unable to determine what would be the best strategy to pursue. For some games it is at least possible to identify an equilibrium (sometimes more than one) at which all participants see no advantage to changing their behavior. As Bicchieri (1993) notes, though, economists tend to ignore the fact that such equilibria depend on all participants sharing a perception of the rules of the game. She is less successful at showing how people would come to share such perceptions, but can be applauded for showing that even economic theory depends on assumptions of a shared culture.

2. TIME PREFERENCE

The troubles experienced by Mexico in financial markets in 1995 have underlined an important point: while foreign investment can be useful in the process of economic development, heavy reliance on it risks financial crisis if foreigners suddenly decide to reduce their exposure to your country's finances. Moreover, despite the large global movements of capital in the modern world, there is still a very strong correlation between the rate of investment in a country and the rate of savings. These facts taken together imply that the rate of investment that is sustainable over a long period in any country will depend crucially on that country's savings rates. And investment rates are in turn an important (though not the only) determinant of economic growth.

Savings rates differ markedly across societies. Some of this is due to income differences: people with higher incomes tend everywhere to save a larger proportion of their incomes. Institutions also matter: people's savings depend on the reputation of banks (including central banks), the structure of pension funds, and even the degree of political stability. A substantial proportion of cross-society differences in savings rates cannot be readily attributed to either income or institutional differences, however. Asian economies have higher savings rates than those in either Latin America or Africa, for example. Why? Time preference is an obvious candidate: societies that live for the present are likely to have lower savings rates than those that value the future (feedback is possible here in that poor people may feel that have no choice but to live for the present; remember, though, that equally poor societies have quite different savings rates).

Other aspects of culture are also important. In societies in which one is expected to share money with either relatives or the local community, people display a natural tendency to either avoid the accumulation of savings or to save in the illiquid forms of large houses or herds which community standards do not require to be shared. Alternatively, savings rates will be higher in societies in which rites of passage such as marriage and death must be marked with huge celebrations (and perhaps dowries).

Time preference is not only important in the modern world. Economic growth rates will have been influenced throughout history by time preference. It is noteworthy that real interest rates (that is, the market rate minus inflation) have generally been much higher than the 4% or so common in the postwar West. The number of investment projects that will be judged worthy when real interest rates are 10% will be a mere fraction of those that pass the 4% test (and decisions by farmers to build fences or even to use natural fertilizer qualify as investment decisions). And the market interest rate should be primarily influenced by time preference (mediated by the institutional structure). The economic impact can be huge: Gellner (1989) argues that the switch from hunting-gathering to agriculture can only happen if the society in question has a sufficiently long-term orientation.

3. ATTITUDE TO ACHIEVEMENT

Perhaps the most famous attempt to describe a link between culture and economy is McClelland's research on achievement motivation. Since the 1960s he has used various sorts of psychological tests to show that people in many poorer societies have a lesser drive to achievement. This, he suggests, could be a key element in economic growth. His approach has been criticized both methodologically and empirically (C→I2). One objection is that his measures of achievement are culturally biased themselves: he is thus actually testing for whether people exhibit "Western" attitudes toward achievement. However, if people in other societies seek achievement exclusively through rising in the priesthood, military, or government, then we would still get the result that economic growth would be hindered. We should be open then to suggestions that societies may differ not only in their attitude toward achievement in general, but in what sort of achievement they favor. (Note that those who seek achievement for the fame it brings may "slack off" when nobody is looking, while those who value achievement for its own sake will not; Smith and Bond 1993.)

This leads to a second and more serious critique. To what extent are the values observed a result rather than a cause of economic conditions? Children in an urban slum may value (economic) achievement little if they believe that they have few opportunities for success: we would be misguided to attribute dropping out of school, teenage pregnancy, or welfare abuse entirely to values rather than schemas. Alternatively Japanese dedication to the service of their employer may reflect the institution of lifetime employment (see DiMaggio 1994). The economic development literature is full of rural peasants who decided to work harder and produce more once institutions or transport changed so that they had access to markets. It would be interesting to know if their attitudes toward achievement changed as well.

The approach of this book guides us to be skeptical that any one phenomenon is entirely dependent on only one other. Nor is it difficult to think of noneconomic forces that could shape cultural attitudes toward achievement: religion is an obvious candidate (though it too is shaped by the economy). Krugman (1994) feels that the denigration of the value of work from the 1960s has had a negative impact on economic performance: if true, this indicates that values can turn against achievement even in a time of prosperity.

Moreover, there is much evidence of significant differences in cultural attitudes among modern Western societies. Britain has been the focus of much of this literature, with many writers suggesting that "bad" attitudes toward education and/or business have hurt British economic performance in this century (e.g., Hannah 1993). Egnal (1996) argues that in the early nineteenth century those in the northeastern United States were more driven to succeed than those in the South or in French Canada. He attributes the southern preference for gentlemanly leisure to a mixture of climate [N →C], the social divisions inherent in slavery [S→C], and the sources of southern immigration, while French Canadians' focus on the present, tradition, and the family is attributable to the dominant role of the Catholic church in people's lives. Harrison (1992) more generally argues for the importance of stimulating respect for both business people and teachers if one wishes to encourage economic growth.[9] And enthusiasm and drive are everywhere the key to business success.

4. RELIGION

Early in this century Max Weber gained fame with his thesis that at least some branches of the Protestant religion instilled values of work and ambition (for success in this life) which were in turn largely responsible for rapid economic growth in northwestern Europe. Calvinists, for example, felt that God would reward the worthy, and thus economic success was a sign of divine favor. More generally, individuals were free to decide what god wanted from them; thus few activities were forbidden, and occupational mobility was enhanced. The emphasis on individualism and literacy was also important (see Gellner 1989). Fukuyama (1996) speaks of frugality, rationality, future-orientation, punctuality, reliability, and trust (especially among small groups of Protestants). Bruton (1997) mentions a belief in both progress and mastery of nature. Lessnoff (1994), in one of very few works on the subject in recent years, stresses the work ethic and profit ethic associated with Protestantism. Fukuyama (1996, 44–45) feels that most scholars who have examined the issue recognize on the one hand that the correlation between Protestantism and growth is imperfect, and that some of the links posited by Weber are misguided, but on the other hand feel the general hypothesis has merit. He notes that the harsh reaction of the Catholic church to Protestantism may have acted to inhibit change of all sorts in Catholic Europe, and that recent growth in Latin America is associated with conversions to Protestantism. Beyond the effects through values posited by Weber, one can think of a number of other possible links between religion and economic activity: religious institutions are large economic players, religious leaders speak out on major economic issues (either as forces for change or apologists for the status quo), religious groups provide aid for people in economic distress, some religions discourage certain occupational choices, and cults provide an escape from the wider economy for some individuals (Wuthnow 1994). Many of the authors in Jeremy (1998) stress the networking that occurred within religious communities, though Patrick O'Brien in that volume is skeptical of their evidence, and wonders why networking was more common in some communities than others.

Economic historians in recent decades have given little space to Weber's thesis in their attempts to explain the economic success of northern Europe and North America. This may reflect in part the fact that cultural arguments of any kind are hard to squeeze into the mathematical models favored by modern economists. But historians could also make sound arguments that Catholic communities in France and Belgium fared rather well. Also, they could point to a lag of some centuries between the Protestant Reformation and the era of rapid growth in northwestern Europe. Finally, it is not clear why England should have been the economic powerhouse of Europe for so long, given that its brand of Protestantism fit Weber's ideal less well than continental varieties.

It is noteworthy that all major religious tracts speak of matters such as work, money, and possessions. Most societies make some attempt to justify their economic system and its resulting income distribution in terms of dominant religion(s). This raises the question of to what extent religions come to reflect the values needed to support the economic system. Religious leaders may, by virtue of heading powerful economic organizations and interacting regularly with other economic and political leaders, tend to interpret their religion in a supportive fashion (they may in some cases fear political or economic penalties for doing otherwise; [P→E]). Moreover, we will see below that the economy influences culture, and we saw in chapter 5 that values influence religion. Still, once religious beliefs have been codified in revered texts, they can adjust sluggishly at best to changing economic circumstances.

Some religions attribute poverty to fate. Hinduism is a key example: the belief that one's role in this life was determined by behavior in a previous life is thought by some to encourage quiet acceptance of one's lot in life. Most religions encourage charitable work, but often reserve this task for private charity (due to an emphasis on a personal responsibility to do god's will on the part of both giver and receiver). All are willing to accept significant differences in income. In the modern United States, religious belief is positively associated with dedication to school and work, but has no effect on attitudes toward income distribution. Islam requires its more successful adherents to donate a significant portion of income to the poor; there appears to be widespread evasion at present, and thus no greater support of the poor (or shunning of conspicuous consumption) than in Western societies.

Studies of the economic effects of non-Christian world religions must not ignore the fact that these have not had as much time to adapt to modern economic conditions as has Christianity. What appear at present to be negative characteristics may prove adaptable over time. Islam, for example, takes a very harsh view of the payment of interest. So did Christianity several centuries ago. A combination of reinterpretation of the Koran and innovative practices of Islamic banks may well yield a solution that does not hamper the development of financial institutions. Some Islamic economists argue that rules forcing depositors to bear risk rather than just earning a fixed rate of interest can be advantageous, though Western economists are skeptical and point to efforts by Islamic banks to imitate the payment of interest as closely as possible.

Eastern religions differ even more than Islam from Christianity. They tend to emphasize harmony with nature rather than mastery over it; this may have limited the advance of say mining or even agriculture (but note that East Asian societies built massive irrigation schemes over the centuries). They also tend to emphasize personal responsibility to play the role fate has dealt rather than the pursuit of one's individuality. The gains in terms of trust, honesty, and a sense of duty (and strong interpersonal networks) may or may not be greater than costs in terms of personal initiative. Not surprisingly, the evaluation of the effects of Eastern religions has changed as Eastern economies have fared well over recent decades (Weber felt Confucian ideals would inhibit growth). Some

scholars suggest that Eastern religions would have restrained the indigenous development of modern capitalism, but are conducive to borrowing
and improving upon it. Fukuyama (1996), for example, argues that only
the fusion of Confucian and Western liberal thought created cultural support for economic growth. Others would suspect that religion was far from
the most important determinant of Asian economic performance (G.
Hamilton 1994).

5. VARIOUS OTHER CULTURAL ATTRIBUTES

Harrison (1992) claims that a number of other cultural attributes have an
important impact on economic performance: individualism (coupled with
responsibility; he warns against the excesses of selfishness), openness to
innovation, tidiness, courtesy, punctuality, and optimism (subgroups that
feel alienated, inferior, or marginalized will have little success). He is
especially critical of an attitude common in Spanish-speaking countries of
elevating one's responsibility to family well above one's responsibility to
the wider society: he feels that this saps the sense of trust and fairness so
necessary to economic growth.

Harrison's attempts to explain the relative success of different societies
is controversial (and I would be skeptical of a line of argument which
suggests that only culture matters). He argues that the emphasis on family
in Asia is less dangerous because it is coupled with a sense of responsibility toward the wider society. Spanish child-rearing practices are accused of
encouraging selfishness, vanity, emotional instability, dishonesty, and authoritarianism. Brazilian success, given a similar ethnic mix as other South
American countries, is credited to size (which encourages optimism and
competition) and the willingness of the Portuguese elite to integrate with
immigrant groups. Conjectures such as these must be approached
carefully, but with an open mind.

6. CULTURE → CONSUMER WANTS

Economic analysis tends to assume that consumer tastes are given. Pressed
on the point, economists readily admit that billions would not be spent on
advertising if individual preferences could not be shaped by the wider
society. Indeed, to deny this possibility would reduce individuals to mere
automatons blindly pursuing genetic drives oblivious to information they
could obtain from others (Trigg 1985, 134). Fine, Heasman, and Wright
(1996) describe how culture and social structure influence the demand for
various foods in Britain [S→E]. Several contributors in Miller (1995)
argue that all disciplines have understudied the social (and psychological)
influences on individual consumption decisions. Yet economists are hesi-

tant to ascribe too great an importance to this link for a simple reason: we can only be confident that market exchange makes people better off if we can be sure that they are not induced to pursue misguided goals. If in fact many of our wants are cultural creations rather than reflections of internal drives then all market outcomes are suspect.

Traditional societies are often mocked for religious and other ceremonies or practices in which a significant portion of societal output is "wasted." Yet all societies can be accused of engaging in ceremonial waste (Ayres 1978). We can hardly evaluate market outcomes properly without recognizing this fact. In our society waste serves a similar function: it allows rich and powerful people to spend resources in ways that satisfy no other basic drives than their wish for status. Noneconomic signals of status, if they existed, could thus allow everyone to satisfy the same needs as before at a lower level of output. Our culture determines that fancy cars are a means of impressing others, and thus some members of society come to want cars with features they rarely if ever need (note, though, that their consumption may encourage product innovations that later serve a mass market).

7. ORGANIZATIONAL CULTURE

As I switch attention from how culture influences the economic behavior of individuals to how it shapes institutions, it is useful to look at organizational culture. Whether we speak of private firms, nonprofit entities, or government bureaucracies, the views of managers concerning worker motives will shape how they structure organizations, while the actual motives of workers will determine whether the organization operates as intended. While some scholars focus on the question of whether organizations naturally function better in certain societies (e.g., does the loyalty and dedication of Japanese workers increase the efficiency of Japanese firms?), others inquire as to how firm managers can affect the internal culture of an organization so as to encourage work effort.

Management theory oscillates between a stress on control, whereby managers tell workers what to do and monitor their behavior closely, versus an emphasis on morale, loyalty, and giving workers some freedom to determine how best to achieve the organization's goals. Today, this debate can be seen in discussions of the Japanese emphasis on work teams and cooperation (with many scholars being surprised that this system seems to produce results even when transplanted to North America, though notably less wonderful results than in Japan itself). There is also a concern that the ongoing wave of corporate and government downsizing may be destroying the sense of morale and loyalty on which organizational success rests. In particular, workers may be hesitant to suggest means of enhancing productivity if they fear losing their own job as a result.

One variable that is often the focus of inquiry is employee turnover. North American firms are already characterized by much more turnover among both middle management and employees than is the case in Europe or Japan. Loss of loyalty or fears of job loss can encourage even greater mobility. While mobility can be advantageous for the economy if it serves to make information more widely available, the downside is that organizations may be unable to sustain either strong relations with customers or any sense of what the organization stands for. Some firms struggle against the tide—devoting large sums to training workers (e.g., MacDonald's University); there is some evidence at least at the level of senior managers that retention and promotion from within is a superior strategy in terms of firm performance.

Trust becomes even more essential within an organization if the ranks of middle management are thinned to such an extent that detailed monitoring is not possible. Organizations can only trust workers if those workers in turn feel both that the organization is basically fair and that they have a future with it. Firms can institute and advertise rules of fair play. Some key portions of the work force can be granted some job security. Firm rituals (e.g., company picnics) and an espoused corporate culture may help, though many scholars suspect that these are better for external public relations than internal (see Selznick 1992). Still, a recent survey found four worker attitudes to be strongly correlated with firm performance: a belief that firms give workers the opportunity to do their best work, a belief that the firm listens, a belief that coworkers care about quality, and a belief that the worker's efforts contribute to firm success.

How closely should managers and employees work? Some hold that a sharp distinction needs to be maintained: otherwise managers will be hesitant to discipline or dismiss workers who fail to perform. Others emphasize that a sense of common purpose between managers and workers cuts both ways: miners are more likely to strike than surface workers in regular contact with managers.

A positive organizational culture can work to enhance the natural tendency of most people to (want to) behave honestly. One key question concerns the tradeoff between emphasizing teamwork versus individual responsibility and initiative. If workers identify with coworkers, they will be more likely to pull their weight. An extreme example is provided by religious communes, where workers are observed to be very productive despite the lack of monitoring. In general, though, workers may work hardest in response to financial incentives. But pay differentials may sap the sense of identity (and fairness) that encourages worker dedication (Frank 1988). The theory of efficiency wages suggests that paying all workers more may help the firm attract and keep better workers, while also encouraging a greater sense of loyalty. And some recent research suggests that the best results occur when incentive pay and teamwork are combined [I→E].

We should not ignore the possibility that loyalty to organizations may drive individuals to behave in a manner which hurts the wider society. Even in the military, we now tell soldiers that they should disobey orders that violate human rights. Yet within some firms salespeople feel pressured to mislead and workers to ignore environmental or safety laws—though there are rarely precise instructions to this effect (see Davis and Stasz 1990). That such deviant organizational cultures are possible indicates a failure of the wider culture to inculcate values of honesty and responsibility.

We should also not lose sight of the numbing conformity that afflicts many larger bureaucracies. For decades, IBM insisted that all managers wear white shirts. Corporate cultures, if pushed too far, can cause individuality to be threatened. And conformity is hardly conducive to recognizing the problems which any bureaucracy possesses, or to innovation.

What works best within a particular organization will depend on the type of work the organization is trying to accomplish. High-tech firms need a loose structure so that all employees are able to innovate.[10] More traditional firms may require a greater dose of command. Kuhn (1993) feels that all organizations need to encourage a creative culture in our ever-changing world. If pundits are right that the future of both manufacturing and services involves the tailoring of output to the needs of small groups of consumers, workers can no longer be treated like mass production machines. Best practice likely also varies across societies. Relying on salary incentives may make more sense in North America with a long tradition of individualism than in Japan with its emphasis on collective effort.

If different organizations have different cultures, how can they cope with mergers or the increasingly common business alliances (where firms cooperate in the production of particular goods or services)? It is essential that managers from different organizations have frequent informal face-to-face meetings so that they can understand each other. They can thus strive to seek compatibility in values, while respecting different customs. It is also important that the managers who will work together play a role in determining the new structure: what looks like a good combination to the lawyers may be unworkable (Kanter 1995).

Salaries within bureaucracies tend to be tied to promotions; these in turn tend to be based on seniority for blue collar positions but not for white collar (and hence there is the possibility that discrimination and other biases affect white collar promotion decisions). Economic theory pays little attention to these internal promotion mechanisms, despite the fact that many positions, especially those you can only be promoted into, seem to be rewarded quite differently from what a competitive labor market would suggest. Do the best people get promoted (or do people often get promoted out of jobs they were good at into jobs they perform poorly)? Does the occasional promotion act as a spur to worker effort, or is it a source of divisiveness and anger? (and decreased self-image among subordinates; J. Blau 1993). Do hierarchical job classification systems interfere with teamwork and cooperation? Why do some jobs provide greater opportunities for advancement than others, and do firms make enough effort to ensure that the "best" people get a chance to shine in those positions? Are the raises that accompany promotions bigger than necessary? Answers to these questions cannot flow simply from economic theory but require both psychological understanding of worker motivation and sociological analysis of how workers function in groups (see various chapters, especially those by Sorenson and Meyer, in Smelser and Swedberg 1994).

I close by emphasizing that firm owners need to be concerned with loyalty of senior managers as well. They too can be encouraged to act out of loyalty or honesty in the firm's interest. The difference here is that shareholders often have much less influence of any sort over the activities of senior managers than these in turn have over the rest of the firm. Corporate culture may thus reflect what senior managers want, since they are the locus of power (similar arguments can be made with respect to government bureaucracies and elected officials, or nonprofits and their boards). Ownership of large blocks of shares by individuals or institutions might allow better oversight of senior managers, and thus encourage a corporate culture reflective of shareholder desires.

8. CULTURE → ECONOMIC INSTITUTIONS

Formal institutions arise when people will not obey particular informal rules (or when informal rules do not exist that cover particular situations) to the extent that (some) people think the benefits of formal rules outweigh the costs. Thus formal institutions are designed and created on a foundation of informal values (Knight 1992). This limits the possibilities available to those who frame the new rules (who will try to bend the rules to suit their own personal interests). While special interests will try to influence both informal and formal rules, Knight fears that formal rules are much more likely to perpetuate inequality.

The growth in size of a community (or firm) may make informal governance impossible, and thus induce the creation of institutions.[11] If the interests of members diverge considerably, institutions are unlikely to affect all equitably. When closely knit communities feel the need for formal rules, they are more likely to succeed in developing effective and acceptable policies (Sabel 1994).

Institutions evolve over time; today's institution is a direct descendant of yesterday's. It is important to remember that at any point in time the effect of institutions depends on informal rules as well. A rule against pilfering at work will be very successful if workers value honesty highly, less successful if workers value secrecy. Those favoring institutional change must be conscious of how culture will influence the effects of the changes they promote, as well as how evolving culture is changing the effect of existing rules (Sabel 1994; Selznick 1992). North (1990) notes that societies which value honesty or hard work will be able to fashion "better" institutions; he hopes that economic change itself can encourage such beneficial value formation (e.g., market expansion could encourage a sense of fair play) [E→C].

9. CULTURE → MARKET INSTITUTIONS

I could apply the foregoing analysis to the huge cross-country differences that exist in finance, labor law, or firm structure. Instead, I will focus on how culture influences institutions governing exchange. Economists tend to assume that free markets are something natural that exist everywhere in similar form (Barber 1993). Such an assumption blinds us to the effects of institutional form in our own society and severely limits our ability to give advice to other societies with quite different histories.

We suggested earlier (G→C4) that we have four inherent models governing exchange—authority, equality, community sharing, and market exchange—and that all cultures will sanction each of these for certain situations. If true, then those who have argued that economists are wrong to think market exchange ubiquitous are themselves misguided. But so too are those economists who feel that the situations in which market exchange will be condoned are unaffected by the wider culture. An obvious example is slavery: markets for people only exist where the society believes this is ethically justifiable. Few goods or services, if any, have not had constraints put on their sale in some time and place.

The question, then, is one of degree. Karl Polanyi, while recognizing that market exchange had been around since at least the Stone Age, devoted most of his career to arguing that it had only become dominant in Europe within the last few centuries (but even there, and to this day, restrictions on market activity are maintained). Most economic historians would argue for a much greater role for the market in history than Polanyi grants, especially for Asia and medieval Europe, but also Africa and the New World. Fernand Braudel, a famed economic and cultural historian, felt that market exchange was essential to any large-scale society—it was only the problem of monopoly that had risen to new levels in early modern Europe (Haskell and Teichgraeber 1993). Fiske (1991), however, argues that the market model is still less important than the others in West Africa today.[12]

Much of Polanyi's work focused on the markets for land and labor. Markets for land can only develop as societies abandon the principle that all members of society must have access to land to feed their families. Markets for labor likewise depended on a breakdown in the view that each laborer was tied to particular pieces of land and/or political overlords. While both changes have advantages, they can be viewed as relying on societal denial of a guaranteed livelihood for all.[13] Many writers since Polanyi have objected to this treatment of individuals as merely the owner of their talents rather than as an ethical whole or part of a larger society. In any case the culture/economy link should be clear.

Culture is not the only determinant of the relative prevalence of different types of exchange. If we observe two tribes engaging in a complex exchange of gifts rather than haggling over market prices, it could be because mutual antagonism between the two has rendered market interaction too dangerous and/or costly. Yet each tribe desires something the other has, and so they are forced to develop a different method of exchange. North (1990) argues that we should not lose sight of both the costs of transactions (negotiating, acquiring information, enforcing contracts) and political circumstances [P→E] when discussing modes of exchange. He emphasizes that changes in modes of exchange can often more easily be explained in terms of these variables rather than culture (this may reflect in large part the difficulty to date in measuring cultural attributes).

Even the transactions costs stressed by North are greatly influenced by culture. In a society pervaded by honesty and trust, the costs of getting information about both goods and people will be much lower. Shared values will also reduce the costs of negotiation. Trade occurs when both sides feel they benefit: the higher the transaction costs the more mutually beneficial trades that will not occur (you may be willing to sell an apple for a dollar, and I may be willing to pay $1.50, but if the transaction costs are more than the fifty-cent difference the trade never happens). The level of economic activity depends crucially, then, on culture.

It is not just the existence of but the structure of markets that is influenced by culture (as Braudel 1979, noted when he surveyed the great range of market forms over the course of human history). Markets, to work, must be more than places for exchange. They are necessarily a venue for competition (as Weber emphasized),[14] and thus shaped by norms for honesty, cooperation, and courtesy. They are also a mechanism for the exchange of information. Markets are not a place but a process in which buyers and sellers learn about each other and those they compete with. Their institutional form is thus shaped both by our genes and our culture. If markets do not allow for positive feedback among participants with respect to a certain commodity, then exchange will not occur (T. Smith 1992).

E → C: Economy → Culture

I have noted before that culture can act to limit the fitness of a particular group. There are, however, strong pressures on culture to evolve in a fitness-enhancing direction. We would expect, then, that changing economic circumstances would (imperfectly) act to change culture in ways that allowed the society to take better advantage of its economic opportunities. Egnal (1996, ch. 12) thus argues that the discovery of oil in Texas, and urbanization elsewhere in the South, changed cultural attitudes so that these were more favorable to economic growth. We should not, of course, go overboard and assume that societies will naturally and quickly gain the cultural attributes conducive to growth. Even if Israel were ideally suited to pork production, a cultural prohibition strongly rooted in tradition will not readily be changed.[15]

As anthropologists have long noted, dispersed hunter-gatherer groups display a lack of complex cultural practices. A few simple rules governing mate selection, gender roles, and communal decision-making are all that exist. To some extent, the lack of culture can be attributed to the simple fact that small mobile groups will find it difficult to stage elaborate rituals. However, many anthropologists feel that there is also less need for elaborate cultural guidelines in a society of self-sufficient families (Johnson and Earle 1989). As economies become more complicated, and especially as people turn to settled agriculture, greater elaboration of values becomes necessary.[16] No longer able to move in search of food, communities develop norms of sharing, gift exchange (with prestige flowing to those who give most), and interest-free loans and/or kinship obligations to insure against hunger and starvation (Eggertson 1990). Religious belief in a creator god concerned with human morality supports many of these values; such beliefs are only common in agricultural and industrial societies (Lenski, Lenski, and Nolan 1991).

According to Parsons (1966), though, cultures could not increase in complexity as quickly as economies, at least over the last few centuries. He felt that economic development is inherently a process of differentiation (though the process unfolds differently across societies). The number of occupations increases. Work moves from home to factory. In a simple world, cultural rules can guide every sort of interaction. In a complex world, values evolve so that they become more general. Individuals thus find themselves questioning how to behave in particular situations.

Modern industrial society has surely wrought tremendous cultural changes. Many anthropologists believe that there are huge differences (on average) in values between those in developed countries and those in less developed countries (DiMaggio 1994). Smith and Bond (1993) compile a lengthy list of characteristics of "modern man": belief in self-efficacy, low social integration with relatives, egalitarianism, openness to change, high achievement motivation, independence, future orientation, secular religious beliefs, and individualism. Individualism is credited with being the key element of the modern outlook; many of the other characteristics flow from it. (Other scholars question the strength of the link between income and individualism; they suggest that differences in work ethic are more important.)

In the 1970s, it was commonly argued that economic convergence would inevitably lead to cultural (and political) convergence. One argument along these lines stressed that economic ideology was strongly intertwined with all cultural elements (Smith 1993). I would, of course, be wary of such a blanket hypothesis, and suspect that some cultural traits would be much more strongly influenced by economic changes than others. Certainly, casual empiricism tells us that there are still vast cultural differences between developed countries (though the gap may be narrowing). Given that cultures evolve gradually, convergence must be slow. Some scholars hope that the cultures of nations catching up economically will combine the best of the old and the new (e.g., that the Hong Kong Chinese will retain a respect for authority while being achievement oriented).

Scholars disagree about whether the changes associated with development are "good" or not. Individualism and achievement-motivation, if taken too far, become selfishness and workaholism; we might all disagree on where the dividing line is. Good characteristics may also have bad side effects, such as consumerism or worker alienation. This is not the place for a debate on values. The existence of this debate does, however, illustrate the difficulty of predicting how economic change will affect culture. Selection arguments require that we know what is fitness enhancing; if we cannot even agree on what qualities would maximize human happiness, we can never be sure how societies will or should react to change.

I. INDIVIDUALISM

The working of the market, whereby selfish individual motives are translated into the public good, likely serves to decrease the individual's sense of responsibility toward the wider society. As we have seen (C→E1), though, we tend to underestimate the degree to which a market economy depends on shared values of trust, honesty, and fairness. Economic ideology thus pushes cultural values in a direction that limits economic efficiency. Etzioni (1988) feels that developing a system that assumes that people will behave selfishly acts to weaken ethical behavior.

Over a century ago, the banker Alexander Bryan Johnson claimed that the market was making life look like the theater: duplicity was always a danger, and people's actions were presumed to be self-interested. Herman

Melville voiced similar concerns. Emile Durkheim, the founder of modern sociology, worried that the unhindered market caused people to be less able to rely on others (various forms of social support disappeared; see also Adams 1993), and blamed this for a common sense of "anomie" (life being meaningless) as well as increased suicide rates. On the other hand, of course, many thrived on the new-found freedom from strict community control (not to mention the ever-widening range of occupational choice, itself a source of individualism).

Peasant communities develop various guidelines for sharing as a protection against starvation.[17] Such rules limit the individual's incentive to increase output. As markets allow peasants to store money in banks, borrow, buy insurance, or purchase food from other villages, communities tend to abandon their sharing rules. This process is not painless; the most successful peasants are naturally more willing to change. Yet the pain is not without benefit, and we must be careful not to lose sight of the advantages of individual freedom.

2. CULTURAL CHANGE

We have seen that modern market economies encourage individualism. This in turn has the effect that culture can evolve more rapidly than in more conformist societies. Many people feel that Western cultures are changing too fast, and we must be open to the possibility that rapid change may undermine the very role of culture in facilitating interaction between group members.

3. LEISURE

Throughout the nineteenth and early twentieth centuries, economic growth was accompanied by decreases in the standard work week. Livingstone (1994) describes how values of hard work and saving were replaced by an emphasis on consumption and leisure. Otherwise, production threatened to outstrip people's desire to consume. Henry James and others struggled to define how workers who had been alienated from work by mechanization could find meaning in life through leisure.

In the postwar world, the standard work week has decreased more slowly, and many salaried employees today put in much longer hours than would have been common decades ago. This at first sight seems odd: as people can more easily satisfy their basic needs we should expect them to desire more time for enjoyment and self-actualization. People have tended to express their individuality through consumer purchases, however, and have thus decided to take the benefits of increased productivity mostly in the form of stuff rather than time (Cross 1993). We should not be too critical of this: high wages and better consumer goods have increased the value of our time whether in work or leisure. People can legitimately choose to work a little harder so that they can enjoy their leisure time with a nice car, stereo, and television (and dishwashers and microwaves and electric can openers save on time spent in mundane household tasks), or a movie or restaurant meal. Moreover, we should not view work as merely a means to earn money: people need meaning in their lives and get much of this from involvement in productive employment [E→I].

Cross (1993) argues that the experience of the Depression served to increase the value that people placed on work while giving leisure a bad name. Many today would fear that Western societies still place too much importance on work and on purchases of goods and services. People might be happier if they were less focused on earning money and buying things, and more comfortable with leisure time.

Americans work longer hours than Europeans on average, though shorter hours than the Japanese. More attention has been focused on the first distinction. One possible explanation is that Europeans may place more value on and thus get more pleasure from time spent with family and friends. In other words, many Americans may work hard to escape the emptiness of their private lives. Or, it could be that American bosses are more demanding/punitive, and thus white collar workers put in long hours just to protect their jobs. A more benign explanation is that lower American income tax rates tip the balance away from leisure toward increased consumption. Finally, a recent survey suggests that two-thirds of Americans would take a pay cut averaging 20% in return for a proportional decrease in work time. This suggests that institutional inflexibility may be the biggest single cause of long hours. It also raises the possibility that employees could be made much happier and perhaps more productive (at least per hour) if allowed more leisure time.

Hunter-gatherer groups generally have abundant leisure time, but do not develop complex rituals or celebrations. Agricultural communities do tend to devote a considerable portion of their leisure time to public rituals. Gellner (1989) wonders if modern industrial societies can/will develop new rituals that put meaning into people's lives. The individualistic nature of modern societies suggests that the problem of finding meaning in leisure time will not be solved on a society-wide basis. Some people find meaning in volunteer work, cult membership, or political activism. Others write or paint or juggle (Szostak 2002).

4. UNEMPLOYMENT → ATTITUDE TO WORK

It is hardly surprising that those without jobs are much less likely to value work than those who have jobs [S→I]. The direction of the causal forces at work can be debated. Do the unemployed change their values to avoid feeling that their life is meaningless? Or do negative attitudes toward work encourage unemployment in the first place? There is likely some truth in both conjectures. As for the effect of welfare support, it is undoubtedly true that some people "abuse" the system in the sense of not trying to find work. Among certain subgroups in society, the stigma of long-term welfare reliance has disappeared. Yet for most recipients the system likely still works as intended—temporary support during hard times. Nevertheless, the societal willingness to support those in need inevitably suffers as the incidence of abuse increases.

5. ECONOMIC GROWTH → AMBITION, SHARING

For much of human history, intensive economic growth (increase in per capita income) occurred if at all at rates so slow as to be imperceptible. People in such environments naturally view economic activity as a "zero-sum" game: one person can only benefit at the expense of another. They thus tend to be suspicious of ambition and creativity. In an environment of economic growth, however, success is appreciated. Especially in the first postwar decades, growth was also associated with a willingness to help the less fortunate members of society. In part this may have reflected an appreciation of the role that luck could play in an ever-changing economy. More importantly, it is true that it is easier to share with others when your income is growing (you do not have to decrease consumption). It is not clear to what extent the more sluggish growth of recent decades has been responsible for a decreased willingness to share (versus, say, a rising concern with welfare abuse).

6. INSTITUTIONS AND VALUES

It is noted that in countries where it is possible to be paid for blood there are fewer donations. People who will not sell their blood do not donate it; the act of giving is apparently 'cheapened' by the fact a price has been put on it (see Hausman and McPherson 1996). If so, we must worry that many other economic institutions will discourage values we treasure.

7

Politics

THE PHENOMENA

POLITICS IS THE EXERCISE OF POWER. AND "ANY POWER RELATIONSHIP ultimately rests on the possibility of using force" (Schwartz 1990). Leaders in other fields of endeavor may exert considerable influence, but states reserve for themselves the legitimate use of force (at least outside the family, and even here the state places limits). Nonsanctioned use of force is by definition criminal; crime is thus a political act and will be treated in the appendix to this chapter. Radcliffe-Brown in 1940 noted that all societies must determine the appropriate use of force, and thus politics so-defined is ubiquitous; even stateless societies must have politics (though Gledhill, 1994, wonders if cultural constraints might suffice). However, while the identity of politics with physical force guarantees universality, it provides little guidance on how to unpack the category.

Institutions have always been a key focus of interest for political scientists. Recent scholarship has tended to emphasize institutions to an even greater extent. In part, this is a reaction to the behavioral revolution in the field in the 1950s and 1960s. At that time, scholars recognized that institutions alone could not explain particular political decisions, and turned instead to the study of political behavior. With public opinion polling becoming much easier both to perform and analyze at the time, public opinion emerged as an alternative focus of the discipline. At present, there is a general appreciation that both behavior and institutions (and their interaction) should be studied (Thelen and Steinmo 1992).

How might we categorize political institutions? I can begin with Frey's (1992) tripartite division into decision-making systems, organizations, and rules. Note first of all that these are interrelated: the shape of our decision-making system will have a large effect on the formal rules by which we live. The rule category is the easiest to disaggregate. I can first distinguish the laws and bylaws of various levels of government from the rules which operate within organizations. In both cases an important distinction can be made between rules that are very hard to change (constitutions) and the rest. Although space constraints will prevent me from discussing individ-

227

ual rules in much detail below, these can be defined by purpose. Remember that informal rules are subsumed under the category "culture."

With respect to decision-making systems, I must first distinguish between autocratic and democratic forms of governance. There are numerous types of the former: monarchy, military dictatorship, one party states and so on. Elster (1993) would view authoritarian and totalitarian as two separate types of government; he notes that the boundaries between his types are not always clear. Finer (1997) speaks of three nondemocratic types of government: palace regime (one acknowledged leader), church polity (e.g., Papal States, Tibet), and nobility polity (oligarchy, where the aristocracy jointly rules); he notes that the latter two types are very rare historically. Due to space constraints, I will focus more on democratic governance in what follows. Democracy also comes in many forms. There are almost as many electoral systems as democratic states in the world. Legislative assemblies function differently too.[1] Finally, and of crucial importance, we need to recognize the differential reliance on direct democracy (e.g., referenda) as opposed to representative democracy.

Kuhn (1974) recognized that organizations were a means for decision-making when neither cultural consensus nor market transactions could suffice, and thus must be a key focus for students of politics.[2] The primary organization of interest to us is the state itself. Finer (1997) feels that states have several characteristics: defined territory (though borders have often been unclear), a civil service, an army (or a police force that maintains order), and recognition by other states (a shared sense of community is desirable, at least in modern times, but not always achieved; C→P2). We would want to know about the relationship between the judiciary, executive, and legislature, and how each operates. The size and structure of government bureaucracies is also important. These can be distinguished in terms of the degree to which they are rule-governed or subject to the caprice of individual bureaucrats, and also whether they extend to the local level (rare before the twentieth century) or rely instead on local nongovernmental authorities (Finer 1997). Military and police/judicial organizations are of special interest, for here the use of physical force is manifest. Armies have taken three forms historically: the standing paid army, the voluntary citizen militia, and a nobility-based army (Finer 1997). We would also look at affiliated organizations such as publicly owned firms, regulatory boards, schools, public hospitals, and public universities. Finally, there are numerous nongovernmental organizations: political parties, interest groups, unions, clubs, churches, and associations. I might note that many of these organizations serve an economic function as well, with each role influenced by the other. (See Mann [1986] or Thelen and Steinmo [1992] for a further discussion of classification, and Peterson [1990] on the role of churches and clubs.)

Two points should be emphasized. The first is the variety of political institutions with which we must be concerned. Some scholars have tried to develop categorization schemes whereby states are rated along one or two dimensions. We should instead be conscious of the fact that the relative importance of different institutions depends on the question being asked. For example, economists debate the role of the South Korean government in the rapid economic growth achieved by that country in recent decades. In some areas the government allowed market forces to operate, in others it interfered. Our understanding of the link between politics and economy will be enhanced more by focusing on the effects of particular institutions than by attempting to reliably classify South Korea on a continuum from laissez-faire to interventionism.

The second point is that I have striven to define institutions in a fashion that allows comparisons across the whole range of human societies. I have thus not followed Lewellen (1992) and others in defining the three main forms in which pre-state governments occur: chiefdoms, tribes (which can be governed by lineages, age grades, secret societies, village councils, ritual groups, or big men), and bands (even less centralized, with families often the major locus of power; he notes that some scholars question the utility of the distinction between band and tribe). Instead, I define our institutions in terms of what they do, and can then search for how that function is performed in all societies.[3]

How might I capture schematically the concern of political scientists with political behavior? Some of these concerns require no additions to our schema. "Leadership" (or political involvement of any sort) is not a phenomenon but a causal link between personality and institutions ($I{\rightarrow}C3$). Much of the "behavioral" research in political science has in fact been exploring the interdisciplinary links with personality, culture, and social structure. Still, there are three types of attitude which require special representation. One is the supportive attitude toward the institutional structure of the state, or "ideology." Another is the attitude toward the collective citizenry of the state, or "nationalism." The third is "public opinion."

I should clarify the dividing line between ideology and public opinion. I define ideology as a general appreciation of one's political system. (Thus, as Karl Mannheim advocated in 1946, I define ideology functionally.) Views about particular issues will be treated as public opinion.[4] In common parlance, ideology is often viewed as defining people as conservative or liberal or socialist. I would view these self-definitional schemas as part of public opinion. This seems appropriate, since scholars have been frustrated in their efforts to understand particular policy positions in terms of these self-definitions. They are only one of several sources of opinions on particular issues.

Like many terms in this book, we think we know what "public opinion" is, but find it difficult to define precisely. Noelle-Neumann (1993) refers to the vast number of different definitions that can be found in the literature, and recognizes that there is still no consensus. Her own definition, "opinions one can express in public without fear of isolation," would be too broad for my purposes, for it would include much of my cultural category. I would limit public opinion to matters only of political importance: "People's views acquire the status of public opinion because they relate to an event, an issue, or a personality of topical relevance" (Himmelweit 1990). Table manners are culture; views on whether to enforce fines for littering are public opinion. Noelle-Neumann's definition does convey an important characteristic of public opinion: it is a collective product. The opinions I voice, and even the opinions I feel in my heart, will be shaped by the opinions I observe in those around me.

C → P: Culture → Politics

Politics in a sense begins where culture fails. All societies strive to limit their recourse to violence or coercion, and prefer to rely on persuasion and reason (Burk 1991). If informal rules are not enough, then legal sanctions are introduced to encourage appropriate behavior. If the community does not agree on how to act, formal decision-making structures are necessary. While humans are designed for culture, it is nevertheless true that even the simplest societies have recourse to politics.

I. TRUST (IDENTITY) → DEMOCRACY

Within any form of democracy there is always the possibility that majorities, however constituted, will abuse their power over minorities. Many democracies have constitutional provisions that protect minorities of various types from various sorts of attack. Some even have explicit power-sharing provisions. Such formal arrangements cannot by their nature protect people from every sort of abuse (even if one ignores the difficulty of inducing the majority to enshrine minority rights in the first place). Widespread public support of democracy, then, requires a sense of trust that those in power will not favor (excessively) some groups over others.

The easiest situation, of course, is where a strong sense of national identity causes the bulk of a society to feel that they are part of one large group,[5] though small minorities may feel especially uneasy in such a situation. Common language and religion in early Greek city states supported democratic institutions, though these excluded slaves and foreigners (Finer 1997). Most societies have significant groups that perceive themselves as minorities, whether on the basic of ethnicity, gender, class, or sexual orientation. In such situations, many scholars feel that local governments are more trusted because different groups can meet and establish personal ties (though local governments are often the most corrupt). In countries like Canada or Belgium where major ethnic groups are separated geographically, it can be difficult to maintain the necessary level of trust in national political institutions.

There are likely positive feedbacks here. If politicians are viewed as servants of the public good rather than of particular interest groups, they may be less likely to engage in discriminatory policy-making or corruption. They will thus be more trustworthy. States in which there is a strong sense of unity may be more likely to pursue egalitarian policies (e.g., Costa Rica), and thus encourage trust in the political process. On the other hand, African states are often corrupt and ineffective precisely because ethnically divided nations have not developed an ethic of civic responsibility (Bayart 1999; Chabal and Daloz 1999).[6]

2. IDENTITY → STRONG STATE

I have noted above that a sense of cultural identity can encourage trust in political institutions. Political philosophers have been divided for centuries on the advisability of defining the state in terms of the dominant ethnic group (C→P6). John Stuart Mill argued that a strong state required a sense of "fellow-feeling" that could only come from a shared culture (but recognized that many parts of the world were too culturally diverse to achieve this ideal). The treaties that ended the First World War were based on this principle, and attempted to divide Europe into homogenous nation states. Unfortunately the explicit association of state and ethnicity left millions of Europeans as ethnic minorities distrustful of the state. The fascist excesses of the next decades naturally caused many political philosophers to question the advisability of defining the state in ethnic terms.

Tamir (1993) tries to describe a compromise between the two positions. He feels that states must both on the one hand respect the autonomy of the individual and on the other encourage a sense of belonging. Thus states must embrace their role as an expression of the dominant culture while ensuring that minority cultures are also respected. Such a system will only work, he feels, if individuals are able to choose their cultural identity. If this is thrust upon them at birth, as it tends to be, then ethnic rivalry will be difficult to avoid.

Sociology in the 1970s could be characterized as split between those who emphasized the conflict and change inherent in any society and those who instead (following Durkheim and Parsons) emphasized the stability of societies due to the absorption of values. This dispute was paralleled in political science by a dichotomy between those who emphasized the pluralistic nature of modern democracy and those who stressed dominance by a small political elite (Mizruchi 1992). Yet little attempt was made to link the debates in these two fields. Does ethnic diversity reduce the possibility of elite domination in the political sphere? Does it weaken the strength of the state?

Tamir feels that regional integration, such as in the European Union, can increase the sense of trust among ethnic minorities. Many ethnic minorities in Europe—notably the Catalan—have been among the strongest support-ers of integration. Integration can only work if the activities of the regional body do not depend on the sort of cultural consensus which Tamir feels is useful at the national level. This suggests that we need to be more careful in our analysis. States perform many functions, and we should be clear about which of these (if any) are facilitated or hurt by association with ethnic identity. We might then be able to decide rationally which powers should be associated with particular levels of government.[7]

Identification of states with particular groups can be a source of interna-tional conflict. Indeed, Huntington (1991) argued that with the end of the Cold War future political conflicts were most likely to come from cultural differences. Fukuyama (1996) suggests alternatively that cultural differences could instead be a source of creative change (C→C1). His more harmonious projection depends, of course, on the degree to which we accept cultural diversity as a good thing. The argument made in this book—that it is ludicrous to consider one culture (as opposed to particular cultural elements) as superior to another—would serve to decrease inter-national tension. So, too, would the recognition that cultures are not mono-lithic. Huntington speaks at length about an Islamic world view, for exam-ple. Many scholars would argue that cultural differences among Islamic countries are of a similar magnitude to those that separate them from the rest of the world. And all of these cultures are in transition, and may well be converging in certain respects (E→C) with the rest of the world (C→N6).

3. INSTITUTIONS

To what extent are political institutions themselves reflective of culture? Pye felt that political structure was "inevitably rooted in the creative ge-nius of the ruling nation," and Geertz argued that everyone knows but cannot demonstrate that "a country's politics reflect the design of its cul-ture" (both in Tamir 1993). One can easily point to symbolic effects: the Israeli Knesset uses Hebrew as a language, respects the Jewish Sabbath and holidays, and utilizes a range of rituals and symbols. While such practices may serve to alienate ethnic/religious minorities from the state, it remains to be shown that culture has more substantive effects on the shape of political institutions.

Václav Klaus was able to achieve a great deal of support for economic reform in the Czech Republic, even as per capita income dropped by a third, by appealing to Czech traditions of rationality, democracy, and individualism. Fiske would argue that it is only natural that cultural preferences among his four models (G→C4) would be reflected in political institutions. Societies that approve of authoritarian allocation of resources will support forms of government that market-oriented or equality-based societies will not. We should be careful, though, to remember that institutions do not always reflect the values of the whole community. Political elites may be successful in establishing authoritarian systems against the wishes of the population. Alternatively, group conflict may make it impossible to establish state authority to the degree desired by the population. At the level of particular laws, one needs only to think of how radical feminists and religious conservatives have joined forces in the fight for laws against pornography to realize that laws need not reflect shared values.

It is worth noting as well the degree to which laws are the same in different countries. This is especially so across modern democracies, which suggests that political circumstances play a bigger role than culture in lawmaking. Even the civil law tradition of the European continent (and its colonies) and the common law tradition of Britain and her colonies have come to look more and more similar over the years. There is still a major difference in that judges play a much greater role in assembling evidence and asking questions within the civil law tradition. However, whereas judicial precedent used to be much less important in civil law, there is now little difference (though civil law perhaps evolves in greater accordance with clear principles than common law). The two traditions are also very similar in terms of safeguards against injustice.

The cost of enforcing laws depends on public opinion, which in turn is influenced by culture. If a large proportion of the citizenry believe that gambling, drugs, or littering should be legal, enforcement will be extremely difficult. This in turn may (should) affect the form that particular laws take.

4. RELIGION

At the level of public opinion, it is clear that religious views play a major role in influencing political preferences. Indeed, the recent shift in votes from the Republican to the Democratic parties in the United States is better understood in religious terms than any other way. Catholics, who a couple of decades ago voted overwhelmingly for the Democrats, are now as likely to vote Republican. Evangelical Protestants, who had tended to have low participation rates, now vote Republican by overwhelming margins. One might attempt to attribute the shift in Catholic preferences to religion becoming a less important influence on politics. Or, it might reflect the fact that Catholics no longer feel themselves to be a persecuted minority; religious beliefs themselves thus have little to do with voting behavior. The changed behavior of Evangelicals, though, is much harder to explain in any other terms than that they have come to think that Republicans better reflect their religious values. Since many Catholics share Evangelical concerns about the family or abortion, it is likely that this argument applies there as well.

Certainly, surveys have found major differences in attitudes across religious groups. Jews in America tend to be liberal, tolerant, and have a high participation rate. Fundamentalists are conservative on both social and foreign policy (see Peterson 1990). While Jewish liberalism may well reflect minority status more than the tenets of the faith, the social conservatism of religious fundamentalists can be traced to the orientation of their faith toward personal salvation and voluntary acts of charity. Recent research has tended to move beyond a focus on denominations. It recognizes that the larger denominations, especially Catholicism and Judaism, are too broad for analytical purposes. Those with conservative religious views, such as Orthodox Jews and Catholics who believe in papal infallibility, are observed to be more likely to espouse conservative political views and vote conservatively, while the theologically liberal tend also to be politically liberal.

The degree of religious influence in American politics has ebbed and flowed over time, in large part as different issues came to the fore. The early decades of this century witnessed a religious crusade for prohibition and the teaching of creationism; political success in both areas proved transitory, and may have encouraged a backlash against religious influence. Even at its weakest, though, religion tends to be much more important in American politics (and society more generally) than in Europe (see P→C2).

Laws concerning abortion or divorce give proof that the religious views of a society can affect political institutions. Does this effect carry over, though, to the organizing principles of the state? Certainly, many Islamic fundamentalists preach the overthrow of both autocratic and democratic political structures in the Middle East. Lenski, Lenski, and Nolan (1991) feel that the Protestant Reformation provided a great encouragement to democracy in northwestern Europe; by debunking the authority of Catholic clergy, it encouraged skepticism of all appeals to authority, including the divine right of kings. Gellner (1989) posits an indirect link through Protestant encouragement of literacy. Centuries later, though, the Catholic Church is credited by many with a major role in the democratization of Poland. In any arguments such as these, there is considerable room for debate: were/ are political changes a cause or effect of religious changes, and is religious behavior guided by the central tenets of the faith or by transient historical circumstances and/or manipulation by religious leaders?[8]

Taking a longer-term historical perspective, Finer argues that religious and political development have been mutually reinforcing. He feels that authoritarian governments have always required religious justification (in the modern era, some autocrats have instead claimed popular support). He associates hunter-gatherer groups with mythical (men as gods) religions. These are succeeded by "archaic" religions, with many gods, who interact with humanity through religious intermediaries; such religions are naturally associated with societies characterized by a political/religious elite.[9] The succeeding "historic" religions (e.g., Christianity, Islam) were monotheistic and stressed a sharp distinction between this world and another, better world. The focus on salvation formed the basis for codes of behavior. While religious elites became separate from political, and sometimes acted as a brake on secular authority (with the medieval papacy being an extreme example of religious authorities wielding power), these religions also provided a justification for political and social stratification, as well as a sense of community solidarity (forced conversion was common, and religious fervor often supported military conquest). The early Jewish state, he argues, was the first in human history to place the king under an obligation to behave according to religious guidelines. Historic religions both justified and limited the power of kings.

Lewellen (1992) is skeptical of a strong correlation between religion and type of polity, noting the existence of both very religious hunter-gatherer societies and atheistic states.[10] He does recognize three types of effect, however: some governments are directly based on a particular religion, others are legitimated by religion, and religion also provides an underlying set of beliefs that constrain governments.

Finally, I should note that religious bureaucracies are powerful political institutions in their own right. They often control substantial economic resources, whether from donations or land ownership. They exert power over the populace not just by mediating their intercourse with god but by more down-to-earth roles like sanctioning marriages and births (and thus inheritance). The religious hierarchy inevitably interacts with the secular political leadership. Ceremonies like coronation can serve to legitimate both church and state. The views of religious leaders on policy matters can carry great weight. Shakespeare's Henry V seeks out the view of leading clergy on the just nature of his war on France. This is important not only for his own conscience, but helps ensure that his army will remain loyal and steadfast in battle. As Shakespeare tells it, the clergy are hardly guided by scripture in responding; note that the actions of an organized religion need not be guided by belief.

5. IDEOLOGY

As political philosophers well know, one cannot answer the question of what is the ideal political system without first contemplating what is the best way of life. The goals and means accepted by a particular cultural group should influence their choice of political institutions. Individualism versus collectivism, egalitarianism, and sense of community are just three key cultural attributes here. There is room for debate, though, about how great the differences in political preferences will be across groups. When Middle East leaders suggest that democracy is inconsistent with the Islamic belief that god guides major decisions, or Asian leaders suggest that it is antithetical to "Asian values" (particularly respect for authority), many, especially but not exclusively in the West, suspect that self-interest has caused them to severely exaggerate their case.

Openness to innovation, along with other cultural elements, will affect a community's acceptance of ideology in general. The dangers of blind adherence to ideology have long been obvious. The status quo becomes entrenched (Marx was very critical of ideology for this reason). Individuals lose their sense of judgment and are too easily compelled to commit unethical acts at the behest of the state. Yet there are dangers as well in being too casual about ideology. Polls tell us that most citizens of Western democracies are cynical about the character of politicians, and doubt that a clash of special interest groups is likely to yield good public policy. Many of these people give little thought to the advantages that flow from democracy and the rule of law, much less appreciate the fact that a messy system often yields decisions the bulk of the populace can respect. The very advantages which flow from democratic governance exist because of the efforts of past generations that believed in the system, and will slip away if future generations cease both to believe and to strive to make the system work.[11] (This is, incidentally, evidence that group preferences for political institutions do change over time.)

The difficulty in encouraging the right degree of ideological support for the system—recognizing both its advantages and faults, and coping with change—causes some to advocate basing state institutions on unchanging religious or scientific principles. Yet we have seen that these change too; there is no obvious higher principle that can save us from the messy business of incremental institutional change (Maier 1987).

6. NATIONALISM

All modern states encourage some sense of belonging, some emotional attachment of citizenry to state. Nationalism is more than just an ideological appreciation of the basic institutions of the state. It must also embody a sense of the difference (if not superiority) between this state and others. Appreciation of institutions may be an important part of this, but given the strong similarity in both economic and political institutions across modern Western democracies this alone could provide only a weak sense of loyalty. One does not exult in German rather than British citizenry because of a heightened appreciation of proportional representation as an electoral system. At the very least nationalism must be rooted in an appreciation of the country's history and geography [N→P].

Most often, nationalism also embodies an appreciation of shared values. In some cases these values are explicitly stated. The Swiss take pride in their efficiency and their flexible attitude toward ethnic differences (some Swiss will doubtless reject these values while still feeling "Swiss"). Bangladeshis can rejoice in a shared religion. In other cases, there may be considerable room for debate about what the shared values are, but nevertheless a strongly felt belief that such exist. Canada is an example here. This author believes that Canadians (both French and English-speaking) are on average more laid-back, more prone to certain sorts of humor (especially friendly insults), more willing to sanction government intervention in the economy, and less likely to feel or voice their sense of nationalism than Americans. But he is well aware that many—perhaps most—Canadians would proffer a substantially different self-definition. This does not prevent a strong attachment to Canada.

Nationalism tends to be at its most virulent in that minority of world states in which one ethnic group provides the vast bulk of the population. Ethnic purity encourages a sense of shared values (despite the fact that genetic differences do not lead to cultural differences except as we believe them to do so; G→C1) and shared history. It tends also to encourage an emotional attachment to a certain territory on which most of the group's history has played out, though not always exactly the same piece of ground which the group presently inhabits (N→C). Especially if the group feels some "right" to land controlled by others, this ethnic-based nationalism can lead to great hostility toward other states (Hooson 1994).[12] While people tend to develop an emotional attachment to their land, Chisholm and Smith (1990) doubt that this is inherent but rather culturally determined. Aboriginal people often have a mystical association with the land, while other groups have a more pragmatic attachment. One common source of attachment is the veneration of ancestral burial grounds (Ignatieff 1994). In any case, it is generally easier to get citizens to fight for land than for institutions.[13]

Nationalism seems such a natural part of the modern world (so much so that the words "nation" and "state" are often mistakenly used as synonyms) that it is easy to mistakenly think that it has been with us forever. Yet there is scholarly agreement that nationalism as we know it is an eighteenth- or nineteenth-century creation (e.g., Hobsbawm 1990). Ethnic loyalties have existed for millennia (G→C2), but identification with the state as an entity is new. It is thus a mistake to view recent nationalist excesses as a return to a "primitive" mentality (Wrong 1994). In the days of kings and emperors, one's loyalty was to these leaders (and beyond them to a shared religion or shared civilization). When William Wallace rose against the king of England on behalf of the Scottish people in the thirteenth century, he was viewed with suspicion by the Scottish lords; men were to fight on behalf of lord or king, not country. The idea that the lower classes of society had "culture," much less a common cultural bond with rulers, was equally laughable at the time (Namenwirth and Weber 1987).

As the feudal system broke down in Europe, to be replaced by centralized states with growing bureaucracies, states could no longer depend on old feudal loyalties. (Marxists tend to blame nationalism on the rise of capitalism, a view not incompatible with this. Gellner has argued that industrialization was the key influence.) The French state ensured that the French language of Paris replaced regional dialects and languages throughout its realm. This had administrative advantages no doubt, but served most importantly to provide a sense of common identity.[14] This was especially important given the ideals of the French Revolution: popular sovereignty, and exercise of the national will.

The British government was somewhat less successful in establishing English as a common language. As it moved steadily toward democracy, there was both a greater need for attachment to state rather than king, and an opportunity to rely on loyalty to democratic political institutions rather than ethnic purity. Still, those European states that encouraged/relied upon a strong sense of nationalism fared much better militarily and otherwise over the next centuries than states like the Austrian Empire which were divided by ethnic loyalties (the "ideal" of ethnic nationalism having spread with Napoleon; Mann 1986). It is no surprise, then, that English philosophers wrestled through the nineteenth century with the question of whether loyalty to the state was best founded on loyalty to (democratic) institutions or on loyalty to a group. Some viewed the first as an appeal to reason while the latter was a mere appeal to emotion. While we must be cognizant of the dangers of ethnic-based nationalism, we can on the other hand recognize that, since we are programmed for a sense of group identity, the latter may provide both psychological benefits and a stronger state. As Wrong (1994) notes, while we often focus on the divisive qualities of nationalism, by superseding more local or tribal loyalties it has bound humanity into larger groupings. Many African states would be well served if nationalism could replace these narrower loyalties.

Nor were debates among the intelligentsia of little significance. A point to be emphasized is that national identity does not spring "naturally" from the creation of a centralized bureaucratic state, but must be shaped by opinion leaders (see Toland 1993). The citizenry must be convinced of a shared history, geography, and values. "Professionalized intelligentsias have been absolutely central to the design of such imaginings" (Milner 1991, 23). I myself have come to think of Canadian history as my own because that is what I was taught, despite the fact my ancestors arrived less than a century ago. There is no (genetic or other) logic which decrees that Provencals feel a sense of community with Bretons rather than Lombards; the French government's language policies made it so. If Serbian and Croatian leaders had chosen to emphasize their similarities rather than their differences, the recent history of the former Yugoslavia might have been quite different.

How should a nascent state focus its efforts to instill nationalism? Kedourie (1993) feels that it is no coincidence that the French state and others focused on language. Languages are the easiest way of distinguishing one group from another (C→C3), and thus are often seen as the best guide to appropriate national boundaries (see also Hobsbwam 1990). Yet language alone would provide a weak sense of identity. Thus it was precisely in the early stages of nation-building that the idea of a strong link between language and other cultural elements gained currency (e.g., German philosophers associated Latin languages with a low ethical standard). Many writers went beyond this to posit a link between genetic ethnicity and language: each race had its own natural language (Kedourie 1993). This view of language, which emerged to serve the interests of early nation-building, stays with us today [P→C].

Opinion leaders are limited in the degree to which they can shape a community's views. Those who would instill a national identity will be constrained by preexisting loyalties. American opinion leaders were able to convince most ethnic groups to embrace an ideal of shared values and history. While the thirteen colonies had little in common, and indeed divergent reasons for rebelling, a history was constructed that stressed the principles of the declaration of independence, hero worship, and a belief that American colonists had always fought for freedom, while ignoring slavery and the religious orthodoxy of most early colonies (Appleby, Hunt, and Jacob 1994). Leaders of the Austrian Empire faced a perhaps impossible task of convincing Hungarians, Czechs, Croats, and Italians that they shared a common bond. Linguistic diversity was an important barrier in the latter case (though it has not prevented a sense of Swiss nationalism). It is noteworthy in this regard that the spread of ideas from Western Europe that equated language with culture, ethnicity, and nationality made the Austrian situation untenable.[15] That is, political changes in Western Europe (the rise of the nation states) caused cultural changes (emphasis on role of language) which when transferred to other states prevented the same political change from occurring [P→C→C→P].

What is the relationship between democracy and nationalism? I suggested above that while nationalism was important to all centralized states, it was especially important to those attempting to shift allegiance away from hereditary kings. Democracy by its nature embodies power in the collective citizenry and can thus only work to the extent that citizens feel that they have something in common. Proponents of "civic nationalism" felt that ideally this should come from a shared appreciation of political institutions. Yet these institutions themselves may require a firm grounding in popular support for the state. With the fall of communism in Yugoslavia, fledgling democratic institutions commanded little respect and thus provided little security. Citizens not surprisingly turned to ethnic nationalism for security (Wrong 1994). The process is self-reinforcing: if one group in an area invokes nationalist fervor, others respond in kind in order to survive (Kedourie 1993). Yet this result was not inevitable: a slower transition may have allowed faith in democracy to emerge. In particular the experience of groups working together during this transition would calm fears, and the emergence of political parties that crossed ethnic lines would have encouraged cooperation (M. Brown 1993, Ignatieff 1994). Experience shows that most practical political problems cannot be solved by an appeal to ethnic values, but require pragmatic compromises between groups.

Under the guise of self-determination, nationalism has been viewed as a stepping stone to democracy through much of this century (C→P,1,2). Thus, Woodrow Wilson argued for ethnically homogenous states in Eastern Europe in the aftermath of the First World War. Asian and African leaders picked up the cry in their search for independence after the Second World War. In neither place was a transition to democracy automatic. Dictators could easily turn nationalism to their own use, as had fascists in the interwar period or Napoleon in the nineteenth century, by convincing enough of the population that autocratic leadership was necessary for the nation to achieve its destiny (Ignatieff 1994; Finer 1997).

Even in states that are not based on a sense of common ethnicity, minorities may feel a need for specific constitutional protections (Shehadi 1993). When a state is based on common ethnicity, those who fall outside this definition must fear if not persecution at least second-class status.

Even nonethnic minorities, such as homosexuals, foreigners, or those who disagree with the leadership, may feel uncomfortable if not pursuing the "way of life" the state explicitly is striving to uphold (Chisholm and Smith 1990). Ethnic minorities must at the very least lose in terms of the sense of dignity that is attained by the national majority (Ignatieff 1994). If the dominant culture is viewed as "correct" then minorities must worry that their behavior will be judged inappropriate (Toland 1993); they inevitably come to see themselves as outsiders. They will also lose financially to the extent that their tax dollars are used to finance cultural celebrations of which they are not part. They may face overt discrimination or a simple inability to rise in government or business bureaucracies in which particular cultural attributes are valued. Constitutional protections of minorities may be especially difficult to achieve in a state which sees itself as the embodiment of the majority.[16] But not impossible: Swedes in Finland, Germans in Italy, even Basques and Catalans in Spain, have achieved enough in the way of minority protections to feel comfortable and loyal to their states. One of the keys to success here may well be a belief in fairness among the dominant group (Toland 1993).

7. SOCIALLY EXPECTED DURATION

Many rules have a temporal element: prison sentences, terms of office, statutes of limitations, duration of employment contracts. Such time limits should reflect what Merton terms "socially expected duration" and "constitute a class of social expectations that significantly affect the current behavior of groups and individuals" (1996, ch. 14). This class of expectations would depend on the group's attitude toward time in combination with various other aspects of culture (e.g., individualism versus collective responsibility in establishing prison sentences).

P → C: POLITICS → CULTURE

1. ENFORCEMENT OF VALUES

We have seen that politics begins where culture leaves off, providing sanctions for behavior that social pressure alone could not control (C→P). Political rules, once put in place, can act to change a society's values. We must be careful, though, to distinguish between behavior elicited from fear of sanction and behavior which—though not in our self-interest—is pursued because we believe it to be right (Taylor 1993). Many people in developed societies obey speed limits only from fear of penalty. In this case, laws do not affect values. In the case of drunk driving, however, one could argue that laws—in concert with a public relations campaign—have served to alter values. Historically, one can point to a number of cases in which enforced rules became values; the Catholic Church enforced rules against polygamy, concubinage, and incest in its early days (to enhance its chances of inheriting estates, according to Taylor); Western society accepts all of these prohibitions as only natural today.

All modern states encompass a large number of potentially diverse local societies. In some states the process of welding these into a unified nation has progressed over the course of centuries, while in the newly independent states of Africa it is still in its infancy. In all cases, the state attempts to promulgate laws that can be internalized as values by all subgroups. They can never wipe out local cultures in this way, but can strive for a common national culture with local variants (Gellner 1989). Organized religions are often important sources of unification, though early missionaries tend to push a mixture of orthodoxy and local beliefs; local elements such as belief in witchcraft can have enormous staying power (Pounds 1989; Migdal 1988).

As in the case of drunk driving, mere enforcement of a law will not change internal beliefs. The state (or other organization) must also try to justify its laws. One powerful tool the modern state has in this endeavor is an educational system. Through schools the state can try to teach the young that its laws are valid. It can also encourage a sense of national identification by glorifying the common language,[17] history, and geography.

2. "CULTURAL INSTITUTIONS"

I have placed all institutions in the economic or political categories. Yet many organizations—churches, theater groups, television networks, and schools—play a large cultural role. States, by exercising control over the leadership of these organizations, can exert a strong but indirect influence over culture. This political control may come in the form of nationalization, regulation, or subsidization.

Historically, religious organizations have been the most important. They could have a huge impact on the values of a population (and cuisine and dress and ritual). Religious leaders could at times be quite critical of political leaders who violated these values. Yet this was a dangerous course, for political leaders would in turn attack religious authorities who threatened their position. In most societies, then, secular and religious leaders achieved some truce. Religious leaders could remain critical of some aspects of state policy (e.g., treatment of the poor), but would for the most part accept the status quo. In Europe, this relationship was symbolized and legitimized by the idea of the divine right of kings to rule. No matter how scandalized religious leaders might be by the behavior of kings, they would be unlikely to call for their removal. Kings could encourage even greater support by threatening to confiscate church property (though this might not be popular with the peasants). The church was not powerless, though; beyond its hold over the people it alone could recognize marriages and legitimate births on which the inheritance of positions of power rested. Still, the overall effect was that organized religion supported the ideology of the status quo, though at times serving as a force for moderate reform.

It was long thought that the separation of church and state—such as occurred with the American Revolution, and with the "disestablishment" of state religions in many European countries—would lead to a decrease in religious observance, for the simple reason that state coercion and reward no longer compelled it. Yet the United States has become more religious over time. In Japan as well the postwar disestablishment of state Shintoism led to an increase in overall religious observance. It appears that competition allows a wider range of people to find a denomination that fits. Moreover, while established religions may become bureaucratic and stuffy over time, new religions are more zealous in their efforts to attract members. Competition between a variety of religious groups may have an important feedback effect as well, for religious plurality is associated with, and may well support, democratic institutions.

In premodern times, artists and writers needed a wealthy patron. This ensured that art was in general not too critical of the existing political and/ or economic elites. In modern times, artists have gained a certain degree of freedom as they are able to serve a wide market. Both the middle class and to a lesser extent the working class have some money to devote to works of art and literature. Although these groups also accept the basic ideology of their state, they are likely more open to critical works of art than the elite. Government subsidies to the arts are ubiquitous in the modern world. Yet democratic governments strive to place their granting agencies at arms length from the political leadership. It is not clear therefore whether subsidies serve to encourage conformist art or the opposite (but see Hufford 1994 on how governments through their museums can overvalue the role of dominant cultural groups in history) (P→A).

Coming closer to home, similar arguments can be made with respect to governmental support of universities and intellectuals. Milner (1991) suggests that sociologists are more critical of the status quo than economists because they are less often drawn into political discourse. University professors have a great degree of freedom to speak their mind, but also face pressures to conform to the dominant views in their disciplines if they want to get published or promoted. Do these pressures encourage intellectuals to be too forgiving of the status quo?[18]

3. IDEOLOGY AND VALUES

When Alexis de Tocqueville traveled through the United States shortly after the American Revolution, he was struck by the effect that the new political institutions had on people's values. Much of his writing was devoted to this theme. Democracy encouraged a utilitarian philosophy, where all acts were to be judged by whether they enhanced the welfare of society as a whole. Intellectual skepticism, a belief in public opinion, and certain novel precepts also resulted. While changes in political institutions and ideology seem likely to have cultural impacts (Barber 1993), it is safe to say that this link has been explored only to a limited extent.[19]

APPENDIX 7-A: CRIME

Not only does most crime involve at least the threat of physical force, but crime by definition involves the violation of the formal rules of a society. It is thus a political activity within the schema. It is, of course, rather different from other political activities; hence the study of crime has come to be housed in sociology rather than political science departments, and I have placed it in an appendix.

I stressed in chapter 1 the fact that a sense of the interrelatedness of phenomena in the human sciences can be invaluable in the formulation of public policy. There is perhaps no better place to see this point than in public debates about crime. All too often these degenerate into a battle between those who stress personal responsibility for behavior, and thus favor harsh penalties, versus those who emphasize societal causes of crime and argue for preventive measures aimed at these causes of crime. Even scholarly debate is not above reproach. Eide (1994) notes that one's discipline is the best predictor of where one stands in this unproductive debate, and urges all scholars to share rather than compete. The fact is that both personality and environment are causes of crime, and an effective policy to deal with crime must reflect both. Indeed, I would argue that genes, culture, individual differences, the nonhuman environment, the economy, politics, social structure, and demography all affect crime rates, and thus the ideal societal response must be multifaceted indeed.

I will discuss various types of crime together here, but should note that further insight can be gained by focusing on particular types of crime. Indeed many scholars would argue that another major problem with public debate is precisely that people, say, urge tougher treatment of all criminals, when perhaps what is advisable is longer sentences for some and shorter for others. To be sure, those with a strong tendency to criminal behavior are often observed committing a range of crimes. Yet especially between sex crimes and economic crimes, and less so between violent crimes and burglary, one can discern significant differences in motivation (such that sex criminals generally have to be segregated from other prisoners). Major types of crime are crimes versus persons (including violent crimes such as murder, political crimes such as treason, and public order crimes such as vagrancy) and crimes versus property,[20] which can be further unpacked according to the explicit use of violence, or directly to the level of individual crimes.

Finally, I should note the difficulties in interpretation of crime statistics. Since many—perhaps most—crimes go unreported, one must always treat these with a certain skepticism. However, unless one can point to some obvious reason why reporting rates would have changed (friendlier police, support for victims of crime), changes in reported crime likely reflect changes in the incidence of crime. It is noteworthy then that public concern with crime has risen over the last decade while crime rates for most types of crime have fallen in most developed countries. This is perhaps because television news crews are increasingly able to bring gory live pictures from the crime scene, or because of some well-publicized crimes, especially those perpetrated by young offenders. Still, while comparisons over longer time periods are difficult, it is quite possible that crime in the twentieth century is high by historical standards (Pepinsky and Jesilow 1984). Moreover, the increase in violent crime among adolescents could be a harbinger of worse to come.

C→P_c: CULTURE → CRIME

Most centrally, culture plays an important role in determining which activities a society labels as criminal. To be sure, murder, theft, and rape are considered to be worthy of punishment in all societies. Yet a number of other activities, such as possession and sale of drugs, polygamy, collusion, suicide, spousal beating, child spanking, and sexual mutilation would be considered crimes in some societies but not in others. Other activities, like corruption or pollution, may be judged wrong universally, but accepted as inevitable in some societies while punished severely elsewhere. It is culture, in concert with the self-interest of political elites [P→P_c] which is primarily responsible for these cross-societal differences.

Culture also affects the treatment of criminals. I noted above that public policy clashes often center on a simplistic debate concerning individual responsibility versus social responsibility. We might expect, then, that societies which value individuality would be harsher in their treatment of criminals than societies which value collective action. This may explain, in part, why the United States imprisons a much larger proportion of its population than Western European nations. As noted above, there are dangers in both extremes. To deter people from crime requires both a sense that we are responsible for our own actions, as well as a sense of our responsibility to the rest of society. Societal attitudes toward crime may also have a major impact on the possibility of rehabilitation: Pepinsky and Jesilow (1984) feel that halfway houses work better in Sweden than North America because Swedish society feels that criminals deserve their help.

Culture also affects the likelihood of particular individuals transgressing their society's rules. Beyond the individuality/communalism distinction discussed above, attitudes of society toward ambition, charity, the role of women, aggression, time, and honesty will affect the degree of criminal activity. Religions that promise eternal damnation for present transgressions may limit crime (but remember the time preference problem; $G{\rightarrow}C11$). Societal cohesiveness is also important: if one feels oneself to be part of a cohesive and supportive community, one will be less likely to commit crime. If, however, society is divided into a number of competing groups, one may feel little compunction about stealing from other classes or ethnic groups $[S{\rightarrow}P_c]$. In such a case, cultural subgroups will likely emerge in which the attitude toward crime is much less critical than among dominant groups in society.

One area of intense debate these days concerns the effect of television on behavior, especially of children $[E{\rightarrow}P_c]$. Does television serve to glorify violence and deaden our senses to the human costs of violence? Academics are quite divided on this issue, and the empirical evidence is far from clear. It is not hard to sketch a compelling theoretical argument, drawing on how we each develop schemas to guide our behavior, and recalling the role of repetition in learning. It would seem that witnessing thousands of murders and rapes in one's life could certainly lead one to a misguided appreciation of such acts. The question is whether these effects can fairly readily be overwhelmed by the influence of role models and everyday experience (see Wilson and Herrnstein 1985; they note that television may also encourage a desire for instant gratification).

8

Social Structure

IDENTIFYING SOCIETAL SUBGROUPS

THIS CHAPTER EXAMINES THE SUBGROUPS INTO WHICH EVERY SOCIETY IS divided.[1] In the case of one of these divisions, gender, biological distinctions provide a clear demarcation line between male and female. Note, though, that even here there are some who possess the genitalia of both sexes, and a much larger number who would wish to identify themselves with the other gender. In the case of all other social divisions (e.g., racial/ethnic, class, occupation) the dividing lines are much more blurred. Many postmodern scholars have thus moved away from a rigid focus on class, with its implicit assumption that class boundaries are obvious, to ask instead how people form their self-image. How do they come to see themselves as members of certain groups? Classes, especially, but other social divisions as well, exist only to the extent that people believe them both to exist and to be important.

Looking at how self-image is formed yields three methods by which we could attempt, albeit imperfectly, to identify subgroup membership (Books and Prysby 1991). The first method flows from the conjecture that social divisions only matter (and will be seen to matter) if social groups differ significantly in their average attitude toward certain groups or values. Note that a group may be judged distinct according to this criteria if the only difference observed between it and other groups is that others feel group members to be different.

The second method for discerning group boundaries is to measure social interaction. Are group members many times more likely to interact with each other than with people outside the group? If so, then we have good reason both to suspect that group members will perceive their group to be distinct, and that some differences in values will exist relative to outsiders. Gross and Rayser (1985) describe a variety of measures we could use: the proportion of time spent within a group, proportion of one's links with others that are shared with others in the group, frequency of interaction, and presence of other group members when interacting with outsiders.

247

The third method is to look for defining characteristics of groups. We can come up with three classes, for example, by defining one in terms of ownership of the means of production, another in terms of manual labor, and a third as possessing neither of these two characteristics. This is often the easiest strategy, but carries the danger of suggesting that boundaries are both more clear and more important than they really are. Are workers with mutual funds to be counted in the upper class? Are skilled workers with high incomes to be viewed as middle or working class? The best answer to these and other questions may well be—as suggested above—that it depends on which class if any they (and others) see themselves as members of.

I close by noting that social differentiation need not imply stratification, but often does. One can be proud of one's Polish heritage without necessarily thinking that Poles are better or worse than any other group. One could identify oneself as middle class without feeling any sort of superiority over the working class. Yet humans like to compete, and need to value their own characteristics (I→I2), and these two tendencies together encourage us to think that our group is better than others. Conversely, a tendency to blame others for our misfortune, and to respect authority (even hunter-gatherer societies are hierarchical; G→S), allow us to treat some other groups as higher in status. The end result is that most social distinctions will be associated with status distinctions [G,C→S]. This will be especially so if there are power differentials; Kuhn (1974; ch 10) even defined "status" as apparent or perceived power [P→S]. Wilson (1998, 147) included "status differentiation" in his list of universals.

THE PHENOMENA

GENDER

As noted above, gender is the easiest of our social divisions to identify. Yet I should note that feminist scholars make an important distinction between sex and gender. When they speak of two sexes, they refer only to the biological differences between men and women. When they speak instead of gender they refer to cultural attitudes that treat men and women differently. I would capture the first sort of distinction under G→S, and the second primarily under C→S. In both cases, though, the boundary between men and women is the same (see Golombok and Fivush 1984). I will leave it as an empirical question for now as to the precise roles of genes and culture in gender differences. In this, I follow Brody and Hall (1993), who use the word "gender" to refer to both "sex" and "gender." They note that to do otherwise prejudges whether observed differences are caused by genes or environment. (We should also be open to at least a third "ambiguous" gender which, while only occasionally observed physiologically, has been recognized in some societies.)

While gender differences are easily identified under our first and third criteria from the previous section—genders differ physiologically, and in terms of various values such as attitude toward aggression—gender divisions do not fare well under our second method. Most people—at least in Western society—would claim that their most important relationship is with a member of the opposite gender (though beyond this there is some tendency toward within-gender interaction). Note also that to the extent that differences in values are shown to be culturally determined, and men and women both come to perceive their genetic differences to be slight, gender differences become much less important. If gender identity—how we define ourselves in gender terms—ceases to be a major component of our self-schema, then gender ceases to be a key social division.

FAMILY

Just as all societies (to date) treat men and women differently, all societies are also divided into families. Although marriage is ubiquitous, family form differs markedly across societies. Most obviously, grandparents and cousins are more likely to be found under one roof in some societies than others. Among some tribes in Papua New Guinea, it is common for the men to live together; strong economic and social ties nevertheless exist between individual men and their mates and children.

This latter example suggests that defining families by the external criterion of living under one roof is fraught with danger (see van der Poel 1993). If you have regretfully placed your aging mother in a nursing home, but pay her bills and visit her regularly, is she any less a part of your family than if she lived in your house? We are guided, then, to think of families in terms of both economic and emotional support. It is children, of course, who most rely on the support of others. The family unit plays its greatest role in any society in nurturing the young. Yet particular families do not cease to exist just because children mature.

One external criterion by which we might define families is degree of kinship. All societies have terms that define kinship (aunt, nephew, and so on). While some societies may view cousins as family members and others not, in all societies there is a strong tendency for those within a family to be more closely related than those without. Both marriage and adoption cause nongenetically related individuals to share family units, though. While kinship provides us with some guidelines, then, the real defining characteristic of a family is that its members perceive it to be a family. If you are dependent on the financial and emotional support of others (but what of cult members or mental patients?), or vice versa, then you can consider yourself and these others a family unit.[2]

In the appendix to chapter five I dealt with parental and sibling relationships. Our concern here is with different family structures (nuclear, extended, and so on), and with differences in the role played by families in the wider society. Of course, family relationships and family structure will influence each other.

Since kinship systems are important in some societies, and the borders between kin groups and families not identical, I must include kinship groups as a separate phenomenon.

CLASS

The most contentious social division is "class." Marx argued forcefully that class conflict was the major engine of social, political, and economic transformation in societies: the rise of capitalism had depended on the bourgeoisie overcoming the power of the landowning class; the victory of the workers over the bourgeoisie would in turn usher in a socialist utopia. While scholars within the Marxian tradition have added many caveats to Marx's analysis, most—but far from all—still hold that an emphasis on class relations is a central tenet of the Marxian tradition. Many non-Marxian scholars have concurred that class divisions are the most important characteristics of any society.

Increasingly, though, other scholars have maintained that class boundaries—at least today—are too blurred for class to be a meaningful unit of analysis. It is notable that this line of argument is much more common in North America than in Europe. This, Dogan and Pelassy (1990) suggest, reflects the fact that North Americans are much less likely to define themselves in terms of class. Rather than debating endlessly whether class matters, a more constructive approach, they argue, is to ask whether we need a more flexible typology of class than that employed by Marx. If members of the working class do not see themselves as being at the bottom of a hierarchical class structure our typology should reflect this.

Sanderson (1995) reviews recent attempts to provide less aggregative definitions of classes than Marx's division of the world into owners and workers. Rassides spoke of five classes, an upper class identified by wealth, an upper middle class composed of managers and professionals, a lower middle class of small businesspeople and lower level managers and professionals, a working class, and a lower or underclass of those who are often unemployed. Goldthorpe expanded this list to eleven classes by, for example, separating skilled and unskilled workers (though leaving man-agers, businesspeople, and professionals together). Eric Wright, respond-ing to a criticism that such divisions reflect merely prestige and income, focused instead on control. He suggested that there are three basic classes: the bourgeoisie who own large companies and thus exercise control over large numbers, the working class who are subject to such authority, and the small businesspeople class (petty bourgeoisie) who, having no workers, neither exert nor suffer control. There are also three contradictory classes, who both exert and suffer authority: managers, small employers, and semi-autonomous professionals (those that are not employees) (Wright has in later writings suggested further divisions).

I must be careful to distinguish social structure from other elements of the schema. If classes perfectly reflect either the economic or political organization of a society, I could save space by combining these elements. "While wealth and status can be used to acquire power, and the three are frequently correlated, each needs to be understood as part of a separate domain" (Schwartz 1990). While classes may be rooted in the distribution of income and power in a society, they matter only to the extent that people believe them to. Remember, though, that we can distinguish groups if insiders *or* outsiders view them as different, and/or if there are differences in attitudes between them. Wright's emphasis on control serves to remind us that we must be careful in relying on self-definition: even if workers are unaware of the control exercised by others, or managers perceive them-selves as indistinguishable from owners, their roles in society would still be quite different.

Where does that leave us? Our experience with unpacking in this book suggests that disaggregation is no bad thing. I can leave as an empirical question the level of disaggregation which has most explanatory power. If managers and professionals and small businesspeople are observed to believe the same things, then the idea of an upper middle class is shown to have much scientific merit. If, alternatively, doctors, lawyers, and pro-fessors are found to be more aware of their differences than their sim-ilarities, and thus behave quite differently, we would be guided to unpack yet further.

Crompton (1993) proposes a fairly disaggregated set of classes, which she argues reflects a fair degree of consensus. Like all typologies, hers has an upper class comprising a small group of people with substantial wealth and ownership of the means of production. She divides her middle class into professionals, small businesspeople, and middle management (I could follow Rossides and divide these each into upper and lower groups). She divides the working class into white collar—routine office, sales, and clerical duties—and blue collar (I will further disaggregate these into skilled and unskilled). She concludes with an underclass of chronically unemployed. Such a classification scheme suits my purposes well enough for now. I should emphasize, though, that it lacks the universality I have generally striven for in this book. Crompton herself recognizes that she would have suggested a different typology mere decades ago; certainly the conception of a white collar segment of the working class would have surprised scholars a century ago. Dogan and Pelassy (1990) discuss the difficulty of applying any Western conception of class divisions to less-developed countries.

This classification scheme does meet our criteria for group divisions. People do tend to define themselves in terms of categories like professional, skilled labor, or unemployed. The different economic roles played by these groups leads us to suspect that they may well be differentiated by attitudes as well. Most social activity tends to occur within these groups. Moreover, while we have not required that children remain in the same class as their parents in order for class to be a meaningful concept, the tendency of children to do exactly that makes it much more likely that differences in attitude across groups will be maintained.

Our mention of children brings us to a further problem. Classifications by class were first designed in a world in which one family member was the primary "breadwinner." The rest of the family was then assigned to the class of the breadwinner. But what do we do when a bricklayer marries a lawyer? The common usage of "middle-class family" or "working-class family" easily breaks down in a world where both parents work. And what of single parents? Are they automatically members of the underclass, or do they become working or middle class when they land even part-time work?

OCCUPATION

Having disaggregated this far, it is but a small step to disaggregate further to the level of occupation. Casual empiricism suggests that people are even more likely to define themselves in terms of occupation than class. Thus, I must leave a place for occupation in the schema, and be open to the possibility that at least in some respects occupation may play a more important causal role than class (see Blau 1992).

RACE/ETHNICITY

I have suggested elsewhere (G→C1) that genetic differences between racial/ethnic groups are slight indeed. Differences in skin pigmentation, physical appearance, language, and location can nevertheless be used to distinguish one group from another. Such distinctions matter only if people inside and/or outside the group believe that they do.

OTHERS?

So far I have divided societies into groups on the basis of gender, family, kinship, class/occupation, and ethnicity. There are a host of other characteristics by which humans can be differentiated. Height and weight are obvious candidates: both the short and the overweight are often discriminated against [I→E]. There are now organizations that fight for fair treatment of each group (remember that special interest organizations are political institutions). At the moment, though, neither the short nor the above-average in weight have anywhere near the level of self-consciousness associated with our other groups. We can thus recognize that height and weight have significant influences on individuals (just as intelligence, eye color, and hair density do), without recognizing their group identity as worthy of special study (but this could change with self-awareness).[3] A stronger case might be made for the disabled.

Sexual orientation can likewise be treated as an individual difference or a group difference. As with height and weight, it made sense to treat the causes of homosexuality at the level of individuals. Societal attitudes toward homosexuality are an element of culture.

Age and marital status are two other characteristics that have important effects on individual outlook and behavior. In both cases, mobility between groups is so endemic as to limit the degree of societal division. Still, we are all conscious of how age and marital status affect us, and know that others use these criteria to judge us. All societies discriminate in many ways on the basis of age and marital status. Social interaction tends to occur predominantly with others of similar age and marital status. And organizations do exist to further the aims of the elderly, and the single. The young, especially, are prone to using their youth as a reason for having different values. I would be tempted to include age as a phenomenon here, but can capture its effects as easily in our discussion of age distribution in chapter 10.

The approach taken here accords well with that of Payne (2000). He devotes most attention to class, ethnicity, and gender, noting that these are what most sociologists would view as social divisions. Lesser attention is devoted to age, sexuality, disability, and nationality. Payne notes that stratification is one common element across diverse divisions.

Some sociologists approach the study of social structure in terms of the network of social contacts that each individual develops, rather than in terms of groups. The two approaches are far from incompatible. Since people choose friends on the basis of shared values and customs, they are much more likely to form contacts with those of similar class/ethnicity. Rather than treating networks as a separate category, then (which would create enormous problems, since each individual's network is inevitably unique), I will view networks as a causal link: one way in which group membership affects behavior.[4]

SOCIAL IDEOLOGY

I have argued in the last two chapters that inequalities in income or power must be justified ideologically (Law 1994, ch. 7). To the extent that any of our social divisions can be viewed as having different status or prestige within society, this too must be justified. A key distinction is that the very existence of social structure depends crucially on perception. Rather than rationalizing differences in status, then, we can attempt to downplay the size of such differences.

C→S: Culture → Social Structure

For many sociologists, the unit of social structure is the "role." The question they ask is how a person's gender, ethnicity, class, and occupation constrain both their behavior and the way others view them. While cognizant that genes play a part in at least gender differences, the natural focus of such scholars is on how cultural attitudes define roles. In other words, the position of any group within the wider society depends crucially on cultural attitudes, both of insiders and outsiders.

With regard to the attitudes of one group toward another, I should note that the exact same behaviors may be valued quite differently depending on whether they are performed by insider or outsider. Abe Lincoln is hailed for thrift while Abe Cohen is castigated as a miser.

I. GENDER ROLES

While gender roles have changed markedly in modern societies over recent decades, men still dominate political (including educational) and economic institutions, and women predominate in home, childrearing, and the provision of emotional support. Further differences are widely observable in dress, speech, movement, interests, occupation, and sexual behavior. We have seen before (chapter 4) that genes can explain some but far from all of these observed differences.

In their attempts to define a handful of key personality dimensions decades ago, psychologists often had recourse to a masculine/feminine dimension where the masculine end was associated with such traits as assertiveness and competitiveness, while feminine traits included nurturing and submissiveness. This personality dimension has fallen out of favor with psychologists, in large part as it was recognized that many people scored highly (or poorly) in terms of both supposedly masculine traits such as assertiveness and feminine traits such as nurturance. In common parlance, though, masculine and feminine are still terms used to cover a host of culturally sanctioned personality differences. People who deviate from the behavior expected from their gender—wimpy men, ambitious women—will be ostracized or worse as a result. Scholars thus often refer to "sex typing," the degree to which people conform to culturally sanctioned gender roles.

While we can point to many commonalities across societies in attitudes toward gender, it is nevertheless true that accepted gender roles differ not only by country and time period, but also class and ethnicity. Whereas it was considered admirable for men to display their emotions in the eighteenth century, they are now expected to do the opposite. In the United States, the working class, as well as many ethnic minorities, takes a less favorable view of female ambition than does the middle class [S→S]. It might be thought that there would be huge gender differences in attitudes toward gender roles. Yet these appear to be very slight compared to ethnic and class-based differences. The acceptance by many women of gender stereotypes naturally serves to reinforce these. If women believe themselves to be submissive, they are less likely to fight for a change in gender roles [S→I].

How do men and women learn gender roles? This learning starts very young. By the age of two children display a strong preference for playing with members of the same gender (even though they have as yet a very limited understanding either of the genetic base of gender differences or of the exact cultural expectations of gender).[5] From this point on, they inevitably learn more about their own gender than the other. Remember that preschool children are struggling to form schemas that make sense of the world: the fact that the world is comprised of men and women, and these are distinguishable by dress, hair style, and occupation, can hardly fail to be incorporated in the child's earliest schemas. Slight differences between genders will likely be exaggerated (Golombok and Fivush 1984). Role models are especially important for young children. Having identified themselves by gender, they will naturally ape the behavior of adults of that gender. Their goals in life will reflect what they see members of their gender doing. Books, movies, and television reinforce gender roles. Most books, especially historically, have been written by men. They tend naturally to have male heroes, with women in supporting roles.[6] While there have been changes in recent decades, movies and television shows still tend to showcase male exploits. Television advertisements may be of special importance here: ads for home care products and clothing in particular tend to provide a very limited perspective on women's role in society. Finally, both parents and teachers tend to treat boys and girls differently (often subconsciously). Teachers, for example, often reward boys for brilliance and girls for obedience.

Culturally defined gender roles both encourage and are reinforced by gender discrimination. Men who believe that women are less assertive will be less likely to promote them. Even men who merely recognize that other men think so will have fears about the reaction of male workers to female promotion. Women who accept gender roles will be less likely to protest. While there is much debate about the extent of gender discrimination, Blau (1993) calculates that about half of male/female income differentials in the United States are due to discrimination. This affects young women's aspirations in two ways: it limits their access to role models, and it discourages them from striving to succeed because of the extra barriers they will face.

Religion has a special role to play in gender roles. All major Western religions give a privileged position to men. God is often viewed as male, the prophets are almost exclusively male, and positions in the clergy have historically been limited to men. Passages of scripture describe men as the head of the household, and even give men instructions to physically discipline spouses. Men are hailed as rational, women viewed as creatures of passion. Many modern theologians argue that these elements of their religions reflect the patriarchal nature of middle eastern society millennia ago rather than the design of god. Religions do evolve over time: the position of women within both Christianity and Judaism has improved over the last generations (though the Catholic Church and Orthodox Judaism still ordain only men). Islam at the moment appears to proscribe women's role more than any other world religion. Yet a casual journey through Islamic countries quickly betrays the fact that women have much greater freedom in Malaysia or Turkey than in Saudi Arabia or Iran. While the Koran does suggest discreet clothing for women, the idea of head to toe covering results from later interpretations, and is ignored in many Islamic lands. In a handful of places, indeed, the Koran speaks more highly of women than the Bible or Torah. Eve is not created from Adam's rib in the Koran, and it is Adam rather than Eve who gives into temptation. There is thus some cause for hope that Islamic attitudes toward women may soften as has happened within Christianity and Judaism.

Resistance to cultural change can be a barrier to the evolution of gender roles. South Africa provides a useful example. Feminists there dislike many traditional practices among some elements of the black community: arranged marriages, dowry, polygamy, and inheritance of property only by males. Yet many hesitate to voice these concerns in the immediate post-apartheid era because the ideology of the new state involves protecting the traditional black cultures (traditional rights are enshrined in the constitution). Only once it is recognized that cultures can and should change can this sort of barrier to gender equality be vanquished.

2. CLASS

I have stressed already that class matters only to the extent that people believe it to do so. Occupational and income differences need not yield great differences in attitude or behavior (but almost always do). This is especially so if it is believed that there is substantial occupational mobility. Many sociologists would define caste systems as the extreme end of a continuum wherein culture dictates inherited class and prohibits mobility between them (based, I might note, on misguided notions of genetic purity). Moving away from caste on that continuum, then, the degree to which culture (and economic and political circumstances) permits mobility will decrease the importance of class in that society.

We should not ignore, though, the reinforcement that seemingly insignificant cultural attributes can provide to class divisions. Different views of etiquette can embarrass those attempting to cross class boundaries. Different tastes in dress can distinguish one group from another. Different preferences in recreation can limit cross-class contact.[7]

3. RACISM

Racism, purely speaking, refers to a belief that one group is genetically superior to another. It should be distinguished from ethnocentrism, the belief that one group's culture is superior to another's. In the latter case, culture plays a dual role: we must first believe that two groups have quite distinct cultures, and then believe that one is superior to another. In practice, racist and ethnocentrist ideas are often voiced together, and clearly reinforce each other. Remember that I have suggested previously (chapter 3) that, while it is legitimate to judge particular cultural attributes on ethical grounds, it is a mistake to think entire cultures can be so evaluated. We have likewise seen that genetic differences between groups are generally insignificant relative to within-group differences ($G{\rightarrow}C1$).

Many scholars would question my simultaneous treatment of racism and ethnocentrism. Both, though, have roots in the genetic drive to identify with groups ($G{\rightarrow}C2$). Moreover, we have seen that "cultures" are defined in terms of ethnicity (by scholars as by the general public): to feel ethnically superior to another group must mean that one doubts the validity of their culture. To doubt another group's culture can all too easily lead to suspicion of substandard genes.

Gilroy (1991) discusses the practical difficulties in identifying race with culture. First, it reduces the immediacy of race problems: if blacks are viewed as separate rather than an integral part of the wider society, then it is easier to either ignore or give up on racial problems. More centrally, if it is taken for granted that black culture is forever different, then it is easy for racists to claim that integration is impossible. If instead we were to recognize that cultures evolve and borrow from each other, an entirely different view of race relations follows. And a casual moment's reflection on the role of blacks in entertainment and sports, or the contributions of black slang to the national vocabulary, suggests that black contributions to "white" culture in both Britain and North America has been far from insignificant. Gilroy concludes that racist attitudes depend not on color but on culture and identity. If we were to concentrate more on the elements of history and culture we share than on our differences, racist tensions would decline.

Racism/ethnocentrism is embodied in stereotypes about how members of groups behave. It is now widely recognized that these stereotypes are formed just as any other schema (I→I1; Hamilton 1994).[8] We could potentially measure the degree of racism in a society in terms of the likelihood that a member of one group will expect a member of another to behave in a certain way, compared to a baseline of the average expectation in society. These stereotypes have a huge influence on cross-group behavior: if I believe members of group X to be lazy I will not hire them nor let them date my children, if I think they are dishonest I will not do business with them, and if I think they are untidy I will oppose their living in my neighborhood. Note that stereotypes serve to limit the degree of cross-group contact, which in turn serves not only to maintain cultural differences, but people's exaggerated perceptions of these differences. Even when contact does occur, I will act according to my stereotypes: if I expect you to be hostile, I will be hostile myself and elicit the expected behavior from you. And if you do surprise me, I will view you (or the situation) as an exception to the rule, rather than revising my view of your group. Only frequent contact with a variety of members from other groups is likely to shake my stereotypes.

It should be admitted, though, that we are far from a full understanding of how we can change stereotypes. I have suggested that intergroup contact is one way, but neither it, nor movies, lectures, or schooling is always successful (Monteith, Zuwerink, and Devine 1994). Those for whom prejudice forms a key element of their schema system may find that they risk losing their identity if they abandon their stereotypes of others [I→S].

While scholars used to focus on those with the strongest racial attitudes, it has become common in recent years to emphasize subtler forms of racism. Cultural attitudes have changed significantly in the United States and other Western countries over the last generations. Most citizens, when asked, would indicate a strong belief in equality between people, and opposition to discrimination. Yet in their daily lives they are still constrained by a host of subtle stereotypes (some perhaps subconscious, especially those learned early in life) that cause them to act differently toward members of different groups. Such people, in contrast to extreme racists, may be quite receptive to attempts to change their stereotypes, and may indeed try to consciously override their subconscious stereotypes. Yet the very subtlety of these stereotypes makes it difficult to identify them in the first place.

4. VALUES→FAMILY

The terms by which we denote kinship ties differ across societies. In extended family situations, it is common for the word for cousin to be identical to that for brother/sister. This symbolizes the fact that one's responsibilities are the same in either case. In other societies, uncles on one's mother's side are denoted differently from those on one's father's side, symbolizing the fact that one side is more important than the other.

While marriage is ubiquitous, societies differ greatly in how marriage decisions are reached, and in attitudes toward divorce. Societies that view mutual love and consent as the key to successful marriage will leave marriage decisions primarily to the young. By weakening the power of parents over their adult children, this arguably increases the role of the nuclear family over the extended family. Indeed some have claimed that the early Catholic Church pushed the ideal of consensual marriage in order to reduce the power of extended family and clan.

S→C: SOCIAL STRUCTURE → CULTURE

Within any society, we are likely to find that certain values are more widely shared than others. Various subgroups will differ in terms of various cultural attributes (chapter 3). Our concern here is with how the division of society into groups affects the evolution of a society's culture. It has long been suspected that dominant social groups had a disproportionate effect on culture. The upper class would encourage beliefs that supported their position. Powerful ethnic groups would encourage public support of their language and ritual. While few would doubt the importance of such influences, it is now widely recognized that relatively powerless minorities can also exercise a considerable cultural influence (Smith and Bond 1993). Mugny and Perez (1991) argue that any view (cultural or political, [S→P]) adhered to strongly by any minority (however composed) will inevitably influence majority beliefs. While people may resist agreeing publicly with the minority for some time,[9] in order to disagree with them they will have to learn the basis of the minority view. In doing so they will tend naturally to absorb its more palatable elements. The position of the minority in society affects the degree of influence. If they are viewed as outsiders, the majority may not bother to enter into dialogue with them. On the other hand, if they are seen as integral members of society, others may be deeply offended by their apostasy. It can be of crucial importance, then, that the minority be willing to engage in debate.

I have noted in previous chapters that individuals will accept some ideas on authority. If the scientific community tells us that $e = mc^2$, so be it; we will not even attempt to verify this judgment. Cultural values can also be accepted on authority. The relevance of myths depends on our respect for the storyteller. Cross-group transmission will be enhanced, then, to the degree to which authority figures are respected by more than one group. It might be thought that dominant groups would have an advantage here, but other groups may resent their claim to authority.

I. MAINTAINING SOCIAL ORDER

Any hierarchical social structure will be destabilized to the extent that it is not supported by an ideology that justifies differences in status. This ideology may in turn affect a host of cultural values. Foucault spent much of his career arguing that cultural attitudes toward diverse phenomena such as sex, crime, and mental illness reflected little more than the desire of those at the top of the social hierarchy to maintain social order. Note, though, that once a culture absorbed these values, even the upper class would not be immune from their effect. In Law's (1994) words, social ordering must be represented (culturally), and these representations in turn will have influences on society.

Along with values, symbols and rituals will reflect social structure. Ethnologists have indeed long operated from the assumption that one of the main purposes of these would be to express social differences (Lemonnier 1992). Most obviously, the common practice of traditional groups whereby those with wealth throw huge feasts in which they dissipate much of their wealth serves to justify social structure. Status is gained not from the accumulation of wealth, but through substantial sharing with the wider community. Antipathy toward the rich is lessened by a recognition that the whole community will periodically benefit (and in many societies leaders would share their wealth especially during times of hardship). Some anthropologists would argue that visible philanthropy may be just as essential to the maintenance of social stability in modern societies.

De Tocqueville felt that the egalitarian ethos he observed in early America reflected the lack of an aristocracy. While a society based on inherited privilege will be threatened by egalitarianism, substantial class cleavages are not incompatible with it. Two conditions are necessary: equality must be defined primarily in terms of opportunities rather than outcomes, and there must be a widespread (if not necessarily accurate; see Brezis and Temin 1999) belief in mobility.

2. THE PERSISTENCE OF ETHNIC SUBCULTURES

Despite the tendencies of both dominant groups and "minorities" to influence the wider culture, ethnic subcultures persist. This is hardly surprising. If both our family and peer groups come from within a particular group, we will naturally absorb the values of that group. We will tend to define ourselves in terms of membership of that group rather than the wider society. To the extent that individuals interact across ethnic boundaries, become exposed to other ideas (including through the media), and come to identify with the larger society, these ethnic subcultures will weaken.

Kephart and Zellner (1991) analyze a handful of American ethnic—and other—groups that have maintained a very distinct subculture (see also Pitzer 1997). In their case studies, religion looms very large.[10] The Amish religion requires its members to shun many elements of modern society (e.g., automobiles). By adhering to this religion, the Amish must necessarily abandon the aspirations of the wider society. By seeing other Amish as their reference group, they are willing to accept a life of harder work and lower incomes. Amish society also penalizes heavily those who digress from the accepted way (banning those who commit extreme transgressions).

Gypsies too have a distinct "religion," in which the lower part of the body is viewed as profane (though gypsies may adhere to mainstream religions too). Since non-gypsies do not obey the strict rules that gypsies obey in terms of the profane, intimate cross-group associations are limited. The geographic mobility of gypsies, and their tendency not to send children to school (and resulting illiteracy), further limits cross-group contact. Extended families and arranged marriages also encourage an emphasis on within-group relations.

Just as different religious beliefs can serve as a powerful barrier to ethnic integration, so a shared sense of ethnic hardship can encourage greater emphasis of religious differences.[11] Many would attribute the rise of Islamic fundamentalism in recent decades, both on the world stage and within the United States, to a shared sense of injustice at the hands of white Christians. Emphasizing religious differences will in turn increase the barriers to communication, and thus the chances of further ethnic conflict.

3. RELIGION

We saw in the previous section that religious differences can enhance social differences (with a feedback effect).[12] Often, though, religious beliefs are shared by diverse groups. In this context, religions must provide some justification for social divisions. A classic example is the "divine right of kings," a belief with limited scriptural justification that was used for centuries to justify not just kingly but noble pretensions in Europe. Elite groups also have an incentive to encourage religious belief in rewards in the next life; this can divert attention from injustice in this life (Barkow 1989). Subservient groups may find relief in religions which argue that suffering in this life will lead to rewards in the next.

Cultural beliefs often differ by gender. Values relating to male dominance in particular were/are likely at the very least interpreted differently by women. Women may, for example, decide that activities in which they participate are more important. One area that has seen considerable exploration by feminist scholars in recent years has been religion (C→S1). Some have pushed for gender-neutral terms (especially for god) in sermons, or for female ordination. Others have wondered whether inherited religious traditions are not so biased toward male dominance that reform is impossible.

In the modern United States, there is virtually no correlation between income and religious observance. The poor are more likely, though, to belong to fundamentalist denominations. Educational attainment has a slight positive effect on religious observance overall. University professors are as likely as others to be religious, though in certain disciplines such as anthropology and psychology religious observation is well below the national average. Blacks, women, and the elderly are more religious. Some of the increased attendance among the elderly may simply reflect the lesser pressure on their time.

4. CLASS SUBCULTURES

Given that many scholars question the importance of class divisions in modern society, it comes as no surprise that there is debate about the significance of class-based cultural differences. DiMaggio (1994) argues that upper-class solidarity is maintained through shared values and leisure activities, but recognizes that others suspect that solidarity depends instead on personal ties (networks) and shared economic interests. Some scholars would maintain that the working class is more violent, less ambitious, less respectful of authority, less emotionally inhibited, and less gender-neutral than the middle class; others would argue that such differences are steadily disappearing, in large part due to common exposure to mass media.

Class differences in attitudes toward sexual intercourse have been the subject of much study. In many societies in which there are cultural prohibitions against extramarital intercourse (this is, I should note, far from a universal characteristic of human societies), the lower classes are generally observed to have the most liberal attitudes (though they are sometimes quite puritan). The upper classes may flout the rules as well. Those concerned with mobility and reputation will be the most likely to adhere to cultural values. Thus, the middle class is generally the most devoted to "traditional" values.

5. GENDER AND LANGUAGES

Most North American scholars—if recent surveys are correct—strive to use gender-neutral language in both their teaching and publications. This practice reflects a recognition that using male descriptors—chairman, craftsman, or referring to leaders habitually as "he"—may send a subtle message that such positions are a male preserve. This is only the most obvious way in which changing gender roles affect (and are affected by) languages. Many feminists also decry the fact that there are many more derogatory terms for promiscuous women than men, or that there are many derogatory gender-based expressions (drive like a woman, throw like a girl). We also denigrate those who speak shrilly. Given that women on average have a much higher pitch to their voice, this suggests that women's speech is less preferred (Romaine 1994).

Some elements of languages are harder to change than others. The very fact that we use gender-based forms of address (Mr., Ms.) may serve to exaggerate the significance of gender differences in everyday life. Yet the struggle to replace Mrs./Miss with Ms. indicates that changes in forms of address are not easy. And what of other languages, such as French, where all nouns, articles, and adjectives must be either feminine or masculine? It is not at all clear that this practice has a significant impact on gender relations. Nevertheless, if we were to build a new language from scratch today we would probably eschew gender-sensitive nouns.

6. CLASS AND LANGUAGE

As with gender, linguistic norms can become established that serve to exacerbate class divisions. In English, it is common for high-status people to be addressed as Sir/Madam, Dr., Mrs. or Ms./Mrs., whereas low-status people are addressed by first name. In French, a further complication arises in the distinction between the singular "tu" and plural "vous" (both translate as "you"). Traditionally "tu" was used for friends and "vous" for less close acquaintances. But low status individuals could not use "tu" when speaking to those of high status. Both traditions have been breaking down in recent years.

7. SOCIOLINGUISTICS

One of the major branches of linguistics, sociolinguistics deals with the apparently natural tendency of social groups to develop distinct dialects.

Despite decades of radio and television broadcasting, which tends to strive for a standard dialect, not to mention the long-standing existence of standard dictionaries, dialects remain very strong (though many feel that their importance is dwindling). Sociolinguists are interested in differences in pronunciation (accents), grammar, and vocabulary (Figueroa 1994). While regional differences are the most obvious, sociolinguists also examine the nature and effects of class, ethnic, and gender differences in speech patterns. In all these cases, the rise of dialects can be attributed to two key influences. First, people have a greater tendency to talk to other group members than outsiders. Thus, any linguistic mutation (and languages are always evolving) will spread more quickly within a group than across groups. Second, people's inherent desire for identity encourages dialect formation as a very public signal of difference.

With regard to the first influence, it is noteworthy that the middle class, which tends to be more geographically mobile than either the upper or working class, exhibits far fewer regional dialect differences (Chambers 1995). This, plus the prominence of the middle class, encourages a tendency to recognize the middle-class dialect as the standard from which others deviate. However, there is no reason for viewing one dialect as superior to others, except perhaps the number of people who can comprehend it. All dialects are mutations of previous dialects, and all are equally good at facilitating within-group communication.

When cross-group contact is great, dialect convergence is likely. The greatest historical instance occurred with European settlement of North America, Australia, and New Zealand. In all these cases, English, Irish, Welsh, and Scottish immigrants created a common dialect (which in all cases resembled dictionary English more than the dialects of their homelands). While regional dialects did emerge in these new countries, they tend to be much more similar than in the British Isles, perhaps in part because of greater regional mobility.

What are the effects of dialects? Like distinct languages, they provide a barrier to between-group communication, and a source of within-group identity.[13] In countries in which classes are readily distinguishable by dialect, they serve as an important barrier to social mobility. Both employers and teachers will, consciously or not, judge those with lower-class accents or syntax to be less able. The latter may strive to speak "properly" when, say, interviewing for a job, but will be unlikely to succeed perfectly (sociolinguists, I should note, strive to put interviewees at ease, so that they can measure their "casual" rather than "formal" speech patterns). [S→C]

In the areas of grammar and vocabulary, mastery of a different dialect may be possible if time-consuming. In matters of accent, though, shaking one's roots can be much more problematic (though differences in accent by class tend to be smaller than differences in grammar). Studies of regional migration show that those who move after the age of fourteen never completely master the new dialect, while those who move before seven lose all trace of their original dialect. Ambitious working-class children, though, have been shown to be more aware of class-based dialect differences, and tend to attempt middle-class speech patterns from a young age. Indeed, once successfully ensconced in the middle class, they are observed on average to be even more 'grammatically correct' than those born into the middle class [C→I].[14]

Working-class women are generally observed to use a more "standard" speech than men. Some scholars have suggested that this reflects greater status-consciousness among women (perhaps because they tend to have lower status than men) or simply a greater facility with language. Others stress instead the greater cross-class contacts of working-class women. The jobs such women perform—waitress, maid, typist—require regular interaction with the middle class. Working-class men, on the loading dock or the assembly line, tend to interact primarily with each other, and thus favor a dialect that sets them apart from their bosses. Yet even among the middle class, men are much more prone to using nonstandard grammar; this may reflect a lesser concern with status, or a desire to imitate working-class men.

Dialect diversity may aid the process of linguistic evolution, just as cultural diversity may aid the process of cultural evolution (C→C). But can we think of languages as in any sense getting better? Chambers (1995) speaks of, for example, regularizing verb tenses, and argues that the "standard" dialect may be slower to eliminate inconsistencies. But the empirical question of whether languages have in fact improved over time remains unanswered. The fact that there are no obvious differences between existing world languages in ease of communication suggests otherwise.

8. BILINGUALISM

What about ethnic minorities who speak a different language than the majority? These linguistic differences will form a very strong barrier to between-group interaction. Some minorities try to limit members' access to mastery of the majority language. This ensures linguistic and thus cultural separation (as Breton 1991, notes, bilingualism is a necessary intermediate step if people are ever going to abandon the minority language). Yet members of the minority group may find it essential to learn the majority language for economic and political (including educational) purposes. If their mastery of the dominant language is less than perfect, they will find themselves at a disadvantage in dealing with those for whom it is a first language. In most multilingual societies, languages differ in status, and limited mastery of higher status languages can place one at a disadvantage. Experts differ on the best means of teaching minority children more than one language when young (with debates often influenced by the interest of community leaders in ensuring imperfect grasp of the second language).

9. FAMILY FORM AND CULTURAL CHANGE

The form that families take in a particular society will influence the rate of cultural change. Close-knit families, such that children learn predominantly from parents and grandparents rather than peers, will be inherently conservative. The adults with whom children interact the most will exert particular influences: mothers exert the greatest influence on music appreciation, moviegoing, and religion, and fathers on sports, museums, and partying ($I_R \rightarrow C$; Cavalli-Sforza 1981). While the family has lost some of the roles it used to play—for example in education—it still remains the primary source of cultural transmission in all societies.

9

Technology and Science

A COUPLE OF DECADES AGO, THE TREATMENT OF SCIENCE AND TECHNOLOGY in one chapter would have raised many eyebrows. Although scholars of science and of technology have each been distributed across a range of academic departments, they had tended to have little contact with each other. Historians of science often felt that their subject matter was more worthy (as intellectual history) than the history of technology, while historians of technology could argue that their subject matter had a greater practical impact on people's lives. Sociologists of (scientific) knowledge and economists concerned with technology had even less cause to interface. In the last decades, though, many universities have established science and technology studies programs, in which scholars of science and technology have inevitably cooperated. While such scholars are still largely organized in separate scholarly societies (e.g., the Society for the History of Technology) these occasionally hold joint conferences, and often feature sessions that cross the science/technology boundary. Increasingly, scholars have explored the various ways in which science and technology influence the other.[1]

What exactly are science and technology? With the usual warnings about the problems inherent in brief definitions, I can define science as our understanding of how the (both human and nonhuman) world works, and technology as the set of techniques we use to produce goods and services. While these definitions may appear deceptively simple, a few remarks are necessary. Note that the word "knowledge" appears nowhere: it is now recognized by philosophers of science that we can never "know" anything with certainty but can only amass more and more evidence so that our confidence in certain hypotheses approaches certainty (see chapter 2). Note also that I have avoided defining technology as applied science. Much of even modern technology has no firm scientific basis. Engineers often follow rules of thumb based on past practice rather than a strict application of the laws of physics. Chefs develop recipes without any understanding of the chemistry of flavor. Indeed, technological exploration often precedes scientific explanation: nineteenth-century developments in steelmaking both preceded and encouraged metallurgists' understanding of the chemical reactions involved. Finally, as our reference to recipes implied, we must recognize that technology need not be embodied in a machine, nor even written down.

UNPACKING

Science and technology can each be unpacked in terms of field of inquiry. Within human science, I have argued throughout this book that it is dangerous to disaggregate to the disciplinary level without having due regard for the connections among disciplines. While disciplinary boundaries are less problematic in the natural sciences, even there we must be careful of not losing sight of how one discipline influences another. The same argument applies to technology: historians of technology have long recognized how diverse technologies affect each other. With this important caveat in mind, then, I can feel free to speak of physics or military technology in what follows (though much of the discussion will be at a more general level).

We will see while discussing technological and scientific evolution below that there are a handful of distinct stages involved in the development and adoption of new technology. When examining *→T links, then, I can unpack in terms of these stages of innovation as well. These can be analyzed with respect to a particular innovation or field, or more generally. For example, we could ask how a particular government encourages technological diffusion [P→T].

TECHNOLOGY AND SCIENCE AS BOTH CAUSE AND EFFECT

Bijker (1995) describes the development of studies of technology thus: before the 1940s the subject was largely ignored (with a couple of exceptions, such as Lewis Mumford), then the pendulum swung sharply to technological determinism: historians, economists, and philosophers pointed to the many ways in which technological developments affected the rest of society.[2] Then, the pendulum swung sharply to the other extreme, and technology became entirely a social construct for several years. Happily the pendulum now oscillates less wildly about a middle ground where it is recognized that technology both influences and is influenced by other phenomena. While this point of view fits well with the approach taken in this book, Bijker notes that some modern scholars object to the very idea of a technology/society dichotomy. They argue that any production decision is simultaneously technical and "social" (e.g., do we use machines or slaves?). Yet this view is also compatible with my approach: it recognizes that all aspects of human endeavor are interrelated, and that we cannot fully understand any one phenomenon without reference to others. Many of the articles in Bijker and Law (1992) stress that new technologies are generally born out of conflict—since they create both winners and losers—and thus cannot be understood without reference to political, economic, cultural, and social phenomena.

Naturally, some scholars emphasize the causes of technological change and others its effects. Within the latter group, a number of seminal historical transitions have been credited a technological root: the cotton gin made a dying slavery profitable again, while the much later mechanical cotton picker encouraged black migration northward, the compass and other navigational tools made the discovery of the New World almost inevitable, the printing press ushered in the Reformation, the automobile created the suburbs, and the birth control pill induced the sexual revolution. In all of these cases, the actual course of history was undoubtedly more complicated. Yet the T→* links are undeniable, and the very tangibility of technical artifacts (you can touch a cotton gin) lends these an aura of causal power (Smith 1994).

One key insight behind the recognition of technology as both cause and effect is the unpredictable nature of technological development. If innovators were fully cognizant of the effects their ideas would have, one *could* argue that technology itself plays no causal role. However, Marconi developed the idea of wireless transmission primarily to allow ships at sea to contact shore stations in an emergency. He did not foresee the role that radio would come to play a short couple of decades later. We can see, then, both that the development of radio was influenced by various factors—the nature of shipping, Marconi's personality, and the resources at his disposal—and yet in turn influenced culture and economy in ways nobody imagined. Rosenberg (1994) asserts that it is practically a general rule that developers of a new technology cannot foresee all of its effects: along with radio he refers to the laser, telephone, computer, and transistor as technologies that had a much greater impact than predicted. In these and other cases, several factors contributed to difficulties in prediction: the technologies were radically improved over time, they developed in concert with other technologies (e.g., the transistor revolutionized the computer industry), adjustments in the wider society were necessary for them to have their full effect (think of the automobile) and/or they met previously unrealized human "needs" (as the radio fulfilled a previously unappreciated desire for mass entertainment) (see also Smith 1994).[3]

An understanding of science as both cause and effect has emerged over a long period. Early scholars tended to view science as a "natural" process of discovering nature's laws. Though even within this perspective one could still argue a role for, say, education in determining the rate at which these

discoveries were made, and historians made much of the changes in intellectual attitudes associated with the Enlightenment, the greatest attention
was paid to how this unerring march forward aided humanity. In recent
decades, as philosophers showed that scientists could neither prove nor
disprove theories, and sociologists described the biases that could influence scientific inquiry, a view of science as both cause and effect has
inevitably emerged.

THE EVOLUTION OF SCIENCE AND TECHNOLOGY

It is not a surprise that nobody experimented with television in the fifteenth
century nor pondered the theory of relativity in the seventeenth. While
popular historiography tends to hail the successful scientist or inventor as a
special genius [I→T], the fact is that all thinkers and tinkerers are limited
in their efforts by the existing body of knowledge. We can thus speak of an
evolutionary process wherein every scientific or technological advance is a
mutation of previous ideas. It is important, though, to recognize many
ways in which this evolutionary process differs from biological evolution.

CHOICES

Genes mutate without a plan. People must almost always consciously
design new ideas. In rare circumstances, a new technique may be
discovered by accident: an artisan attempting to duplicate an existing
machine might inadvertently improve upon it, for example (Elster 1985).
The vast bulk of technical advances, though, occur by design rather than
accident. Genes adapt to nature; we manipulate it. One can thus think of
the process of scientific or technological advance as a decision tree. After
any development, there will be decisions to be made about what further
lines of inquiry to pursue. Different individuals or organizations may
choose differently. If a certain line of inquiry proves disappointing, it may
be dropped in favor of an alternative. Both technical and societal factors
can influence evaluation of which is the best path to pursue. Note that
success along a particular trajectory will encourage further research along
the same lines; we may thus never know the potential of other lines of
inquiry.

STAGES OF INNOVATION

Since scientific/technological mutations must be created, we can identify a
handful of stages of innovation. Since innovation is a creative act, these
stages naturally bear a close resemblance to those in other creative processes (I→C2). First, at least one individual must come to see a particular

line of inquiry as worth pursuing (even the rare cases of accidental discovery must involve some recognition of their utility). Second, research is undertaken that draws together relevant pieces of existing information. Generally, more than one individual is involved. Trial and error experimentation is ubiquitous at this stage (and thus some scholars think it may yield new information, beyond just new combinations). Once the right package of previous information and/or experimental information has been put together—we will only know after the fact what this package comprises—we move directly to the act of insight. This is the stage that often gets the most attention, thus leading to the mistaken impression that both technology and science advance through isolated acts of inspiration. While it is true that inspiration often occurs when one has left one's desk or laboratory and is in the bath or sailboat, it is equally true that inspiration usually only follows lengthy periods of inquiry. Nor does the process end with the act of insight; minor refinements are almost always necessary to make a new technique useful or a new theory persuasive. This stage is called critical revision. Finally, the idea must be communicated to others, and these convinced that it is indeed an advance. This diffusion stage generally involves years if not decades (this typology of stages was first developed by Abbot Payson Usher, and is discussed in greater depth in Szostak 1991). Note that in the case of technology the critical revision and diffusion stages will be oriented toward the commercial (not just technical) feasibility of an innovation.

SIMULTANEOUS DISCOVERY

We suspect that advantageous biological mutations happen once and spread gradually through the population. The history of science and technology bears witness to many simultaneous discoveries: calculus by Newton and Liebnitz in 1671, oxygen by Priestley and Scheele in 1774, the telephone by Bell and Gray in 1876 (Lenski, Lenski, and Nolan 1991). If we rule out incredible coincidence, we are forced to recognize that often the time is right for a particular development, and thus many people will be involved in pursuing a particular line of inquiry. Previous scientific or technological advances may have set the stage for a new combination (in which case science and technology are seen to have a certain internal momentum), or social/cultural/political developments may have opened up previously closed lines of inquiry.

CROSS-FERTILIZATION

Within biology, the evolution of one species affects the selection environment for others. Think of giraffes and tall leafy trees, or the speed of predators and prey. The same happens in technology. More and faster cars induce more and safer roads, not to mention advances in roadmaking, petroleum refining, and tire manufacture (Cross and Szostak 1995). Historians have long suspected that advances in spinning technology during the Industrial Revolution induced greater efforts to mechanize weaving (the argument is often overdrawn; see Szostak 1991). In science, too, advances in atomic theory encouraged developments in chemistry and biology.

While it is exceedingly rare for species to crossbreed, in both science and technology it is all too common for the most diverse elements to be combined.[4] The modern airplane depends on engine design, material advances, superior fuels, advances in aerodynamic theory, computers, radio, and a host of other elements, most of which were not developed in their early stages with the airplane in mind. It is as if nature had somehow merged the elephant, cheetah, and eagle. Gilfillan in 1935 argued that all new technology was simply a novel combination of prior ideas. Even if this is not strictly true, the importance of combinations in technological advance bodes well for the future rate of innovation: as we develop more and more new techniques we increase (geometrically) the number of possible combinations.

SELECTION CRITERIA

One can readily characterize the major approaches to philosophy of science in this century as differing in terms of selection criteria. The positivism of Karl Popper argued for selection in terms of rigorous tests and falsification: scientists were able to test their theories against reality in such a way that the misguided theory could be disposed of. In this ideal state, the selection criteria was really how close a theory approximated to reality. With the passing of positivism, various alternatives have arisen. Sociology of knowledge, at least in its most extreme version, would argue that selection is solely in terms of the opinions of scientists, each of whom advocate their own pet theory. Most scholars would argue for some middle ground, with neither external reality nor scientific whim being the entire source of selection. For Thomas Kuhn, scientific inquiry could proceed for some time within a particular paradigm in which the basic precepts were unquestioned, but if enough evidence was compiled that contradicted these basic precepts, a scientific revolution would replace them (in evolutionary terminology we would speak of a punctuated equilibria, or sudden large mutation). In other words, scholarly preferences govern until reality checks overwhelm them and push inquiry in other directions. Imre Lakatos added a further wrinkle: scientists need research ideas. Thus theories that suggest lots of research avenues will be accepted. Again, though, external reality will intrude if research throws up too many objections to basic theory.

The fact that science gives us an increased ability to manipulate both nature and human endeavor provides the best evidence that external reality is part of the selection environment. In the case of technology, we could expect an even stronger role for nature. People, after all, should only adopt technologies that bring them better results.[5] Only mousetraps that actually do a good job of catching mice will be used and remembered. Still, while inventors can never ignore the market for their product [E→T], they can be influenced by many other forces: a desire to impress other researchers (elegance may then win out over efficacy), the institutional environment in which they work, or cultural taboos against certain avenues of exploration [C→T].

Technology, like science, evolves through a process of steady research along particular lines, punctuated by occasional introductions of whole new research trajectories. The first few decades of airplane development focused on propeller-driven flight. In the 1940s, some researchers started to work on the jet; they recognized that while the propeller would be much improved there were limits to how fast a propeller-driven craft could fly. Genetic mutation of the piston-to-jet magnitude must be exceedingly rare (chapter 4), but such changes are very common in science and technology where human agency guides research.

Rosenberg (1994) defines major innovations—in both science and technology—as those from which a series of minor innovations flow. Once the jet engine became a reality, many naturally set to work on improving it. The jet thus opened up a new set of choices for researchers to make. We should be open to the possibility that the relative importance of societal and technical considerations as selection criteria may be different for major and minor innovations. In the case of the latter, external reality may be the greater influence: a development either makes jets work better or it doesn't. In considering a major innovation, though, which by its nature will emerge in highly imperfect form (despite critical revision), societal influence may dominate (C→T).

C→T: Culture → Technology and Science

Despite their holistic approach, ethnographers have spent very little effort examining the technology or science of the groups they study. Tools and pots are examined for their aesthetic rather than practical value. Theories concerning the world around them are treated as mysticism rather than science.[6] Even economic anthropologists have tended to ignore technical details in favor of squeezing traditional societies into simple economic categories. We thus have only barely begun to explore most aspects of this causal link.

Lemonnier (1992) notes, though, that scientific/technological schemas are necessarily nested within the larger body of schemas that govern societal behavior. Ideas about how best to build a house must fit the community's view of what a house means. A complete understanding of any house or tool must incorporate technical, cultural, and artistic elements. Lemonnier points to a few particular ways in which culture can affect technique. Men in some societies are observed to shun the use of materials associated with women. Some groups avoid advantageous techniques that are associated with other groups. Often, though, he can only point to evidence that culture is at work, without being able to pin down a precise causal mechanism. Both arrow and house design show regional variation among Highland New Guinea tribes that cannot be explained in terms of environment. Moreover, those groups that choose a certain type of arrow also choose a certain type of house, even though there is no functional relationship between these technical domains. Lemonnier, recognizing that technology evolves over time, suggests that the cultural causes of such technical choices may be lost in the mists of time. Groups long ago chose certain technical paths for long-forgotten reasons, but having mastered certain ways of doing things are loathe to adopt the techniques of others (especially if the advantages of doing so are not obvious).

The study of modern Western technology can add to the limited insights to be gleaned from the ethnographic record. Lemonnier himself discusses how some modern airplane technologies (e.g., flying wings) have faced intense resistance from pilots because they do not look like a plane: this illustrates both how culture still affects technology, and how earlier technical developments constrain the later path of change. Thomas Hughes, one of the leading figures in the history of technology, has argued at length that it is in the earliest stages of a new technical system that cultural forces are most important. Once a certain technique has become dominant, the skills and tools and institutions associated with it will constrain further innovation (in Smith 1994).

The idea that some groups are unwilling to borrow from others gains much support in the historical literature. Europeans appear to have been more willing to borrow ideas from Asia than the reverse for much of the last couple of millennia. Wind and water mills, stirrups, and gunpowder were among the key innovations borrowed by Europe (note, though, that Europe was technically backward in most spheres until a few centuries ago). When Europeans took the technical lead in recent centuries, Asian civilizations—or at least their governments [P→T]—disdained Western technology (Mokyr 1991).

I. DIRECTION AND SPEED OF CHANGE

Most obviously, perhaps, culture influences what each of us wants, and therefore the avenues innovators decide to pursue. "We cultivate technology to meet our perceived needs, not a set of universal ones legislated by nature" (Basalla 1988, 14). Vegetarians are unlikely to develop meatpacking technology. Those who think television the tool of the devil will hardly work to improve reception. Technology, despite the adage, is rarely the child of necessity, but serves rather to allow humans to live well above subsistence.

Culture influences not just the direction of technical advance but its speed. Groups differ in whether they equate change with progress or destruction. Western societies have long been distinguished by a tendency to fantasize about a bright technological future (from Da Vinci's musings to modern science fiction). This, Basalla suggests, encouraged Westerners to innovate. Etzioni (1988) concurs that societies that rate economic goals like efficiency and growth higher than social cohesion, stability, and religious orthodoxy will be more conducive to technical change. Even in the West, however, there has, at least since the Industrial Revolution, been a sizeable and often vocal minority who have spoken out about the negative effect of technological innovation on jobs, the family, privacy, the environment, and a host of other variables.

Innovation depends on one or more people being willing to expend scarce time, energy, and resources in pursuit of technical improvement. Their willingness to do so will depend on how well rewarded they would be for successful innovation. In societies in which military prowess or poetry or mastery of the scriptures are most highly esteemed, we might expect the most talented individuals to perceive better avenues to wealth and prestige than innovation. Societies that value tradition highly may provide a serious disincentive to the prospective innovator (Mokyr 1991).

2. CULTURE AND SCIENCE

Once we accept that science evolves not through conclusive tests of theories, but through argumentation and compilation of diverse evidence by a scholarly community, then culture inevitably comes to play a role. (Scientists tend to believe that their own theories are empirically verified truth, while competing theories reflect sociocultural influences.) What sorts of argument and evidence are most appreciated? McCloskey (1987) and others have recently noted that modern scientists use similar rhetorical tools to those employed by Greek philosophers. This may be evidence of a genetic propensity toward certain types of argument [G→T], but at worst leaves room for subtle cultural distinctions (e.g., some cultures may respond favorably to arrogance, and others with hostility).

As with technology, culture will also influence the goals that scientists deem most worthy. In some cases, culture may dictate that certain questions be ignored.[7] And culture has a huge impact on the institutional structure in which science operates. We take for granted in the late twentieth century that governments are the primary sponsors of scientific research. It was not always so: medieval alchemists were for the most part privately financed, and much Renaissance science was sponsored by aristocrats. If citizens in Western countries did not have a strong cultural appreciation of science, much less research would be funded.

3. RELIGION

Throughout most of human history, individuals have faced enormous pressure to conform to the religious beliefs and practices of their group. These beliefs and practices, we have seen, were themselves responsive to environmental changes. Yet at any point in time they could severely limit the range of acceptable behavior.

Most innovations involve some alteration of nature. A society whose religion opposed mastering nature, then, should see very little innovation. Some religions hold that humanity should live in harmony with nature, while others proclaim that humanity was placed here to master nature. Note, though, that all human societies manipulate nature to some extent. Consider the Amish, who shun the automobile and television; they have turned brush into farmland and embrace most pre-eighteenth century technology. The Amish may still innovate but are much less likely to do so than the average American. Religions may thus not eliminate all innovative behavior, but arguably can influence the rate of innovation. Indeed, many scholars have suggested that Christian dogma was a key reason for Europe's technological advance over the past millennia (though some branches of Christian thought were inimical to change, and important innovations occurred within all major world religions). Perhaps mainstream Christianity stressed mastery of nature more than other faiths. Or perhaps the Western belief in a benevolent god stimulated the pursuit of the natural laws such a god would create. We must, though, be wary of the possibility of reverse causation: if for some other reason Europe became more innovative, and people were impressed by the gains that technology could bring, we might expect religious beliefs to move toward favoring change (Mokyr 1991).

Religions also differ markedly in the degree to which they stress rewards in this life versus the next. Within strict Hinduism, nobody could rise above the caste they inherited. However, a life of noble deeds and thoughts could yield a better status when reincarnated. Calvinism, alternatively, has been hailed by Max Weber and other scholars for its claim that God would reward the chosen in this life. Again, I must stress that differences are likely of degree rather than absolute. Yet the poor innovative record of India, which rarely figures in chronicles of technical advance despite obvious skills in metallurgy and textiles and irrigation, suggests that it may be an important difference of degree (Mokyr 1991).

Religion also influences the evolution of science.[8] Some religions claim that all that we need to know about nature is to be found in holy texts, whose words are not to be doubted. Indeed, some element of this attitude can be found in all major religions at some time. Many have claimed that Protestantism was very conducive to the rise of science in Europe. Yet Protestants often preferred a more literal reading of the Bible than Catholics, and some of the leading early "scientists" were Catholic. It could well be that once the Catholic church reacted with hostility to, for example, claims that the earth revolved around the sun, it was advantageous for the future advance of European science that no one religious authority dominated Europe. Even granting this, we must note that both Protestant and Catholic authorities have remained hostile to scientific theories that are inconsistent with a strict reading of the Bible (e.g., evolution). By its nature, any religion that holds a set of beliefs as unquestionable must from time to time find itself at odds with a scientific approach that is willing to ask any questions and be guided by experiment rather than scripture. Arguably, though, (some branches of) Christianity has been more open to the scientific exploration of nature (as with the technological mastery of nature) than other religions. Again, we must be concerned with reverse causation: as science has gained increased status over the last centuries in the West, religious opposition has diminished (see Restivo 1995). (T→C)

T→C: TECHNOLOGY AND SCIENCE → CULTURE

While much ink has been spilled on the place of science in modern culture, there has been little general discussion of the effects of technology on culture. Rather, historians of technology have explored the effects that particular innovations have had: the railroad brought a national cultural identity, the automobile a sense of freedom, household appliances a changed view of the role of women, and the birth control pill a radical change in attitudes toward sex (see Cross and Szostak 1995). There can be little doubt that a variety of such innovations have had a huge impact on the way we live and thus see our lives.

I. THIRD WORLD DEVELOPMENT

If technology does indeed have far-reaching effects on culture, then it might be conjectured that the adoption of "Western" technology would lead to cultural convergence. Nor is this merely a scientific conjecture, but has been the subject of debate in many countries. The experience of Japan, which has a similar technology but a quite different culture from Western nations, suggests that wholesale cultural convergence is not a danger. Of course, it is likely that technology has a greater impact on some aspects of culture than others. We can well imagine, for example, that the adoption of modern factory technology encourages a respect for punctuality. And it appears that the economic growth that innovation brings is conducive to a desire for political freedom [E→P]; many scholars would argue that as innovation frees people from starvation and backbreaking physical labor, it supports an increased respect for the individual and for self-actualization (see also E→C).

2. THE IDEA OF PROGRESS

Intellectuals in nineteenth-century Europe commonly embraced the idea of progress: they felt that human societies were evolving toward a better state. It is not a coincidence that this belief in progress became so popular at the same time that technological innovation was producing unprecedented rates of economic growth. In North America, Egnal (1995) has found that the idea of progress was much more common in the rapidly industrializing northern states than in either the south or French Canada. And Nye (1994) has shown how particular technological marvels such as the railroad, suspension bridges, electricity, or skyscrapers induced a sense of awe previously reserved for nature.

This belief in progress has been battered by two world wars, the Depression, and a growing concern with environmental degradation. Technology must share the blame for each of these negative developments. It should be clear, then, that technological innovation can have both good and bad effects. This leaves room for argument about whether the net effect of technological innovation is positive, which is closely tied to a debate about whether it makes sense to speak of progress at all.[9] I personally would not trade life in the twenty-first century for life in previous centuries when extensive physical labor and poverty were the lot of the vast bulk of humanity. But I can also appreciate work that details the negative impact of technology (e.g., Segal 1994).

3. MASS PRODUCTION

Technology has enabled us to dramatically increase our productivity [T→E], which in turn allows modern people to have both more stuff and more leisure than their ancestors. One drawback is that many modern workers have been required to perform monotonous tasks [E→I]. Henry Ford, when he introduced the assembly line to the auto industry, actively appealed to an emerging cultural belief that males should be breadwinners for their families, in order to urge men to take well-paid but unsatisfying employment. He even refused to hire women, even for sewing jobs, in deference to this cultural belief on which he depended [C,T→S].

4. SCIENCE AND RELIGION

Science and religion were once closely associated. Astronomers detailing the orderly movement of heavenly bodies were viewed as elucidating the god-given order of the universe. Even after discoveries of a non-orderly non-Earth-centered universe, many scientists, including Newton, felt themselves to be illuminating god's divine plan. On the whole, however, religion and science have operated as separate and often hostile enterprises over the last centuries. In Christian Europe, scientific theories that posited that the Earth was not the center of the universe or that humanity was descended from apes were attacked by church leaders. In turn, disciplinary fragmentation reflected the scientific community's recognition that they were not uncovering god's unified plan (Toulmin 1982).

While some theologians remain harsh critics of the evolution of species, in general Christian churches have become less hostile to science. This might change if, say, cognitive psychologists were able to explain brain functioning so completely as to render the concept of a soul highly questionable at best (but see Chalmers 1996, and note that recent developments in particle physics suggest that the world is not really made of solid matter at all). And not all world religions have reached a solid truce with the scientific community. Still it must be said that science and religion cohabit more easily today than a century ago.[10]

That result would come as a surprise to many early scientists. They felt that the scientific emphasis on rational and open-minded analysis of various data sources was the only way to approach any question. As scientific exploration steadily expanded our understanding of how the world works, they were confident that more and more people would recognize the superiority of this type of inquiry. People would thus turn away from the reliance on tradition, faith, intuition, and emotion, on which religious belief is based. Science, though, has provided no compelling answers to such questions as the existence of god,[11] the meaning of life, or the possibility of an afterlife. Even in terms of how humans should live with nature, science alone cannot tell us what to do, though it can elucidate some effects of our actions. Most people, then, have—explicitly or implicitly—decided that there are some questions best left to science and others where they must be guided by their hearts. We do not, after all, choose our spouses on the basis of cold rational calculation. If science has no place for intuition and emotive experience, then a world devoted to science alone would lack meaning (Adams 1993; Melzer, Wenberger, and Zinman 1993).

Some writers suggest that recent developments in the philosophy of science lend further support to the idea that there is still a place for religion. While positivist philosophers disdained religious beliefs for their lack of falsifiability, it is now recognized that even scientific theories can not be falsified. Trigg (1985) concludes that we cannot call religion irrational in a post-positivist world. Adams (1993) suggests that religious beliefs are tested in two ways: their consistency with scientific understanding of the world, and an internal personal test of whether they give meaning to one's life. While he feels that this makes them as legitimate as scientific beliefs, others would worry that a test as to whether a certain belief makes one feel good is too biased to be considered a real test. Ironically, post-positivism may serve to introduce a greater flexibility into major world religions: rather than taking every sentence of holy texts as incontrovertible truth, nonpositivist theologians may be willing to examine whether certain rules are reasonable or desirable in a modern context.

5. ETHICAL DILEMMAS

New technology often poses ethical dilemmas for business and government alike. Where is the best tradeoff between freedom to drive and public safety? How careful should we be with chemical and nuclear waste? (How much should we tell local people?) Mitchell (1994) worries about digital photographic technology, which makes it all too easy to manipulate content, and studies attempts to develop new ethical standards.

10

Health and Population

As IN CHAPTER 9 I DEAL HERE WITH TWO CLOSELY RELATED PHENOMENA: health and population (see also Szostak 2000b). One of these, population, is completely determined by the experience over time of three constituent phenomena: mortality, fertility, and migration. These in turn determine not just the size of a group's population but a fourth phenomenon worthy of our consideration: the age distribution of a population.

The health of a population has a predominant impact on mortality, a significant impact on fertility, and a lesser role in encouraging migration. It also has strong causal links with various other phenomena. Nevertheless, while the study of population has long been a staple of sociology, economics, and geography departments, health receives much less attention. Students of population at times worry about the causes of disease or famine, and health economists worry about the institutional structure for health service delivery. But for the most part health is left to those in medical schools (and nursing, pharmacy and so on). Medical students are rarely required to gain much familiarity with human science, even though most practitioners spend much of their time dealing with social and psychological problems.[1] Medical research is rarely grounded in human science theory; this in turn deters human scientists from engaging in health research. Inevitably, then, these causal links receive less attention than they deserve.

All of our phenomena—except age distribution—can be unpacked. Mortality can be divided between death by injury and death by disease. For fertility we can distinguish between fecundity—the biological capability of a population to reproduce—and the degree to which this biological maximum is approached. Hornsby and Jones (1993) review the many attempts to establish a typology of migration: migration experiences can be distinguished in terms of international versus internal, temporary versus permanent, and by distance traveled. (They also attempt to distinguish migration experiences by cause.)

281

Health lends itself to an even greater degree of unpacking, for we can identify thousands of diseases or illnesses.[2] Note, though, that those maladies, including mental disorders, which have their roots in genetics, have already been treated under individual differences. That leaves us here to worry about diseases of viral or bacterial origin, as well as any maladies caused by environmental pollution (including cigarette smoke). Disease is not the only component of health; we must also worry about nutrition. Nutrition can be unpacked in terms of the diverse nutritional requirements of our bodies.

Measuring Phenomena

For the most part, the phenomena unpacked in this chapter are among the most readily measured in human science. For population itself, one needs only a census. While these are still dodgy affairs in some of the world's poorest countries, we have accurate measures of population for most countries. Likewise, most countries keep fairly accurate records of births and deaths. Dividing these by population gives us crude birth and death rates (usually reported as annual births or deaths per thousand people). Age distribution requires somewhat more meticulous record keeping. Nevertheless for most countries we can report the number of people falling into particular age categories (usually in five or ten year intervals, and represented graphically in age "pyramids"). When age-specific data is available, demographers prefer to calculate age-specific death and birth rates. These provide much better predictors of future population behavior than crude birth and death rates. For example, a society with a disproportionately large number of people in their 20s and 30s (as North America in the 1970s and 1980s) would be expected to have lower death rates and higher birth rates than a society with a majority of people in their 50s or 60s.

Migration presents greater problems. Censuses that record place of birth give us only a limited grasp of migration. Temporary and permanent migrants will be confused. Those who moved from place A to B to C will be mistakenly recorded as moving from A directly to C. Those who move from A to B and back again will likely be recorded as not migrating at all. Students of migration thus prefer more detailed examination of particular populations.

With respect to health, modern medical technology allows a fairly precise diagnosis of the cause of the vast majority of deaths and the bulk of serious illnesses. In developed countries, at least, then, we have fairly good estimates of the prevalence of major diseases. Diseases with less recognizable symptoms, or which modern medicine has no or very limited understanding of, will be poorly measured in all societies. At the aggregate level, there is a tendency to use life expectancy as a proxy for the health of a given population. While increased life expectancy does generally signal an improvement in health, there are a couple of problems. First, there are important causes of mortality, such as murder and car accidents, that have little to do with health. Second, health involves more than just staying alive: some would in particular question the degree to which an ability to keep the elderly alive in a semivegetative state for decades should be viewed as rendering society healthier.

Before leaving this section, I should note that one can observe positive trends in most indicators. Life expectancy is increasing in most but not all countries (the former Soviet Union providing a regrettable case of decline). Many diseases, notably smallpox, have been eradicated or are on the verge of being so. Unfortunately, others, such as AIDS, have emerged in their place. Birth rates have fallen in almost all countries (except Africa), and thus worldwide population growth fell from a peak of 2% per year in the 1960s to 1.6% in the 1990s. While the youthful age distribution of many developing country populations guarantees that crude birth rates will remain high for some time, most demographers predict that the world will achieve zero population growth sometime in this century.[3]

C → H: Culture → Health and Population

1. REPRODUCTION

In most human societies, childbearing is casually assumed to be such a normal part of life that most couples will have at least one or two children without much conscious decision making (Daugherty and Kammeyer 1995). Indeed, while European societies have long accepted that a significant percentage of the population would remain childless—priests, nuns, spinsters—most historical societies have exhibited suspicion of any childless adult. And even in the modern West, childless couples still face subtle pressures to reproduce.

How many children should parents have? Here too culture influences decisions. Whereas a century ago families with several children were common in most developed countries, the common social expectation today is that families will have two or three children. Those who have seven or eight will be viewed with amazement, and perhaps disdain, especially if they are poor or members of religious or ethnic minorities. This sea change in cultural attitudes in turn reflects the economic, social, and technological factors which have encouraged a decrease in family size [E, S, T → C; see below], though note that this does not mean that the causal role of culture can be ignored.

I have stressed before (C→C) that any society will strive for consistency among cultural norms. A society that encourages small families could not simultaneously embrace early marriage, frequent sexual intercourse, and no birth control. It is thus likely no coincidence that Victorian prudery about sexual matters replaced a long-standing cultural belief that sex, at least within marriage, is healthy and good, at the same time as English society became worried about population growth. As for birth control, while the rhythm method, coitus interruptus, and even sheepskin condoms had been employed for centuries, legalization of mass-produced birth control devices or abortion did not occur until well into the twentieth century, as cultural objections to such practices ebbed. As birth control became increasingly accepted, it was possible for societies to embrace both small families and the idea of sex for enjoyment.

2. RELIGION AND REPRODUCTION

In many Western countries, Catholics have long been observed to have higher birth rates than Protestants, though at least in North America this difference is disappearing. Worldwide, most of the countries with the highest birth rates are Islamic. While a strong correlation between religion and reproduction is thus clear, one must be careful in suggesting causal links. Scriptures are generally ambiguous on the question of ideal family size, with both children and the well-being of parents being valued. This gives both religious and secular leaders scope for interpretation. French Canadian Catholics moved from having one of the highest birth rates in the Western world to one of the lowest in just a generation, a generation that witnessed a dramatic decline in the role of the church in everyday life and also a changing political leadership which suggested non-demographic means for French Canadian cultural survival. In the United States, Catholic attitudes toward birth control are now no different on average than mainstream Protestants (though the most fervent Catholics still display less acceptance); it is now fundamentalist Protestants and Mormons who are observed both to be suspicious of birth control and to have larger families. On the other hand Jews are observed to have below-average birth rates; this may simply reflect their above-average educational attainment. The high birth rates observed in Muslim countries are widely attributed to the relative powerlessness of women [S→H], aided by relatively anemic efforts at birth control by governments [P→H].

3. PERCEPTIONS OF HEALTH

Societies differ in how seriously they view particular illnesses (based largely on the incidence of such illnesses), whether they view illness as a problem to be borne stoically by the individual or a cause for collective support, whether they stress cures or the alleviation of symptoms, and the degree to which they rely on traditional versus modern medicines. Health professionals crossing cultural boundaries need to keep such differences in mind. So must any who look at statistics on disease across societies.

Rothman, Marcus, and Kiceluk (1995) examine how culture has influenced the practice of medicine through the ages. Drawing on brief excerpts from countless authors, they look at attitudes toward the body, the relationship between mind and body, disease and purity (e.g., treatment of lepers), the healer, medical experimentation, hospitals, pain, suffering, and death. Unfortunately, they neither define nor disaggregate either culture or medicine.

4. ATTITUDES TOWARD DEATH

Ironically, cultural attitudes toward death may have an increasing impact on mortality as medical technology extends our life spans. Indeed, the grave disagreements within all societies about such issues as doctor-assisted suicide and requests for nonresuscitation reflect the novelty of the situation whereby those who have limited consciousness and/or are in great pain can be kept alive for many years. Various values are in conflict: we value both life itself and the ideal of personal choice, we believe in human dignity but worry that impatient family members will hasten death.

5. CULTURAL IDENTITY AND MIGRATION

Needless to say, members of close-knit communities are less likely to move away (excepting those who find the very closeness suffocating). Thus, when Western Canada opened for settlement, French Canadians proved much less willing to move west than English Canadians (French Canadian church leaders were generally hostile to long-distance migration). Instead, French Canadians were much more likely to move just across the border into the United States (where most families nevertheless became English speaking over time). The low population of New France at the time of Conquest was also in large part due to the hesitance of community-minded French to leave France (Egnal 1996). If circumstances nevertheless cause some members of close-knit communities to depart, early migrants will act as a magnet for later migrants. Thus European migration to North America resulted in a pattern of pockets of ethnic groups.

6. VALUES AND HEALTH

We are far from having a complete inventory of the effects of values on health. It is likely that societies with a preference for overly large meals and/or the wrong foods will suffer in health terms. Proxemics may affect the rate of disease transmission. In other cases we are much less sure. Do individualistic societies cause enough self-examination to compensate for the decrease in helpful advice from concerned friends? Studies have found that the very religious tend to be healthier (at least in North America); this may be due to the support people get within religious communities, the antipathy of these communities toward certain habits such as smoking and drinking, or the reduced stress associated with belief (note that the suicide rate is much lower among the very religious, as are rates of drug abuse).

H → C: Health and Population → Culture

There can be little doubt that the health of a population, as well as fertility and mortality, will influence societal attitudes toward disease, family, children, and death. For example, parents in environments in which half of children die before adulthood may well be more reserved in their parental affection than parents who can reasonably anticipate child survival. These links, not to mention possible links to other elements of culture, have received little attention.

Even the more obvious effects of migration on culture have received little scientific attention, at least relative to the attention public figures have devoted to the topic. In the United States, high levels of migration have variously been alleged to encourage individualism, conformity, tolerance, practicality, nationalism, and optimism, but there is little convincing evidence of any of these links (Daugherty and Kammeyer 1995).

As seen before (C→C), there is a natural process of cultural borrowing when groups come in contact. Migrants tend to borrow more than they give in this respect. Fellman, Getis, and Getis (1990) note that the first group(s) of settlers in an area tends to establish a culture to which later migrants adapt. But the size of migrant groups relative to residents, not to mention power relations, play a role as well; otherwise North America would have an Indian culture with European adaptations. The tendency of migrants to locate where others of similar background have located can lead to a diversity of cultural islands (as in the western United States—see Fellman, Getis, and Getis, 1990), though migration between diverse locales will work against this.

Culture also depends on age distribution. Many commentators spoke of a return to "family values" in North America in the 1990s. Few recognized that this in large part reflected the fact that the large baby boom generation was now married with children (Foot 1996).

11
Art

WHAT IS ART? PHILOSOPHERS HAVE AGONIZED OVER THIS QUESTION FOR millennia, with the perhaps inevitable result that there is no precise definition possible. As with various other terms encountered in this book, however, a "good enough" definition is not hard to find. In chapter 1, I suggested that works of art were those objects (including musical compositions) created for aesthetic purposes rather than for use.[1] I recognized at the time that many objects, such as decorative pottery, served both practical and aesthetic purposes. Such objects can only be fully appreciated if both their economic and artistic functions are recognized.

What is "aesthetic?" I will argue below both that we are genetically programmed to appreciate certain sights and sounds (other senses are involved; Herbert Reed claimed sculpture was an art of touch), and that individuals differ in which works of art they appreciate [G,I→A]. This latter fact opens the door for both popular and scholarly debates over whether certain works qualify as "art." Until such time (if ever) as our understanding of genetic drives places some limits on our understanding of art, we can only take a subjective view: that which any one person perceives to be art is therefore art. We have no scientific grounds for saying to anyone that they are mistaken and that the object before them cannot possibly have any impact upon them.[2]

It is thus quite possible that works created for solely economic reasons may nevertheless be hailed as art. The artisan focused consciously only on utility may somehow shape an object so that others acclaim its appearance. While I will in what follows emphasize objects intended by their creator to be (at least in part) art, I should recognize that our whole world has artistic potential.

There are some characteristics of art that receive frequent attention from art scholars. While there is much dispute as to whether these characteristics apply to all art, and could thus be included in its definition, their ubiquity is worthy of note. First, art is not a realistic portrayal of our world; rather the artist distorts reality in order to send a message (even photogra-

phers distort reality in their selection of subjects). Second, art, since it has
messages, does not provide just enjoyment but understanding as well.
Third, art can provide us with a glimpse of a better world than the one we
inhabit.

While I have taken a very broad definition of art here, this does not
necessarily preclude there being standards by which we can hope to judge
the relative quality of works of art. Nobody who has read several critical
analyses of particular works of art will imagine that these standards are
transparent or that we are anywhere near to consensus on what they should
be. Some scholars have therefore concluded that any attempt to define
certain works as masterpieces can only be entirely subjective, and therefore offensive because subject to class/race/gender bias. Others have argued that there is something more than a conspiracy of white males that
has caused Shakespeare, Michelangelo, and Beethoven to remain popular
for centuries, even if we cannot readily agree on what that something
might be. I tend to agree with Denby (1996): there are works that deserve
to be viewed as masterpieces, though we can as individuals reach different
conclusions about which works to include in this category. The fact that
white males dominate the Western canon should guide us to search for
works by women and non-whites that may have been underappreciated,
but should not encourage us to elevate these works to higher esteem than
they merit. Given the subservient role of women through most of history,
we should not be surprised if they produced less work of superior quality
(see also Gillowy 1993).[3]

If we accept that there are qualitative differences in art works, should we
try to unpack our art category in this way? Scholars often attempt to
distinguish between "real" art and popular art on the grounds that the
former responds to higher artistic motives. If we were to distinguish between these types of art, we might wish a more solid grounding for our
distinction. We could, for example, distinguish works of art in terms of
intended audience: an educated elite versus the masses. Or we could
distinguish art works in terms of the degree to which works served a
utilitarian as well as aesthetic purpose. I am skeptical, though, that either of
these distinctions would accurately reflect distinctions in aesthetic quality.
Happily, little of what I have to say in this chapter requires that I make any
such distinction. This is, I suspect, because all art provides some degree of
aesthetic satisfaction (though some art provides more or better satisfaction
than other art).

Art can be unpacked in terms of art forms: painting, sculpture, music,
dance, prose, poetry, theater, film, photography, and architecture are the
main divisions, with textiles, pottery, and performance art being examples
of the variety of art forms possible.[4] One key distinction is between non-
reproducible (one of a kind) art works, such as a sculpture, and reproduc-

ible art, such as a movie (though the border between these is often unclear; are plays reproducible or is each performance necessarily unique?).[5]

I will in this chapter focus for the most part on art as a category rather than particular types of art. That is, there is much less unpacking than in previous chapters. This likely reflects both the inherent unity of art and the fact that research on many of our links has not progressed to an extent that distinctions among types of art have been identified. Yet surely some distinctions exist. Students of music, especially, tend to emphasize its distinctiveness. It is noteworthy that in the seventeenth and eighteenth centuries, music was viewed as the least valuable of the arts due to its inability to represent external objects, while in the nineteenth century it was hailed as the purest of the arts for the same reason. In the twentieth century scholars have debated the degree to which music does refer to external objects.

EVOLUTION OF ART

Like many branches of history, art history began by describing how successive generations of artists borrowed from their predecessors and their own ingenuity to create new art. This "internalist" history, with its emphasis on both personality and the relationships between works of art, has increasingly given way to an interdisciplinary focus on the societal influences on the evolution of art. Nevertheless, Zolberg (1990) argues that those trained in the humanities are still most likely to focus internally on technique, artist personality, and aesthetic influences of one work on another, while those with a social science background are most likely to look at links between art and social phenomena. While Zolberg bemoans the limited contact between humanist and social science scholars, we can at least take solace in the fact that between them they cover most of the relevant causal links.[6]

How does art evolve? The internalist/humanist tradition makes an important point. All artists wish to create something new and different, but they naturally begin by looking at previous art works. One reason for this is that their audience will be more readily able to appreciate art that bears some resemblance to that which has gone before. As well, the artists themselves will find it easier to build upon past works than to start from scratch. This yields us an evolutionary process where mutation is endemic but generally limited in degree.

When discussing technological evolution (chapter 9), I noted that new ideas were often a combination of old ideas. The same is true of art. Gauguin, for example, combined elements of European and non-European art. Note here that artists can borrow across art forms, with sculptors learning from painters or architects, and poets from musicians. One difference between art and technology is that "old" art forms are not superceded to the extent that old technologies are (Sporre 1992). Da Vinci's technical drawings are a historical curiosity, his paintings a continuing source of inspiration.

Artists do not just learn from the past, but also must take note of what contemporaries are doing. While each artist in isolation might mutate in a unique direction, in any society some mutations will achieve greater acclaim, and thus other artists will be encouraged to mimic the successful (due in part to our predisposition toward fads; G→C10). In other words, while mutation is endemic, the societal reward structure ensures that only a small subset of mutations are accepted at any point in time. A diversity of political, social, economic, and other phenomena serve as the selection environment. This conformist mechanism is strong enough that art historians are able to describe a dominant style for virtually every time and place in history.[7]

Kuchler and Melion (1991) describe this process in terms of schema formation [G→A]. Both artists and their audience must learn to appreciate a new style. An artist makes a creative breakthrough, others strive to appreciate it, and eventually the social memory of a society incorporates this new style.

In the last century or two, this tendency for one style to dominate has given way to the acceptance of diverse styles. Zolberg (1990) attributes this development to the expanded market for art as incomes rise, and the associated fact that no narrow elite group in any society can any longer dictate what is considered good art [E, S→A]. In such a world, art dealers and critics have striven to carve out niches in particular styles. Moreover, since new art styles tend to be combinations, the very proliferation of styles has a dynamic effect of its own, favoring the proliferation of yet more styles.

C→A: CULTURE → ART

In distinguishing art from culture in the first chapter, I defined art as that which appealed to universal tastes. We have seen throughout this book, however, that culture influences the behavior of all humans. Artists being no less human than the rest of us, any work of art will reflect both cultural and aesthetic influences. The artist may (or not) strive for universal appeal, but will inevitably speak a bit more clearly to their own society.

If I wanted to play semantic games, I could claim that culture does not influence art, but merely the expression of art. That is, if we think of art as only that which is universal, then by definition cultural elements that are not universal could not influence it. Even so, culture must at least influence the ability of any artist to express that which is universal. For example, culture might dictate the use of only certain colors or designs or religious motifs. More generally, we must recognize that art is a struggle, with the artist striving for inspiration but never being completely satisfied. Societies that encourage individual expression will be more likely to produce masterpieces.

Any work of art will combine the cultural and the aesthetic. We can think of a continuum of relative influence. At one end are works that seem at first glance to be entirely cultural, such as religious rituals, but even these will have aesthetic value (Gillowy 1993). At the other end, we could think of those modern artists who claim to be only interested in expressing their subconscious; even they cannot escape their culture. Most of the art in our museums lies toward the middle of our continuum: religious themes or expressions of harmony with nature or the glory (or horror) of war are combined with elements of universal appeal. No matter what time and place a work of art was created, we should look for both aesthetic universals and cultural expressions within it (Layton 1991).[8]

Cultural influences on works of art are so ubiquitous as to require little description (and their diversity renders enumeration impossible). The study of literature has long proceeded country by country, based on the assumption that there are important differences across countries. Nor can this practice be blamed entirely on linguistic barriers: English and English Canadian literature is distinguished from American (with many scholars feeling that both French and English Canadian literature is concerned with survival and/or American hegemony). Denby (1996) is struck by the violence, betrayal, and ethical conflict at the center of ancient Greek plays; he associates it with a community in touch with its subconscious. In music, too, scholars distinguish the Italian focus on stringed instruments and singing, the English concern with quality, and the French and German determination to maintain distinct national traits. Religious art tends to be sensuous within Eastern religions such as Buddhism which stress feelings, and austere within Western religions such as Christianity which stress belief. Changes occur over time as well: classical architecture emphasized firmness and utility, while appearance has become of increasing importance. In all art forms culture influences content, symbolism, and style.[9]

Early anthropologists tended to view artworks from the societies they studied as purely cultural. Given that their focus was on understanding the cultural peculiarities of varied societies, this emphasis is hardly surprising. However, as early modern European artists—particularly the cubists— came to admire the art of traditional societies and incorporate it into their own work, anthropologists naturally came to appreciate the aesthetic qualities of traditional art as well. While Coote and Shelton (1992) applaud this development, they recognize that it poses problems for the objective analysis of these societies. Just as a sort of "methodological atheism" is desirable for the study of traditional religion, anthropologists can not become so enamored of the aesthetic appeal of traditional art that they lose sight of its cultural elements.[10] Their task is rendered especially difficult by the lack of consensus on what exactly are the aesthetic universals in art.

I close by noting that art has come to play a quite different role in modern society than it had previously. Art has come to be applauded as a separate activity. But this very separation has meant that for many people artistic creation plays almost no role in their lives. In traditional societies, almost all members exercise their artistic impulses in craftwork. Art seems just a natural part of life to such people. In the modern world, it tends to be viewed either as the special focus for a talented few or as entirely superfluous. If art has an important role to play in our lives, we have lost something of value (see Szostak 2002).

A→C: ART → CULTURE

In common parlance, art is viewed as a subset of culture. I have distinguished these by defining art as that with universal appeal. To what extent, then, does the purely aesthetic affect the cultural? I have suggested above that all works of art will embody both cultural and artistic elements. If the artistic elements serve to grab the attention of the audience, they will enhance the effect of the cultural elements. Layton (1991) gives an interesting example of this: in many societies the more beautiful spirit masks are generally assumed to better attract the attention of the spirits. Likewise Picasso's antiwar message in the painting "Guernica" is felt more strongly because of the widely recognized aesthetic appeal of the work.

Philosophers of art have thus long agonized over the ethical role of art. They take as their starting point the belief that works of art can communicate ethical sentiments. Some, including Plato, various religious leaders, and communist functionaries, then argue that it is therefore incumbent upon artists to communicate only "good" values (e.g., love stories must celebrate monogamy and expose the dangers of adultery).[11] Others react with horror to what they see as incipient censorship, and argue that art is too important to society for us to curb artistic expression in any way (especially given our limited understanding of how art "works"). All might agree that since art often communicates its message subconsciously, it would serve society well to be aware of its ethical influence (Szostak 2002).

Art may be naturally biased toward doing good. One of the functions of art is to aid our understanding of the world we live in and help us imagine a better world. Literature, for example, puts the reader inside the lives of diverse people, and therefore helps readers to overcome prejudice. We thus appreciate our common humanity. By causing our imagination to soar, art may serve as an antidote to provincialism (but can also support a narrow sense of identity; see below). Aristotle and other philosophers have claimed for art a cathartic function: by expressing views not socially sanctioned or by allowing us to experience the urges and pain of others, it may make us less angry and competitive in our own lives. DiMaggio (1994) feels that art plays a special role in times of change. Theater, movies, and novels especially can then educate people to new ways of behaving. This education can involve diverse elements: social roles, personal and group identity, and strategies for success in a new environment.

Even art works recognized as masterpieces internationally, and which thus act to some extent as a signal of our common nature, may nevertheless be a source of ethnic pride. Wagner's operas are widely praised, but especially so in Germany, where they are thought to be evocative of German culture. Even where such cultural connections are weaker, people will still take pride that a widely acclaimed artist was "one of theirs." And privileged access to the literary heritage of one's group is one of the strongest arguments for maintaining the group's language, though languages inevitably evolve over time (C→C).

The twin facts that art can communicate values and provide a source of group identity has meant that religious authorities have always attempted to use art in support of belief. Indeed, throughout much of human history the world of art was so closely tied to the world of religion that the precise relationship between them is difficult to uncover. Batson, Schoenrade, and Ventes (1993) have investigated the stages by which a person converts to a new religion and the factors which facilitate this transition. Along with drugs and meditation, they suggests that two types of art are key facilitators. Religious imagery is important in three of their transition stages: encouraging the original crisis, guiding the eventual illumination of the new faith, and guiding life within the new faith. Music facilitates all of these as well as the self-surrender stage, due to its ability to elicit strong emotions: tension, letting go, elation, and joining with others.

12

Concluding Remarks

LESSONS LEARNED

THIS BOOK IS CLEARLY NOT THE SORT WHOSE ENTIRE CONTENTS CAN BE summarized in a few brief pages. Yet that in itself is a powerful insight, for the history of human science is littered with great books that have claimed to be able to explain everything within the compass of one narrow theory. If I have succeeded in highlighting the inherent complexity of human interaction in these pages, I will have achieved much.

I have striven for brevity throughout, but this idea of complexity warrants repetition. As humans, we all form schemas that guide our behavior. Scientists also try to bring order to their observations by developing theories. The all-too-obvious temptation for scientists no less than others is to oversimplify. They can recoil from the true complexity of our existence and seek consolation in a too simple world view. Let us broadly proclaim, then, that our understanding of human interaction will never be simple or tidy. "Those who fear complexity and uncertainty should avoid science" (Zuckerman 1991, 427).[1]

As chaos theorists have long recognized, a complex system of interaction is virtually impossible to predict. A small change along any one causal link can over time have effects throughout the system. As an economist, I have long bemoaned the damage that faulty prediction has done to the discipline's reputation. It is time for the human science community as a whole—and the public at large—to recognize the severe limits on our ability to see into the future. But do not despair: Our inability to predict does not mean that we do not understand. This book gives evidence of the great strides that we have already taken. Scholars who are cognizant of the variety of causal links at work can do a respectable (and ever-improving) job of explaining past transformations. In the same way, they can analyze the likely effects of any given public policy proposal. If we stop trying to build sandcastles in the sky, we can help to fashion a better life on earth.

Having embraced complexity, the next quality we should adopt is open-mindedness. No one person can master each of our causal links. To boldly state that a particular change in X *must* yield a particular change in Y is to

294

assert that one knows exactly what will transpire along each of the virtually infinite number of causal chains connecting X and Y. Since nobody should be proud of the sort of arrogance implicit in the latter statement, all of us should be open to arguments in opposition to our pet beliefs.

Openmindedness translates into schema flexibility. Given that people devise schemas in order to guide behavior, it is not easy to leave every schema open to adjustment in the face of new information. This is especially so given that one's self-definition and thus self-esteem are often tied to one's schemas. And humans seem programmed to respect assertiveness and disdain indecision.[2] Finally, some schemas may be subconscious; only through perhaps painful self-examination can these be uncovered. Yet one can only strive for openmindedness if one recognizes the barriers that stand in the way.

A liberal arts education should teach students how to rationally analyze complex questions. While it is inevitable that students will take much on authority—nobody has the time to analyze every question in human science—they should nevertheless be equipped with the skills to evaluate competing arguments on their own merits. They must also, I would suggest, be equipped with the zeal to question, to analyze, and to change. And they must, sadly, also be trained to recognize that not everyone they encounter will have succeeded in overcoming their baser motives in order to pursue honesty and openmindedness.

Once we have accepted complexity and openmindedness, we must also abandon the idea that any one theory can give us the answer to all of life's questions. Who can imagine that any "great" thinker could have encompassed each of our causal links within their gaze? We must recognize that by embracing some simplistic view of the world, we are giving in to our inherent desire to feel that we have schemas to cover every eventuality. It is noteworthy in this regard that ideologues of both "right" and "left" tend to be simple thinkers while those in the "middle" or more pragmatic tend to be complex thinkers (Simonton 1990).

Rather than completely jettisoning what are commonly termed ideologies, we should recognize that these are a mixture of values and beliefs. Our quarrel is with the second of these rather than the first. People must be free to choose guiding values, and are likely to differ in the relative importance they ascribe to personal responsibility versus social responsibility or collective rights versus personal rights (see Szostak 2002). These decisions are likely to influence their public policy preferences. The problem comes with the next step when one leaps to the conclusion that, for example, either markets or governments are the best way of dealing with any situation. One can develop theories which purport to provide such results, and expose these to various sorts of empirical tests, but should strive not to assume the result beforehand.[3]

I would not attempt here to decide a value-driven debate such as whether we should design our institutions with individuals or collectivities foremost in mind. I should note, though, that my analysis has shown that there is two-way causation between the individual and the wider society. This at least suggests that the ideal public policy should not be focused exclusively on one or the other. Individuals should neither be viewed as entirely the masters of their own fate nor as entirely victims of societal forces. Individuals in turn must avoid the temptation to define themselves only externally (by occupation, ethnicity, political affiliation, and marital status), while not losing sight of the fact that their lives are influenced by societal forces. Culture must be recognized as a glue that holds societies together, while every cultural element should be subjected to rational evaluation.

IMPLICATIONS FOR THE STUDY OF CULTURE

I have in this book surveyed analyses of diverse causal links to and from cultural phenomena by scholars across all human science disciplines. There are several lessons that can be drawn from this exercise (lessons that apply by extension to the study of other categories). These lessons may seem obvious (at least at this point), but they are nevertheless all too commonly ignored in research and teaching on culture. First, culture is best understood as, and can only be defined precisely as, an amalgam of (for the most part closely related) subsidiary phenomena. Analysis of influences on or effects of culture are *always* better performed in terms of one or more of these subsidiary phenomena than with reference to a vaguely defined cultural aggregate. That being said, I would emphasize that explanation is *not* always best pursued in terms of the lowest level of aggregation: this has not been a reductionist exercise, and indeed the analysis suggests that second-level phenomena have important effects on third- and fourth-level phenomena. I would also emphasize here that by disaggregating culture it becomes possible to ethically evaluate individual cultural elements while foreclosing the possibility of claiming that one culture is better than another culture (since there is no objective metric for weighting outcomes in terms of different phenomena).

Second, cultural phenomena influence and are influenced by hundreds of other phenomena (and exert diverse influences on each other as well). While some of these causal links are more powerful than others, a full understanding of the role of culture in human society, especially over the long term (when even small influences can have a huge cumulative effect) and across time and place (effects that are small in one place may loom large elsewhere) *must* encompass all of them. Grand theories necessarily touch on only a subset of these, and must *necessarily* be incomplete and thus misleading. This leads to a third crucial point: this book differs from the vast majority of books on culture in that there is no attempt to identify a key organizing theory or method. The schema alone serves to organize the material. And a casual perusal of these pages will show that a wide variety of theories (and less obviously scientific methods) have shed light on different causal links. At times, these were grand theories purporting to cover a large number of links, at times they were theories aimed at a handful of related links, and at times they were narrow theories focused on only one link. All have their place. It is sheer folly to imagine that any one theory or method can illuminate all or even most of the role of culture in human societies. Books or courses that attempt to do so may shed valuable light on some links, but do so at the tremendous cost of steering our attention away from (indeed often denying implicitly or explicitly the importance or even existence of) other important links. This book may seem a "messy" collage of link-based analyses. I would stress that it is better to be messy and accurate than to attempt the impossible task of fitting the study of culture into a tidy theoretical package. Note that advance in our understanding of culture will occur gradually link by link, not (primarily) through the development of exotic grand theories that purport to explain all.

I noted in the first chapter that some human scientists stress how individuals affect societal aggregates, and others stress the reverse lines of causation. We have seen in this book that individuals both affect and are in turn affected by culture. The same applies to the interaction of culture with other societal aggregates. A fourth lesson, then, is that it is a mistake to view cultural phenomena exclusively as cause or effect. Scholars will often wish to specialize with respect to one or the other relationship, but should not lose sight of the fact that causation runs in both directions. They should always be open to the possibility of feedback effects.

If we will embrace complexity rather than shrink from it, we will need some mechanism for organizing our thoughts. If we reject, as we should, the possibility of a theoretical or methodological organizing principle, then we can only hope for an organizing schema such as that utilized in this book. The fifth lesson, then, is that such a schema is essential to the task of coping with the complex interactions among cultural and other phenomena, without being seduced by the siren song of grand theory or method.

In the first chapter I reviewed Cornwell and Stoddard's (1998) critique of interdisciplinary cultural studies courses. Some courses fail to recognize that cultures evolve, and argue that we cannot evaluate individual cultural practices. Others act as if there is such a thing as a "normal" culture. Still others are unable to deal with subcultures. Cornwell and Stoddard advocate an interdisciplinary study of causal links, and a recognition that cultures evolve. Why is their prescription not more commonly fulfilled? I would argue for a sixth lesson of this book: an appreciation of the true complexity of culture is difficult or even impossible to convey or receive without an organizing schema. Instructors and students are too tempted to simplify and thus mislead in the absence of a schema (which also guides them to unpack culture into its constituent parts). Of course, the material presented in this book is daunting in its own way. The lack of a false theoretical or methodological unity forces instructors and students to master a number of distinct arguments. Better, though, a rocky road to understanding than a smooth ride to oversimplification. And it is unnecessary to master or teach every causal link in order to gain an appreciation for the complexity inherent in the study of culture. Indeed, students should be required to write papers or make presentations on causal links not covered in class. They can thus pursue their particular interests, without losing sight of the big picture.

IMPLICATIONS FOR PUBLIC POLICY

The most obvious implication here is that public policy analysis must strive to encompass a diverse body of causal links. It is all too common for policymakers to focus on the links that they (think they) understand best, and then be surprised when their policies have effects they had never imagined. One can understand their desire to simplify the tough decisions they have to make. But we can only conquer the complexity of the modern world by facing up to it.[4]

Often, when we cast our gaze widely, we can find that diverse causal links all point toward the same policy. If it is true, for example, that urban landscapes have an important effect on happiness, and also that unemployment has severe psychological effects, then hiring the unemployed to spruce up the city appears more advantageous. Some might argue that other causal links argue against such a policy (e.g., we would have to finance these programs somehow). I have avoided any attempt to develop a scoring system that could indicate which causal links are more important than others. It would have been possible to take a stab at such a system, since much of the scholarly literature is indeed concerned with how important various causal mechanisms are (though our understanding of some causal links is much greater than our understanding of others). But this would necessarily have detracted attention from the key point that all links are important to some degree. Further elucidation of relative importance will greatly aid policy formulation.

Although some scoring is certainly possible and desirable, we should not lose sight of the stochastic nature of most causal links. We can rarely say with certainty that X→Y, but rather that X increases the likelihood of Y. This may reflect either the inherently stochastic nature of human inter-action or merely our inability as scholars to precisely identify the conditions under which X will cause Y. Whatever the cause, the simple fact of stochasticity has several important implications. First, it is a yet further reason for recognizing that no one causal link will determine an outcome. Second, we must be open to the possibility that certain historical events had "unlikely" causes. Third, we must recognize that no one public policy can solve a problem. I discussed in Appendix 7-A the many factors that encourage criminal behavior. Any policy aimed at any one cause cannot have perfect success. It is too easy to attack such policies by pointing to these failures: "We've tried tougher penalties, or more counseling, or youth employment, and there's still crime." Of course. But the question that should be asked is whether a particular policy reduced the incidence of crime. If we insist on perfection, we will be unable to achieve improve-ment. Fourth, and as mentioned before, we will never be able to predict the future with deadly accuracy.

Despite my pleas for openmindedness and rational analysis of policy alternatives, I must recognize that our subconscious intuitive side can also provide useful input into policy decisions. A policy may look good on paper, but we may be wary of it either because it conflicts with values we are unaware of or because subconscious schemas suggest that the policy will have effects that we do not consciously recognize. Yet our sub-conscious cannot be depended on to give reliable advice; unresolved child-hood traumas cannot be allowed to determine our attitude toward adult decisions of any sort. The best compromise is not to ignore our feelings, but to attempt to find rational arguments which justify them (see Szostak 2001).[5]

CURRICULAR IMPLICATIONS

I have long embraced the combination of specialization and breadth re-quirements that make up the standard liberal arts degree. While this book has given an overview of the interrelationships that characterize human science, even the author does not pretend to be able to master every nuance of every area of exploration. Specialization is to some degree both inevi-table and desirable. Yet the danger of overspecialization is all too obvious: scholars and students alike can think their area of expertise the only one that matters.

While the dual goals of specialization and breadth are thus laudable, existing curricula do not achieve either goal as well as they might. In the absence of a schema such as that outlined in this book, students have great difficulty in integrating course material from different disciplines. The fact that each discipline has its own jargon, theory, and method only serves to exacerbate this problem. In terms of specialization, the problem is that disciplinary boundaries provide an arbitrary division of scholarly inquiry. A student interested in how ethnic subcultures affect inner city economic growth would struggle to piece together the bits of anthropology, economics, geography, and sociology involved. For some questions, existing disciplinary boundaries may not be much of a problem; for others they may present insurmountable barriers.

A superior curricular structure is possible.[6] A first-year course could provide students with an overview of the causal relationships that characterize human science. (If that course, like this book, emphasized links to and from culture, it would also serve many of the goals Cornwell and Stoddard speak of). Students could then choose which causal links they wished to specialize in for future studies. Instructors would in turn design courses focused on particular sets of causal relationships.

New technology will encourage and support this new curricular structure. CD-Roms and the Internet both excel in allowing students to explore links between diverse subjects. "The availability of interactive hypermedia and Internet access invites learners to cross disciplinary boundaries" (Farmer 1997; he notes that students need an overarching structure in order to avoid getting lost while following hypertext links). They thus become aware of how the subject matter they are most interested in spans disciplinary boundaries. This will likely lead to curricular change: "Knowledge will be restructured by application area to be usefully organized . . . To the extent that students' objectives come to drive the curriculum, traditional departments may well be replaced by new structures" (Farmer 1997).

New technology also facilitates the constant editing of both text and graphics. It thus replaces the ideal of the finished work (which has inspired Great Books programs) with a recognition that we are steadily but gradually adding to our body of understanding (Lanham 1993).[7] Guedon (1996) wonders if the near future will not see the eclipse of the present individualistic approach to research by linked global communities advancing cooperatively in their understanding of particular questions. A world that recognizes that knowledge is expanding gradually in all directions should appreciate a schema and curriculum that give students a framework for readily integrating new information.

Disciplinary divisions would not be necessary in such a model. In large universities, however, administrative convenience might require some subdivision. Moreover, we have learned above that traditions tend to evolve in a path dependent manner; it is thus likely that existing disciplines will display considerable staying power. These can be pushed, however, to divide up the body of causal links in a more coherent manner (with, one expects, a large number of cooperative agreements to jointly teach certain causal relationships). The present tendency of each discipline to favor a particular methodology would and should be severely diminished in such an environment. And of course scholars working cooperatively on particular links should also endeavor to attenuate the barrier to scholarly communication that is jargon.

We must be aware that the maintenance of departmental administrative structures will at least slow the process of curricular reform. Disciplines exert their present power through departments and professional associations, power structures which interdisciplinarians tend to lack (Davis 1995). "The triumph of the academic department as an autonomous unit capable of demanding greater loyalty than the institution to which it is a part is certainly the primary cause of the splintering of the liberal arts curriculum that we see all around us today" (Dean Chambers of Bucknell University, quoted in Lucas 1996).[8]

Some interdisciplinary programs have supplemented course grades with a mix of skills tests and multiyear portfolios. In this way, one can test whether students are integrating knowledge as desired. A curriculum focused on particular phenomena or causal links would be very amenable to comprehensive exams or capstone essay requirements (or, as at Portland State, capstone team community problem solving). Such a curriculum could also be modularized so that students were required to master certain information or skills before moving on (as advocated by Goodlad 1995).

I argued in chapter 1 that the schema would help students develop important skills such as critical thinking, coping with diversity, appreciation of diverse viewpoints, awareness of bias, and suspicion of authority. Klein (1996, 224) provides a list of desirable skills which interdisciplinary programs can and should impart: students should know how to structure a workable but flexible analytical framework, know how to recognize and overcome ignorance in an area, know how to analyze relationships and assess their importance, know how to balance depth and breadth of knowledge, know how to identify and integrate salient concepts, and know how to clarify and present material. I think it clear that the curriculum I have outlined would serve all of these goals.

This new curricular structure would serve not just to enhance education but research as well. At present, it is all too easy for disciplines to become ingrown, to waste their energy in pursuit of intellectual puzzles of limited practical import.[9] Research needs to be focused on questions rather than methods. A curriculum designed around explicating causal links rather than developing arcane theory and methods would make it much more difficult for scholars to ignore the areas in which our knowledge is fuzzy at best (and I have noted many times in this book causal links or parts thereof that have received scant attention). Moreover, the increased interaction of scholars trained in different disciplines can only serve as an antidote to misguided disciplinary values.[10] At present, many scholars—economic model-builders, literary theorists, geographers—rejoice in applying their pet methods to the subject matter of other disciplines. Yet these other disciplines often pay little attention. The future could so easily be brighter than the present.

Methodology would be treated quite differently within a new curricular structure. The same principles of breadth and specialization should operate. At present, we teach econ majors how to build and test mathematical models, English majors how to read texts, geography majors how to draw and interpret various sorts of maps, and political science majors how to do surveys. Many of these students are never exposed to even the basics of any other method. A better approach would be to provide first-year students with an overview of the dozen or so methods employed throughout human science (there are several texts which cover, albeit unevenly, the methods of the social sciences, but I am unaware of any similar treatment of the humanities). Note that the methods employed by natural scientists are a subset of those employed by human scientists. Note also that citizens are regularly confronted in their lives with evidence resulting from the application of each scientific method, and should thus have some capacity to evaluate these. Students could then choose one or two methods to specialize in. Since different methods *may be* of different utility for different links, students could be guided to coordinate methodological and subject matter choices. But students who wanted to apply literary theory to economic questions should not be prohibited from doing so. Instructors of nonmethod courses could assume that all students had a basic understanding of all methods. Intermediate courses in particular methods could still be required, if necessary, for senior question-oriented courses.

Students should also be provided with some introduction to the study of rhetoric and philosophy of science. I have included some discussion of these in the first two chapters of this book. However, I would still favor a full course devoted to the exploration of the philosophical insights into what science is and how it is best pursued. In particular, I think it possible to provide students with a sense of the strengths and weaknesses of different types of scientific theory. As with method, they will be confronted with diverse theoretical arguments in their lives. Moreover, we do our students a disservice by not exposing them to rhetoric: the study of how scholars, politicians, and others convince us of the correctness of their views. Philosophy teaches us that proof is impossible: we must thus learn how to evaluate the veracity of conflicting arguments. Students will be better armed to spot erroneous arguments if they are aware of the "tricks" the unscrupulous can employ to give their arguments power. To the extent that our other curricular reforms do not overcome disciplinary barriers, a training in rhetoric can also help students to appreciate the different styles of argumentation employed across the human sciences (see Lanham 1993).

I would also recommend a broader philosophical course for first-year students. This book has outlined how various phenomena affect each other. I have tried to avoid value judgments. But students also deserve some grounding in the philosophical evaluation of various phenomena. Is cultural diversity good? Democracy? Economic growth? Are some art forms better than others? The list goes on. We could ask ourselves what we might deem to be "progress" with respect to virtually all of our phenomena. Students who developed answers to these questions would in turn find exploring causal links more interesting, just as football games are more exciting if you are cheering for one side.[11] Note that such a course would also enquire into how to live a "good life" and expose students to ethical questions. Students would thus gain early exposure to the sorts of principles that might guide their own life choices. They would learn to accept confusion and insecurity. This would not only prepare them for life, but for the choices and challenges inherent in a college education.

At the risk of overloading students, I would suggest some other courses: a writing course (at least for those who need it, and with an element of literature appreciation), one or two survey courses in the natural sciences, and one or more history courses designed to show how various causal links operated during historical transformations. I would be tempted to add practical fine arts and/or physical education courses, but am conscious that specialization in terms of both subject and methodology will absorb a huge amount of curricular space.[12]

The curriculum I have outlined would have a handful of courses required of all students. This is a departure from present practice: a 1989 survey found that only 10% of American undergraduates had to take a required course. But this curriculum restores the principle that there is some material that all students should master.

While I have focused here on undergraduate training, many of the same principles should apply to graduate school: this too should require/ presume some understanding of the big picture, should be focused on particular questions, should train students in more than one method and type of theory, should expose students to the insights of philosophy of science and rhetoric, and should involve philosophical discussions relevant to the phenomena under study (see Davis 1995). Discipline-based graduate programs are at present the mechanism by which disciplinary boundaries are passed between generations. Human science can only become coherent if the curriculum of graduate schools is transformed (see Davis 1995).[13]

The above may seem a rather lengthy list of proposed changes. This is hardly unusual in curricular debates. And one could argue that it is better to make a coherent attack on present curricula rather than nibble away with often contradictory changes. Moreover, Gaff (1997) finds that large reforms yield much much larger improvements in faculty morale and student learning than small reforms.

RECENT DEBATES ABOUT CURRICULA

University and college curricula have come in for a great deal of public criticism over the last couple of decades. I cannot attempt a detailed analysis of these criticisms here, but can briefly discuss the degree to which my proposed curricular reforms would meet these criticisms.

Sadly, most recent critiques have been "ideologically" driven (Gaff 1991; Lucas 1996). Those on the "right" have yearned for a lost golden age in which the great works of Western civilization formed the backbone of the curriculum. They worry that there is no longer a clear vision of what an educated person should know. Those on the "left" push for greater diversity, especially with respect to the views and issues important to women and minorities. Such suggestions only further aggravate the critics of the right.

The first value of my approach, then, is that the schema itself alerts us to the dangers of viewing the world through the lens of any one narrow world view. No one view sheds light on all links. Lucas (1996) worries that people both inside and outside the academy have become convinced that the curricular debate is being driven by political agendas. This belief squeezes out those who might search for solutions with a broad appeal. Since my schema is politically evenhanded, the curriculum that it encourages is likewise evenhanded. And, as Gaff (1991) notes, it is possible to find room in a curriculum both for an appreciation of Western traditions and of minority perspectives. My schema and curriculum restore the ideal of core concepts that all should know, while simultaneously emphasizing the value of diverse perspectives. Courses structured around links to and from Culture or Social Structure (see Szostak 2001) would show students how diversity issues are causally linked to all other phenomena.

Fuhrmann (1997) provides a list of recent critiques of university education. My schema and proposed curriculum provide at least partial solutions to all. Against criticisms that university curricula have lost their purpose, and that universities are just degree mills, I can hold out the promise of providing students with an overview of relationships in human science that will aid them in lifelong learning. Some argue that we presently prepare students poorly for a complex world and global economy; my schema gives them a mechanism for coping with complexity, and highlights various ways in which societies influence each other. Critics worry that universities serve faculty rather than society, that faculty do not work effectively, and that much university research has little value; the schema breaks down the barriers between disciplines and encourages a problem-oriented approach to both teaching and learning.

Critics worry about outdated teaching methods; my curriculum allows students to link diverse course material and encourages students to explore issues on their own (making presentations and so on). Such innovations might even (marginally) decrease the cost of education. Concerns that universities do not encourage economic growth to the degree possible should be alleviated by a curriculum that shows how the economic sphere is connected to other phenomena. Those who worry about ethical decline should take solace in a schema that shows the advantages of shared values such as trust and honesty, and stresses the need for both personal and social responsibility. My curriculum also contains a key course that focuses on philosophical issues related to the purpose of life (see Szostak 2002).

Fuhrmann's final critique concerns the need to reflect women's and minority concerns. I could note here that scholars who share this concern have recognized that we must move past one or two courses focused on these questions (whether required or optional).[14] My schema captures these issues primarily in its S↔* (see Szostak 2001) and C↔* links. Every student thus gains an early acquaintance with how social structure and culture both influence and are influenced by other phenomena. A curriculum in which specialization is focused on particular phenomena or sets of causal links would force students to recognize how S and C are related to their area of interest. Students who choose social structure and/or culture as a focus of their studies would gain an even greater insight, while not feeling isolated from the broader curriculum.

Long before the recent wave of criticism, a minority of scholars had been fighting for curricular reform under the heading of "general education." Ratcliff (1997) reiterates the goals of this movement as enumerated by Gaff in 1983. Ratcliff and Gaff stress breadth of knowledge (including diverse methodologies), and integration, synthesis, and coherence. They wish to encourage an appreciation of one's own and other cultures. They hope to examine values and controversial issues. They want all to have a common educational experience. They expect mastery of linguistic, analytic, and computational skills (Hendershott and Wright 1997, speak of the need for students to be able to think logically, openly, and independently, cope with complexity, and recognize limits to knowledge). They wish to foster personal development and an expanded view of self. Various authors in Gaff et al. (1997), while optimistic about the future, concur that they are still far from achieving these goals. Again my schema and curriculum can help.

Glassick et al. (1999), following upon the work of Ernest Boyer, urge the recognition of four types of scholarship: research, integration, teaching, and service. By providing a structure for placing specialized research in perspective and integrating such research into a larger whole, which in turn supports curricular reform and improved public policy advice, I hope to encourage advances in all four types of scholarship. I hope also to have illustrated how these are interconnected.

A NOTE ON ELEMENTARY AND HIGH SCHOOL CURRICULA

High school curricula are subject to considerable debate these days as well. Brady (1989) lists several problems, including curricular fragmentation, the fact that schools lack criteria by which to choose among an ever-increasing body of knowledge, and the fact that there is no attempt made to link various pieces together. He feels that the solution lies in placing a comprehensive model of our sociocultural system at the core of the curriculum.

At the very least, my schema could give some cohesion to the social studies curriculum. At present, this is all too often a mishmash of different topics. At the college level, I have recommended starting with an overview of the whole schema, and proceeding in later years to specialization. For pre-college education, a reverse process may be superior. Children, after all, are accustomed to building up their super-schemas piece by piece. A curriculum that gradually exposed children to the unpacking of various phenomena and explication of particular casual links could be capped with a discussion of how all of the pieces fit together. Younger children, not yet capable of complex theoretical speculation, would thus be required only to understand simple causal relations. The larger edifice would be built as students' mental capabilities expanded to embrace it. Since students find it easier to learn when they can place new knowledge into an existing conceptual structure, it would be advisable to relate each new subject to previous ones.

Brady (1989) also worries that education is not tied as closely as it might be to real world experiences. It thus fails to stimulate children's natural curiosity. Martinello and Cook (1994) advocate a question-oriented curriculum, where the questions are drawn from child experiences. They note that if one starts with questions, one is led naturally to an interdisciplinary analysis, for real world questions have complex answers. Even very young children can thus learn of the interrelatedness of various phenomena. Young children, after all, when they have learned how X causes Y, tend naturally to wonder what causes X in turn. An ideal curriculum, then, would involve a series of questions that trigger curiosity, each illuminating a variety of causal links, and gradually coalescing over the years to give students a feel for the overarching schema.

DISCIPLINARY FUTURES

I have emphasized throughout this book that despite arbitrary disciplinary boundaries a great deal of useful research has been undertaken which sheds light on many facets of the human science undertaking. I have suggested in a previous section that at the very least curricular reform requires a change in the focus of existing disciplines. A brief review of where these are and where they might go thus seems in order.

ANTHROPOLOGY

As with most disciplines, a survey of the main subjects covered by anthropology yields a mixed bag. Bulick (1982) divides the discipline into three areas of physical anthropology—namely paleontology, primatology, and neontology—and three areas of cultural anthropology: archaeology, ethnography, and ethnology (with the possible addition of linguistics).

If we start with paleontology (the study of skeletal remains) and archaeology, what we really have is a historical method. By studying the bones and buildings of past societies, we learn about nutrition, trade, social structure, culture, and a host of other phenomena. As argued above, methods should not be viewed as the sole property of any one discipline.

Primatology deals with the study of those animals closest in genetic makeup to humans. Neontology focusses on genetic bases of behavior, often comparing human behavior to that of animals. To the extent that these inquiries do not more properly belong within the natural sciences, they can be seen as elucidating certain $G \rightarrow *$ links. They would thus most logically be grouped with psychology, which has the exploration of $G \rightarrow *$ links as one of its primary goals.[15]

That leaves ethnography and ethnology (comparative ethnography). These also are to some extent methodological in nature. Ethnographers have developed guidelines as to how best to observe a society different from one's own. When observing other societies, ethnographers—like archaeologists—do not limit themselves to any one phenomenon but consider technology, economy, politics, social structure, demography, culture, and art all within their purview. The isolation of this method within one discipline has had the inevitable effect. Ethnographers have gathered an enormous amount of data. Only very rarely have scholars attempted to use this data to test theories about causal relations in human science. Even rarer is the ethnographer who takes a solid grounding in theory into the bush in the first place.[16] Much could be gained if ethnographers were brought into closer contact with theorists across human science.

While ethnographers have been necessarily holistic in approach, the phenomenon of culture has always held a special attraction. When cross-societal comparisons are made, culture is the most common subject. Thus, if anthropology departments of the future wished to lay claim to part of our schema, the $* \rightarrow C$ and $C \rightarrow *$ links would be the natural focus (with perhaps a subset of these left to linguistics departments). To do even this would require that anthropologists more regularly move beyond data collection to theory. It would certainly require a recognition that culture can and should be unpacked. Finally, it would require that anthropologists widen the scope of their inquiry from traditional societies to culture wherever it may be found (absorbing a minority of sociologists in the process). One can discern signs that anthropology is already moving in these directions. Certainly in terms of the latter point, many anthropologists have recognized that as traditional societies disappear a broadened perspective is essential (see Gledhill 1994).

GEOGRAPHY

Parsons (1989) describes geography as a discipline that has expanded in so many directions that it now has no center. Our analysis of geography will bear an eerie similarity to our analysis of anthropology. Here again, two large subdivisions can be identified—physical geography and human geography. As with anthropology, one of these divisions—human geography—is best viewed as a method applicable across a wide range of causal links, and the other—physical geography—while being more narrowly focused on a small number of causal links, has tended to be descriptive rather than analytical in practice.

Geography is most commonly defined as the relationship between humans and "land." For "land" we can read more broadly the category we have defined as "non-human environment." When I introduced that category in chapter 3, I noted the important distinction between the study of the effects of particular elements of the nonhuman environment, and a more general discussion of the spatial component of human interaction. Since all human activities take place in space and time, spatial concerns are relevant to each causal link.

Human geography is focused on the spatial analysis of various of our phenomena: key subfields include population geography, cultural geography, social geography, economic geography, urban geography, political geography, medical geography, and historical geography. In all of these areas, geographers have developed techniques for representing important aspects of these phenomena cartographically and for measuring diffusion, interaction, and migration. Unfortunately, works of geography are very

rarely consulted by other human scientists (Bulick 1982). As with ethnography, then, we have a potentially powerful method cut off from those
in other disciplines studying the causal links which it helps to elucidate.

Physical geography (and some elements of human geography) is
focused on $* \rightarrow N$ and $N \rightarrow *$ links. While texts in physical geography
devote most of their space to detailed descriptions of the topography, soil,
climate, flora, and fauna of particular locales, almost all go beyond this to
the more obvious effects of these variables on economic activity and
population distribution. Some geographers look at links to other phenomena. Humanistic geographers, for example, focus on the emotional attachments that people develop to particular landscapes (though often at a very
general level).

ECONOMICS

The blessing and curse of economics is that $E \rightarrow E$ links are both important
and conducive to isolated study. Unlike other disciplines that envelop a
hodgepodge of poorly related topics, the problem with economics is that it
is too focused. Mainstream economists have so much fun playing with
$E \rightarrow E$ links that they casually ignore the relationships between the economy and other phenomena. They show far less interest in other disciplines
than any of the other social sciences (Bulick 119). In areas where these
links are important, notably in the understanding of the causes of economic
growth, the scientific endeavor has necessarily suffered. While greater
study of $* \rightarrow E$ and $E \rightarrow *$ links is desperately needed, economics departments as presently constructed have provided a poor home for such in-
quiries. Perhaps in an interdisciplinary future, economics departments
could safely be entrusted with their stewardship.

Economics suffers further from its identification with one method: construction of mathematical models and their testing with complicated statistical procedures. Economists are naturally suspicious of work done with
any other method, and thus insights that could only be gained in other ways
are lost (see Szostak 1999). Some economists have boldly invaded other
disciplines with their pet method in recent decades. Hostile though I am to
methodological hegemony at home, I agree that the standard approach of
economists can shed useful light elsewhere in human science. This will
best occur in an environment where scholars cooperate rather than compete, and this cooperation will be enhanced if this method ceases to be
identified with one discipline.

POLITICAL SCIENCE

While political scientists bemoan the lack of a theory of politics that would
give the discipline a better sense of identity, in terms of our schema

political science appears as one of the more sensible disciplines. Like economics, its very title focuses its attention on just one of our major categories. Unlike economics, its subject matter has not for the most part been conducive to isolated study. The major exception is the field of international relations, which not coincidentally boasts the most well-developed body of theory in the discipline (and suffers from a too limited appreciation of how domestic conditions shape international political behavior, and vice versa).

Other areas of political science, such as voting behavior, public opinion, bureaucracy, or comparative political institutions, have always required an interdisciplinary perspective. While political scientists may view their tendency to borrow insights from other disciplines with embarrassment, in the bold interdisciplinary world of tomorrow their longstanding interdisciplinary focus should serve them well. Having recognized that psychology, sociology, anthropology,[17] and economics (at least) have much to say about political processes, political scientists need also to realize that one comprehensive theory is a misguided goal; rather they should concentrate on developing a better understanding of each causal link $*{\rightarrow}P$ and $P{\rightarrow}*$, and then put these together into a necessarily messy understanding of political processes.

PSYCHOLOGY

I have, in my schema, several categories of societal behavior, but only two concerned with individual characteristics. From the vantage point of my schema, then, psychology can easily appear more focused than social science disciplines. Within the field, however, many scholars worry that it is fragmented both by subject area and differing theoretical perspectives.

Some of this fragmentation may reflect the fact that psychology has two distinct tasks: to understand the genetic mechanisms that operate within us all, and to understand differences between individuals. Some psychological fields are primarily focused on our genes: developmental psychology, learning, and "sense and feeling" (perception, consciousness, and so on). yet even here elements of individual differences in intelligence, motivation, and emotion are important. Other psychological fields, such as personality or abnormal psychology, focus on our differences. It could well be that psychology would be strengthened by a more explicit recognition of the distinction between our similarities and our differences (while of course recognizing the importance of $G{\rightarrow}I$ links).

Psychology, like economics, has suffered from insularity. It is all too easy to study individuals in isolation from the wider society. The prominence of the experimental method within the discipline has served to strengthen the tendency to focus on isolated individuals in a laboratory setting. Many scholars have questioned whether the results of laboratory

experiments can be carried over to the understanding of how people behave when interacting with others in the real world.

One field that has focused on links to other categories is social psychology (it is viewed with suspicion by other psychologists as a result). However, social psychologists in psychology departments have generally
focused only on *→I links, such as how social interaction shapes individual self-image, personality, attitudes and prejudices (with researchers in
one area often ignoring research in others; Vallacher and Nowak 1994).
The study of how G and I affect social aggregates has generally been left to
social science departments. Most sociologists ignore psychological links,
and those who study them rarely call themselves social psychologists but
operate in distinct fields such as sociology of the family and gender studies
(Klein 1996, 81). The human science endeavor would benefit if both
psychologists and sociologists were more aware of the causal links connecting their subject matter to other phenomena.

SOCIOLOGY

Barber (1993) criticizes sociology texts as "disorderly and often diverse
collections of topics that are supposed to tell the reader something about
behavior in society." Even Bulick (1982) despairs of easily defining the
boundaries of sociology. He notes the breadth of most definitions of the
field: "scientific study of human interaction," 'science of society," "systematic study of human relations." As a result of this broad self-definition
many "big picture" works of sociologists are filed by libraries in the
general social science category. While I must applaud the efforts of souls
brave enough to extend their gaze over a range of causal links, I must also
note that there is no good reason why such efforts should be limited to the
denizens of one discipline (and Bulick notes that sociologists are almost as
likely as economists to shun extra-disciplinary reading).

Sociology was institutionalized as a discipline without any distinctive
method, content, or point of view; by the 1970s a focus on functionalism,
surveys, and the work of a half dozen theorists gave the discipline some
sense of unity. Since then, it has fragmented into subdisciplines; most
sociologists are optimistic about the prospects of their specialties but pessimistic about the discipline as a whole. Citation analysis shows that the
discipline has lost its core: there is no general body of work referred to by
all sociologists. Abbott (2001, 6) worries that sociology has no intellec-
tually effective way of excluding topics, and thus that it tends only to add
new topics. Calhoun (1992) notes that a general sociological theory would
have to encompass both culture and social structure, and thus that sociology may be not one discipline but many, but worries that the discipline is
too small to be able to fragment.[18]

Looked at from the perspective of my schema, sociology can be broken into four groups that have no more in common with each other than with the foci of other disciplines. Sociology, in essence, took "what was left" after the earlier development of economics, political science, and geography. Trying to argue that there is some logical unity to these four categories both discourages students from fully appreciating the intrinsic value of each of the four, and steers them away from an appreciation of other interdisciplinary links (Calhoun 1992). The confusion that results discourages some of the best students from pursuing careers in sociology (Halliday 1992). Sociology, its students, and human science more generally would benefit from a reorganization around its four core categories.

First, there are those sociologists whose primary concern is with societal norms or values. They are thus focused on a subset of the causal links of concern to cultural anthropologists, and would best work in closer concert with these. Sociologists have, regrettably, shown little concern with where values come from and thus how they might change, but have done invaluable work in describing how once in place values constrain individual behavior. A definition of their task as concerned with both $*\rightarrow C$ and $C\rightarrow*$ links would thus encourage scientific advance.

Second, there are criminologists. This, within my schema, is properly a subset of politics. It is, however, a subset so distinct that there is value in maintaining some distinction between the two spheres.

The third group is demographers. While demography formally defined is concerned only with mathematical aspects of population—birth and death rates, migration rates, age and sex structure, population projections—scholars in the area have looked at links with genes, economy, geography, politics, social structure (especially families), psychology, and culture (Daugherty and Kammeyer 1995). This is where most work on $*\rightarrow H$ and $H\rightarrow*$ links is done in human science. A rational division of academic labor would have this group in closer contact with population economists and population geographers than with criminologists. It would also ensure that health was a more frequent subject of scholarly analysis.

The fourth group of sociologists deals with social structure as I have defined it. They could thus form yet another discipline focused on $*\rightarrow S$ and $S\rightarrow*$ links.

One might identify a fifth group of interpretive sociologists who analyze how individuals interpret their interactions with others. Their predominant focus is thus interpersonal relationships.

WOMEN'S STUDIES, GENDER STUDIES, RACE STUDIES

Both within and outside these departments, there is considerable debate about their ideal place in the academy. Some argue that they have a role to play only because of a previous white male bias in human science; if this were to be overcome such disciplines would no longer be necessary. Others view them as disciplines in their own right with an eternal message.[19] From the perspective of my schema I can see some truth in both arguments. Gender and race/ethnicity are phenomena with causal connections to diverse other phenomena. As long as society treats genders or races differently, these links will deserve our attention (I leave to individual universities the question of whether separate departments are desirable). One of the causal links is indeed to science itself, and thus scholars (all scholars) need to strive to overcome gender and racial bias in science.

There has been considerable concern in recent decades within women's studies departments that these were dominated by white middle-class women. Many in the field have thus striven to be sensitive in their research to questions of class and ethnicity as well as gender (Parsons 1989). This, of course, fits well with the approach of my schema which considers these as similar phenomena.

HISTORY

History as a discipline has rarely been mentioned in this book. The work of historians has, however, appeared often in these pages. This is not surprising, for all causal relationships take place in time, and historians will have naturally studied many of them in various times and places. This is one great contribution that history can make to human science. Most human science research is focused on modern Western democracies. Causal relationships may operate quite differently in other times and places. We have seen above that ethnographers have not seen their vocation as testing the boundaries of human science theory. Historians tend not to see themselves in this light, either. Yet the fact is that their work can be an invaluable input into human science theorizing.

This is especially the case when historians study major historical events such as revolutions or wars. During such times of rapid change, causal links that are virtually invisible in quieter times will leap to the fore. It is all too easy to take for granted a host of behaviors and attitudes observed in peacetime, unless exposed to times and places when these were different. We can think various phenomena are static if we do not observe them changing.

It would be advantageous, then, if historians had a wider exposure to human science theory. They could then see to what extent this theory had to be modified in order to fit various historical circumstances. History courses could also be structured so that students—exposed elsewhere to an overview of human science—could see how various causal links operated in history. In this regard, it might be useful for some history courses to be focused thematically, and thus illustrate some set of causal links through history, rather than being always focused on particular time periods and places as at present. However, we should not lose sight of the advantages of the latter focus. A course on, say, the French Revolution, could/should be structured to show how economic, political, cultural, social, technological, personal, demographic, and artistic variables interacted at that time.[20] This would provide students with an invaluable reminder of the complexity that is human science. And scholars could see whether our existing body of causal understanding provides a satisfactory explanation of the French Revolution, or whether there are not parts of the puzzle needing further elucidation. If the latter, historians should not be shy of attempting to add to our body of theoretical knowledge.

Abbott (1994) is skeptical of the conjecture of Skocpol and others that historians could provide a comparative perspective on individual causal links in different times and places. He worries that any historical event is too complicated to be broken down into component parts. Part of his concern stems from a fear that theory-driven historians will ignore the historical importance of individual personalities. Since such individual differences retain an important place in our schema, this need not happen (though his concern is understandable). Beyond this, I would suggest that to abandon hope of disentangling causal links is to give up on convincing and useful explanation. This book itself should provide compelling evidence that we can profitably study individual links in isolation. The works of many historians—such as M. Mann, 1986—give further evidence that tracing the operation of a limited set of causal links through time is both possible and very informative.

Historians have long suspected that big events can have "small" causes. A disturbed king, a minor food shortage, a chance meeting: all can set off a chain of causation with major consequences. Kindleberger (1996, 8) views exposing such occurrences as history's greatest purpose. Such an attitude need not be discouraged, as long as a convincing set of causal explanations (and evidence) is provided.

Historians also tend to stress the uniqueness of each historical event. This again is consistent with the thrust of this book. In discussions of the evolution of various of our phenomena, I have often noted the likelihood of path dependence. Our situation tomorrow depends on what it is today. A similar harvest failure striking two communities will have different effects depending on the preexisting culture, politics, and economy. Rather than uniqueness being a problem for us it is a blessing for it allows us to identify under what conditions certain results flow from certain causes.

Since culture evolves over time, we can only fully comprehend any society's beliefs—including our own—if we know where they came from. Gellner (1989) deplores the paradox that "the ideas of nineteenth century philosophers of history such as Hegel, Marx, Comte, or Spencer are treated with scant respect and yet are everywhere in use." He recognizes that knowing the roots of beliefs cannot tell us whether they are right or wrong but can help us to understand our choices. A similar argument can be made with respect to institutions. A further role for history, then, is to help us understand and maybe even change our world by telling us how we got here (and that in turn depends on making complex causal arguments).

Ironically, there is a danger that historians have become so specialized in particular times and places that they are poorly equipped to appreciate changes that occur slowly over long periods. Goudsblom, Jones, and Mennell (1996) blame this tendency not just on the scourge of specialization that afflicts us all but also on an excessive adherence to functionalist/ structuralist thinking, and interpretations of positivist philosophy which opposed explaining the present with the past. We have seen in the first chapter that we must not allow our curiosity about structure to deflect us from focusing on change. We also saw that the past does matter, as long as there is a causal chain linking past and present. Perhaps the fact that many historians are now called upon to teach survey courses with a broad temporal and spatial sweep will encourage an enhanced focus on the very long run (while stimulating comparative analyses of how particular links work in different times and places).[21]

AREA STUDIES

Most of what I have said about history can be said as well about area studies. Here too we can find how particular causal links operate in different circumstances. Moreover, we can trace the myriad effects of differences in individual phenomena across societies. For example, if we accept that Japanese culture is different in certain aspects from American culture, how are these differences related to observed differences in other phenomena? As with history, then, the schema provides an obvious framework within which area studies departments could operate.

Many area studies departments began with a focus on language and literature. Interests have broadened over time, though a stress on cross-societal differences can generally be observed. Recently, prominent political scientists in the United States have criticized area studies scholars for doing bad political science. They felt that area studies experts were prone to amassing institutional description in an atheoretical manner (Tessler et al, 1999). Area studies specialists responded that they were in fact trying to perform comparative political science and understand the causes and effects of different political institutions. There is evidence, then, that area studies is in fact headed in the direction I would like. Concerns within area studies that they borrow eclectically from disciplinary theories should be assuaged by use of a coherent organizing schema.

Our schema would also alleviate three concerns identified by Klein (1996). The first is that while area studies has moved beyond language and literature, it has done so unevenly: anthropology, political science, and history are well represented, as these emphasize particularities, but because of their universal principles psychology and economics (and sociology to a lesser extent) are severely underrepresented. Area studies departments at present thus examine only a subset of relevant causal links. My schema would encourage a more evenhanded approach. Klein's second concern is that political scientists (for example) within area studies departments generally aim their research primarily at a political science audience. This creates the odd result that area studies is often not very interdisciplinary. Again, my schema could guide scholars to explore interdisciplinary links. The third concern is with the limited linkages across areas: Latin Americanists having little reason to consult the work of Africanists. The difficulty of mastering several languages must always limit the number of scholars capable of working in more than one area. Still, my schema can make it clear when scholars of different areas are discussing the same link, and will thus facilitate the synthesis of analysis across areas.

Tessler et al. (1999) reprise several longstanding criticisms of area studies: that it lacks rigor, favors description over explanation, lacks analytic cumulations, shows no interest in generalizations, and emphasizes detail and specificity. Area studies specialists have in turn criticized the social sciences for faddishness, oversimplification, and irrelevance. The schema provides a superior link between theory and empirics so that we can examine the same link across diverse societies and seek generalizations (and the limits to these). By understanding cross-cultural differences in detail, we should be guided to formulate theories that are neither trivial nor obvious.

PHILOSOPHY

Philosophers may cringe or rejoice at my suggestion that there should be at least two courses with a large philosophical base required of all human science undergraduates. The philosophy of science course would fall most clearly within their domain (though note that there are—or should be—scholars in all disciplines with a substantial knowledge of philosophy of science, and that I would emphasize the evaluation of different types of theory). The second course, on how to ethically evaluate realizations of diverse phenomena, might best be team taught by representatives of various disciplines. There would, however, be a clear place for philosophers to set the overall tone. Philosophical concerns with ethics, knowledge, and the meaning of life must be taken care of first (see Szostak 2002).

Philosophers need not, of course, spend all of their time teaching the basics to all students. There will still be a place for those who wish to specialize in philosophy of science or ethics or in the philosophy of some particular category. Political philosophy, religious philosophy, philosophy of mind, and linguistic analysis have of late been major areas of philosophical concern, though philosophers have a long tradition of concern with art, economy, and social structure as well. As noted in chapter 1, such philosophical concerns lie on a different plane of analysis from the scientific exploration of causal links. A greater intercourse between philosophers and the human scientists studying such phenomena would nevertheless be desirable.

THE ARTS (ART, MUSIC, DRAMA, FILM STUDIES, LITERATURE)

The reader may have noted that the humanities have fared well in our discussions so far. Departments of history, area studies, and philosophy have a more obvious claim to independence than is the case with the social and behavioral science disciplines. The arts disciplines discussed here also fare well, but for a completely different reason. Much of the teaching that goes on here is of a professional nature: how to sculpt, play the piano, shoot a movie, or, to a much lesser extent, how to write. Just as there are law schools, education faculties, and social work schools that draw on human science for professional training, so these departments train artists in how to do art. I have in this book said little about such professional programs, but can note here their importance.

My schema shows, though, that there is a further role for these disciplines to play. The arts are an integral part of human existence, and thus the links between art and other phenomena deserve our attention. Yet the arts have been seriously isolated from the rest of human science. Much more attention deserves to be paid to the causal links between art and other categories. Whether this is best done by scholars in each department devoted to this sort of study or by some new "human science of art" department is unclear. In either case, as with other causal links it is necessary that these scholars interact with those interested in art elsewhere in human science.

Harris (1997) discusses a number of problems with the present state of arts education: required arts courses for human science majors are rarely integrated with their other courses, arts programs at both undergraduate and graduate levels divorce practical training from the study of art in society, courses in the study of art do not build upon one another to create a systematic body of knowledge, and the links between art and both culture and technology are under-studied. The use of my schema would immediately solve the first and last problems. It would also suggest how students specializing in art could be offered a set of courses that would give them a detailed understanding of one or more causal links A↔*. Finally, those intending to become artists should recognize the value of understanding art's place in society and in the lives of individuals. Just as law schools should teach more than cases, and education faculties more than how to run the projector, artists should be exposed to some understanding of how their vocation is related to other societal phenomena.

English departments often face a conflict between those who specialize in literature and those who specialize in composition. The former have more prestige in the discipline, but the latter often cross-subsidize the former by teaching large numbers of students. This is especially the case where there are required writing courses and/or when poorly paid graduate students or sessional lecturers handle most of the writing courses. The dichotomy will seem strange to any who have tried their hand at writing fiction. My own attempts in that direction have greatly enhanced my appreciation of literature, for I can now see what the author is trying to do (ah: what a clever way of introducing a new character, describing their emotions, setting the scene). From my naive viewpoint, at least, a case can be made for integrating literature and composition. The schema provides a further justification, for an understanding of A↔* links must simultaneously guide us to improve our writing and to better comprehend how and why the literature of others moves us.

We must, as elsewhere, close by speaking of methodology. Despite the paucity of links between scholars of the arts and those elsewhere in human science, the former have made numerous methodological contributions to the latter. This is hardly surprising when one considers the ubiquity of written texts and visual/auditory stimuli in our lives. Scholars of the arts have developed a number of methods by which they can 'read' texts or objects or sounds, and discern not only their aesthetic properties but hidden meanings. None of these methods is perfect—as can be said about any method—but once again scholars and students throughout human science deserve some exposure to what is possible.

FINAL THOUGHTS

I should emphasize in closing that I am not at all sure that we are not better off without disciplines. If they serve an administrative purpose, it is important that this not be allowed to limit cross-disciplinary interaction. By redrawing disciplines so that each is focused on a particular category (we would have to add a technology/science discipline to our list), we have ensured that each external causal link is covered by more than one discipline. That is, C→P would figure both in anthropology and political science. There are both advantages and disadvantages to this approach relative to an alternative where we make each discipline responsible only for causal links where the arrow points toward their category. The first advantage is that it forces cross-disciplinary cooperation. The corresponding disadvantage is that we end up with a fragmented understanding if such cooperation is not forthcoming. The second advantage is that feedback effects are often important. One learns about C→P as one studies P→C. The second disadvantage is administrative: disciplines would have to cooperate in offering courses and programs. With the right attitude, this might turn out to be the greatest advantage of all.

APPENDIX 12-A: THE PHENOMENA

In chapter 1, I divided the human science subject matter into ten logically distinct categories. In the introductory sections of chapters 3–11, I then unpacked (disaggregated) these into hundreds of subsidiary phenomena. I provide here a summary of the unpacking that took place in this book. I close with a tabular list of phenomena. Naturally, I follow the same order in which the categories were introduced in the body of the book. Throughout, second-level phenomena are underlined and third-level phenomena italicized:

CULTURE

Languages can be classified in terms of line of descent. Such a classification ignores the extensive cross-fertilization of vocabulary that has occurred. Moreover, there is little evidence that such divisions have major causal significance. And all languages share important structural and grammatical elements, such that disaggregation along those lines is of limited utility.

Religion is a second component. Religious dogma can be distinguished under the sub-headings *providence* (godly intervention versus cosmic order), *revelation* (past or present; may involve prophecy), *salvation* (various afterlives, paths to entry), and *miracles* (almost a universal feature). Religious *doctrine* comprises the arguments used to support dogma.

Stories can be classified as *myths, fairy tales, legends, family sagas, fables,* or *jokes and riddles,* though their causal function tends to be similar.

There are also a number of expressions of culture: *rituals, dance, song, cuisine, attire* (including fashion), *ornamentation of buildings,* and *games.*

The broadest cultural subcategory I term values. I confess, though, that I have stretched this term to cover not just what sociologists normally refer to under the headings of value or norm, but several other attitudes that fit here better than anywhere else.

I begin with a number of values which concern the goals group members should pursue: *ambition, time preference, optimism/pessimism,* and *atti-*

tudes toward wealth, power, knowledge, prestige, beauty, honor, recognition, love, friendship, sex, incest, marriage, physical well-being, and *psychological well-being.*

I then list a number of values broadly concerned with the means group members should use to pursue their goals: *honesty, ethics, righteousness, belief in fate versus individual initiative* (justice), *work valued intrinsically, attitudes toward violence and vengeance, curiosity, openness to innovation,* and *attitude toward nature.*

While all communities encourage some *sense of identity,* they differ in *relative value of family vs. community, openness to outsiders, egalitarianism versus competitiveness, attitude toward young and old, responsibility for others, trust, authoritarianism versus cooperation,* and *respect for the individual.*

A number of everyday norms serve to facilitate interaction among group members while minimizing misunderstanding: *courtesy, manners, proxemics* (e.g., how close we stand while conversing), *tidiness, cleanliness, punctuality, conversational rules* (interrupting, shouting, eye contact, acceptability of gossip), *locomotion rules* (walk on right, face front in elevator), *tipping.*

THE NON-HUMAN ENVIRONMENT

Geographers generally focus on soil, topography, climate, flora, and fauna, and can further disaggregate these phenomena in terms of categorization schema for *soil type, land forms, climate pattern,* and *species.* Resource availability deserves separate treatment. Water (availability and quality), depending as it does on soil, topography, and climate, also deserves separate treatment. Natural disasters (*flood, tornado, hurricane, earthquake, volcano*) could be left as subsets of climate and topography, but possess common and special characteristics. We should also appreciate the effect which the Earth's rotation has on our lives: *day and night.* While the effects of humanity on the environment in terms of pollution, species extinction, and resource depletion can easily be captured with reference to the above phenomena, three other phenomena are required to reflect human shaping of the environment: transport infrastructure (which can be disaggregated by *mode*), built environments (*offices, houses, fences,* and so on) and population density.

GENETIC PREDISPOSITION

We can consider genetic predispositions of three distinct types: abilities, motivations, and emotions. Among abilities I identify *consciousness, subconsciousness, vocalization, perception* (five senses, all subject to distortion), *toolmaking, learning* (which involves a need and ability to form conceptual schemas concerning ourselves and our world, and may well be grounded in the 'hard-wiring' of certain concepts/approaches in our brains), *decision-making,* and various *other physical attributes* (locomotion, eating, breathing, and so on)

We are all aware of certain basic motivations: *food* (we share various preferences), *clothing, shelter, safety, sex* (again, we arguably share certain mate preferences with respect to age, appearance, and so on). These various drives may well have yielded a more general *drive to better ourselves* (which some would call self-actualization). *Aggression* is another shared motivation. Yet we are also endowed with motivations that support group cohesion: *altruism, fairness* and a *desire to identify with (and be accepted by) a larger group.*

Our emotions serve as reward or punishment (e.g., guilt for lying), and/ or as an incentive to act (e.g., fear encourages flight). Among emotions I distinguish *joy, love, anger, jealousy, fear, grief, guilt, empathy, anxiety, disgust* and *fatigue. Humor* is an emotional reaction shared by all. We also all take pleasure from nature and art, which is grounded in a common *aesthetic sense.* Perhaps most important of all, we *display our emotions physically,* even when we try not to.

Time preference, by which we willingly trade off present pleasure for future gain, does not fit easily in these three subcategories, but is nevertheless an important human characteristic. This characteristic, as well as our abilities, motivations, and emotions, changes as we age, a point which must be remembered when looking at causal links. Another point that must be emphasized is that our motivations are often in conflict; and our brain is best perceived as a loose refereeing mechanism among competing drives and emotions, rather than an all-knowing utility maximization program. Finally, I should note that the existence of a small minority who are blind, deaf, or psychotic (i.e., incapable of guilt) should not prevent us from speaking of seeing, hearing, and feeling guilt as universal traits. And differences in abilities, motivations, and emotions across individuals will be captured under "individual differences."

At a lower level of aggregation, we can, at least potentially, speak of the role of individual genes. Likewise, we can refer to individual fetal hormones which, while not technically genes, have a similar effect on individuals.

INDIVIDUAL DIFFERENCES

We can begin with individual differences in ability. Physical abilities could be described in terms of *speed, strength of various muscle groups, endurance,* or in terms of various physical competitions. I also include physical appearance here, even though it stretches the definition of the word ability, to reflect the fact that various attributes such as *height, weight,* and *facial symmetry* affect how others treat us. People also appear to differ in their *physical* and/or *mental* energy level. In terms of mental ability, I distinguish various sorts of intelligence(s), including *musical, spatial, mathematical, verbal, kinesthetic* (physical movement), and *interpersonal.* (These six, plus an intrapsychic intelligence best dealt with under schemas below, were first suggested by Gardner [1983]. He also unpacked these: interpersonal intelligence, for example, includes leadership, relationships, conflict resolution, and recognition of others' relationships.)

Drawing on the work of various psychologists I propose five major personality dimensions: sociability (extroversion/introversion), which subsumes *talkative, assertive, adventurous, enthusiastic,* versus *reserved, withdrawn,* and so on; emotionality (stable versus moody), which encompasses *contentment, composure,* versus *anxiety, self-pity,* and so on, conscientiousness, which embodies *thoroughness, precision, foresight, organization, perseverance,* versus *carelessness, disorderliness, frivolousness,* and so on; affection (selfishness/agreeableness), which includes *sympathetic, kind, appreciative, generous* versus *cruel, quarrelsome, faultfinding,* and so on; and intellectual orientation (holistic versus analytical), which aggregates such traits as *openness to innovation, imagination, curiosity,* and *artistic sensitivity* versus *closemindedness.*

 Many scholars have suggested that certain personality continua, including *dominant/submissive, independent/dependent, strong-willed/weak,* and *future versus present oriented* (time preference), are poorly captured by this categorization schema. It could be that these, like *humor*—which seems to reflect both holistic thinking and selflessness—*aggression,* and *happiness,* are combined effects of more than one of the traits discussed above.

Personality disorders likely reflect for the most part extreme positions along one or more personality dimensions. Many scholars (e.g., Miller 1990) have attempted to describe how particular disorders can be defined in this way. Still, since cultural attitudes and scientific judgment will determine how extreme one must be before being judged to have a disorder, individual disorders could be viewed as distinct phenomena. Certainly, those disorders that are hard to categorize according to personality dimensions, such as *schizophrenia,* and *psychoticism,* must be given special treatment.

Sexual orientation, despite popular stereotypes, appears to be poorly comprehensible in terms of, or even strongly correlated with, other characteristics, and must thus be given separate treatment.

We are distinguished as individuals by more than the differences in personality and ability listed above. While intellectual orientation tells us about how we think, and intellectual ability describes how well we think, my schema so far has no place for what we think. Yet surely individuals differ markedly in what they think. I capture these differences with the phenomenon of schemas, by which individuals organize their thoughts. Like my organizing schema, these schemas involve definitions of phenomena and/or understandings of relationships among them. Our understanding of the world comprises a large number of schemas comprising relationships among different sets of phenomena. While we strive for consistency among our schemas, we are also capable of ignoring some inconsistencies. We are also capable of ignoring certain questions, or organizing our schemas so that only particular approaches to questions are possible. We can distinguish various types of schema. Arguably, the most important schema is *view of self*. Recent scholarship suggests that this is formed like other schemas, and involves a loose combination of beliefs about different abilities and personality characteristics we possess, along with estimates of how others perceive us. We also have *views of others*. We tend to perceive others, at least when we do not know them well, as group members, and can conceive of hierarchical systems of stereotypes: blacks, black men, black basketball players, those on the home team. Individuals can be analyzed within the same categories as ourselves. Note that positive views of individuals can be maintained along with negative views of their group by judging the individual as special. The largest set of schemas deals with *causal relationships*. We must on a daily basis depend on our understanding of how umbrellas deflect rain, cars slow down for pedestrians, and strangers react to rudeness, and thus require a large number of separate causal schemas.

Interpersonal relationships are not properly a subset of individual differences, but fit here more comfortably than anywhere else in my schema (they may well deserve treatment as a separate category). Kuhn (1974) devotes much of his book to discussing the common elements in all human relationships. He would approve of disaggregating this category in terms of type of relationships: *parent/child, sibling, employer/employee, romance, friendship,* and *casual* being some of the more important types. These can generally be further disaggregated, notably by gender of participants.

THE ECONOMY

A single phenomenon, total output, because of the dynamic framework I use, will allow us to analyze both economic growth and economic fluctuations. Two closely linked phenomena are thus *price level* and *unemployment rates*. And we can disaggregate total output into the output of *individual goods and services* and further to individual artifacts. This allows us to look not only at industrial structure, but also technological effects on the economy and the wider effects of individual goods and services (e.g., the effect of violence on television).

We must also discuss how the output is shared, or income distribution. Societal stability requires some economic ideology which justifies this distribution.

The economy's functioning depends on a variety of economic institutions where institutions are defined as codified rules or laws such that sanctions can be potentially imposed on transgressors. The chief sorts of institutions govern *ownership, production, exchange, trade, finance,* and *labor relations.* All can be disaggregated to the level of individual rules. Note that since institutions depend on the possibility of sanction, they must be embodied in some form of organization. *Organizations* are also properly a subset of institutions; key organizations include firms, unions, employer groups, and nonprofit organizations. Organizations, economic and political, are of four types, depending on purpose: profit, cooperation, service, and pressure.

POLITICS

Institutions loom large in my discussion of politics as well. In some cases (e.g., government regulatory agencies) particular institutions may serve both economic and political purposes. In such cases I would classify them under the most appropriate heading, and capture the dual influences with causal links.

Political institutions can be captured under three main headings (see Frey 1992). *Decision-making systems* can be autocratic (including such variations as monarchy, oligarchy, military dictatorship, one-party state, and religious state) or democratic (with wide differences in electoral and legislative rules and role of referenda; see Elster 1993, Finer 1997).

Rules include both the laws of various levels of government and the rules that operate within organizations. In both cases it is often valuable to distinguish constitutions from more easily changed rules.

Organizations include the state itself and subsidiary organizations, especially the police and military, but also bureaucracy more generally. Schools and hospitals also belong here. So too do political parties, interest groups, clubs, churches, and associations, indeed any organization not primarily economic in nature.

As with the economy, so the distribution of power in society will require some sort of supportive political ideology. We need to distinguish this support of political institutions from nationalism, the support for the collective group embodied in the state, though the two may be closely linked. I have defined ideology differently from common parlance, where it is generally used to refer to attitudes toward a range of political choices. I would capture these under public opinion, or attitudes toward public policy choices, which can be disaggregated by *issue*. (Note that a general preference for honesty qualifies as part of culture, while views about the punishment to be meted out for various types of dishonesty are public opinion.)

Finally crime must be considered a political activity of a peculiar type. Activities are defined as criminal because they violate political institutions. The criminal usurps the role of the state as the only legitimate agent of physical force and/or ignores institutional protection of personal liberty and personal or collective property. Major types of crime are *crimes versus persons* (including murder, treason, and vagrancy) and *crimes against property,* which can be further disaggregated according to the explicit use of violence, or directly to the level of individual crimes.

SOCIAL STRUCTURE

I use the term "social structure" to refer to the subgroups into which a society will be divided. Gender is a ubiquitous social division; the two genders have never been treated exactly the same way (and we should remain open to the possibility of a third "indeterminate" gender). All societies are also divided by family, though both the internal structure of families (*nuclear, extended, one-parent*) and the relationships between families vary markedly. While some small societies may have no occupational differentiation, these are at present exceedingly rare; division by *occupation* is thus at least at present an almost-universal. In many societies, it makes sense to aggregate certain occupational groups into *classes.* The most attractive typology includes an upper class, professionals, small businesspeople, middle managers (the previous three categories could be subdivided into upper and lower), white collar workers, blue collar workers (the last two could be skilled or unskilled), and an underclass (see Sanderson 1995). Some would identify further subclasses, such as an intellectual subclass of the professional class. While there is scholarly debate over, for example, whether class boundaries are too blurred in the present-day United States to be meaningful units of analysis, this very observation is worthy of note. We can leave it as an empirical question for particular societies as to whether class-based analysis adds anything to occupational-based analysis.

Most modern societies are also characterized by ethnic/racial divisions. Differences by age are also important, but will be captured within the population category below. Differences by height and weight and appearance have been captured under individual differences above. A case could be made for treatment of sexual orientation here as well as in individual differences (to the extent that the gay community operates as a group).

Sociologists speak at length of the roles people are expected to play because of their membership in various groups, and of the status differences inherent in social divisions. These concerns will be reflected in our analysis of each of the social divisions listed above: how does membership in a particular subgroup affect the status and behavioral expectations of individuals? As with differences in income and power, status differentials will be justified by some sort of social ideology. (NB: sociological concern with the networks of personal relationships in which we are all embedded will be captured by causal links within the schema.)

TECHNOLOGY AND SCIENCE

Although technology and science are definitionally distinct—the former involving understanding of the world which is applied in the production of goods or services, the latter referring to theoretical knowledge—they are not only closely related but can be disaggregated in the same manner. We can most obviously disaggregate in terms of field (military technology, chemistry, and so on) and then by *individual innovation.* In explaining scientific and technological innovation, it is useful to think in terms of five distinct steps: recognizing the problem (this may be subconscious, and very rarely occurs simultaneously with recognition of a potential solution), setting the stage (gathering information, often through trial and error experimentation), the act of insight, and critical revision (in which the insight is tested and refined), followed by diffusion and/or transmission (the domestic or international spread of the technology). This latter step can be further disaggregated into two steps: *communication of an innovation,* and *decisions to adapt* (see Szostak 1991). I have considered these steps to be first- or second-level phenomena because they can be analyzed in both general and innovation-specific contexts.

HEALTH AND POPULATION

Although closely connected, these two phenomena are best disaggregated separately. As genetic determinants of health were captured earlier in the schema, health matters of interest here are nutrition and disease. Nutrition can be disaggregated in terms of the *diverse nutritional needs* of the human body. Diseases can be considered in terms of major categories such as *viral, bacterial,* and *environmental,* and these disaggregated to the level of thousands of individual diseases.

Population divides logically into three phenomena: fertility, mortality, and migration (which combine to influence a fourth, age distribution). Fertility can be considered in terms of *fecundity,* the biological capacity to reproduce, and a measure of a society's *deviation* from the biological maximum level of reproduction. Migration can be disaggregated by *distance, international versus internal,* and *temporary versus permanent* (see Hornsby and Jones 1993).

ART

Art can be divided into nonreproducible art, which includes *painting* (collage, drawing, and so on), *sculpture, architecture, prose,* and *poetry,* and reproducible art, including *theater, film, photography, music,* and *dance.* The border between reproducible and non-reproducible can be blurred (that is, the distinction is one of degree, not an absolute); the same blueprint could be used for more than one building, while individual performances of a play or dance are necessarily unique. At times, it is useful also to distinguish fine from popular art, and to speak of particular schools of art.

Table One

TABLE ONE: THE PHENOMENA

CATEGORIES	SECOND LEVEL PHENOMENA	THIRD LEVEL PHENOMENA
Culture	Languages	
	Religions	By descent? Providence, revelation, salvation, miracles, doctrine
	Values (Goals:)	Ambition, optimism, attitudes toward wealth, power, prestige, beauty, honor, recognition, love, friendship, sex, incest, marriage, time preference, physical and psychological wellbeing
	(Means:)	Honesty, ethics, righteousness, fate?, work valued intrinsically, violence, vengeance, curiosity, innovation, attitude toward nature
	(Community:)	Identity, family versus community, Openness to outsiders, trust, egalitarianism, attitude to young and old, responsibility, authoritarianism, respect for individuals
	(Everyday Norms:)	Courtesy, manners, proxemics, tidiness, cleanliness, punctuality, conversational rules, locomotion rules, tipping

CATEGORIES	SECOND LEVEL PHENOMENA	THIRD LEVEL PHENOMENA
Culture (continued)	Stories	Myths, fairy tales, legends, family sagas, fables, jokes and riddles
	Expressions of culture	Rituals, dance, song, cuisine, attire, ornamentation of buildings, games
Non-Human Environment	Soil	Soil Types (various)
	Topography	Land forms (various)
	Climate	Climate Patterns (various)
	Flora	Species (various)
	Fauna	Species (various)
	Resource Availability	Various Resources
	Water Availability	
	Natural Disasters	Flood, tornado, hurricane, earthquake, volcano
	Day and Night	
	Transport Infrastructure	Mode (various)
	Built Environments	Offices, houses, fences, etc.
	Population Density	

CATEGORIES	SECOND LEVEL PHENOMENA	THIRD LEVEL PHENOMENA
Genetic Predisposition	Abilities	Consciousness, subconsciousness, vocalization, perception (five senses), decisionmaking, toolmaking, learning, other physical attributes (locomotion, eating, etc.)
	Motivations	Food, clothing, shelter, safety, sex, betterment, aggression, altruism, fairness, identification with group
	Emotions	Love, anger, fear, jealousy, guilt, empathy, anxiety, fatigue, humor, joy, grief, disgust, aesthetic sense, emotional display
	Time Preference	
Individual Differences	(Abilities:) Physical Abilities	Speed, strength, endurance
	Physical Appearance	Height, weight, symmetry
	Energy Level	Physical, mental
	Intelligences	Musical, spatial, mathematical, verbal, kinesthetic, interpersonal
	Sexual Orientation	

CATEGORIES	SECOND LEVEL PHENOMENA	THIRD LEVEL PHENOMENA
Individual Differences (continued)	(Personality:) Sociability (Extro/introversion)	Talkative, assertive, adventurous, enthusiastic versus reserved, withdrawn
	Emotionality (Stable/moody)	Contentment, composure versus anxiety, self-pity
	Conscientiousness	Thoroughness, precision, foresight, organization, perseverance versus carelessness, disorderly, frivolous
	Affection (Selfish/agreeable)	Sympathetic, appreciative, kind, generous versus cruel, quarrelsome, faultfinding
	Intellectual Orientation (Holistic/analytical)	Openness, imagination, curiosity, sensitivity versus closemindedness
	Other dimensions?	Dominant/submissive, independant/dependant, strong/weak, future/present oriented, humor, aggression, happiness
	Disorders?	Schizophrenia, psychoticism, …?
	Schemas	View of self, others, causal relationships
	Interpersonal Relationships	Parent/child, sibling, employee/employer, romance, friendship, casual

CATEGORIES	SECOND LEVEL PHENOMENA	THIRD LEVEL PHENOMENA
Economy	Total Output	Price level, unemployment, individual goods and services
	Income Distribution	
	Economic Ideology	
	Economic Institutions	Ownership, production, exchange, trade, finance, labor relations, organizations
Politics	Political Institutions	Decisionmaking systems, rules, organizations
	Political Ideology	
	Nationalism	
	Public Opinion	Issues (various)
	Crime	Versus Persons/Property
Social Structure	Gender	
	Family Types, Kinship	Nuclear, extended, single parent
	Classes (various typologies)	Occupations (various)
	Ethnic/racial Divisions	
	Social Ideology	

CATEGORIES	SECOND LEVEL PHENOMENA	THIRD LEVEL PHENOMENA
Technology and Science	Fields (various)	Innovations (various)
	Recognizing the Problem	
	Setting the Stage	
	Act of Insight	
	Critical Revision	
	Diffusion/transmission	Communication, adoption
Health	Nutrition	Diverse nutritional needs
	Disease	Viral, bacterial, environmental
Population	Fertility	Fecundity, deviation from maximum
	Mortality	Causes of death (various)
	Migration	Distance, international?, temporary?
	Age Distribution	
Art	Non-reproducible	Painting, sculpture, architecture, prose, poetry
	Reproducible	Theater, film, photography, music, dance

Notes

Chapter 1. The Big Picture

1. Some philosophers argue that the reasons people use to justify acts are logically distinct from causes; both would count as influences in my schema. Braybrooke (1987) identifies three types of inquiry in human science: a "naturalistic" search for causal regularities which apes the natural sciences, an "interpretive" look at what makes certain acts appropriate or what they signify, and a "critical" analysis of such questions as "whose interests do certain rules serve?" While practitioners tend to view these approaches as in opposition, Braybrooke establishes that they are complementary, and that all three use causal statements.

2. I should stress that hierarchy here refers to levels of abstraction rather than any sort of value judgment. Phenomena at one level are disaggregated into (lower-level) phenomena, which together comprise the original phenomenon. Each phenomenon fits in only one place in the schema, though it will be causally related to other phenomena. I do not claim that the *only* way to organize phenomena is hierarchically, but rather that those who have wrestled with the issue have recognized that this is in fact the way that phenomena are "organized" in the real world.

3. I have noted that our ten highest-level phenomena or categories are only rarely the subject of causal analysis. Lower in the hierarchy, causal links exist between phenomena at varying levels of aggregation. We must keep in mind that affecting a lower-level phenomenon must imply affecting those phenomena of which it is a component.

4. It is thus common for interdisciplinary scholars to make a plea for question-oriented research (Klein 1990, 188). Scholars who start first with a question will be more likely to recognize that a variety of theories and methods can illuminate it. One can think of our causal links as questions to be answered.

5. The word *phenomena* has been given precise and conflicting definitions by philosophers over the years. For Husserl, it referred to the essence of things, or "things in themselves," which we with our limited sensual apparatus could only approach understanding of. Conversely, philosophers both before and after him have used the word to refer instead to our sensory perceptions of things. In this book, I will attempt to define our phenomena as precisely as possible, but recognize that our understanding is everywhere imperfect; our use of the word *phenomena* is thus distinct from either of these philosophical usages.

6. As society becomes more complex, we may become aware of new phenomena that deserve a place in our schema. Note, though, that logically our schema is designed so that it encompasses societies at all yet-realized levels of complexity. While most of the examples used in this paper are modern, the schema was designed with an eye to earlier societies.

7. Elster (1989, 3) notes that it is more fundamental to explain facts (that is, realizations in terms of particular phenomena) in terms of (facts and) events than the reverse.

8. Further, we can conceive of what Barber (1993) calls changes in type versus changes within type. Another element of culture is standards of personal attire. One type of such standard is modern western fashion, wherein we expect styles to change from year to year. If this type were to give way to a more traditional and relatively unchanging standard of attire, we could speak of a change in type. Changes in type will be our predominant focus. However, we could also think of changes within type: there are inevitably yearly changes in styles of clothing for both men and women. The particular form these take are of much less interest to the human scientist, though they may still be at least in part causally related to changing artistic tastes or gender roles or a host of other phenomena.

9. Ironically, the schema outlined here, while highlighting the artificial nature of the boundaries between the social sciences, serves to highlight the potential advantage of area studies (and history) departments. These can, for example, show how differences between Chinese and American culture are related to political, economic, social, and artistic differences, among others.

10. Bulick (1982, 162) describes how the Library of Congress classification system, having taken disciplinary self-definitions as its starting point, has been seriously distorted as disciplinary boundaries have shifted.

11. The author, though, should confess his preferences up front, in case biases have crept unbidden into the work. A strong believer in economic growth, he is also skeptical of ideology, preferring openminded discussion and pragmatic solutions to individual problems. While he values cultural diversity, he nevertheless believes that people are people, and worries that we place too many barriers between groups of people. He believes in both personal and social responsibility and thus disagrees with ideologues of both right and left on many points. He is wary of the human tendency to abuse power of all types. While cognizant that all innovations hurt some people, he remains confident that technological advance is a predominantly beneficial process. He believes that art is a central part of human existence.

12. In Szostak (2002), I show how the schema, in conjunction with a recognition that there are five broad types of ethical "theory," can be used to organize ethical analysis, and to identify an "ethical core" of phenomenon-based statements for which there is wide ethical consensus.

13. All phenomena belong in only one place in the schema. Occasionally, as with love, the same word appears twice. The emotion of love is nevertheless a distinct phenomenon from social attitudes toward love.

14. Kant, in his own nineteenth-century efforts to categorize the world of experience, suggested that some categories were so intrinsically obvious as to be inherent (hardwired) in our brains, while others required scientific verification.

15. What if disease X provides immunity from disease Y, and thus decreases mortality? Sosa and Tooley (1993) wonder if it makes sense to speak of disease X causing a decreased risk of death. I would argue here that the problem is not with (definitions of) stochastic causation, but with misspecified causal links. Disease X, like any disease, has a direct positive effect on mortality. It also has an indirect negative effect through Y. While decisions about how hard to fight X will require evaluation of both links, they are nevertheless distinct. Note that while some definitions of stochastic causation only allow for causation when probabilities are increased, it also makes sense to speak of X reducing the probability of Y.

16. While some have shied away from a focus on causation due to a belief that it detracts from the exercise of free will, Hutcheon (1996) notes that a better understanding of causal relations will improve our ability to have the impact we desire on the world. I would stress that behavior is jointly determined by our personalities and external circumstances. The fact that we try to comprehend how personality affects behavior does not at all detract from the ability of any individual to exercise their best judgment in order to achieve their goals.

Nor do our attempts to comprehend personality as influenced by both genes and environment interfere with free will, especially as our understanding is necessarily incomplete.

17. While our focus is on causal links among phenomena, we cannot ignore whatever internal dynamics may exist within certain phenomena. Note, though, that whatever forces for change *may* be inherent in a phenomenon, the course of change will nevertheless be shaped by interactions with other phenomena.

18. Shweder and Fiske (1986) note that generalizations in human science tend to apply only to particular historical circumstances. Some have suggested that we are achieving ever greater generalizations. Alternatively, Rosenberg has suggested that social science is impossible, and Geertz has argued that we should focus on the particular rather than the general. I would respond that recognizing the complexity of human experience should not cause us to give up hope of increasing our understanding.

19. Kuhn (1974) defines "system" more loosely as any set of one or more causal links "regular enough to deserve attention." He then goes on to define several different types of systems. As noted before, in studying any causal link we are concerned primarily with identifying general patterns rather than explaining individual occurrences. Still, while Kuhn (1974) focuses on static relationships, our schema is flexible enough to capture the dynamics of societal change. In this context, note that even if we were able to detect a Parsonian subsystem defined by weak links to other phenomena, in the long run these weak links will still have a large cumulative effect (see Hodgson 1993, 242–50).

20. Bhaskar's tendency to use the word "structures" or "systems" as a synonym for his "things" implies the existence of relatively autonomous social subsystems. To avoid such an implication I have used the term "phenomena." Yet this seems to be only a semantic difference: Bhaskar is merely emphasizing that scientific investigation occurs at many levels, and that the phenomena we investigate will turn out to have subcomponents which need analysis in their own right. Thus, to understand why any phenomenon changes in a particular way, we need to understand its composition as well as its causal links with other phenomena.

21. A minority of deconstructionists argue that the problem of ambiguity is so severe that an attempt such as ours to increase understanding is doomed. "Most philosophers and critics would be quite willing to admit that slippage of meaning occurs (poetry works on just such a principle), but would draw the line at saying that *nothing but* slippage occurs: it is hard to see how, if that were the case, we could even communicate such a state of affairs." (Sim 1992, 109).

22. Carlisle (1998) often stresses that any phenomenon is "simultaneously a number of things." In a key example, she notes that "Thomas Jefferson was a philosopher, politician, farmer, landholder, architect, slave holder, writer, husband, and father—and he was all of these at once. Scholarship, however, has needed to divide him into separate parts." Note first that Jefferson would not be a "phenomenon" in our schema, but a collection of personality characteristics, which we could attempt to comprehend in terms of his political, cultural, and family environment. Second, it is only by disaggregating and then synthesizing across links that we can hope to understand a complex event, process, or individual. Third, we should appreciate that different causal links can have quite different qualitative as well as quantitative importance.

23. Cornwell and Stoddard (1998) note that we do not suggest that only white males should teach Milton. They argue that we should both appreciate the complexity of individuals (we are more than members of a group) and the advantages of learning from members of other groups. We should want to hear all voices. In chapter 4, I will argue that individuals should move beyond stereotypes to an appreciation of the uniqueness of other individuals.

24. Science can be thought of as an evolutionary process, involving variation and selection. Our schema will enhance variation by limiting the loss of certain discoveries, and enhance selection by juxtaposing diverse sorts of information.

25. And there are many different types of instrumental interdisciplinarity: topically focused, professional preparation, life experience focused (e.g., ethnic studies), shared components, crosscutting organizational principles, hybrids, and syntheses (Ray Miller, in Klein 1996, 34).

26. To be sure, while we may accept or critique disciplines, we must understand them (Klein 1996, 212), at least until we achieve greater synthesis. There is, however, a danger of interdisciplinarians coming to revel too much in disciplinary distinctions. Rather than searching for synthesis, they stress how students are stretched by exposure to incompatible world views. The Association of Integrative Studies, in its guide on syllabus preparation, stresses efforts at integration; yet its May 1997 newsletter suggests that most inter-disciplinarians may secretly appreciate the strength of the boundaries between disciplines, for it makes their struggle heroic. They thus come to see the value of interdisciplinary studies in pointing out disciplinary disagreements, rather than trying to see how scholarly understanding fits together. Their very focus on disciplinary differences may blind them to the arbitrary nature of modern disciplines, their limitations, and their biases.

27. The problem affects the K-12 system as well as college education. Brady (1989) surveys an eloquent and critical literature: "It is a well known scandal that our educational system is geared more to categorizing and analyzing patches of knowledge than to thread-ing them together" (Harlan Cleveland); "We have lost sight of our responsibility for synthesizing learning" (Robert Stevens); "To dump on students the task of finding coherence in their education is indefensible" (Ernest Boyer). He concludes: "If all knowl-edge is related, then any curriculum in which the major elements are not related is not a good curriculum."

28. By reducing student frustration, the schema might help encourage their joy in learning. And some of the less studied causal links would present great opportunities for student assignments and presentations. The schema should also help students pursue con-tinuous learning after graduation. In my ongoing research, I argue that, in addition to the overview of phenomena that the schema can provide, students should also be exposed to a broad overview of the dozen or so distinct methods used by scientists, the handful of different types of theory, and the five types of ethical analysis. These elements too can be readily integrated into existing curricula.

29. Indeed, perhaps very little of what is said will entirely escape revision. Much of the task of science is to place caveats on previous knowledge. Even our schema itself will not survive without some changes. I echo the sentiments of Robert Musill: "I am convinced not only that what I say is wrong, but that what will be said against it will be wrong as well. Nevertheless, a beginning must be made" (in Samuels 1993). Still, I am confident that the basic structure as outlined here will survive.

30. Elster (1989) notes that rational choice analysis will be indeterminate if an individ-ual identifies equally good actions, is unable to compare options (perhaps because they cannot estimate the likely implications of, say, going to law school, or they cannot foresee how others would react to their choice), or has no way of establishing how much informa-tion it is worth collecting. Individuals may flip a coin or mislead themselves into thinking that they did have a rational basis for choosing. Elster identifies three types of irrationality: acting on impulse, wishful thinking which generates misguided beliefs (though some bias toward optimism may be beneficial), and "irrational desires" (such as only caring for the present).

31. Lemonnier (1992, 100) reaffirms the primacy of society: those who speak of individ-ual decisions altering cultures neglect the fact that all individuals are socially embedded. His statement can be broken into a recognition that causation does work in both directions, and an assumption that one direction is dominant. Sampson (1993, ch. 11), following Bakhtin, makes a similar point about how our personalities are shaped by our relationships

with others, and thus it is silly to speak of autonomous individuals. Just because X influences Y does not, however, necessarily mean that Y does not influence X. Sampson decries the fact that scientists often design theories which have no place for their own behavior; one must wonder if he views himself as just a social construct.

32. We thus largely concur with Mann: "It is a basic tenet of my work that societies are not systems. There is no ultimately determining structure to our entire social experience— at least, none that we, situated in its midst, can discern" (1986, 736). Elsewhere (1986, 10) he speaks of a "mess" of continuous interactions of various forces. Conversely, Barber feels that interdisciplinary research would be greatly enhanced by a "systematic model of the various functional subsystems important for each discipline" (1993, 380).

33. Wrong (1994) feels that the central question in sociology is what keeps people together in society given the human tendency toward conflict. Most analysts focus on one explanation: coercion for Machiavelli and Hobbes, self-interest for Locke and Marx, consensus on values and norms for Durkheim and Parsons. He is critical of this unnecessary focus on one causal factor, the tendency of theorists to use the same explanation for why individuals cooperate locally and why groups or even nations cooperate, and of the tendency to ignore change. No society is either perfectly orderly or disorderly; rather than viewing change as evidence of the breakdown of social understanding it should be recognized as a natural state of affairs.

34. Nevertheless, Otto Neurath, in conjunction with Rudolph Carnap and others, attempted an "Encyclopaedia of Unified Science" in the 1930s, in despair of the dangers of overspecialization. When 19 of some 260 proposed contributions were assembled in *Foundations of the Unity of Science* (University of Chicago Press, 1970), Neurath noted on the first page that, "The classification of sciences may be interesting in itself and sometimes also stimulating; but the premature drawing of boundary lines does not help us much in research work, not even in arranging its results, as long as we are not able to combine the classification of simple items with the presentation of interrelations between them." Logical positivists and general systems theorists also attempted syntheses early in this century, as most disciplines were just becoming established, with high hopes of dovetailing disciplines so that advance in one would mean advance in the others.

35. Tooby and Cosmides (1992) are horrified by the lack of consistency in human science. They hypothesize that in part this situation reflects the distaste many felt about the implications of Darwinian theory for the place of humanity in the universe; human scientists thus decided their efforts need not be consistent with those of natural scientists, and thus with each other.

36. Bechtel (1986, 22) discusses how disciplinary ethnocentrism exacerbates this problem. Disciplines "decide" that central questions are more important than peripheral areas close to other disciplines. Graduate training, leading journals, and so on emphasize these central topics. At the same time, the necessity of competing for resources within universities encourages a negative attitude toward other disciplines. Interdisciplinary work must inevitably be viewed as shallow by the real disciplines. Following a similar logic, Klein (1990, 138) concludes that the "organization of research along disciplinary lines will continue to stand in the way of interdisciplinary research."

CHAPTER 2. PHILOSOPHY OF SCIENCE

1. Thomas Kuhn showed that new theories are usually accepted for a long time on the basis of equivocal evidence, while more compelling evidence is accumulated. Previously, it was commonly believed that new theories were established by some crucial experiment.

2. Simplicity, elegance, compatability with other beliefs and/or theories, comprehensiveness, and creation of further research possibilities are among the criteria referred to. We should note that at least some of these criteria have nothing to do with whether one theory is a closer approximation to reality than another.

3. If science disappears, philosophy is threatened. "If there is no canonical grid of concepts in terms of which the world is best divided up and classified, then the traditional role of philosophy as the discipline that analyses such concepts is also thrown into doubt" (Skinner 1985).

4. Barber (1993) uses the "strong" program in the sociology of knowledge, which denied the existence of an external reality, except as socially constructed, as an example of misplaced absolutism in theory. Historians were instructed to ignore the truth or falsity of a particular hypothesis when studying why scientists adopted it.

5. Scholars of persuasion have developed four models of successful persuasion. One relies on rationality, the belief that good ideas will sell themselves. The second focuses on social interaction, recognizing that opinion leaders—those respected in the community— and skilled rhetoricians will be most successful. The third holds that ideas which solve pressing problems will naturally spread. The final model is political, and notes that those in power can force others to change their views. All four models can be applied to science.

6. Deconstruction is an extreme form of hermeneutics. As Hey (1985) notes, hermeneutics need not be at odds with a belief in science, but sometimes is. While hermeneutics emphasizes that understanding need not always lead to knowledge, it need not insist that it can never do so. See also Lanham (1993).

7. Note though that Foucault has criticized Derrida for focusing on the text rather than the social context in which it was written.

8. Chalmers (1982, 166) disagrees with Feyerabend, and asserts that there are ways of judging whether an enterprise is suitably scientific: "We can attempt to criticize any area of knowledge by criticizing its aims, by criticizing the appropriateness of the methods used for attaining those aims, by confronting it with an alternative and superior means of attaining the aims, and so on." Note, though, that Chalmers avoids use of the word "science" here.

9. Elster (1989, 6–7) accepts that explanation should involve laws, but nevertheless urges scientists to focus on individual causal mechanisms and try to define these ever more precisely.

10. Abbott (2001, x) discusses the incentives away from openmindedness in academia: "An eclectic is always losing arguments. One lacks the closemindedness necessary to treat others' positions with the contempt they so easily display for one's own . . . And I have never managed that happy disregard of whole areas of intellectual life . . . that so simplifies the lives of some of my colleagues." I too have chosen the eclectic approach in life.

11. "He who knows only his own side of the case knows little of that. His reasons may be good, and no one may have been able to refute them. But if he is equally unable to refute the reasons on the opposite side, if he does not so much as know what they are, he has no ground for preferring either opinion. The rational position for him is suspension of judgment, and unless he contents himself with that, he is either led by authority or adopts, like the generality of the world, the side to which he feels most inclination. Nor is it enough that he should hear the arguments of adversaries from his own teachers, presented as they state them, and accompanied by what they offer as refutations. That is not the way to do justice to the arguments or bring them into real contact with his own mind. He must be able to hear them from persons who actually believe them, who defend them in earnest and do their very utmost for them. He must know them in their most plausible and persuasive form; he must feel the whole force of the difficulty which the true view of the subject has to encounter and dispose of, else he will never really possess himself of the portion of truth which meets and removes that difficulty. Ninety-nine in a hundred of what are called

educated men are in this condition, even of those who can argue fluently for their opinions." (John Stuart Mill, *On Liberty,* 35).

12. "It is quite natural that we should adopt a defensive and negative attitude towards every new opinion concerning something on which we already have an opinion of our own. For it forces its way as an enemy into the previously closed system of our own convictions, shatters the calm of mind we have attained through this system, demands renewed efforts of us and declares our former efforts to have been in vain." (Schopenhauer 1851, quoted in McCloskey 1996, 52)

13. This point was made by Richard Feynman, a Nobel laureate in physics: "But there is one feature . . . that is generally missing in . . . [pseudo-science.] It's a kind of scientific integrity, a principle of scientific thought that corresponds to a kind of utter honesty—a kind of leaning over backwards. For example, if you are doing an experiment, you should report everything that you think might make it invalid—not only what you think is right about it." (1985, 311).

14. Experiments might seem superior, but in human science especially experimental results can be critiqued on many grounds. Shweder and Fiske (1986), for example, note that small changes in experimental design are often observed to have a large impact on outcome (even in natural science). Expectations of scientists, paid subjects, and laboratory settings all affect results. This raises the question of whether experiments reliably duplicate real world conditions. In Szostak (1999), I have pointed out the damage to economics that has resulted from exclusive reliance on statistical analysis.

15. This problem is exacerbated by the fact that human scientists are often driven to explain particular events. Since each event is unique it will inevitably be the result of a unique confluence of causal factors. It will thus be inherently difficult to achieve consensus on causes. Note that natural scientists also have trouble with particular events: predicting earthquakes for example. Yet while we can learn much from the analysis of particular events the focus of science must remain on generalizations—the discovery of causal relations that apply over a well-defined range of circumstances. And since such generalizations can contain stochastic elements (X will likely cause Y), human idiosyncrasy need not be the barrier to science it at first appears.

16. One reaction is to search for and celebrate past achievements of woman scientists. As Hutcheon (1996) notes, though, these were inevitably a minority due to societal restrictions. A more productive path is to encourage increased female (and minority) participation in science, while continuing to subject received theory to real world tests.

17. McDonald (1993) is thus very skeptical of social reformers who embrace a postmodern rejection of science. She notes that earlier generations of reformers (and especially feminists) tended to value research. She stresses the value of empirical research, noting that exposing our theories to real world data is a powerful means of exposing and surmounting our biases. This does not prevent her from recognizing problems with existing scientific practice: the lack of openmindedness, focus on petty questions, and lack of historical perspective, which we have had cause to criticize, not only slow the advance of science but encourage bias.

18. Woolgar (1988) takes the self-admittedly extreme view that external objects do not exist prior to our representation of them. Such a perspective would likely be hostile to our idea of enduring phenomena. Woolgar extends his "logic of inversion" to various cultural phenomena, arguing in particular that norms do not cause behavior but are merely a means for after-the-fact evaluation of behavior. He would view as epistemologically misguided the varied research I will discuss below which suggests that norms (and rules and logic) do indeed influence behavior. But his argument fails if we allow the existence of an external reality.

19. A. C. Crombie developed a list of six "styles of reasoning" employed in science:

postulation and deduction (as in mathematics), experimental exploration, models by analogy, ordering of variety by comparison and taxonomy, statistical analysis, and historic
derivation (of genetic development). Each has advantages and disadvantages. What scientists believe depends on their style of reasoning. Individual disciplines privilege one or two
styles and thus lose the potential benefits of synthesizing diverse styles (Hacking 1990).

20. Clyde Kluckhorn compared disciplinary boundaries to walls between gardens: "But
just because some students of man have believed in the reality of these walls, some of the
most precious flowers in the gardens have failed to bear fruit. Moreover, some rich lands
were never fenced in because ownership was in dispute. . . . Hence, between and beyond
the boundaries of the several social sciences there is a vast no man's land" (in Brady 1989,
92).

21. Mowery and Rosenberg (1989) have shown how greatly the advance of natural
science has depended on technological experimentation. Many scientific theories were a
direct response to questions raised by those actively involved in industry. Human science
can benefit in the same way from exposure to the difficulties of public policy.

22. "While knowledge is organized by discipline, it is seldom applied that way in the
solution of practical problems. Such solutions tend to require perspectives that draw on
more than one discipline. . . . In preparing people for the solution of practical problems,
therefore, universities face the conundrum of how to provide a broad education with an
appreciation of interdisciplinary approaches when the material to be presented is organized
and taught within disciplinary boundaries" (Smith 1991, 69).

23. Pepper (1942) draws an important distinction between data and what he calls
"danda." Say we hypothesize that a certain chair is durable. We could gather data by having
a range of people sit on it. Or, we could examine the chair's construction in light of our
theory of what makes a chair strong. Both sorts of evidence are valuable. Note that data will
often be ignored if they disagree with theory (e.g., observations of ghosts, UFOs).

Chapter 3. Culture Unpacked

1. Haack (1998, ch.8) bemoans the fact that the word "multicultural," which is prominent in both curricular and public policy debates, has many meanings, some of which are
contradictory. Some of these definitions she views as "good" and others as "bad." She notes
that a large part of the problem stems from the existence of many definitions of "culture."

2. Malinowski felt that a theory of culture had to begin with "the organic needs of
man": food, reproduction, safety, comfort, movement, and so on. These necessitated institutions to deal with such matters as the economy, social control, education, and politics
(Brown 1991, 67).

3. Fukuyama (1995, 34) suggests a residualist approach. He argues that culture should
be distinguished from rational decisionmaking, thus encompassing goals and means pursued from habit rather than calculation. While the role of habit deserves emphasis, we will
find it better to distinguish culture in terms of function.

4. A further overlap occurs here. As we shall see, one of the purposes of art is to
transport the audience to another world. This may serve as a cathartic experience, allowing
individuals to—in their minds—temporarily flout the norms of their society.

5. Barber (1993) suggests that "ideology," "doctrine," and "belief," as well as "myth,"
"legend," and "fable" can all be viewed as synonyms. This is a sad commentary on the
casual usage of terminology in human science. Within my schema, the latter terms are
easily differentiated from the former by the degree of aesthetic input. The most tedious
philosophical tract may still have some aesthetic appeal, but this is not as important as in a
myth or legend.

6. "Axial Age" scholars speak of stages of religious development (e.g., primitive,
archaic, historical, early modern, and modern), and emphasize how the development of

universal religions changed the course of world history. These "stages" could in turn be defined in terms of the religious elements I enumerate below.

7. Billington (1997) reviews a handful of detailed definitions. He is critical of those who define religion so broadly that many nonreligious organizations such as political parties (which also have rituals, myths, and so on) would qualify. He recognizes that we must focus on metaphysical questions concerning god or an afterlife (this justifies our treating ethical codes above under "values"). We cannot, though, make "belief in god" a criterion, for some religions such as Theravada Buddhism are arguably atheistic. It is the questions asked rather than the answers given that identify a religion.

8. Many religions have demons that serve the role of capricious gods. These can also serve to frighten people into believing. Semi-divine angels are also fairly common. Note that angels and demons serve to blur the boundary between monotheism and polytheism.

9. Durham (1991, 9) also quotes Geertz favorably: "culture is best seen not as complexes of concrete behaviour patterns—customs, usages, traditions, habit clusters—. . . but as a set of control mechanisms." While this might seem at first glance a plea for a holistic approach, it is rather a directive to not, as many ethnographers have, focus on the most readily observed cultural elements while neglecting values that guide behavior across a range of situations.

10. Tooby and Cosmides (1992) feel that the combination of cultural dynamism and porous boundaries between most cultural groups renders it silly to speak of homogenous cultures. They feel it is thus best to view humanity as a single interacting population than as a collection of diverse groups. Delisle (1993), critiquing Quebec nationalist thought, writes: "What is a nation? It is an abstract idea. For me, there are groups of humans, changing, constantly in transformation, but whose characteristics nationalists wish to conceal". Gillowy (1993) concurs that in the modern world borders between communities are especially fuzzy; one cannot say "this group believes this" and thus it is best to think of a discourse of values within and between communities.

11. Earlier in this century, while European anthropologists embraced functional/ structural analysis, American anthropologists developed "enormous" trait lists and charted various societies on these; "one suspects this type of inquiry declined through sheer boredom" (Lewellen 1992, 11). Without first identifying both a comprehensive but manageable list of cultural characteristics, and identifying how societies could differ with respect to these, such painstaking empirical work could lead nowhere.

12. Potter and Wetherell (1987) worry that it is tautological to define groups by shared "schemas" that are products of group interaction. One might, I suppose, define groups according to some measure of internal versus external interaction. Yet we would only care about this to the extent that different groups were characterized by different world views. They also worry about the fact that cultural boundaries as presently constructed are themselves an (cultural) opinion resulting from interaction. I share this concern.

13. Given these characteristics, discourse analysis can tell us little about the genetic or psychological causes and effects of culture. It can, however, potentially allow empirical analysis of links between culture and the social, political, and economic realms (see Namenwirth and Weber 1987, for example). Finally, it can be used to identify cultural effects on individuals, such as their emotional expression (White 1993).

14. Fraser and Gaskell (1990) suggest that we use the term "widespread beliefs" to describe such attitudes, for it does not possess the cultural baggage of terms such as values. One advantage would be that it signals the fact that such values can change.

15. Indeed, ethnographers have seemed willing to speak of how economic changes might have negative impacts on a culture, but not positive effects. If all cultures are equal, though, one cannot have it both ways. The same argument can be made with respect to the alleged negative effects of importing cultural values from other groups: the resulting cultural melange should be as valid as its predecessor. Looking at how culture affects the

economy, Fukuyama (1995, 43) notes: "It is fashionable to shy away from value judgments when comparing different cultures, but from an economic standpoint, some ethical habits clearly constitute virtues while others are vices."

16. Gross and Rayser (1985, ix) have noted that no matter how scrupulously an ethnographer avoids making judgments, such study must necessarily be comparative. We only know what to make of an observation if we can compare the group under study to other cultures, including our own. While in terms of some characteristics we need make no value judgments (there is no better or worse, just different), this is not always the case.

17. Merton emphasizes the distinction between the manifest and latent functions of a cultural practice. Those that endure despite appearing ineffective (rain dance) or unethical to outsiders likely serve more than one function. It is difficult to purposefully change these.

18. Generational transmission still leads to change. The psychologist Eric Ericson felt that the younger generation tended to make overt what was covert in their parents' generation. That is, they would take rules and norms which their parents repressed, and express them (see Appleby 1994).

19. It was commonplace mere decades ago to view traditional cultures as inherently static. The United States government thus tried to record native songs and dances as mementoes of a dying culture. Now, the emphasis has changed from preservation to conservation, and the government attempts to document the dynamics of cultural change (Hufford 1994).

20. Boyd and Richerson and Cavalli-Sforza both attach considerable importance to the use of force as a factor in cultural transformation, while Durham emphasizes the role of conscious individual decision-making. They also disagree on how likely cultural evolution is to work against genetic fitness. They all, however, recognize the potential for great cultural variability due to the fact that we can attempt to guide cultural evolution. While the three books do list many similar potential sources of cultural change, mathematical models alone cannot tell us which are most important.

21. Of any cultural attitude or behavior we can ask several questions: who? when? where? with what purpose? object? result? (a point stressed in the HRAF guidelines). Gradual change could occur in terms of any of these. In Lumsden and Wilson's (1981) concept of "culturgens" (similar to Durham's memes) we find a sense of completely independent units of culture. In later formulations, though, it is recognized that "cultural traits" or "memes" can blend together (Barkow 1989, 289). Thus we should feel comfortable with a level of analysis which focuses on clearly identifiable phenomena (while always aware, of course, that further unpacking may yield additional insight).

22. Culture can even affect communication by creating misunderstanding. For example, Apache children were raised to believe that silence is a virtue, and Navajo children that they should only speak on subjects they had mastery of. They were often judged to be stupid by white teachers as a result. Scholarly research can help us overcome such misunderstandings.

23. We must be careful not to confuse observed behavior with culture. Some cultural traits may only be evoked in certain circumstances (e.g., competitiveness in the marketplace). Cultures may be more similar than they appear against a background of economic, political, and other differences. Convergence in these other areas will create the appearance of cultural convergence. Dogan and Pelassy (1990) note that some scholars see differences in behavior and (tautologically) infer differences in culture with which to explain them.

24. Hunter-gatherers may have different values in part because they are viewed as outcasts by neighboring farming communities, and naturally respond with opposing values. Likewise, medieval European Jews may have reacted to the anti-merchant values of their neighbors. Dominant groups, too, can identify themselves by exaggerating their differences with weaker neighbors (Gellner 1989, 37).

25. He devotes most of his book to a quantitative analysis of language distribution. Only recently has the long-standing trend of increased linguistic diversity been reversed. He notes that only a couple hundred languages have books (other than the Bible) or magazines regularly published in them. Like many, he argues that languages should be preserved, but recognizes that he cannot point to any intrinsic qualities of languages as justification. Jahr (1993) feels we should not speak of the death of a language but rather language suicide, and should respect a group's decision that maintaining a separate language imposes more costs than benefits.

26. One possible exception arises if we include alphabet systems within our definition of languages. The complex Chinese alphabet has aesthetic advantages, but arguably is harder to teach, and certainly harder to mechanize (book printing, computer keyboards). This may indirectly influence various phenomena, cultural and otherwise.

27. Collins (1998) makes a number of conjectures about the relationship between Chinese language and philosophy which deserve further study: that a dearth of explicit syntax discouraged epistemology, that a lack of verb tenses encouraged temporal elision, and that multiple meanings of the same word encouraged poetic expression. He notes, though, that as philosophy develops it creates its own vocabulary (and the Greek language once suffered from making no distinction between "similar" and "identical").

28. One possibility raised by Gellner is that myths or rituals may come to be viewed primarily as an expression of cultural identity. Thus someone who objects to a particular element will be castigated for disloyalty, even if people agree with the value expressed by the objector. Gellner stresses the tremendous staying power of cultural elements; as noted above our theory must be flexible enough to account for the fact that cultures—at least modern ones—are constantly changing.

29. Woolgar (1988) and others skeptical of the existence of an external reality would argue that we only "think" that our beliefs shape our actions, when in fact we only rely on beliefs to justify actions after the fact. But then what, if anything, does influence our behavior?

Chapter 4. The Nonhuman Environment and our Genetic Predisposition

1. Culture also influences how we "see" both the built and natural environment. Massey (1994) warns us against being too protective of the "authentic" nature of localities, for people normally remake their environment. The identity of a location is not inherent but created.

2. While there are many schools of landscape design, they all share a concern with use of space, mass, light, color, line, texture, and seasonal variation. All also recognize the tension between unity and variety, and strive for a proportional relationship between elements. One can easily discern some genetic preferences here, likely shaped by prehistoric environments conducive to survival [N→G→C→N].

3. We mentioned the eugenics movement above. It is noteworthy that this had been attacked by biologists long before it was discredited by the excesses of fascist regimes. Given the existence of recessive genes, and the fact that genes combine to shape behavior in conjunction with environmental influences, restricting or outlawing the breeding of those with an observable undesirable trait could not succeed in eradicating such a trait for hundreds of generations if at all (Gordon 1991, 522–29).

4. There is no consensus on what exactly consciousness is. Scholars of philosophy, psychology, artificial intelligence, evolutionary biology, and neuroscience debate these issues. Dennett (in various works) and Chalmers (1996) provide quite different viewpoints.

5. Rapid change is often argued for by students of the evolution of species. Dawkins (1986) devotes much of his book to arguing the reverse, drawing on the argument that large changes are unlikely to be fitness-enhancing. Arguments in favor of some periods of dramatic change include the lack of intermediate species in the fossil record, and the difficulties in explaining how a complex organism such as the human eye could have evolved. Yet only a minute proportion of living beings get fossilized, and it can be argued that gradual increments in sightedness would have enhanced fitness.

6. Just as the heart, liver, and pancreas must obey the laws of cell biology, there may be general rules that govern all mental mechanisms. Thus, those who stress the connections within the brain need not be at odds with those who stress modularity (Jackendoff 1992, 17). Moreover, theorists recognize the advantages of being able to refer to a manageably small set of mechanisms, and therefore are open to suggestions of commonalities (Fodor 1983).

7. The frontal lobes may serve a coordinating function. The left hemisphere dominates linguistic and logical functions, and the right spatial, synthesizing, and intuitive functions. Most mathematical manipulation seems centered in the left hemisphere, with geometry and even long division in the right. Miller (1991) suggests that consciousness itself (requiring logic and language) is largely a left brain function. He emphasizes, though, that the two hemispheres need to cooperate, and discusses the problems faced by epileptics who have the connections between the two hemispheres severed. Much childhood trauma may reflect hemispheral conflict as when the left hemisphere hears a maternal compliment but the right sees a maternal scowl; the lingual left cannot comprehend the surge of negative emotion from the right.

8. We are still far from scholarly consensus on the role of dreams. Culturally, dreams are variously interpreted as reality, portents of the future, or signs of cures (if acted out). Some scholars view them as an extension of waking thoughts, others as a response to internal stimuli while sleeping. Freud suggested that they disguised forbidden desires, and were an essential form of emotional relief; Jung countered that they were a means for subconscious desires to receive conscious attention. Questions remain: Why do we not always remember dreams? Are nightmares an entirely separate phenomenon?

9. A minority of these may be attributed to a peculiar type of mutation. Huntingdon's disease, for example, is caused when a particular part of the genetic code of a particular gene repeats itself excessively. The code is normally repeated 10 to 35 times. Excess of 40 repeats activate the disease. The number of repeats seems to increase with each generation in families of sufferers, resulting in earlier and more severe onset of symptoms. While selection works against the disease, mutation creates new sufferers.

10. It is now recognized that the effects of phenylketonuria, a genetic source of retardation, can be prevented by entirely removing phenylalanine, an amino acid, from the diet. Scientists hope to uncover environmental influences on other genetic diseases.

11. It is a common mistake to confuse linguistic divisions with ethnic divisions. Breton (1991, 25–28) shows that there is no strong correlation between existing racial and linguistic groups. This is hardly surprising, since genes and languages are transmitted so differently.

12. That we all possess similar linguistic mechanisms does not ensure that we are equally skilled, just as the fact that we have two legs does not make us equally good at soccer. Pinker (1994) and others note that the correlation of prestige with language ability provides a strong argument in favor of selection. Moreover, there is evidence that some language disabilities have a genetic component. Differences in the learning environment also affect ability.

13. The plural of schema is properly "schemata." Yet this word is often interpreted as implying a schema system. It also has a pedantic jargon-like sound. I will thus violate the dictates of my dictionary in this one case and use the much more sensible "schemas" throughout this work.

14. Note that we were likely selected to focus consciously only on matters in which learning costs were low and environmental change frequent for hunter-gatherers. If learning costs were high, and the environment stable, we might have been selected to subconsciously mimic others. We might face difficulty consciously exploring such areas today.

15. Memory is highly structured. If asked to remember a string of letters R-A-B-L-E, we will save space if we associate it with a word and a transformation. The choice we make (ABLE plus R, TABLE with a change T to R, RABBLE minus a B) will depend on the previous structure of our memory.

16. We could also speak of more precise child-rearing mechanisms. Adults tend naturally to raise their voice when speaking to infants; this accords with the fact that infants have a higher auditory threshold, and have difficulty separating voice signals from ambient noise. Repeating simple statements over and over seems to be another instinctual adult behavior which enhances infant understanding. Are mothers better equipped with these instincts?

17. Hatfield and Rapson (1993) draw on this analysis to explain the oft-observed distinction between passionate love—an intense desire to be with another, and companionate love—a less intense but more durable tenderness toward those we are close to. Many relationships start with one and progress to the other. Some individuals, however, find this transition difficult. Hatfield and Rapson hypothesize that passionate love bears a close resemblance to what a child feels, while companionate love has more in common with parental affection.

18. Not all signals are genetically determined, though those with a genetic base are more credible because they cannot be so readily imitated. The hand gestures that accompany conversation differ widely. The observation of Frank (1988, 189) that being too eager in the pursuit of love signals that there is something wrong with you, may also reflect culture rather than genes.

19. Lemerise and Dodge (1993) agree that anger is focused on others, and argue that it encourages self-defense, mastery of others, and regulation of interpersonal links. It can also, however, serve to increase interpersonal misunderstanding, lead to rejection by peer groups, and encourage heart disease. Stearns (1993) notes that it is hard physiologically to distinguish sadness from anger. They both are triggered by disappointment; one either responds with resignation or acts out (though sadness does not preclude coping with the disappointment). She also questions the universality of sadness. While most psychologists would likely agree with Izard that sadness is a separate emotion, it has been much less studied than others.

20. Rozin, Haidt, and McCauley (1993) argue that disgust emerged in animals as a reaction to unhealthy foods. They note that humans, too, are disgusted by the very thought of eating, say, cockroaches. While disgust is instinctive in animals, it has a cognitive element in humans. They suggest that it is thus elicited by reminders of our animal nature, such as sex, violence, and dead bodies.

21. One interesting characteristic of time preference is that it is nonlinear. That is, we may prefer $100 today to $110 three days from now, but would hardly choose $100 a year from now over $110 a year and three days from now. Our sense of the importance of the passage of time diminishes as we look farther into the future. This reflects our tendency to overvalue the present.

22. Yet the elderly have played an important role in human societies. They have often been venerated for their wisdom. The tendency of the old to be both powerful and conservative has arguably acted to inhibit societal change (Lenski, Lenski, and Nolan 1991). It is an open question as to whether this conservatism reflects genetic programming to pass on tradition to the young, or perhaps a subconscious desire to recapture youth.

23. Support for this view could be found in the psychological literature of behaviorism, in the Marxist assertion that human nature was molded by material conditions (Brown

1991), and by observations that infants are the same everywhere but adults quite different. However, it is inconsistent with recent developments in cognitive and developmental psychology and artificial intelligence (Tooby and Cosmides 1992). Brown feels that the fundamental assumptions of anthropology were established 1915–34: culture cannot be reduced to psychology, it is the primary determinant of human behavior, and it is largely arbitrary.

24. Hinde (1987, 155) notes that evolutionary psychologists have often gone to great lengths in developing ingenious genetic explanations for those cultural practices which appear to decrease genetic fitness. In doing so, they tend naturally to assume the result: there is no clear separation between their arguments and supporting evidence (see also Durham 1991). He recognizes that dropping the assumption that all cultural traits must enhance fitness weakens the explanatory power of genes. Barkow (1992) discusses at least four means by which culture could decrease fitness: sluggish adaptation to environmental change, good short-term versus bad long-term effects (e.g., soil erosion from over-farming), errors in transmission, and exercise of power (P→C).

25. Trigg (1985, 81) suggests that if she had not been searching for exceptions she would have realized she was being lied to: "Without the assumption of some similarities between humans, any account of their behaviour becomes speculative, and there is no standard by which it can be judged whether people are likely to be telling the truth or not."

26. Cherry (1994) suggests that we have a need for intimacy which encourages us to bond with another, a need to belong which encourages membership in family-sized groups, a need for security (groups of 20 or so), and a need for a place in the world reflected in cultural identity. Those who are not able to form such bonds will have psychological problems, be prone to antisocial behavior or membership in gangs and cults, and may use aggression to establish their place in the world [G→I].

27. Smith and Bond (1993) note similarities between Fiske's analysis and the work of other scholars. For example, Hofstede in the 1980s had suggested that one could identify four distinguishing characteristics of interpersonal relationships within large corporations (and elsewhere). His collectivism, power distance, feminine, and masculine categories bear a strong resemblance to Fiske's four categories [C→E]. There is also a strong resemblance to the grid/group analysis of Wildavsky and others which yields egalitarian, hierarchical, fatalistic, and individualistic possibilities (see Chai and Swedlow 1998).

28. Fiske also suggests that societies, like individuals, may tend to progress from the communal to authoritarian to equality to market models (successive models can be derived from the preceding with the addition of axioms). Given the fact that each model has its merits it is not clear that we should speak of progress. Fiske warns us that social scientists tend to overemphasize the market model because it is easiest to explain. Note that this sequence is at odds with the Marxist dream of a transition from a market to communal orientation.

29. Freud reacted harshly to the idea that we are programmed to avoid incest, for it seemed to contradict his hypothesis that children wished to seduce their parents. It is still possible, though, that children discovering their sexuality would fantasize, recognize such fantasies as wrong, and strive to repress them (Wilson 1998).

30. Barkow hypothesizes that media personalities may become so familiar that they trigger our "curiosity algorithm." This could explain the popularity of celebrity gossip magazines and also the value of celebrity endorsements.

31. Some have suggested that warfare in tribal society was mainly over women. Others, recognizing that the same argument should apply to all societies, suggest that wars were usually over land. More generally, Wenegrat (1990, 89) suggests that violence among men most commonly occurs when they feel they cannot achieve their ends any other way.

32. Male preferences for high cheekbones and a small distance between nose and chin in women serve no obvious fitness goal. Moreover it is noteworthy that selection has not

guided us to a distribution around some "ideal" cheekbone or nose-chin distance. As with the peacock's tail it appears that we are programmed to prefer more of one and less of the other. Makeup suppliers have implicitly recognized this fact by preparing products that allow women to exaggerate the appropriate features (Wilson 1998, 230–32).

33. Wright discusses how this flexible programming can lead to quite different results in different circumstances. Males surrounded by young women will tend to be promiscuous (and magazines and strip shows may send the wrong signals to the subconscious on this score), as will women surrounded by promiscuous men. Unattractive women may maximize their fitness by promiscuity. Wright suggests that we will likely always get a mix of behaviors in both genders since the benefits of either strategy depend on some people doing the opposite.

Chapter 5. Individual Differences

1. Miller (1991) emphasizes a distinction between self-oriented drives (e.g., power) and other-oriented (love), and notes that most people have difficulty finding an appropriate (subconscious) balance between these. While others have reached a similar conclusion, the evidence in favor of this argument is largely circumstantial.

2. Researchers in the Pavlovian tradition—mainly in Eastern Europe—have found that energy levels and capacity for work are very important sources of personality differences in animals, and are trying to extend their analysis to humans (Zuckerman 1991).

3. Messer and Warren (1990) discuss several approaches to therapy: psychoanalytic in which the goal is uncovering subconscious motives; phenomenonological, in which the therapist tries to understand and communicate what the client is feeling; cognitive, in which the focus is on changing maladaptive beliefs; and self-psychological in which through interaction with the therapist the client realizes that everyone is imperfect, needs to struggle, and needs supportive relationships in order to pursue personal development. None seem superior in general; further research is needed to see whether certain therapies work better for certain patients. All can be accused of focusing on symptoms rather than causes. Their main argument is that we need to know why certain symptoms occur together—are they the result of a single cause or does one symptom induce others?

4. Indeed, earlier versions of the APA manual had used the word "borderline" to refer to the mildest cases of a number of disorders. Symptoms of the new disorder include very deep moods (which render patients unable to sustain relationships or careers), frequent changes in goals, and an inability to learn from mistakes. While there has been a fair bit of study of this disorder, there is no consensus on causes. One suggestion is that borderline patients have mild cases of more than one type of disorder (Johnson 1994, 15).

5. Westen (1990) makes a plea for the integration of clinical analysis—the long-term interaction with one person—with academic research. He notes in particular that psychoanalysts would be well aware of the conflicting mental mechanisms at work, and that conflict and compromise are hard to observe in the laboratory.

6. Elster (1989, 13) notes that our opportunity set and desires sometimes work in concert (as when we do not want or get top-notch candidates for political office), or in opposition (as when hardship decreases our ability to revolt but increases our desire), that one can influence the other (as when we desire what we cannot have because we cannot have it), and that we may at times act to decrease our opportunity set if we dislike making choices.

7. Evidence that individual behavior (including verbal expression of disposition) is inconsistent across situations does not mean that we are not able to form reliable judgments of others' personality which allow us to predict their behavior. Such judgments are neces-

sarily stochastic (and the behavior of some people, such as those who feel powerless, is particularly hard to predict), but recent studies show that even statements of attitudes do have great—but not perfect—predictive power. Past behavior is also a very good predictor, unless the situation has changed greatly. The fact that we generally are pursuing many goals simultaneously is perhaps the key difficulty in prediction (Ajzen 1988).

8. We can more easily do so if we put barriers between different realms of analysis, even though all are interrelated (Kelly 1991). I discussed this problem with respect to interdisciplinarity in chapter 1. Just as economists can ignore evidence of nonrational behavior as out of their domain, so we can all classify new information so that it does the least damage to our schema.

9. My own casual empiricism suggests that it is too easy for people to hide behind the distinction: "I'm a wonderful person; it's just that others fail to see some of my qualities." We thus pretend to self-esteem while excusing failure. But this is a copout: we are social animals, and projecting a positive image is a key part of the game we all have to play. Eric Ericson felt that one of the important tasks of adolescence was coming to believe that the way you present yourself is what others will see. Those who fail at this task tend to display a lack of initiative and fear of intimacy (Crook 1980, 278).

10. Religious belief will generally be strengthened by such events. Some scholars suggest that the miracles observed within various religious traditions may well reflect the combined efforts of believers to respond to a crisis of faith (e.g., if a religious leader believed to be "godly" is killed by mere mortals, efforts will be made to attribute religious significance to the event). Such arguments are naturally difficult to verify.

11. In Western societies, psychologists play an important role in determining what qualifies as a disorder. Some argue that the diagnostic manual in the United States fudges cultural and psychological arguments. Note that psychologists can destroy self-esteem by telling patients that they have a psychological disorder.

12. Bem (1993) argues that in Western societies children are "taught" individualism by being weaned early, being given their own room (if possible), and constantly being asked what they want. In traditional societies, neither children nor adults have this range of choice. This encourages westerners to pursue goals that interest them rather than goals that society dictates.

13. Social psychologists spend much time looking at the escalation of aggression (sometimes to the extent of ignoring causes of the initial act). A little bit of misunderstanding can erupt into a major conflagration if each retaliation induces another. Differences in values is not essential to this process, as we all have a natural tendency to evaluate our actions more favorably than others', but will inevitably encourage misunderstanding.

14. This disagreement is largely semantic. I would call the transmission of a cultural representation an effect of culture on the individual, while Sperber would call it a person to person transmission. One powerful argument for an independent causal role for social representations is that these are often combinations of different mental representations: a shaman and audience contribute differently to a ritual, and different classes contribute to our overall perception of our society.

15. I should confess that I have always found Maslow's hierarchy compelling. Many scholars note, though, that the empirical base on which he depended was exceedingly thin. Others note that people are at least to some extent willing to trade self-actualization for goods (perhaps by taking a job that is less demanding but pays better).

16. Storr (1996) looks at several "gurus" who founded new religious movements. He argues that all were introverted and narcissistic, unsure of the affection of others. They generally faced some life crisis, from which they emerged sure that they had "the" answer. The fervent certainty with which they preached was the source of their charisma, and convinced others to convert. They needed disciples to shore up their self-esteem. They might all be classified as manic-depressive or schizophrenic, with their revelations being a

desperate attempt to make sense of the world. Their ability to attract followers assured both themselves and (some) others that this view of the world was reasonable.

CHAPTER 6. THE ECONOMY

1. These phenomena are obviously more important for modern societies. Note, though, that the observation that inflation and/or unemployment are impossible in a certain society, because it relies on barter and/or provides work for all, is itself of great importance.

2. Lenski, Lenski, and Nolan (1991) define institutions as "durable answers to important and persistent problems." Knight (1992) speaks of sets of rules which structure interaction in particular ways, with knowledge of these shared by the relevant community. He notes that rather than the distinction between institution and culture as I have drawn it, one could conceive of a continuum from state enforcement to community pressure. Laws against littering which are obeyed mostly not out of fear of getting caught would, admittedly, fall on the border between institution and culture in my schema.

3. Halperin (1994) argues that treating production, exchange, and consumption as separable activities reflects circumstances in our own society. In many societies much of economic activity is production for own use. In such a case, the institutions that govern family behavior could be seen as simultaneously dealing with production and exchange. While Halperin's goal of developing value-free categories for comparing economies is laudable, it need not prevent us from unpacking institutions to enhance our understanding. We must simply remember that a particular institution may fulfill more than one function.

4. Kuhn decries the fact that organizations are studied in isolation by several disciplines, and proposes the creation of a new discipline focused on organizations. Yet his own approach recognizes the need for both a general understanding of organizations and the analysis of particular cases (and he recognizes that at least some political organizations require separate treatment).

5. Ironically, Alfred Marshall, the turn-of-the-century economist often hailed as the founder of modern "neoclassical" economics, envisioned an ambitious program of research which would categorize societies according to institutional, cultural, political, and social circumstances (Smelser and Swedberg 1994).

6. Knight applies this bargaining approach to cultural values as well. Thus, those who prefer informal rules in order to avoid special interest influence are misguided. As we will see elsewhere (S→C) the powerful have a more than proportionate influence on values as well.

7. Rutherford (1994) notes that institutionalists within economics are not only a minority but riven by conflict. A newer group, which favors the formalism, rationality assumption, and non-interventionist approach of the economics mainstream, condemns the work of an older tradition, and vice versa. Moreover, within both groups there are disagreements over the importance of unintended consequences. Rutherford suggests that these groups could fruitfully cooperate if they recognized that there was some truth in the conjectures of their opponents.

8. Mainstream economic theory has tended to emphasize how markets will discipline the untrustworthy. More recently, scholars have outlined how "incentive compatible mechanisms" (institutions) could be constructed to ensure appropriate behavior. Critics argue that such scholars ignore the huge informational costs involved in establishing and monitoring these. The school of "Austrian economics" (a minority even in Austria) has long stressed that markets work to limit but not eliminate dishonesty.

9. He does not discuss at length how this might be accomplished. He does note a link between teacher pay and respect. It would seem that respect for business people would be tied to the incidence of philanthropy, corruption, and political interference. While Harrison

urges us to overcome our antipathy to ostentation, the perception that successful business people are flaunting their success and are uninterested in the plight of the less fortunate can hardly encourage respect.

10. Most large firms have policies to enhance the ethnic (and gender) diversity of their workforce. These go beyond legal requirements of affirmative action, and appear to reflect a desire to serve the increasingly diverse local and global market. Some suggest that worker diversity may encourage all types of innovation, but there is little evidence for this at present. Economists have begun to investigate how such policies might affect wage differentials (E→S).

11. Fukuyama (1996) argues that values influence the size of firm observed in a particular society. China, France, Italy, and South Korea are each characterized by loyalty to family over community. Large firms only emerged with state aid. Japanese and German entrepreneurs, alternatively, found it easy to draw on a sense of community in establishing large firms.

12. "It is often difficult, both empirically and theoretically, to make a clear distinction between gift exchange and trade. In most cases, the exchange is valued both because of the goods themselves and because of the social relations maintained between exchange partners" (Cashdan 1989, 43). Many people shop at their local store rather than a more distant discount store because they like the store owner and/or think it important to maintain a local operation. Many business people prefer to deal with friends and relatives. These exchanges might seem at first glance to be entirely market-driven, but are not.

13. These views affect attitudes toward material possessions as well as attitudes toward land and labor. In many tribal societies, if the builders of a boat were not using it, other group members could. Ownership was defined, that is, in large part in terms of use.

14. Georg Simmel in 1908 defined competition as a form of conflict, but not one directed at an opponent. One tries to surpass one's opponent(s) in the eyes of a third party. One thus needs to divine the latter's wishes. Exchange only occurs if one succeeds in this. H. White defended markets as in part "tangible cliques of producers watching each other. Pressure from the buyer side creates a mirror in which producers see themselves, not consumers" (in Smelser and Swedberg 1994).

15. We should not be surprised, perhaps, that some "new institutional economists" have attempted to derive models in which social values emerge as the result of rational utility maximization. Rutherford (1994) justifiably urges a broader view of value creation.

16. Berry hypothesized that farming required more cooperation than hunting-gathering, and therefore that farmers would be more conformist. He performed a number of Asch-type tests of this hypothesis, most of which confirmed it (Smith and Bond 1993).

17. Cashdan (1989) notes that the importance of sharing rules depends crucially on whether climate and mobility allow low-cost storage. Californian Indians who stored considerable amounts of fish had very little sharing. Climatic variability also influenced the strength of sharing rules, especially between groups [N→C]. Food sharing customs are commonly associated with norms favoring humility: the successful farmer or hunter is expected to deprecate their success.

CHAPTER 7. POLITICS

1. I would distinguish assemblies like the American where representatives vote with a great degree of independence from parliamentary systems in which a great degree of party discipline is opposed. I would also distinguish assemblies that operate in terms of majority vote from those in which a high degree of consensus is sought. Finally, I could wonder about the degree of logrolling that is possible: in the American Congress bills often contain

quite diverse elements; this allows legislators to trade support for a policy they do not like in return for the support of others on issues of greater importance to them.

2. Kuhn identified several questions: how are dominant coalitions formed, how do organizations establish legitimacy, how is authority exercised, and how do communications and transactions take place?

3. Dogan (1990) expands on this point. Political leaders serve both an executive function and a party leadership function, and these are best evaluated separately (they may also serve a symbolic role, which I would capture under either culture or ideology or nationalism). Likewise, political parties in one-party states serve different functions from those in multi-party states. McGlynn and Tuden (1991) note that efforts to distinguish traditional societies depending on whether they were governed by lineages, chiefs, and so on can hide more than they illuminate because chiefs vary widely in the types of power they wield.

4. As will voting preferences. Morris Janowitz has argued that political systems that perform the duty of maintaining social control well will be characterized by large political majorities. He worried that close elections and swing voters (due in turn to such factors as rapid urbanization and the blurring of class boundaries) indicated a lack of faith in the system (Burk 1991). While one can readily discern a decreased trust of politicians in most modern democracies over the last decades, one could also posit many other sources of discontent than loose party affiliation (which could be taken as a positive sign of open political discourse and of a closing of the differences between political parties). In any case, few go so far in their concern for political practice as to wish to do away with the democratic system itself.

5. Fukuyama (1996, 351) argues that democracy depends on a sense of community rooted in shared traditions. Smith (1993) notes that collectivist cultures tend to be hierarchical, and expect their leader to lead in all ways, while individualistic cultures expect leaders to perform certain roles.

6. Turner (1994) discusses nineteenth-century concerns that democracy depended on a range of cultural attitudes which had developed over a period of centuries. Chai and Swedlow (1998) discuss the possiblity that democracy requires the correct balance between a 'participatory' and 'deferential' orientation.

7. Tamir is in fact quite concerned with the fact that very few of the world's ethnic groups could hope to form a homogenous nation-state. He is thus hopeful of identifying some combination of power-sharing between levels of government and respect for minorities that would allow them to feel secure without the necessity of their own state.

8. The same concerns arise when we consider the international role of religion. The Catholic Church which organized the Crusades now preaches world peace. Similar contradictions can be found in other world religions. Some feel that the future course of religion will be ecumenical, involving an appreciation of the similarities rather than differences between religions. If so, the peaceful side of religion will likely triumph.

9. In the important case of ancient Greece, however, a religion with human-like gods with no claim to a higher morality encouraged rational analysis both of how to design a state and how to live a good life (Finer 1997).

10. Interaction between societies at different levels of development often affects religious beliefs. When traditional societies face external conquest, a common reaction is religious transformation. They may stress traditional ways, or try to integrate their religion with that of the conqueror, or develop a new religion (e.g., cargo cults), which make some sense of the other society, or simply try to encourage new religious practices. These diverse reactions all serve to strengthen identity and change societal values (a similar role is played by religious cults for those who feel marginalized within modern societies) (Lewellen 1992).

11. Morris Janowitz worried that the tendency of political commentary to focus on personalities rather than issues must weaken support for democracy. He felt that the only antidote was increased political involvement: people need to recognize that democracy involves increased responsibility along with increased rights. If community-based groups could be given enough power to feel part of the system, faith in the system would naturally increase (in Burk 1991).

12. Nationalism has many overlapping characteristics: politically it is associated with self-determination, culturally with the nation as the primary source of belonging, and ethically as a justification for violence (Ignatieff 1994; he notes that none of these are obvious results). The combination can yield intense conflict between 'nations'.

13. One gaping hole in international law is how best to determine national boundaries. Even between or within democratic states there are no set rules on how to vote for border changes. Even when plebiscites are held in an area—as was often done in the aftermath of World War One—the decision takes on an odd sense of finality. Why should the same people not have the same right to change their mind years later? (Kedourie 1993). Shehadi (1993) suggests that disputes about borders should be referred to international arbitration rather than as at present decided by force. Perhaps in this way we might develop a set of principles to guide us in drawing borders.

14. The emphasis on linguistic unity is interesting in light of our previous discussion of the role of language in culture (C→C3). We would be skeptical that learning a new language transformed the average Breton into French overnight; rather the common language encouraged the spread of common (often Parisian in origin) values and customs, while maintaining a barrier to German, Italian, or Spanish ideas. If the French government had waited, its opportunity may have been lost: in the late nineteenth century linguistic groups were much more protective of local languages (Mann 1986, Hobsbawm 1990).

15. Kedourie notes that a minority of scholars reject the idea that nationalism spread from Western Europe to the rest of the world. They tend to view it as a characteristic of most world societies for centuries (see Hooson 1994). The problem here may largely be semantic: a confusion between nationalism as we have defined it and ethnic-tribal loyalties which we have recognized as ubiquitous.

16. Note, though, that in liberal democracies in which personal rights are supposed to take precedence over group rights, many find minority group protection offensive. Affirmative action plans and Indian Affairs bureaucracies have come under fire in both the United States and Canada for this reason.

17. Breton (1991) surveys the efforts of states to encourage a national language. While governments have always had a language of operation, it is only in recent centuries that they have cared what language people spoke in their home. Still, only 75 languages (30 European, 40 Asian, and 5 African) have the official recognition of some state. Efforts to codify a national language are still in their early stages in many less-developed countries.

18. Milner would answer yes, arguing that scientists are necessarily influenced by the dominant values in society. While I would accept an ideological bias toward belief in the system as a whole, it is less clear that intellectuals need be biased against reform.

19. One likely effect is on attitudes to violence. States that commonly use and rationalize the use of violence against minorities and dissidents are likely to encourage individuals in society to see violence as a legitimate means to achieve their ends (though they will likely be fearful of using violence against the state itself).

20. I think this distinction the most important, for it captures critical differences in both the motivation for and effects of crime. Of course, this distinction may be blurred in some cases. For some societies, other distinctions, such as religious versus nonreligious crime *may* be of greater importance. If this were true for many societies, we would wish to adjust the schema.

CHAPTER 8. SOCIAL STRUCTURE

1. I discuss the causal links between elements of social structure and phenomena in other categories in Szostak (2001).

2. This is a broader definition of the family than would be countenanced by those who preach "family values." Single parents and their children, and homosexual couples who feel themselves to be so, qualify as families. Divorced and remarried couples, sharing custody of children from previous marriages, pose a trickier question of where one family stops and another begins—the best answer may involve overlapping families.

3. It is noteworthy in this regard that short people and obese people appear just as likely to discriminate on the basis of height and weight as the general population. While gender or ethnic or class groupings will sometimes absorb others' sense of their inferiority, it is rare that such groups would behave so harshly toward in-group members.

4. This accords with Blau's (1992) definition of social divisions as any distinction that has an effect on one's network of contacts (he also appreciates the importance of self-recognition of differences). Note, though, that this definition implies that we should widen our definition of groups to include variables such as education which clearly influence networks. Note also that I have striven to avoid defining phenomena in terms of the causal links that emanate from them, for this smacks of tautological reasoning.

5. Genes likely play some role here. Girls tend to prefer intimate face-to-face play, while boys emphasize motor skill development (Golombok and Fivush 1984, ch. 7).

6. Feminist scholars thus often speak of "the other." The term has been borrowed by scholars of class and ethnic division as well. They aim to point out that white upper/middle class males are taken as the norm by Western societies, with all other groups being inferior by omission (Sampson 1993).

7. Nasaw (1993) discusses how the exclusion of blacks from amusement parks and vaudeville shows early in the century, as well as the negative portrayal of blacks that occurred therein, served to integrate white Americans of diverse backgrounds while segregating blacks.

8. How are particular stereotypes formed? Observation plays a role: if all the blacks I see are performing manual labor it is an easy step to belief in intellectual inferiority, and if the Jews I meet are businesspeople I can easily identify the group with greed. While it used to be thought that all stereotypes had some roots in experience, it is now recognized that stereotypes may simply reflect what one group finds it useful to think about another (Hamilton 1994). One possibility here is projection: Delisle (1993) argues that Quebec intellectuals attacked Jewish solidarity because of their frustration with the lack of French-Canadian solidarity. As with other key schemas, children often form racial stereotypes before entering school.

9. Empirical inquiries with a short-term focus may thus miss the possibility of minority influence. Mugny and Perez rely primarily on experimental evidence. They emphasize that it is the basic principles of minority views, rather than their potential political implications, which are communicated.

10. Despite the mobility of the American people the geographic distribution of religions has proven remarkably stable (Park 1994). Religious beliefs are reinforced by regular interaction with others who share the same beliefs. Some regions thus become hotbeds of religious fervor while others display greater diversity. History (especially of persecution), urbanization, and socioeconomic variables are important influences on regional religious behavior. Geography and a sense of identity are important barriers to external religious influences.

11. Minorities of a nonethnic nature may also indicate their dissatisfaction with mainstream society by pursuing alternative religions and/or values. Kephart and Zellner note that such 'cults' are not just a recent phenomenon. Nineteenth-century America witnessed

some 60 large-scale communal experiments—all espousing a quite different set of values. The Shakers, who preached celibacy, the Mormons, who favored polygamy, and the Oneida colonists, who developed a complex intermarriage system, are among the groups they discuss.

12. Batson, Schoenrade, and Ventes (1993, ch. 2) examine the effects of gender, race, class, education, and urbanization on religious beliefs.

13. When does a dialect become so different that it should be considered a separate language? Measures of ease of cross-group communication could potentially be used. In practice, political circumstances are crucial. Portuguese bears greater similarity to Spanish than does Mandarin to Cantonese, but the Chinese government is adamant that the latter two are Chinese dialects.

14. Sociolinguists focus on group differences rather than individual. There has thus been very limited scholarly explanation of how the manner in which we speak affects our lives as individuals. Yet language is the key means by which we communicate to others who we are. We do know that our changing voice sends clear signals of our age. A tendency to vagueness may cause others to think us deceitful, a monotone voice can encourage boredom, and hesitant speech may create the impression of thoughtfulness—but such links have scarcely been explored (Chambers, 1995) [C→I].

CHAPTER 9. TECHNOLOGY AND SCIENCE

1. It was common mere decades ago to think that scientific advances generally preceded technological advances. While such a sequence of events certainly happens—advances in both physics and chemistry necessarily preceded the development of nuclear power plants, for example—it is now widely recognized that reverse causation may be of even greater importance. Scientific discoveries are increasingly dependent on sophisticated tools and instruments. More centrally, much technical innovation occurs far from the scientific frontier and relies heavily on trial and error experimentation; yet the problems and successes of technical innovators throw up questions which often drive scientific research.

2. While postwar technological determinists have tended to emphasize the negative consequences of technological advance—pollution, nuclear threat, and so on—there has long been a popular strain of technological determinism in the United States that has equated innovation with progress (see Smith 1994, esp. ch. 2).

3. In terms of the conflict approach outlined in Bijker and Law (1992) a further cause of unforeseen consequences is that no individual knows how others—competitors, government regulators, environmental activists etc.—are going to act.

4. "It is my conviction that all innovations, minor or major, result from a cross-fertilization (i.e., synergetic) process in which hints from consumers, from the same or other technologies, or, occasionally, from science, are utilized to develop new concepts" (Klein 1988, 98–99). He attributes the success of a company like 3-M to the purposeful interaction of researchers pursuing various product lines, and praises Japanese companies for frequently shifting workers and managers between jobs.

5. Some economists have such faith in the ability of free markets to encourage the development of ever-better technologies that they doubt the necessity of an evolutionary approach. Like positivist philosophers, they are confident that technology steadily approaches some ideal state. Given that technological advance occurs in small steps, however, a path not followed may never get a chance to prove itself. If the same amount of time and effort had been devoted to electric cars as has been the case with internal combustion perhaps they would by now be far superior to existing automobiles.

6. Watson-Verran and Turnbull (1995) condemn the long-standing tendency to contrast rational and primitive ways of understanding the world. Rather, they argue that these should be compared as "knowledge systems."

7. Arguably, Herrnstein and Murray's (1994) conjecture of racial differences in intelligence violated cultural taboos. This may have had the effect of giving the work an exaggerated sense of novelty. I have argued in the first two chapters for the open-minded exploration of all questions.

8. I discuss this relationship at some length in Szostak (2002). Gellner (1989) argues that the rise of universal religions depended on a coherent set of concepts wherein each statement had one specific meaning. Complex dogma, such as the combination of free will and special role for clergy, required complex rational argumentation. In this way, these religions paved the way for the emergence of modern science millennia later.

9. Any meaningful analysis of progress would require a disaggregated approach, looking at whether we can speak of improvement in terms of various of our phenomena. In ongoing research associated with Szostak (2002), I have evaluated "progress" in terms of more than one hundred phenomema, and across three time periods, and found a diverse experience of progress and regress. While writers as diverse as Karl Marx and Ayres (1978) have treated technology as the sole source of progress, my schema suggests that other factors, including the blood and sweat of men and women dedicated to human betterment, also have a role to play.

10. Adams (1993) argues for the importance of religion. Yet he recognizes that religious beliefs should not contradict scientific understanding. When there are areas of disagreement, he recommends leaning more heavily on the empirical evidence of science. He traces how the Judeo-Christian tradition has changed in response to various scientific discoveries. On a broader scale, I should note that enhanced understanding of climate, volcanoes, and earthquakes lessen the temptation to view these as the acts of gods or spirits (Trigg 1985).

11. Evolutionary theory, to be sure, provides to many a plausible explanation of how our complex world could have come to be without the hand of god. Yet believers can point to the anomalies within the evolutionary explanation: complex organs that seem not prone to gradual evolution, or the absence in the fossil record of intermediate species. Or, they can embrace evolutionary theory and argue that god set it all in motion (just as early astronomers felt that god had set the planets in motion).

CHAPTER 10. HEALTH AND POPULATION

1. In Cuba, medical training includes elements of sociology, philosophy, communications, and even music, as well as nutrition and physiology. Doctors treat not just families but entire neighborhoods.

2. Needless to say, words such as "health," "disease," and "illness" are difficult to define with precision. The word "disease" generally refers to ailments defined by the medical establishment, while "illness" refers to the sense we have that we or others are unwell. A lengthy list of diseases (though with no organizing principle) can be found in the *International Classification of Diseases* (Ann Arbor: Commission on Professional and Hospital Activities), which is regularly updated.

3. Plane and Rogerson (1994) note that the alarmism of 1970s texts on the subject of population growth has largely—but not entirely—dissipated as birth rates have fallen. They note that small changes in birth rates can have a huge impact: if every fertile woman had just 2 children the species would become extinct, but if they had 3 children we would see growth rates much faster than today. Hornsby and Jones (1993) devote a chapter to the difficulties in making population projections.

Chapter 11. Art

1. An article in the 4 Dec. 1998 *Chronicle of Higher Education,* "Wearying of Cultural Studies, Some Scholars Rediscover Beauty," notes that scholars shunned the aesthetic just a few years ago, viewing as elitist the idea of universal tastes that could be cultivated. There is now an increased recognition of aesthetic considerations, though only a small minority of research reflects this.

2. Dickie (1992) surveys a number of failed attempts to define art (as imitation, expression of emotion, and so on), and concludes that a work of art is best defined as an artifact created to be presented to an artworld public. The definition is similar to my own in terms of leaving the identification of art to the audience. His attempt to delimit an "acceptable" audience is, he recognizes, subject to the criticism that this cannot be objectively identified. I would also doubt that art must be intentional.

3. Blau (1993) is hostile to the idea of masterpieces or a canon, and claims that the distinction between high art and popular art is artificial. Yet in reading her work, I sensed that she was most concerned with emphasizing that the work of women and nonwhites has been underappreciated due to social bias. One can recognize this fact without asserting that masterpieces do not exist.

4. Literature is often treated separately from the other arts. "Although the tradition of distinguishing between verbal and nonverbal arts is difficult to sustain, the literary arts are in practice rarely included in the arts curriculum" (Harris 1997). Harris notes not only the basic similarities between literature and other arts, but the fact that text is critical to theatre, film, some music, and even some visual arts.

5. I could also distinguish art by medium: visual, verbal, auditory, or mixed. Scholars of art often focus on particular "styles"—impressionist, cubist, abstract expressionist—where these styles are viewed as cutting across art forms. All of these are legitimate categories of analysis for different purposes.

6. Humanists have often shied away from explicit discussion of causal links, though their attempts to understand the influence of (characteristics of) particular times and places on particular artworks inevitably involved causal arguments. There has been a tendency for the art history discipline to become fragmented as the scope of research has broadened. Students of different links tend to employ different methods (Prezioni 1993). I briefly discuss the links between art and phenomena in all other categories in Szostak (2000c).

7. One key focus of the anthropology of art today is to describe how changes in the art of traditional society come about. It is recognized that such changes may emanate from the artistic community alone—as in Western societies some artistic experiments will be praised and built upon—or they may instead reflect changes in the wider society. Such societal changes may be cultural, social, political, economic, or technological in nature.

8. Lemonnier (1992) notes that the headbands designed by !Kung women sometimes express ethnic identity and other times are more individualistic. While recognizing throughout his book that both cultural and aesthetic forces are at work, he at times seems to suggest that particular works might express only one or the other.

9. As cross-cultural contact has increased, some artists purposely appeal across cultural boundaries. This can most clearly be seen amongst traditional artists catering to tourists: their art often combines indigenous and foreign elements (Layton 1991). This has led to a decrease in quality of much "exotic" art, but may lead to a new synthesis. Perhaps artists will find themselves expressing aesthetic universals to a greater extent?

10. Scholars must also be careful not to become so focused on the cultural that they ignore the aesthetic. This seems to be the case with Kuspit (1993), who feels that art must reflect "nowness" and implies that art only has value to the extent that it expresses the time and place that we live in. The acceptance of stylistic diversity in the postmodern era offends

him because he believes that every epoch should have its style. He believes that the art critic must be prepared to love certain works but abandon them when their time has passed.

11. Duncan (1993) argues that eighteenth-century French artists pushed the emerging middle-class view of conjugal love, joy of parenthood, and the dangers of adultery in arranged marriages. This encouraged the aristocracy to adopt these views.

CHAPTER 12. CONCLUDING REMARKS

1. Unfortunately, the pressure to publish within academia, combined with the arrogance that is selected for among academics, takes scholars away from messy reality with its loose ends and instead encourages them to play with excessively tidy theories (Getman 1992).

2. Singlemindedness is often hailed as a key to success in life. Yet few would doubt that this can be taken to extremes: neither the truly inflexible nor the perpetually indecisive are likely to succeed. It is important to strike a balance: one must be open to new information, but yet treat one's existing schemas with confidence in the meantime.

3. This seems to be the line of argument taken by Holmes (1993). He is adamant that certain core elements of "liberalism" should be unquestioned. The key element seems to be a respect for individual rights. While adamant in defense of these values, Holmes is quite willing to recognize that many elements of liberal belief systems are historical inheritances inappropriate to modern conditions.

4. "We are drowning in information, while starving for wisdom. The world henceforth will be run by synthesizers, people able to put together the right information at the right time, think critically about it, and make important choices wisely" (Wilson 1998, 269).

5. One solution to a conflict between reason and emotion is to search for further empirical verification. Pilot projects are too little used by policy makers, but can allow some measurement of the diverse effects of a particular policy before it is inflicted on everybody.

6. Ratcliff (1997) notes that the ideal curriculum varies by student. There is thus scope for different institutions to offer different curricula. Ratcliff recognizes, though, that all students learn more from an organized sequence of courses, and that all students benefit from opportunities to synthesize material from different courses. Our suggested curriculum does both.

7. Rothman (1996) describes a central electronic database of the near future that would allow scholars and others to readily access published information in electronic form on any subject. Such a database can easily seem overwhelming. As Freeman (1996) recognizes, most discussions of electronic publishing focus on the natural sciences where information is more easily categorized. In human science categorization is a real problem. Our schema could provide a roadmap to human science material.

8. See also Messer-Davidow, Shumway, and Sylvan 1993. Papers in the first section discuss the evolution of particular disciplines, those in the second section show how the ongoing efforts of disciplines to define boundaries have not yielded timeless or logical divisions, and those in the fourth section describe the socialization of students to a particular disciplinary world view via exams and paper grading, and of scientists via peer review. The Gulbenkian Commission (*Open the Social Sciences,* 1996) suggested three radical innovations to reduce departmental autonomy: require all professors to have joint appointments, require 25% of department members to have advanced degrees in other disciplines, and require graduate students to take courses in other disciplines; it may be easier to eradicate disciplines than introduce such changes.

9. Much research explores issues that are only important if we believe in a particular grand theory. Rule (1997) urges researchers to ask themselves whether their analysis would still be useful after the inevitable recognition that their preferred theory is not universal.

10. One can even dream of a brilliant tomorrow where journal editors and reviewers, focused clearly on the questions at hand, rise above their theoretical and methodological biases to judge work by the standard of whether it helps answer important questions or not. Klein (1990) has worried that "interdisciplines," the new combinations which emerge at disciplinary borders, may over time develop the bad habits of disciplines. This need not be the case if a question-orientation is maintained and if a more coordinated human science became suffused with the ideals of theoretical and methodological flexibility.

11. In Szostak (2002), I argue that there are five broad types of ethical theory, apply these to hundreds of phenomena, and identify an "ethical core" of phenomenon-based statements for which all five types of theory provide strong support. In related work, I also evaluate whether we have seen progress in terms of hundreds of phenomena.

12. I am also partial to requiring that all students perform some volunteer work in the community, but will not pursue that tangent here. A final possibility is some sort of Great Books program. My preferred option here would be to allow students to choose from a long and flexible list of "great books" (perhaps being required to choose books from several categories). They would then be required to write a paper and/or face an oral exam focused on how the great book in question illuminates particular causal links. Perhaps of even greater importance, they should be required to show the limitations of each great book selected (or how different great books reach different conclusions about important issues). Students might be expected to apply techniques of textual interpretation as well. As Denby (1996) discovered, different students find different meanings in the same book.

13. A Carnegie Foundation survey found that 40% of graduate students were dissatisfied with their training; this suggests that modifications to graduate programs would be popular. One barrier is that students trained in an interdisciplinary manner may have difficulty finding jobs in universities organized by discipline; non-academic jobs and the growth of interdisciplinary programs must overcome this barrier.

14. "The call is to compare and contrast throughout academic programs and to infuse the undergraduate curriculum broadly with multiculturalism" (Garcia and Ratcliff 1997). Hendershott and Wright (1997) cite recent studies showing that an appreciation of social divisions requires integration across the social sciences and humanities. Musil (1997) recognizes that we must understand how social groups interact with politics, institutions, culture, and personal identity; she thus hopes for "a developmental model" that would allow students to integrate material from various courses as well as personal experience; she also urges us to recognize both similarities and differences between groups. Olguin and Schmitz (1997) concur that we must integrate social analysis with law, politics, art, and so on, and urge students to contribute personal experience to class discussions.

15. As Wilson (1998, 184–85) notes, there is at present an inherent conflict between anthropologists who study the common genetic inheritance of humanity, and cultural anthropologists who deny that such genetic universals exist (or at least are important).

16. "Anthropology has always been a case-based and place-oriented science that aims to produce ethnographic and archaeological data primarily, and comparative treatments only secondarily" (Halperin 1994, 232).

17. Political scientists in Canada have devoted considerable attention to the question of whether cultural differences between Canada and other countries are responsible for political differences. This is a popular pursuit in other countries as well. Success in this endeavor naturally depends on unpacking both culture and politics.

18. Calhoun argues that sociology as a discipline survives because funding agencies, hiring committees, and so on operate in terms of disciplines. Textbook authors are required by publishers to pretend to a false unity, when in fact sociology cannot be distinguished by theory, focus, or method.

19. Some would claim for "feminist theory" the status of a new methodology. If so, then it deserves exposure to all students, just as other methods.

20. "Historians cannot comprehend all the variables bombarding a single event. Human beings participate in a dense circuitry of interacting systems, from those that regulate their bodily functions to the ones that undergird their intellectual curiosity and emotional responses. A full explanation of an event would have to take into consideration the full range of systematic reactions. Not ever doing that, history-writing implicitly begins by concentrating on those aspects of an event deemed most relevant to the inquiry" (Appleby, Hunt, and Jacob 1994, 253). I would be more optimistic, while recognizing that naturally the most attention will be lavished on the links deemed most important.

21. The Gulbenkian Commission (*Open the Social Sciences,* 1996) questioned the value of separate history departments. They are certainly right to bemoan an artificial distinction between present and past, and to urge the study of particular causal links in various times and places. Scholars in other disciplines should indeed be free to apply their theories to the past as well as the present. However, the value of the holistic examination of particular times, places, and events would be lost without scholars focused on history.

Bibliography

Abbott, Andrew. 1994. "History and Sociology: The Lost Synthesis." In *Engaging the Past: The Uses of History Across the Social Sciences,* edited by Eric H. Monkkonen. Durham, NC: Duke University Press.

———. 2001. *Chaos of Disciplines.* Chicago: University of Chicago Press.

Adams, E. M. 1993. *Religion and Cultural Freedom.* Philadelphia: Temple University Press.

Agar, Michael H. 1981. "Ethnography as an Interdisciplinary Campground." In *Cognition, Social Behavior, and the Environment,* edited by John H. Harvey. Hillsdale, NJ: Lawrence Erlbaum.

Ahrne, Goran. 1994. *Social Organizations.* London: Sage.

Ajzen, Icek. 1988. *Attitudes, Personality, and Behavior.* Milton Keynes: Open University Press.

Amabile, Teresa M. 1996. *Creativity in Context.* Boulder CO: Westview Press.

Appleby, Joyce, Lynn Hunt, and Margeret Jacob. 1994. *Telling the Truth about History.* New York: Norton.

Apter, Michael J. 1992. *The Dangerous Edge: The Psychology of Excitement.* New York: Free Press.

Averill, James R., and Thomas A. More. 1993. "Happiness." In *Handbook of Emotions,* edited by Michael Lewis and Jeanette Haviland. New York: Guilford Press.

Ayres, Clarence. 1978. Reprint. *The Theory of Economic Progress.* Kalamazoo: New Issues Press. Original edition, 1944.

Barber, Bernard. 1993. *Constructing the Social System.* New Brunswick, NJ: Transaction Publishers.

Barkow, Jerome H. 1989. *Darwin, Sex, and Status.* Toronto: University of Toronto Press.

———. 1992. "Beneath New Culture is Old Psychology: Gossip and Social Structure." In *The Adapted Mind,* edited by Jerome H. Barkow, Leda Cosmides, and John Tooby. Oxford: Oxford University Press.

Barth, F. 1987. *Cosmologies in the Making.* Cambridge: Cambridge University Press.

Basalla, George. 1988. *The Evolution of Technology.* Cambridge: Cambridge University Press.

Batson, C. Daniel, Patricia Schoenrade, and W. Larry Ventes. 1993. *Religion and the Individual.* New York: Oxford University Press.

Bayart, Jean-François. 1999. *The Criminalization of the State in Africa.* Bloomington: University of Indiana Press.

Bechtel, William, 1986. *Science and Philosophy: Integrating Scientific Disciplines.* Dordrecht: Martinus Nijhoff.

Beckwith, Guy V. 1999. "The Lure of Novelty and the Disappearance of the Public Intellectual." *Issues in Integrative Studies,* 5–20.

Bem, Sandra Lipsitz. 1993. *The Lenses of Gender.* New Haven: Yale University Press.

Berger, Bennett M. 1995. *An Essay on Culture*. Berkeley: University of California Press.

Bethlehem, Douglas W. 1990. "Attitudes, Social Attitudes, and Widespread Beliefs." In *The Social Psychological Study of Widespread Beliefs*, edited by Colin Fraser and George Gaskell. Oxford: Clarendon.

Bicchieri, Christina. 1993. *Rationality and Coordination*. Cambridge: Cambridge University Press.

Bijker, Wiebe E. 1995. "Sociohistorical Technology Studies." In *Handbook of Science and Technology Studies*, edited by Sheila Jasanoff, Gerald E. Markle, James C. Peterson, and Trevor Pinch. New York: Sage.

Bijker, Wiebe E., and John Law, eds. 1992. *Shaping Technology/Building Society*. Cambridge, MA: MIT Press.

Billington, Ray. 1997. *Understanding Eastern Philosophy*. London: Routledge.

Blau, Judith R. 1993. *Social Contracts and Economic Markets*. New York: Plenum Press.

Blau, Peter M. 1992. *Structural Contexts of Opportunities*. Chicago: University of Chicago Press.

Books, John W., and Charles L. Prysby. 1991. *Political Behavior and the Local Context*. New York: Praeger.

Boon, James. 1985. "Claude Levi-Strauss." In *The Return of Grand Theory in the Human Sciences*, edited by Quentin Skinner. New York: Cambridge University Press.

Booth, William James, Patrick James, and Hudson Meadwell, eds. 1993. *Politics and Rationality*. Cambridge: Cambridge University Press.

Boyd, Robert, and Peter J. Richerson. 1985 *Culture and the Evolutionary Process*. Chicago: University of Chicago Press.

Boyer, Patrick. 1990. *Tradition as Truth and Communication*. Cambridge: Cambridge University Press.

Braddon-Mitchell, David, and Frank Jackson. 1996. *The Philosophy of Mind and Cognition*. Oxford: Blackwell.

Brady, Marion. 1989. *What's Worth Teaching? Selecting, Organizing and Integrating Knowledge*. Albany: SUNY Press.

Braudel, Fernand. 1979. *Civilization and Capitalism*. New York: Harper and Row.

Braybrooke, David. 1987. *Philosophy of Social Science*. Englewood Cliffs, NJ: Prentice-Hall.

Breton, Roland J-L. 1991. *Geolinguistics: Language Dynamics and Ethnolinguistic Geography*. Ottawa: University of Ottawa Press (translated from French).

Brezis, Elise S., and Peter Temin, eds. 1999. *Elites, Minorities, and Economic Growth*. Amsterdam: Elsevier.

Brody, Leslie R., and Judith A. Hall. 1993. "Gender and Emotion." In *Handbook of Emotions*, edited by Michael Lewis and Jeanette Haviland. New York: Guilford Press.

Brown, Donald F. 1991. *Human Universals*. Philadelphia: Temple University Press.

Brown, Lawrence B., 1994. *Religion, Personality, and Mental Health*. New York: Springer-Verlag.

Brown, Michael E. 1993. "Causes and Implications of Ethnic Conflict." In *Ethnic Conflict and International Security*, edited by M. Brown. Princeton, NJ: Princeton University Press.

Bruton, Henry J. 1997. *On the Search for Wellbeing*. Ann Arbor: University of Michigan Press.

Bulick, Stephen. 1982. *Structure and Subject Interaction*. New York: Marcel Dekker.

Burk, James [Morris Janowitz]. 1991. *On Social Organization and Social Control*. Chicago: University of Chicago Press.

Buss, David. 1992. "Mate Preference Mechanisms." In *The Adapted Mind*, edited by Jerome H. Barkow, Leda Cosmides, and John Tooby. Oxford: Oxford University Press.

Byrne, Richard W., and Andrew Whiten, eds. 1988. *Machiavellian Intelligence: Social Expertise in the Evolution of Intelligence in Monkeys, Apes, and Humans*. Oxford: Clarendon.

Calhoun, Craig 1992. "Sociology, Other Disciplines, and the Project of a General Understanding of Social Life." In *Sociology and its Publics*, edited by Terence C. Halliday and Morris Janowitz. Chicago: University of Chicago Press.

Cantor, Nancy, and Sabrina Zerkel. 1990. "Personality, Cognition, and Purposive Behavior." In *Handbook of Personality Theory and Research*, edited by Lawrence A. Pervin. New York: Guilford Press.

Carlisle, Barbara. 1998. "Music and Life." In *Essays in Interdisciplinarity*, edited by Bill Newell. New York: College Board.

Cashdan, Elizabeth. 1989. "Hunters and Gatherers: Economic Behavior in Bands." In *Economic Anthropology*, edited by Stuart Plattner. Palo Alto: Stanford University Press.

Cavalli-Sforza, L.L. 1981. *Cultural Transmission and Evolution: A Quantitative Approach*. Princeton, NJ: Princeton University Press.

Caws, Peter. 1993. *Yorick's World: Science and the Knowing Subject*. Berkeley: University of California Press.

Chabal, Patrick, and Jean-Pascal Daloz. 1999. *Africa Works: Disorder as Political Instrument*. Bloomington: University of Indiana Press.

Chai, Sun-Ki, and Brenda Swedlow. (1998). *Aaron Wildavsky: Culture and Social Theory*. New Brunswick, NJ: Transactions Publishers.

Chalmers, A.F. 1982. *What is This Thing Called Science?* 2nd ed. Milton Keynes: Open University Press.

Chalmers, David. 1996. *The Conscious Mind: In Search of a Fundamental Theory*. Oxford: Oxford University Press.

Chambers, J.K. 1995. *Sociolinguistic Theory*. Oxford: Blackwell.

Cherry, Andrew L., Jr. 1994. *The Socializing Instincts*. Westport, CT: Praeger.

Chisholm, Michael, and David M. Smith. 1990. *Shared Space, Divided Space: Essays on Conflict and Territorial Organization*. London: Unwin Hyman.

Cloke, Paul, Chris Philo, and David Sadler. 1991. *Approaching Human Geography*. London: Paul Chapman Publishers Ltd.

Coleman, James. 1990. *Foundations of Social Theory*. Cambridge, MA: Harvard University Press.

Collins, Randall. 1998. *The Sociology of Philosophies: A Global Theory of Intellectual Change*. Cambridge: Belknap (Harvard University) Press.

Coote, Jeremy, and Anthony Shelton, eds. 1992. *Anthropology, Art, and Aesthetics*. Oxford: Clarendon Press.

Cornwell, Grant H., and Eve W. Stoddard. 1998. "Things Fall Together: A Critique of Multicultural Curricular Reform." In *Essays in Interdisciplinarity*, edited by Bill Newell. New York: College Board.

Croft, William. 1990. *Typology and Universals*. Cambridge, United Kingdom: Cambridge University Press.

Cromer, Alan. 1997. *Connected Knowledge: Science, Philosophy, and Education*. New York: Oxford University Press.

Crompton, Rosemary. 1993. *Class and Stratification*. Cambridge, United Kingdom: Polity.

Cronbach, Lee J. 1986. "Social Inquiry By and For Earthlings." In *Metatheory in Social Science*, edited by Donald W. Fiske and Richard A. Shweder. Chicago: University of Chicago Press.

Crook, John. 1980. *The Evolution of Human Consciousness*. Oxford: Clarendon Press.

Cross, Gary. 1993. *Time and Money: The Making of Consumer Culture*. London: Routledge.

Cross, Gary, and Rick Szostak. 1995. *Technology and American Society: A History*. Englewood Cliffs, NJ: Prentice-Hall.

D'Andrade, Roy. 1986. "Three Scientific World Views and the Covering Law Model." In *Metatheory in Social Science,* edited by Donald W. Fiske and Richard A. Shweder. Chicago: University of Chicago Press.

Daniel, Norman. 1978. *The Cultural Barrier.* Edinburgh: Edinburgh University Press.

Daugherty, Helen G., and Kenneth C. W. Kammeyer. 1995. *An Introduction to Population.* 2nd ed. New York: The Guilford Press.

Davis, James R. 1995. *Interdisciplinary Courses and Team Teaching.* Phoenix: American Council on Education/Oryx.

Davis, Nannette J., and Clarice Stasz. 1990. *Social Control of Deviance: A Critical Perspective.* New York: McGraw-Hill.

Dawkins, Richard. 1986. *The Blind Watchmaker.* New York: Norton.

Delisle, Esther. 1993. *The Traitor and the Jew.* Montreal: Robert Davies Publishing.

Denby, David. 1996. *Great Books.* New York: Simon and Schuster.

Dennett, David C. 1981. *Brainstorms: Philosophical Essays on Mind and Psychology.* Cambridge, MA: MIT Press.

De Swaan, Abram. 1990. *The Management of Normality.* London: Routledge.

Devine, Patricia, David L. Hamilton, and Thomas M. Ostrom. 1994. *Social Cognition: Impact on Social Psychology.* San Diego: Academic Press.

Diamond, Jared. 1997. *Guns, Germs, and Steel: The Fates of Human Societies.* New York: Norton.

Dickie, George. 1992. "Definition of Art." In *A Companion to Aesthetics,* edited by David E. Cooper. Oxford: Blackwell.

DiMaggio, Paul. 1994. "Culture and Economy." In *The Handbook of Economic Sociology,* edited by Neil Smelser and Richard Swedberg. Princeton, NJ: Princeton University Press.

Dogan, Mattei, and Dominique Pelassy. 1990. *How to Compare Nations.* 2nd ed. Chatham, NJ: Chatham House Publishers.

Dosi, Giovanni, et al., eds. 1988. *Technical Change and Economic Theory.* London: Pinter.

Dunbar, Robin, Chris Knight, and Camilla Power, eds. 1999. *The Evolution of Culture.* New Brunswick, NJ: Rutgers University Press.

Duncan, Carol. 1993. *The Aesthetics of Power.* Cambridge: Cambridge University Press.

Durham, William. 1991. *Co-Evolution: Genes, Culture, and Human Diversity.* Palo Alto: Stanford University Press.

Eggertson, Thrainn. 1990. *Economic Behavior and Institutions.* Cambridge: Cambridge University Press.

Egnal, Marc. 1996. *Divergent Paths: How Culture and Institutions Have Shaped North American Growth.* New York: Oxford University Press.

Eichner, Alfred S. 1983. *Why Economics is Not Yet a Science.* Armonk, NY: M. E. Sharpe.

Eide, Erling. 1994. *Economics of Crime: Deterrence and the Rational Offender.* Amsterdam: North-Holland.

Elster, Jon. 1983. *Explaining Technical Change.* Cambridge: Cambridge University Press.

———. 1989. *Nuts and Bolts For the Social Sciences.* Cambridge: Cambridge University Press.

———. 1993. *Political Psychology.* Cambridge: Cambridge University Press.

Ember, Carol R., and Melvin E. Ember. 1988. *Guide to Cross-Cultural Research Using the HRAF Archive.* New Haven: Human Relations Area Files Inc.

Epstein, Seymour. 1990. "Cognitive-Experiential Self-Theory." In *Handbook of Personality Theory and Research,* edited by Lawrence A. Pervin. New York: Guilford Press.

Etzioni, Amitai. 1988. *The Moral Dimension: Toward a New Economics.* New York: Free Press.

Eysenck, Hans J. 1990. "Biological Dimensions of Personality." In *Handbook of Personality Theory and Research,* edited by Lawrence A. Pervin. New York: Guilford Press.

Farmer, James. 1997. "Using Technology." In *Handbook of the Undergraduate Curriculum,* edited by Jerry G. Gaff, James L. Ratcliff, and Associates. San Francisco: Jossey-Bass.

Fellman, Jerome, Arthur Getis, and Judith Getis. 1990. *Human Geography: Landscapes of Human Activities.* Dubuque, IA: William C. Brown.

Feynman, Richard P. 1985. *"Surely You're Joking, Mr. Feynman": Adventures of a Curious Character.* New York: Norton.

Figueroa, Esther. 1994. *Sociolinguistic Metatheory.* Oxford: Pergamon.

Fine, Ben, Michael Heasman, and Judith Wright. 1996. *Consumption in the Age of Affluence: The World of Food.* London: Routledge.

Finer, S. E. 1997. *The History of Government From the Earliest Times.* Oxford: Oxford University Press.

Fiske, Alan. 1991. *Structures of Social Life.* New York: Free Press.

Fiske, Donald W. 1986. "Specificity of Method and Knowledge in Social Science." In *Metatheory in Social Science,* edited by Donald W. Fiske and Richard Shweder. Chicago: University of Chicago Press.

Foa, Uriel. 1993. *Resource Theory: Explorations and Applications.* San Diego: Academic Press.

Fodor, Jerry. 1983. *The Modularity of Mind.* Cambridge, MA: MIT Press.

Foot, David K., with Daniel Stoffman. 1996. *Boom, Bust, and Echo.* Toronto: Macfarlane, Walter, and Ross.

Frank, Robert M. 1988. *Passions Within Reason.* New York: Norton.

Fraser, Colin, and George Gaskell, eds. 1990. *The Social Psychological Study of Widespread Beliefs.* Oxford: Clarendon.

Freeman, Christopher, and Luc Soete. 1997. *The Economics of Industrial Innovation,* 3rd ed. Cambridge, MA: MIT Press.

Freeman, Dyson. 1994. *Nature's Imagination: The Frontiers of Scientific Vision.* Oxford: Oxford University Press.

Freeman, Lisa. 1996. "The University Press in the Electronic Future." In *Scholarly Publishing: The Electronic Frontier,* edited by Robin B. Peek and Gregory B. Newby. Cambridge, MA: MIT Press.

Frey, Bruno S. 1992. *Economics as a Science of Human Behavior.* Boston: Kluwer.

Frye, Northrop. 1991. *The Double Vision: Language and Meaning in Religion.* Toronto: University of Toronto Press.

Fuhrmann, Barbara S. 1997. "Philosophy and Aims." In *Handbook of the Undergraduate Curriculum,* edited by Jerry G. Gaff, James L. Ratcliff, and Associates. San Francisco: Jossey-Bass.

Fukuyama, Francis. 1995. *Trust.* New York: Free Press.

Gaff, Jerry G. 1991. *New Life for the College Curriculum.* San Francisco: Jossey-Bass.
———. 1997. "Tensions Between Tradition and Innovation." In *Handbook of the Undergraduate Curriculum,* edited by Jerry G. Gaff, James L. Ratcliff, and Associates. San Francisco: Jossey-Bass.

Garcia, Mildred, and James L. Ratcliff. 1997. "Social Forces Shaping the Curriculum." In *Handbook of the Undergraduate Curriculum,* edited by Jerry G. Gaff, James L. Ratcliff, and Associates. San Francisco: Jossey-Bass.

Gardner, Howard. 1983. *Frames of Mind: The Theory of Multiple Intelligences.* New York: Basic Books.
———. 1995. *Leading Minds.* New York: Basic Books.

Gauker, Christopher. 1994. *Thinking Out Loud.* Princeton, NJ: Princeton University Press.

Gellner, Ernest. 1989. *Plough, Sword, and Book.* Chicago: University of Chicago Press.

Getman, Julius. 1992. *In The Company of Scholars.* Austin: University of Texas Press.

Gillowy, John. 1993. *Cultural Capital.* Chicago: University of Chicago Press.

Gilroy, Paul. 1991. *There Ain't No Black in the Union Jack.* Chicago: University of Chicago Press.

Glassick, Charles E., Mary Taylor Huber, and Gene I. Maeroff. 1997. *Scholarship Assessed: Evaluation of the Professoriate.* San Francisco: Jossey-Bass.

Gledhill, John. 1994. *Power and Its Disguises.* London: Pluto Press.

Golombok, Susan, and Robyn Fivush. 1984. *Gender Development.* Cambridge: Cambridge University Press.

Goodlad, Sinclair. 1995. *The Quest for Quality.* Ballmoor, Buckingham: Open University Press.

Gordon, Scott. 1991. *The History and Philosophy of Social Science.* London: Routledge.

Goudsblom, Johan, Eric Jones, and Stephen Mennell. 1996. *The Course of Human History: Economic Growth, Social Process, and Civilization.* Armonk, NY: M. E. Sharpe.

Gross, Jonathan L., and Steve Rayser. 1985. *Measuring Culture.* New York: Columbia University Press.

Guédon, Jean-Claude. 1996. "The Seminar, The Encyclopedia, and the Eco-Museum as Possible Future Forms of Electronic Publishing." In *Scholarly Publishing: The Electronic Frontier,* edited by Robin P. Peek and Gregory B. Newby. Cambridge, MA: MIT Press.

Haack, Susan. 1998. *Manifesto of a Passionate Moderate.* Chicago: University of Chicago Press.

Hacking, Ian. 1990. *The Taming of Chance.* New York: Cambridge University Press.

Halliday, Terence C. 1992. "Introduction: Sociology's Fragile Professionalism." In *Sociology and its Publics,* edited by Terence C. Halliday and Morris Janowitz. Chicago: University of Chicago Press.

Halperin, Rhoda H. 1994. *Cultural Economies Past and Present.* Austin: University of Texas Press.

Hamilton, Gary G. 1994. "Civilizations and the Organization of Economies." In *The Handbook of Economic Sociology,* edited by Neil Smelser and Richard Swedberg. Princeton, NJ: Princeton University Press.

Hannah, Leslie. 1993. "Cultural Determinants of Economic Performance: An Experiment in Measuring Human Capital Flows." In *Historical Analysis in Economics,* edited by Graham Snookes. London: Routledge.

Harris, Ellen T. 1997. "The Arts." In *Handbook of the Undergraduate Curriculum,* edited by Jerry G. Gaff, James L. Ratcliff, and Associates. San Francisco: Jossey-Bass.

Harrison, Lawrence, E. 1992. *Who Prospers?* New York: Basic Books.

Harvey, John. 1981. *Cognition, Social Behavior, and the Environment.* Hillsdale, NJ: Lawrence Erlbaum.

Haskell, Thomas L., and Richard F. Teichgraeber III. 1993. "Introduction." In *The Culture of the Market.* New York: Cambridge University Press.

Hatfield, Elaine, and Richard Rapson. 1993. "Love and Attachment Processes." In *Handbook of Emotions,* edited by Michael Lewis and Jeanette Haviland. New York: Guilford Press.

Hatton, John, and Paul B. Plouffe. 1997. *Science and Its Ways of Knowing.* Upper Saddle River, NJ: Prentice-Hall.

Hausman, Daniel M., and Michael S. McPherson. 1996. *Economic Analysis and Moral Philosophy.* Cambridge: Cambridge University Press.

Heilbroner, Robert. 1990. "Economics as Ideology." In *Economics as Discourse,* edited by Warren J. Samuels. Boston: Kluwer.

Heise, David R., and John O'Brien. 1993. "Emotion Expression in Groups." In *Handbook of Emotions,* edited by Michael Lewis and Jeanette Haviland. New York: Guilford Press.

Hendershott, Anna Barnhardt, and Sheila Phelan Wright. 1997. "The Social Sciences." In *Handbook of the Undergraduate Curriculum,* edited by Jerry G. Gaff, James L. Ratcliff, and Associates. San Francisco: Jossey-Bass.

Herrnstein, Richard J., and Charles Murray. 1994. *The Bell Curve: Intelligence and Class Structure in American Life.* New York: Free Press.

Hey, David. 1985. "Jacques Derrida." In *The Return of Grand Theory in the Human Sciences,* edited by Quentin Skinner. New York: Cambridge University Press.

Higgins, E. T. 1990. "Personality, Social Psychology, and Person-Situation Relations: Standards and Knowledge Activators as a Common Language." In *Handbook of Personality Theory and Research,* edited by Lawrence A. Pervin. New York: Guilford Press.

Himmelweit, Hilde T. 1990. "The Dynamics of Public Opinion." In *The Social Psychological Study of Widespread Beliefs,* edited by Colin Fraser and George Gaskell. Oxford: Clarendon.

Hinde, Robert A. 1987. *Individuals, Relationships, and Culture.* Cambridge: Cambridge University Press.

Hobsbawm, E. 1990. *Nations and Nationalism Since 1780.* Cambridge: Cambridge University Press.

Hodgson, Geoffrey M. 1993. *Economics and Evolution.* Cambridge: Polity Press.

Holmes, Stephen. 1993. *The Anatomy of Antiliberalism.* Cambridge, MA: Harvard University Press.

Hooson, David, ed. 1994. *Geography and National Identity.* Oxford: Blackwell.

Hornsby, William F., and Melvyn Jones. 1993. *An Introduction to Population Geography.* Cambridge: Cambridge University Press.

Huff, Anne S. 1996. "Ways of Mapping Strategic Thought." In *Social Cartography: Mapping Ways of Social and Educational Change,* edited by Rolland G. Paulston. New York: Garland Publishing.

Hufford, Mary, ed. 1994. *Conserving Culture.* Urbana: University of Illinois Press.

Hugill, Peter J. 1993. *World Trade Since 1431: Geography, Technology, and Capitalism.* Baltimore: Johns Hopkins University Press.

Huntington, Samuel. 1991. *The Third Wave: Democratization in the Late Twentieth Century.* Oklahoma City: University of Oklahoma Press.

Hutcheon, P. 1996. *Leaving the Cave: Evolutionary Naturalism in Social-Scientific Thought.* Waterloo: Wilfrid Laurier University Press.

Ignatieff, Michael. 1994. *Blood and Belonging: Journeys Into the New Nationalism.* New York: Penguin.

Irwin, Michael D., and John D. Kasarda. 1994. "Trade, Transportation, and Spatial Distribution." In *The Handbook of Economic Sociology,* edited by Neil Smelser and Richard Swedberg. Princeton, NJ: Princeton University Press.

Izard, Carroll E. 1993. "Organizational and Motivational Functions of Discrete Emotions." In *Handbook of Emotions,* edited by Michael Lewis and Jeanette Haviland. New York: Guilford Press.

Jackendoff, Ray. 1992. *Languages of the Mind.* Cambridge, MA: MIT Press.

Jahr, Ernst H., ed. 1993. *Language Conflict and Language Planning.* Berlin: Mouton de Gruyter.

Jamison, Kay R. 1994. *Touched With Fire: Manic-Depressive Illness and the Artistic Temperament.* New York: Free Press.

Jaspars, Jos, and Miles Hewstone. 1990. "Social Categorization, Collective Beliefs, and Causal Attribution." In *The Social Psychological Study of Widespread Beliefs,* edited by Colin Fraser and George Gaskell. Oxford: Clarendon.

Jeremy, David, ed. 1998. *Religion, Business, and Wealth in Modern Britain.* London: Routledge.

John, Oliver P. 1990. "The 'Big Five' Factor Taxonomy: Dimensions of Personality in the Natural Language and Questionnaires." In *Handbook of Personality Theory and Research,* edited by Lawrence A. Pervin. New York: Guilford Press.

Johnson, Allen W., and Timothy Earle. 1989. *The Evolution of Human Societies.* Palo Alto: Stanford University Press.

Johnson, Stephen M. 1994. *Character Styles.* New York: Norton.

Kanter, Rosabeth Moss. 1995. *World Class.* New York: Simon & Schuster.

Kaplan, Rachel, and Stephen Kaplan. 1989. *The Experience of Nature: A Psychological Perspective.* Cambridge: Cambridge University Press.

Kavaler-Adler, Susan. 1993. *The Compulsion to Create.* New York: Routledge.

Kedourie, Elie. 1993. *Nationalism,* 4th ed. Oxford: Blackwell.

Kelly, George A. 1991. *The Psychology of Personal Constructs.* London: Routledge.

Kephart, William M., and William K. Zellner. 1991. *Extraordinary Groups,* 4th ed. New York: St. Martin's.

Kindleberger, Charles P. 1996. *World Economic Primacy: 1500 to 1900.* New York: Oxford University Press.

Klein, Burton H. 1988. "Luck, Necessity, and Dynamic Flexibility." In *Evolutionary Economics,* edited by H. Hanusch. Cambridge: Cambridge University Press.

Klein, Julie Thompson. 1990. *Interdisciplinarity.* Detroit: Wayne State University Press.
———. 1996. *Crossing Boundaries: Knowledge, Disciplinarities, and Interdisciplinarities.* Charlottesville: University Press of Virginia.

Knight, Jack. 1992. *Institutions and Social Conflict.* Cambridge: Cambridge University Press.

Koestner, Richard, and David C. McClelland. 1990. "Perspectives on Competence Motivation." In *Handbook of Personality Theory and Research,* edited by Lawrence A. Pervin. New York: Guilford Press.

Konner, Melvin. 1982. *The Tangled Wing: Biological Constraints on the Human Spirit.* New York: Holt, Rinehart & Winston.

Kontopolous, Kyriakos. 1993. *The Logics of Social Structure.* Cambridge: Cambridge University Press.

Kroeber, A. L., and Clyde Kluckhohn. 1952. *Culture: A Critical Review of Concepts and Definitions.* Cambridge, MA: Peabody Museum.

Krugman, Paul. 1994. *Peddling Prosperity.* New York: Norton.

Küchler, Susanne, and Walter Melion. 1991. *Images of Memory.* Washington: Smithsonian Institution Press.

Kuhn, Alfred. 1974. *The Logic of Social Systems.* San Francisco: Jossey-Bass.

Kuhn, Robert L., ed. 1993. *Generating Creativity and Innovation in Large Bureaucracies.* Westport, CT: Quorum.

Kuspit, Donald. 1993. *Signs of Psyche in Modern and Postmodern Art.* Cambridge: Cambridge University Press.

L'Abate, Luciano. 1994. *A Theory of Personality Development.* New York: Wiley.

LaFollette, M. 1992. *Stealing Into Print: Fraud, Plagiarism, and Misconduct in Scientific Publishing.* Berkeley: University of California Press.

Lambert, Karel, and Gordon G. Brittan, Jr. 1992. *An Introduction to the Philosophy of Science.* 4th ed. Alacasdero, CA: Ridgeview Publishing Co.

Lanham, Richard A. 1993. *The Electronic Word: Democracy, Technology, and the Arts.* Chicago: University of Chicago Press.

Lasch, Christopher. 1991. *The True and Only Heaven.* New York: Norton.

Laszlo, Ervin. 1987. *Evolution: The Grand Synthesis.* Boston: New Science Library.

Law, John. 1994. *Organizing Modernity.* Oxford: Blackwell.

Layton, Robert. 1991. *The Anthropology of Art.* 2nd ed. Cambridge: Cambridge University Press.

Lemerise, Elizabeth A., and Kenneth A. Dodge. 1993. "The Development of Anger and Hostile Interaction." In *Handbook of Emotions,* edited by Michael Lewis and Jeanette Haviland. New York: Guilford Press.

Lemonnier, Pierre. 1992. *Elements For an Anthropology of Technology.* Ann Arbor: Museum of Anthropology.

Lenski, Gerhard, Jean Lenski, and Patrick Nolan. 1991. *Human Societies: An Introduction to Macrosociology,* 6th ed. New York: McGraw-Hill.

Lessnoff, Michael H. 1994. *The Spirit of Capitalism and the Protestant Ethic: An Enquiry Into the Weber Thesis.* London: Edward Elgar.

Lewellen, Ted C. 1992. *Political Anthropology: An Introduction.* 2nd ed. Westport, CT: Bergin and Garvey.

Lewis, Michael. 1990. "Self-Knowledge and Social Development in Early Life." In *Handbook of Personality Theory and Research,* edited by Lawrence A. Pervin. New York: Guilford Press.

———. 1993. "Self-conscious Emotion: Embarrasment, Pride, Shame, and Guilt." In *Handbook of Emotions,* edited by Michael Lewis and Jeanette Haviland. New York: Guilford Press.

Linville, Patricia, and Donal E. Carlston. 1994. "Social Cognition of the Self." In *Social Cognition: Impact on Social Psychology,* edited by Patricia G. Devine, David L. Hamilton, and Thomas M. Ostrom. San Diego: Academic Press.

Livingstone, James. 1994. *Pragmatism and the Political Economy of Cultural Revolution: 1850-1940.* Chapel Hill: University of North Carolina Press.

Lucas, Christopher J. 1996. *Crisis in the Academy.* New York: St. Martin's.

Lumsden, C., and E. Wilson. 1981. *Genes, Mind, and Culture.* Cambridge, MA: Harvard University Press.

Mackie, Diane, and John J. Skelly. 1994. "The Social Cognition Analysis of Social Influence: Contributions to the Understanding of Persuasion and Conformity." In *Social Cognition: Impact on Social Psychology,* edited by Patricia G. Devine, David L. Hamilton, and Thomas M. Ostrom. San Diego: Academic Press.

Maier, Charles S. 1987. *In Search of Stability: Explorations in Historical Political Economy.* Cambridge: Cambridge University Press.

Mann, Michael. 1986. *The Sources of Social Power, vol. 2. The Rise of Classes and Nation States, 1760–1914.* Cambridge: Cambridge University Press.

Martinello, Marian L., and Gillian E. Cook. 1994. *Interdisciplinary Inquiry in Teaching and Learning.* New York: Macmillan.

Maslow, A. 1968. *Toward a Psychology of Being.* 2nd New York: Van Nostrand.

Massey, Doreen B. 1994. *Space, Place, and Gender.* Cambridge: Polity.

Mayer, Thomas. 1993. *Truth Versus Precision.* London: Edward Elgar.

McCloskey, Deirdre N. 1996. *The Vices of Economists—The Virtues of the Bourgeoisie.* Amsterdam: University of Amsterdam Press.

McCloskey, Donald N. 1987. *The Rhetoric of the Human Sciences.* Madison: University of Wisconsin Press.

McDonald, Lynn. 1993. *The Early Origins of the Social Sciences.* Montreal: McGill-Queen's University Press.

McGlynn, Frank, and Arthur Tuden, eds. 1991. "Introduction." In *Anthropological Approaches to Political Behavior.* Pittsburgh: University of Pittsburgh Press.

McPhail, Clark. 1991. *The Myth of the Madding Crowd.* New York: Aldine de Gruyter.

Melion, Walter, and Suzanne Kuchler. 1989. "Introduction: Memory, Cognition, and Image Production." In *Images of Memory: On Memory and Representation.* Hanover: University Press of New England.

Melzer, Arthur M., Jerry Wenberger, and M. Richard Zinman. 1993. *Technology in the Western Political Tradition.* Ithaca: Cornell University Press.

Merton, Robert K. 1996. *On Social Structure and Science.* Chicago: University of Chicago Press.

Messer, Stanley B., and Seth Warren. 1990. "Personality Change and Psychotherapy." In *Handbook of Personality Theory and Research,* edited by Lawrence A. Pervin. New York: Guilford Press.

Messer-Davidow, Ellen, David R. Shumway, and David J. Sylvan. 1993. *Knowledges: Historical and Critical Studies in Interdisciplinarity.* Charlottesville: University Press of Virginia.

Migdal, Joel. 1988. *Strong Societies and Weak States: State-Society Relations and State Capabilities in the 3rd World.* Princeton, NJ: Princeton University Press.

Miller, Alan. 1991. *Personality Types: A Modern Synthesis.* Calgary: University of Calgary Press.

Miller, Daniel, ed. 1995. *Acknowledging Consumption.* London: Routledge.

Miller, Laurence. 1990. *Inner Natures: Brain, Self, and Personality.* New York: St. Martin's.

Milner, Alan. 1991. *Contemporary Cultural Theory: An Introduction.* North Sydney: Allen and Unwin.

Mitchell, William C. 1994. *Beyond Politics: Markets, Welfare, and the Failure of Democracy.* Boulder, CO: Westview Press.

Mizruchi, Mark S. 1992. *The Structure of Corporate Political Action.* Cambridge, MA: Harvard University Press.

Mokyr, Joel. 1991. *The Lever of Riches.* New York: Oxford University Press.

Monteith, Margo J., Julia R. Zuwerink, and Patricia G. Devine. 1994. "Prejudice and Prejudice Reduction: Classic Challenges, Contemporary Approaches." In *Social Cognition: Impact on Social Psychology,* edited by Patricia G. Devine, David L. Hamilton, and Thomas M. Ostrom. San Diego: Academic Press.

Morris, Desmond. 1994. *The Human Animal.* London: BBC Books.

Mowat, Thomas W. IV. 1996. "The Timely Emergence of Social Cartography." In *Social Cartography: Mapping Ways of Social and Educational Change,* edited by Rolland G. Paulston. New York: Garland Publishing.

Mowery, David C., and Nathan Rosenberg. 1989. *Technology and the Pursuit of Economic Growth.* Cambridge: Cambridge University Press.

Mugny, Gabriel, and Juan A. Perez. 1991. *The Social Psychology of Minority Influence.* Cambridge: Cambridge University Press.

Mukherjee, Ramkrishna. 1991. *Society, Culture and Development.* New Delhi: Sage.

Mummendy, A., ed. 1984. *Social Psychology of Aggression.* Berlin: Springer-Verlag.

Murdock, George P., Chellan S. Ford, Alfred E. Hudson, et al. 1982. *Outline of Cultural Materials.* 5th ed. New Haven: Human Relations Area Files Inc.

Musil, Caryn McTighe. 1997. "Diversity and Educational Integration." In *Handbook of the Undergraduate Curriculum,* edited by Jerry G. Gaff, James L. Ratcliff, and associates. San Francisco: Jossey-Bass.

Namenwirth, J., and R. Weber. 1987. *Dynamics of Culture.* Boston: Allen and Unwin.

Nasaw, David. 1993. *Going Out: The Rise and Fall of Public Amusements.* New York: Basic Books.

Nesse, R., and A. Lloyd. 1992. "The Evolution of Psychodynamic Mechanisms." In *The Adapted Mind,* edited by Jerome H. Barkow, Leda Cosmides, and John Tooby. Oxford: Oxford University Press.

Newman, Gerald. 1987. *The Rise of English Nationalism.* New York: St. Martin's.

Noelle-Neumann, Elisabeth. 1993. *The Spiral of Silence.* 2nd ed. Chicago: University of Chicago Press.

North, Douglass. 1990. *Institutions, Institutional Change, and Economic Performance.* Cambridge: Cambridge University Press.

Nye, David E. 1994. *American Technology Sublime*. Cambridge, MA: MIT Press.

Oatley, Keith. 1993. "Social Construction in Emotion." In *Handbook of Emotions,* edited by Michael Lewis and Jeanette Haviland. New York: Guilford Press.

Ohman, Anne. 1993. "Fear and Anxiety as Emotional Phenomena: Classical Phenomenology, Evolutionary Perspectives, and Information-Processing Mechanisms." In *Handbook of Emotions,* edited by Michael Lewis and Jeanette Haviland. New York: Guilford Press.

Olguin, Enrique, and Betty Schmitz. 1997. "Transforming the Curriculum Through Diversity." In *Handbook of the Undergraduate Curriculum,* edited by Jerry G. Gaff, James L. Ratcliff, and associates. San Francisco: Jossey-Bass.

Open the Social Sciences: Report of the Gulbenkian Commission on the Restructuring of the Social Sciences. 1996. Palo Alto: Stanford University Press.

Papineau, David, ed. 1996. *The Philosophy of Science*. Oxford: Oxford University Press.

Park, Chris C. 1994. *Sacred Worlds: An Introduction to Geography and Religion*. London: Routledge.

Parsons, Paul. 1989. *Getting Published: The Acquisition Process at University Presses*. Knoxville: University of Tennessee Press.

Parsons, Talcott. 1966. *Societies: Evolutionary and Comparative Perspectives*. Englewood Cliffs, NJ: Prentice-Hall.

———. 1977. *The Evolution of Societies*. Englewood Cliffs, NJ: Prentice-Hall.

Paulston, Rolland G., ed. 1996. *Social Cartography: Mapping Ways of Social and Educational Change*. New York: Garland Publishing.

Payne, Geoffe, ed. 2000. *Social Divisions*. New York: St. Martins.

Pepinsky, Harold E., and Paul Jesilow. 1984. *Myths That Cause Crime*. Cabin John, MD: Seven Locks Press.

Pepper, Stephen C. 1942. *World Hypotheses*. Berkeley: University of California Press.

Pervin, Lawrence A., ed. 1990. *Handbook of Personality Theory and Research*. New York: Guilford Press.

Peterson, Steven A. 1990. *Political Behavior: Patterns in Everyday Life*. Newbury Park, CA: Sage.

Pinker, Steven. 1994. *The Language Instinct*. New York: W. Morrow and Co.

Pitzer, Donald E., ed. 1997. *America's Communal Utopias*. Durham: University of North Carolina Press.

Plane, David A., and Peter A. Rogerson. 1994. *The Geographical Analysis of Population*. New York: John Wiley and Sons.

Plattner, Stuart, ed. 1989. *Economic Anthropology*. Palo Alto: Stanford University Press.

Plutchik, Robert. 1993. "Emotions and their Vicissitudes: Emotion and Psychopathology." In *Handbook of Emotions,* edited by Michael Lewis and Jeanette Haviland. New York: Guilford Press.

Ponting, Clive. 1992. *A Green History of the World*. London: Penguin.

Potter, Garry. 2000. *The Philosophy of Social Science*. Harlow, UK: Prentice-Hall.

Potter, Jonathan, and Margaret Wetherell. 1987. *Discourse and Social Psychology*. London: Sage.

Pounds, N. J. G. 1993. *Hearth and Home: A History of Material Culture*. Bloomington: Indiana University Press.

Pred, Allan. 1990. *Making Histories and Constructing Human Geographies*. Boulder, CO: Westview Press.

Prezioni, Donald. 1993. "Seeing Through Art History." In *Knowledges: Historical and Critical Studies in Interdisciplinarity,* edited by Ellen Messer-Davidow, David R. Shumway, and David J. Sylvan. Charlottesville: University Press of Virginia.

Prus, Robert. 1996. *Symbolic Interaction and Ethnographic Research*. Albany: SUNY Press.

Ratcliff, James L. 1997. "What is a Curriculum and What Should it Be?" In *Handbook of the Undergraduate Curriculum,* edited by Jerry G. Gaff, James L. Ratcliff, and associates. San Francisco: Jossey-Bass.

Restivo, Sal. 1995. "The Theory Landscape in Science Studies: Sociological Traditions." In *Handbook of Science and Technology Studies,* edited by Sheila Jasanoff, Gerald E. Markle, James C. Peterson, and Trevor Pinch. New York: Sage.

Romaine, Suzanne. 1994. *Language in Society: An Introduction to Sociolinguistics.* Oxford: Oxford University Press.

Rose, Gillian. 1993. *Feminism and Geography.* Minneapolis: University of Minnesota Press.

Rosenberg, Nathan. 1994. *Exploring the Black Box.* Cambridge: Cambridge University Press.

Rothman, David H. 1996. "TeleRead: A Virtual Central Database without Big Brother." In *Scholarly Publishing: The Electronic Frontier,* edited by Robin P. Peek and Gregory B. Newby. Cambridge, MA: MIT Press.

Rothman, David J., Steven Marcus, and Stephanie A. Kiceluk, eds. 1995. *Medicine and Western Civilization.* New Brunswick: Rutgers University Press.

Rozin, Paul, Jonathan Haidt, and Clark R. McCawley. 1993. "Disgust." In *Handbook of Emotions,* edited by Michael Lewis and Jeanette Haviland. New York: Guilford Press.

Rule, James B.1997. *Theory and Progress in Social Science.* Cambridge: Cambridge University Press.

Rust, Val D. 1996. "From Modern to Postmodern Ways of Seeing Social and Educational Change." In *Social Cartography: Mapping Ways of Social and Educational Change,* edited by Rolland G. Paulston. New York: Garland Publishing.

Rutherford, Malcolm. 1995. *Institutions in Economics: The Old and the New Institutionalism.* New York: Cambridge University Press.

Sabel, Charles F. 1994. "Learning by Monitoring: The Institutions of Economic Development." In *The Handbook of Economic Sociology,* edited by Neil J. Smelser and Richard Swedberg. Princeton, NJ: Princeton University Press.

Salter, Liora, and Alison Hearn. 1996. *Outside the Lines: Issues in Interdisciplinary Research.* Montreal: McGill-Queen's University Press.

Sampson, Edward E. 1993. *Celebrating the Other: A Dialogue Account of Human Nature.* New York: Harvester Wheatsheaf.

Samuels, Andrew. 1993. *The Political Psyche.* London: Routledge.

Sanderson, Stephen K. 1995. *Social Transformation.* Oxford: Blackwell.

Schelling, Thomas. 1978. *Micromotives and Macrobehavior.* New York: Norton.

Schiffer, Michael B., with Andrea R. Miller. 1999. *The Material Life of Human Beings.* London: Routledge.

Schwartz, Mildred A. 1990. *A Sociological Perspective on Politics.* Englewood Cliffs, NJ: Prentice-Hall.

Secord, Paul F. 1986. "Explanations in the Social Sciences and in Life Situations." In *Metatheory in Social Science,* edited by Donald W. Fiske and Richard A. Shweder. Chicago: University of Chicago Press.

Segal, Howard. 1994. *Future Imperfect: The Mixed Blessings of Technology in America.* Amherst: University of Massachusetts Press.

Selznick, Philip. 1992. *The Moral Commonwealth.* Berkeley: University of California Press.

Shehadi, Kamal S. 1993. *Ethnic Self-Determination and the Break-Up of States.* London: International Institute for Strategic Studies.

Shweder, Richard A. 1993. "The Cultural Psychology of the Emotions." In *Handbook of Emotions,* edited by Michael Lewis and Jeanette Haviland. New York: Guilford Press.

Sim, Stuart. 1992. "Deconstruction." In *Companion to Aesthetics,* edited by David.E Cooper. Oxford: Blackwell.

Simons, Herbert W., and Trevor Melia, eds. 1989. *The Legacy of Kenneth Burke.* Madison: University of Wisconsin Press.

Simonton, Dean Keith. 1990. "Personality and Politics." In *Handbook of Personality Theory and Research,* edited by Lawrence A. Pervin. New York: Guilford Press.

Skinner, Quentin, ed. 1985. *The Return of Grand Theory in the Human Sciences.* New York: Cambridge University Press.

Smelser, Neil, and Richard Swedberg, eds. 1994. *The Handbook of Economic Sociology.* Princeton, NJ: Princeton University Press.

Smith, David M. 1994. *Geography and Social Justice.* Oxford: Blackwell.

Smith, Peter B., and Michael Harris Bond. 1993. *Social Psychology Across Cultures.* New York: Harvester Wheatsheaf.

Smith, S. L. 1991. *Report of the Commission of Inquiry on Canadian University Education.* Ottawa: Government of Canada.

Smith, Thomas Spence. 1992. *Strong Interaction.* Chicago: University of Chicago Press.

Snooks, Graeme, D. 1993. *Economics Without Time.* Ann Arbor: University of Michigan Press.

Solomon, Robert C. 1993. "The Philosophy of Emotion." In *Handbook of Emotions,* edited by Michael Lewis and Jeanette Haviland. New York: Guilford Press.

Sosa, Ernest, and Michael Tooley. 1993. "Introduction." In *Causation.* Oxford: Oxford University Press.

Sowell, Thomas. 1994. *Race and Culture: A World View.* New York: Basic Books.

Sperber, Dan. 1990. "The Epidemiology of Beliefs." In *The Social Psychological Study of Widespread Beliefs,* edited by Colin Fraser and George Gaskell. Oxford: Clarendon.

Sporre, Dennis J. 1992. *Perceiving the Arts: An Introduction to the Humanities.* 4th ed. Englewood Cliffs, NJ: Prentice-Hall.

Staudenmaier, John M. 1985. *Technology's Storytellers.* Cambridge, MA: MIT Press.

Stearns, Carol Z. 1993. "Sadness." In *Handbook of Emotions,* edited by Michael Lewis and Jeanette Haviland. New York: Guilford Press.

Sternberg, Robert J., and Patricia Ruzgis, eds. 1994. *Personality and Intelligence.* Cambridge: Cambridge University Press.

Storr, Anthony. 1996. *Feet of Clay: Saints, Sinners, And Madmen: A Study of Gurus.* New York: Free Press.

Stromquist, Nelly P. 1996. "Mapping Gendered Spaces in Third World Educational Interventions." In *Social Cartography: Mapping Ways of Social and Educational Change,* edited by Rolland G. Paulston. New York: Garland Publishing.

Symons, D. 1992. "On the Use and Misuse of Darwinism in the Study of Human Behavior." In *The Adapted Mind,* edited by Jerome H. Barkow, Leda Cosmides, and John Tooby. Oxford: Oxford University Press.

Szostak, Rick. 1991. *The Role of Transportation in the Industrial Revolution.* Montreal: McGill-Queen's University Press.

———. 1999. *Econ-Art: Divorcing Art From Science in Modern Economics.* London: Pluto Press.

———. 2000a. "Toward a Unified Human Science." *Issues in Integrative Studies.* 115–57.

———. 2000b. "A Schema For Unifying Human Science: Application to Health and Population." Electronic journal, American Association for Behavioral and Social Sciences. http:/employees.csbsju.edu/jmakepeace/Perspectives2k/

———. 2000c. "Unifying Human Science Schematically: The Case of Art." *NSSA Perspectives Journal,* 17.1, 139–51.

———. 2001. "Putting Social Structure in its Place Schematically." *Issues in Integrative Studies.*

————. 2002. *Unifying Human Ethics*. Ms. under review.

Tamir, Yael. 1993. *Liberal Nationalism*. Princeton, NJ: Princeton University Press.

Taylor, Michael. 1993. "Structure, culture, and action in the explanation of social change." In *Politics and Rationality,* edited by William James Booth, Patrick James, and Hudson Meadwell. Cambridge: Cambridge University Press.

Tessler, Mark, Jodi Nachtwey, and Anne Banda. 1999. "Introduction: The Area Studies Controversy" in *Area Studies and Social Science,* edited by Mark Tessler. Bloomington: Indiana University Press.

Thelen, Kathleen, and Sven Steinmo. 1992. "Historical Institutionalism in Comparative Politics." In *Structuring Politics: Historical Institutionalism in Comparative Analysis,* edited by Steinmo, Thelen, and Longstreth. New York: Cambridge University Press.

Toland, Judith D., ed. 1993. *Ethnicity and the State*. New Brunswick, NJ: Transaction Publishers.

Tooby, John, and Leda Cosmides. 1992. "The Psychological Foundations of Culture." In *The Adapted Mind,* edited by Jerome H. Barkow, Leda Cosmides, and John Tooby. Oxford: Oxford University Press.

Toulmin, Stephen E. 1982. *The Return to Cosmology: Postmodern Science and the Theology of Nature*. Berkeley: University of California Press.

Trigg, Roger. 1985. *Understanding Social Science*. Oxford: Basil Blackwell.

Turner, Stephen. 1994. *The Social Theory of Practices*. Chicago: University of Chicago Press.

Vallacher, R. R., and J. Nowak, eds. 1994. *Dynamical Systems in Social Psychology.* San Diego: Academic Press.

van der Poel, Mort. 1993. *Personal Networks*. Berwyn, PA: Swets and Zeitlinger.

Vromen, Jack J. 1995. *Economic Evolution*. London: Routledge.

Walshok, Mary L. 1995. *Knowledge Without Boundaries*. San Francisco: Jossey-Bass.

Watson-Verran, Helen, and David Turnbull. 1995. "Science and Other Indigenous Knowledge Systems." In *Handbook of Science and Technology Studies,* edited by Sheila Jasanoff, Gerald E. Markle, James C. Peterson, and Trevor Pinch. New York: Sage.

Wenegrat, B. 1990. *Sociobiological Psychology.* Lexington, MA: Lexington Books.

Westen, Drew. 1990. "Psychoanalytic Approaches to Personality." In *Handbook of Personality Theory and Research,* edited by Lawrence A. Pervin. New York: Guilford Press.

White, Geoffrey M. 1993. "Emotions Inside Out: The Anthropology of Affect." In *Handbook of Emotions,* edited by Michael Lewis and Jeanette Haviland. New York: Guilford Press.

White, Harrison C. 1992. *Identity and Control: A Structural Theory of Social Action.* Princeton, NJ: Princeton University Press.

Willeband, Ruch. 1993. "Exhiliration and Humor." In *Handbook of Emotions,* edited by Michael Lewis and Jeanette Haviland. New York: Guilford Press.

Wilson, E. O. 1998. *Consilience*. New York: Knopf.

Wilson, James Q., and Richard J. Herrnstein. 1985. *Crime and Human Nature*. New York: Simon and Schuster.

Woods, Clyde. 1978. *Culture Change*. Dubuque, Iowa: William L. Brown.

Woolfson, Peter. 1982. "An Anthropological Perspective: The Ingredients of a Multicultural Society." In *Understanding Canada,* edited by William Metcalf. New York: New York University Press.

Woolgar, Steve. 1988. *Science: The Very Idea*. Chichester: Ellis Horwood.

Wright, Robert. 1994. *The Moral Animal*. New York: Pantheon.

Wrong, Dennis H. 1994. *The Problem of Order: What Unites and Divides Society.* New York: Free Press.

Wuthnow, Robert. 1994. "Religion and Economic Life." In *The Handbook of Economic Sociology,* edited by Neil Smelser and Richard Swedberg. Princeton, NJ: Princeton University Press.

Yankelovich, Daniel. 1991. *Coming to Public Judgment: Making Democracy Work in a Complex World.* Syracuse: Syracuse University Press.

Zolberg, Vera L. 1990. *Constructing a Sociology of the Arts.* Cambridge: Cambridge University Press.

Zuckerman, Marvin. 1991. *Psychobiology of Personality.* Cambridge: Cambridge University Press.

Index

Abbott, Andrew, 311, 314, 342 n. 10
abilities, 66, 166, 192, 320–21; consciousness, 116–17, 121–23, 129, 137, 158, 174, 188, 191–93, 295, 299, 349 n. 14; learning, 12, 91, 122, 125, 128–32, 137, 147–48, 159–60, 174, 182, 195, 246, 290; memory, 132, 192; other physical attributes, 133; perception, 125–26; subconsciousness, 31, 117, 121–23, 129, 136–37, 140, 158, 174, 188, 191–93, 291, 349 n. 22, 351 n. 33; vocalization, 121, 126–28, 130, 164, 198
Adams, E. M., 89, 108, 158, 181, 224, 279–80, 359 n. 10
Africa, 210, 220, 231, 240, 242; !Kung, 360; South Africa, 256; Yoruba, 97; Zulus, 157
Agar, Michael H., 74
age distribution, 142–43, 253, 262, 281–82, 286, 325, 349 n. 22
aggression, 21, 151, 155, 186–87. *See also* violence
Ahrne, Goran, 203
Ajzen, Icek, 174, 351–52 n. 7
Amabile, Teresa M., 192–93, 200–201
ambition, 155–57, 182–85, 207, 211–12, 223, 226, 246, 255, 275
Amish, 261, 276
anthropology, 23, 25, 59–60, 74, 83, 92, 95, 100, 102, 106, 108, 143–44, 180, 185, 188, 207, 222, 262, 273, 291–92, 307–8, 310, 313, 316, 349–50 n. 23, 360
Appleby, Joyce, 43–44, 230, 346 n. 18, 363 n. 20
Apter, Michael J., 169, 189
area studies, 25, 315–17, 338 n. 9
Aristotle, 68, 193

art, 23, 24, 36–37, 83–86, 161, 190, 193, 225, 243, 255, 266, 274, 287–93, 317–18, 327; evolution of, 289–90. *See also* music
Asia, 198, 209–10, 214–15, 220, 236, 240, 274; Bangladesh, 237; China, 209, 223, 347 nn. 26 and 27, 358 n. 13; India, 106, 209, 276; Japan, 106, 113, 212, 216–18, 225, 243, 277; Papua New Guinea, 92, 249, 274
attire, 159–60, 197
Australia and New Zealand, 264
authoritarianism, 87, 99, 100, 104, 107, 149–50, 182, 215, 220, 236, 248
Ayres, Clarence, 207, 216, 359 n. 9

Bacon, Francis, 57
Barber, Bernard, 8, 22, 36, 38–39, 70, 83, 94, 103, 147, 220, 244, 311, 338 n. 8, 341 n. 32, 342 n. 4, 344 n. 5
Barkow, Jerome H., 38, 98, 114, 116, 119, 121–22, 127, 133, 143–44, 146, 150, 152, 154, 163, 180, 262, 346 n. 21, 350 nn. 24 and 30
Barth, F., 92
Basalla, George, 275
Batson, C., 88, 159, 181–82, 190, 192, 197–98, 200, 293, 358 n. 12
Bayart, Jean-François, 231
beauty, attitude toward, 162
Bechtel, William, 40, 66, 78, 341
Beckwith, Guy V., 45
Bem, Sandra, 352 n. 12
Bergson, Henri, 139
Bethlehem, Douglas W., 84, 106
Bhaskar, Roy, 41–42, 55, 339 n. 20
biases, sources of, 28, 43, 45, 53–55, 63, 66, 69, 71, 73–75, 77–79, 130–31, 195, 197, 280, 294, 313, 343 n. 17, 356 n. 18

379